GENESIS

1

Story by George Iida
Manga by You Higuri

Translated and adapted by
Alethea and Athena Nibley

Lettered by
North Market Street Graphics

Ballantine Books · New York

Night Head Genesis volume 1 is a work of fiction. Names, characters, places, and incidents are the products of the author's imagination or are used fictitiously. Any resemblance to actual events, locales, or persons, living or dead, is entirely coincidental.

A Del Rey Manga/Kodansha Trade Paperback Original

Published in the United States by Del Rey, an imprint of The Random House Publishing Group, a division of Random House, Inc., New York.

Publication rights arranged through Kodansha Ltd.

First published in Japan in 2007 by Kodansha Ltd., Tokyo

ISBN 978-0-345-51625-1

Printed in the United States of America

www.delreymanga.com

9 8 7 6 5 4 3 2 1

Translators/Adaptors: Alethea and Athena Nibley
Lettering: North Market Street Graphics

Contents

A word from the creator:

The *Night Head* project starting up again in 2005 has been a good opportunity for me to take another look back at my past projects. I created the story of Naoto and Naoya more than fifteen years ago, and it was like I was groping through the dark, but I was able to reconfirm that I wasn't going in the wrong direction, and I felt like it gave me more than a little courage for my future projects. And people who watched the live action version of *Night Head* when it was aired on TV, as well as people who loved the story as fans, participated on these new projects, and I had many happy encounters. You Higuri-san is one of those people. As their creator, I'm sincerely happy that a new Naoto and Naoya are born again through Higuri-san's work, and that a lot of people will see the story of *Night Head*.

—George Iida

HONORIFICS EXPLAINED

Throughout the Del Rey Manga books, you will find Japanese honorifics left intact in the translations. For those not familiar with how the Japanese use honorifics and, more important, how they differ from American honorifics, we present this brief overview.

Politeness has always been a critical facet of Japanese culture. Ever since the feudal era, when Japan was a highly stratified society, use of honorifics—which can be defined as polite speech that indicates relationship or status—has played an essential role in the Japanese language. When addressing someone in Japanese, an honorific usually takes the form of a suffix attached to one's name (example: "Asuna-san"), is used as a title at the end of one's name, or appears in place of the name itself (example: "Negi-sensei," or simply "Sensei!").

Honorifics can be expressions of respect or endearment. In the context of manga and anime, honorifics give insight into the nature of the relationship between characters. Many English translations leave out these important honorifics and therefore distort the feel of the original Japanese. Because Japanese honorifics contain nuances that English honorifics lack, it is our policy at Del Rey not to translate them. Here, instead, is a guide to some of the honorifics you may encounter in Del Rey Manga.

-san: This is the most common honorific and is equivalent to Mr., Miss, Ms., or Mrs. It is the all-purpose honorific and can be used in any situation where politeness is required.

-sama: This is one level higher than "-san" and is used to confer great respect.

-dono: This comes from the word "tono," which means "lord." It is an even higher level than "-sama" and confers utmost respect.

-kun: This suffix is used at the end of boys' names to express familiarity or endearment. It is also sometimes used by men among friends, or when addressing someone younger or of a lower station.

-chan: This is used to express endearment, mostly toward girls. It is also used for little boys, pets, and even among lovers. It gives a sense of childish cuteness.

Bozu: This is an informal way to refer to a boy, similar to the English terms "kid" and "squirt."

Sempai/
Senpai: This title suggests that the addressee is one's senior in a group or organization. It is most often used in a school setting, where underclassmen refer to their upperclassmen as "sempai." It can also be used in the workplace, such as when a newer employee addresses an employee who has seniority in the company.

Kohai: This is the opposite of "sempai" and is used toward underclassmen in school or newcomers in the workplace. It connotes that the addressee is of a lower station.

Sensei: Literally meaning "one who has come before," this title is used for teachers, doctors, or masters of any profession or art.

-[blank]: This is usually forgotten in these lists, but it is perhaps the most significant difference between Japanese and English. The lack of honorific means that the speaker has permission to address the person in a very intimate way. Usually, only family, spouses, or very close friends have this kind of permission. Known as *yobisute*, it can be gratifying when someone who has earned the intimacy starts to call one by one's name without an honorific. But when that intimacy hasn't been earned, it can be very insulting.

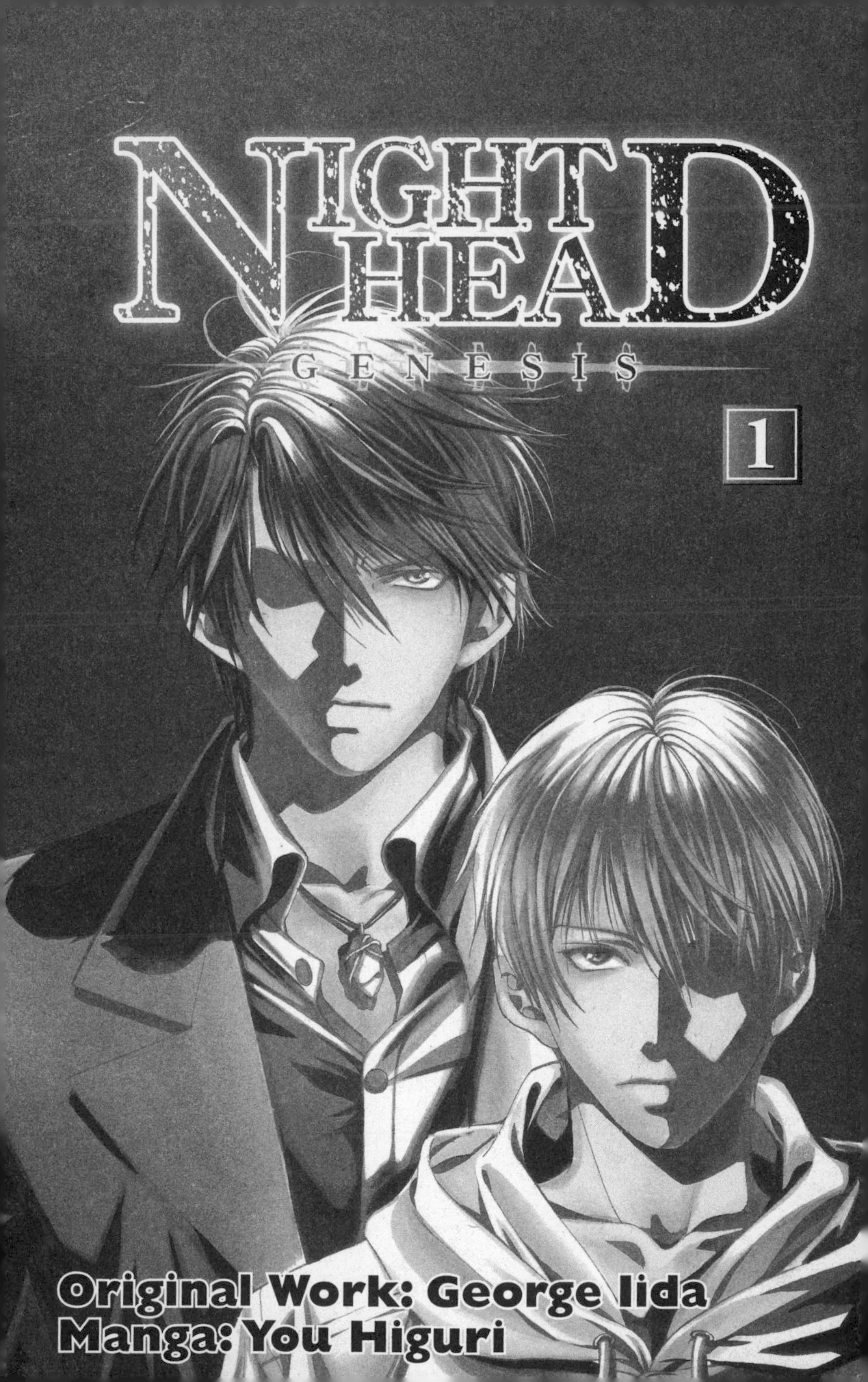
NIGHT HEAD
GENESIS
1
Original Work: George Iida
Manga: You Higuri

CONTENTS

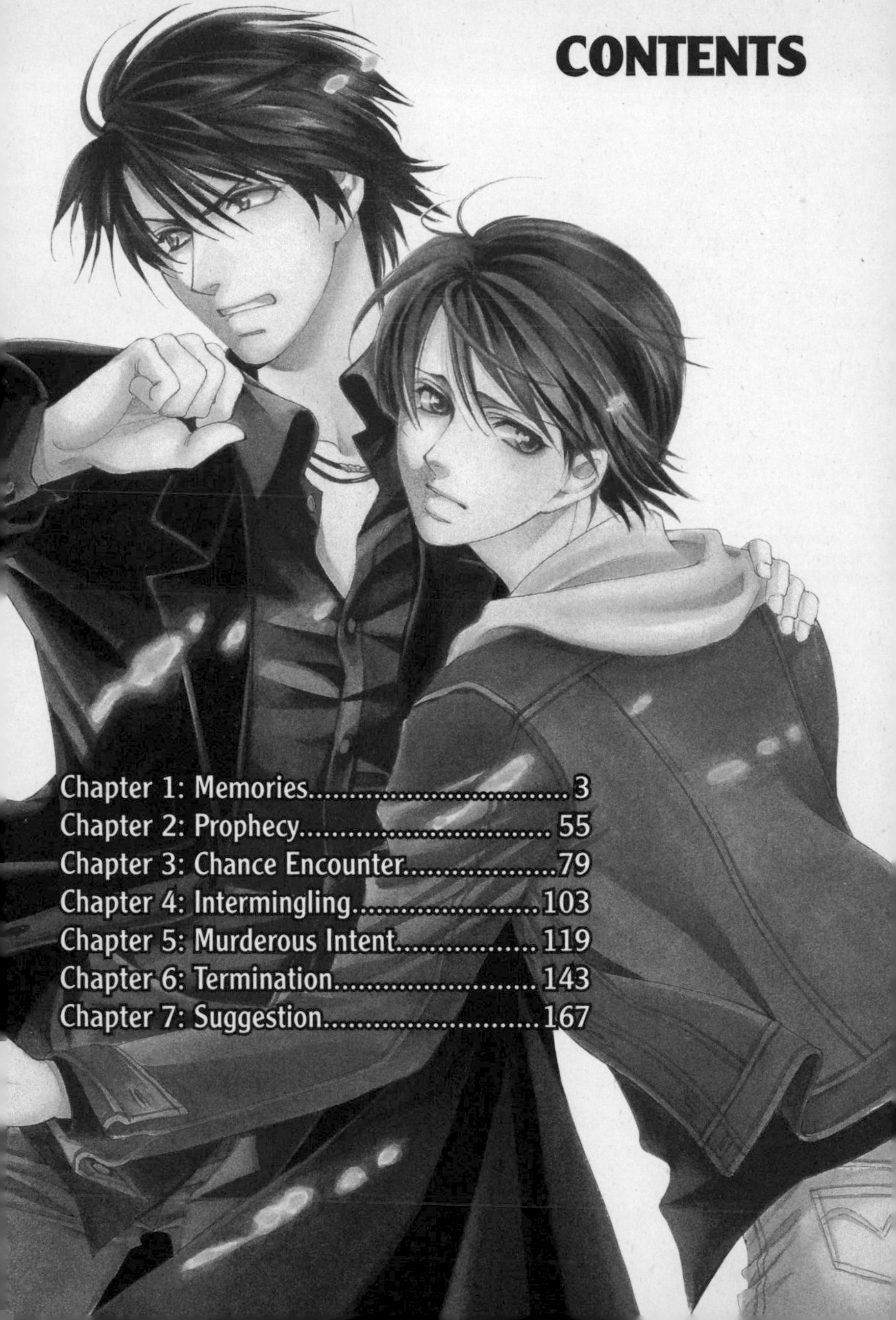

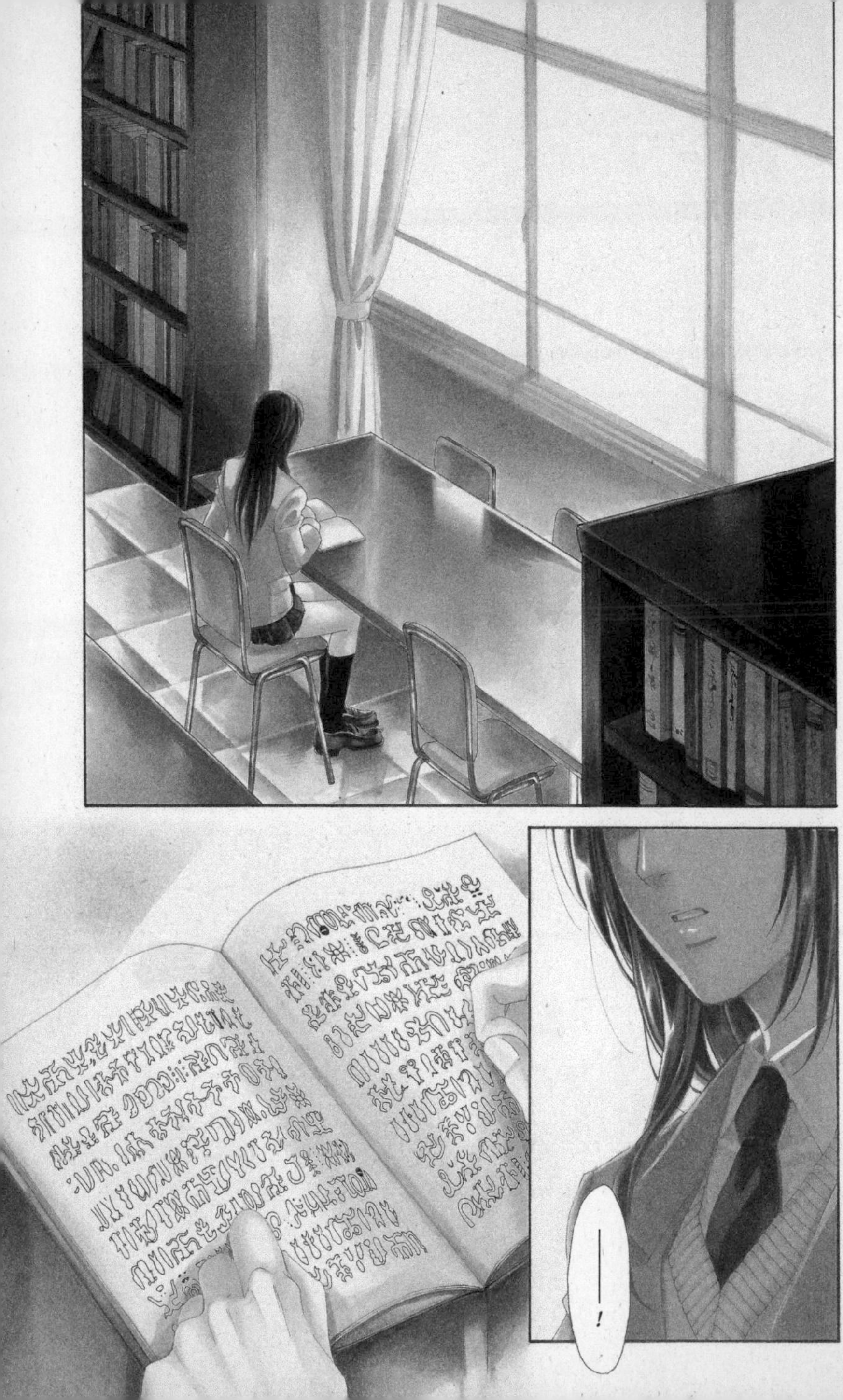
—!

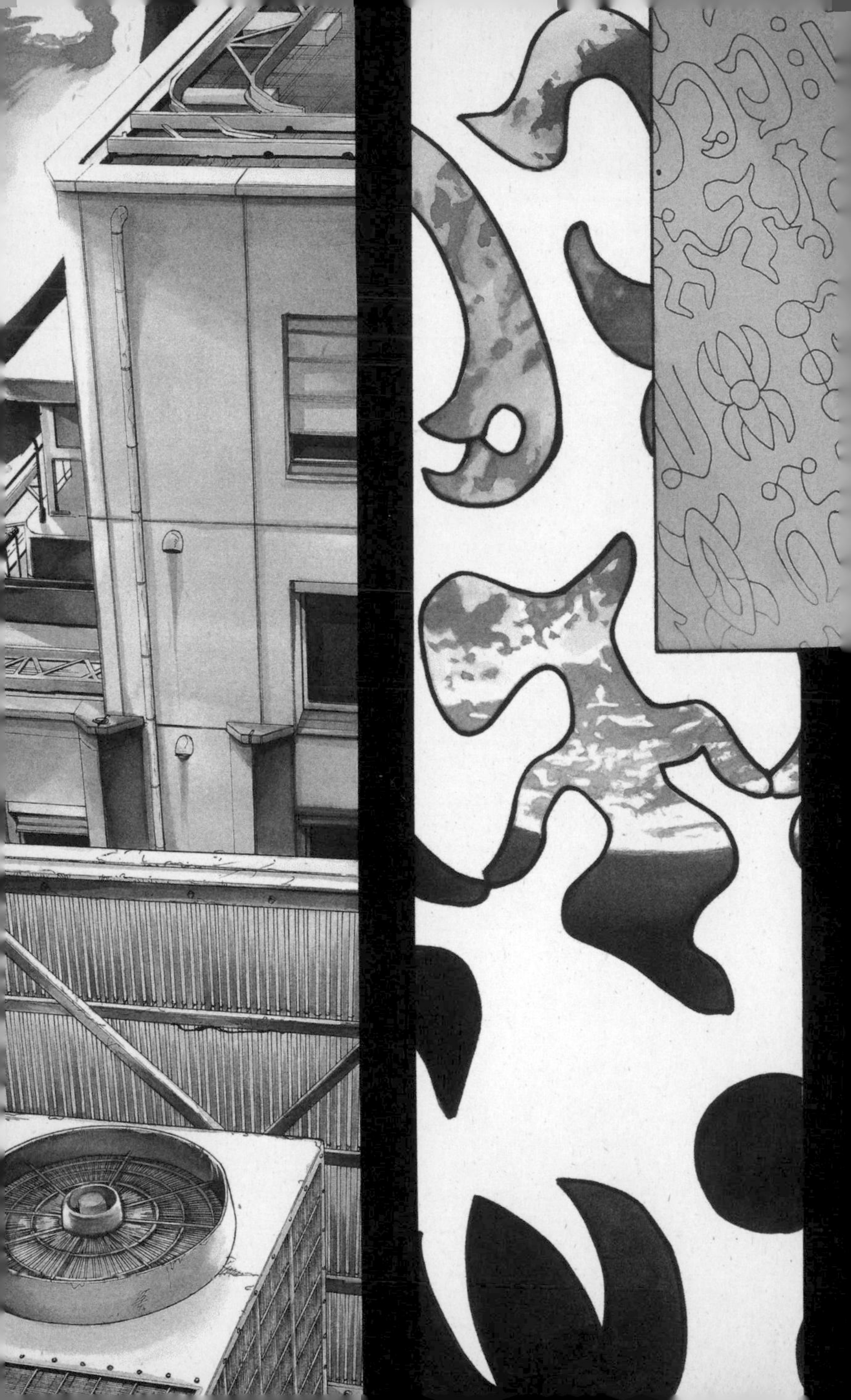

Chapter 1: MEMORIES

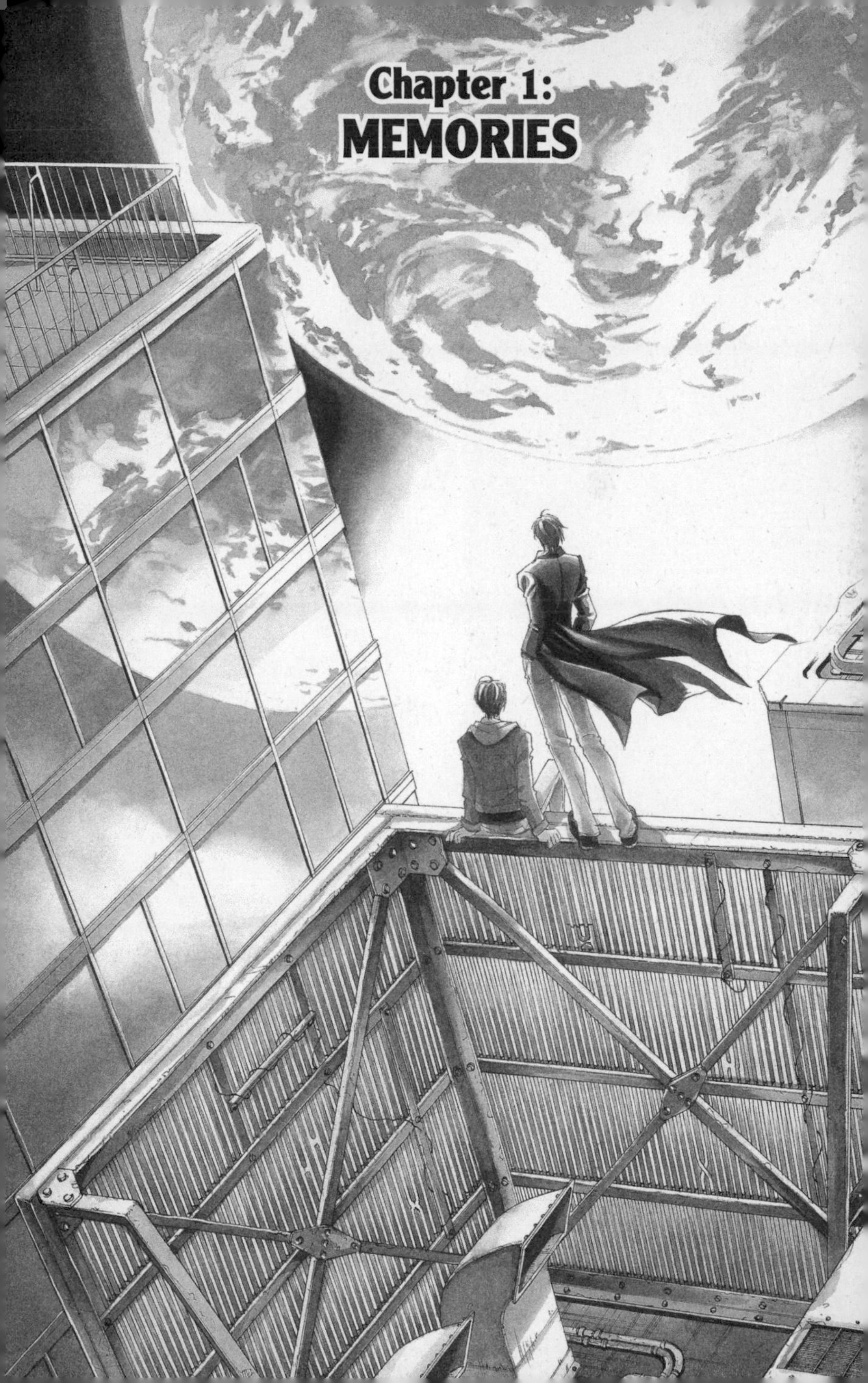

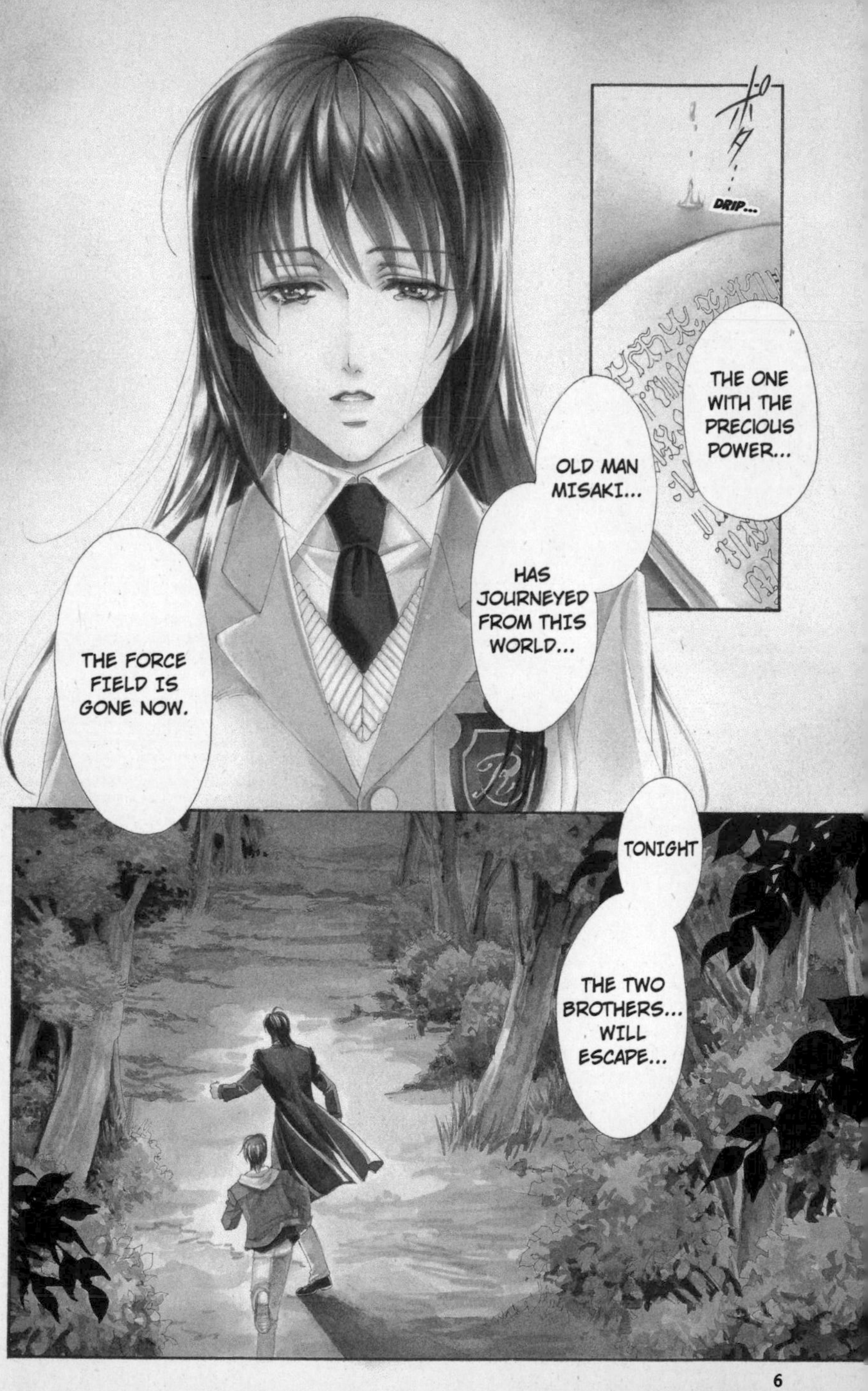
DRIP...
THE ONE WITH THE PRECIOUS POWER...
OLD MAN MISAKI...
HAS JOURNEYED FROM THIS WORLD...
THE FORCE FIELD IS GONE NOW.
TONIGHT
THE TWO BROTHERS... WILL ESCAPE...

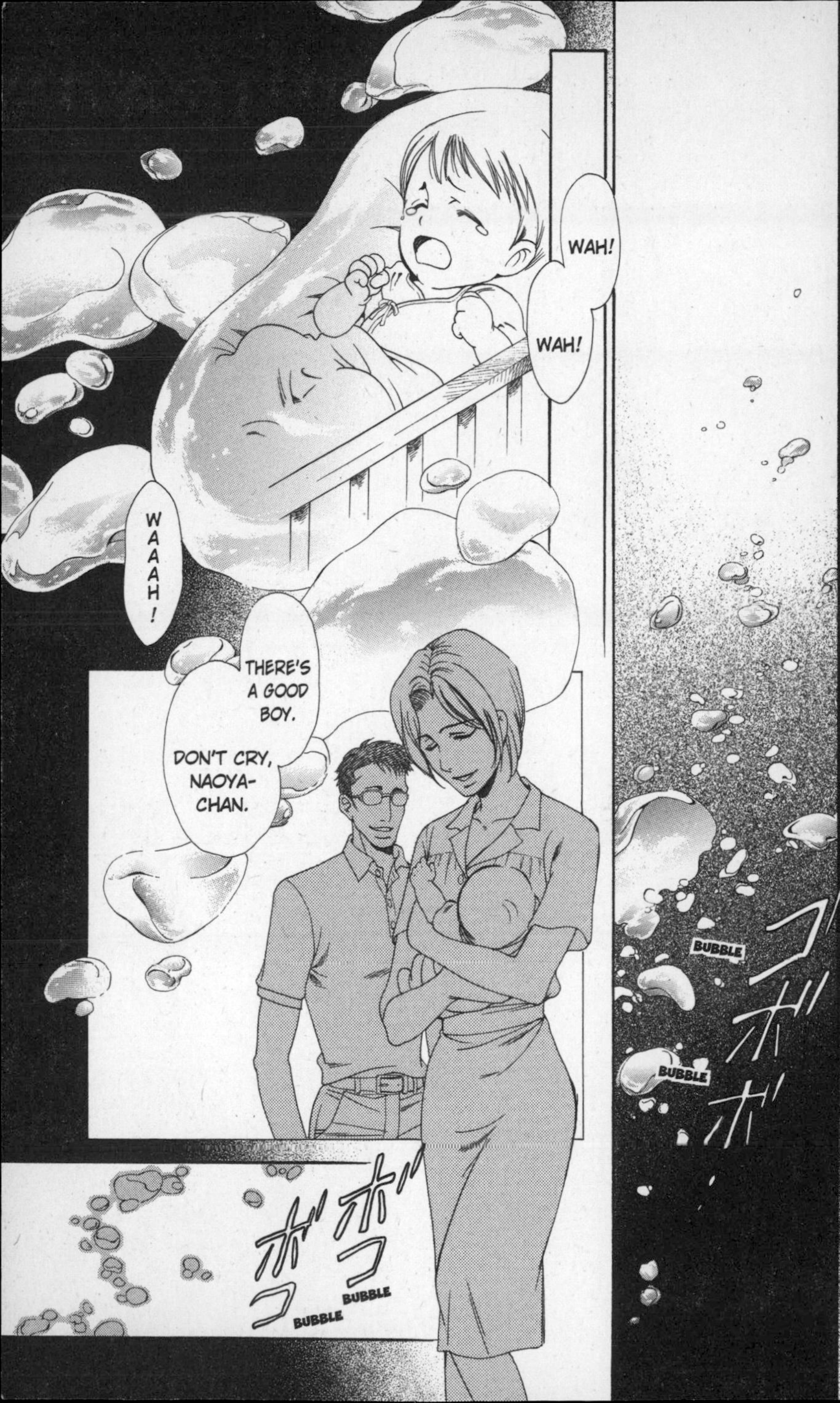
ゴボボボ
BUBBLE
BUBBLE
WAH!
WAH!
WAAAAH!
THERE'S A GOOD BOY.
DON'T CRY, NAOYA-CHAN.
ボッボッ
BUBBLE
BUBBLE

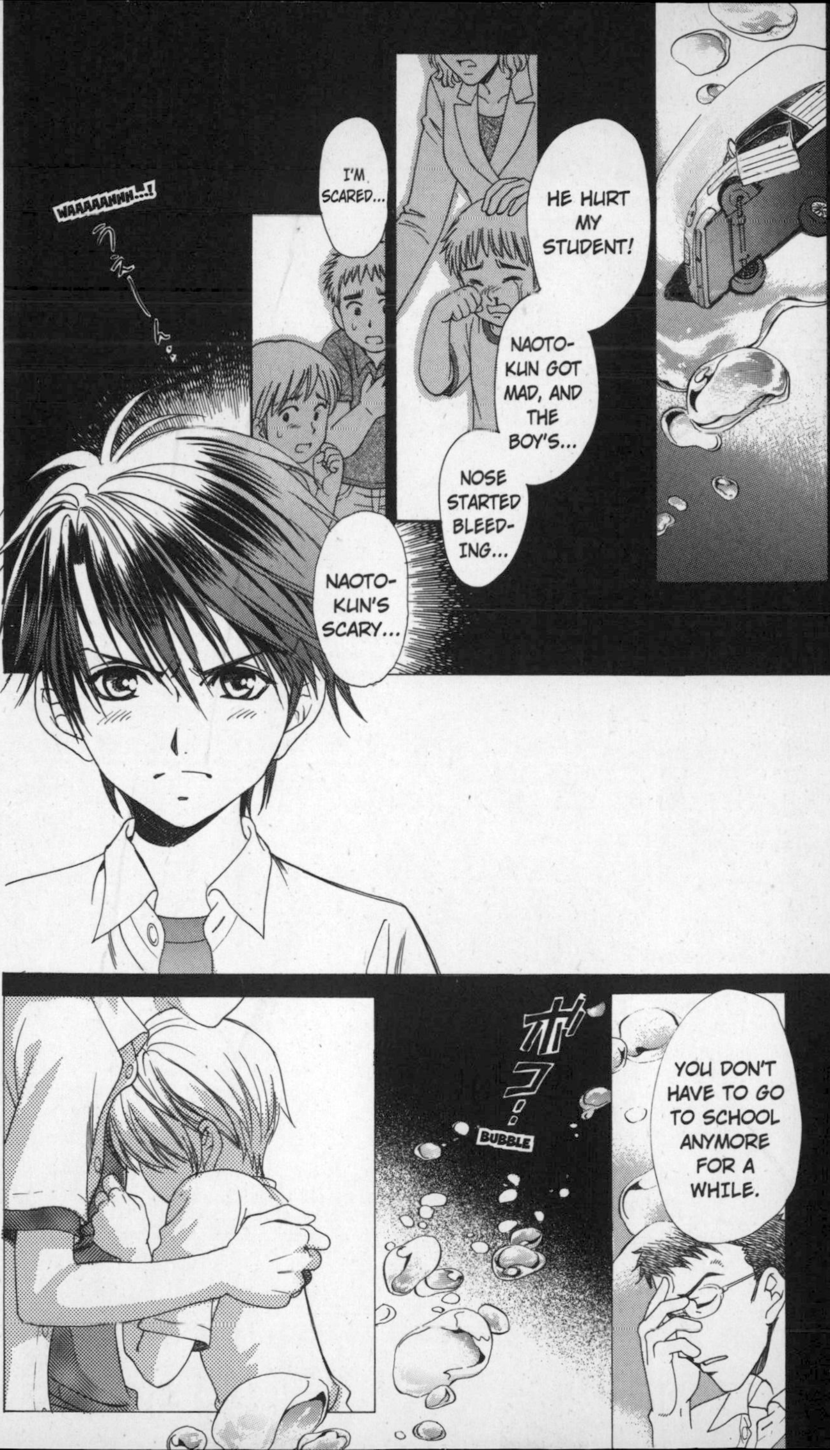
HE HURT MY STUDENT!
NAOTO-KUN GOT MAD, AND THE BOY'S...
NOSE STARTED BLEED-ING...
I'M SCARED...
NAOTO-KUN'S SCARY...
WAAAAAAHHH...!
YOU DON'T HAVE TO GO TO SCHOOL ANYMORE FOR A WHILE.
BUBBLE

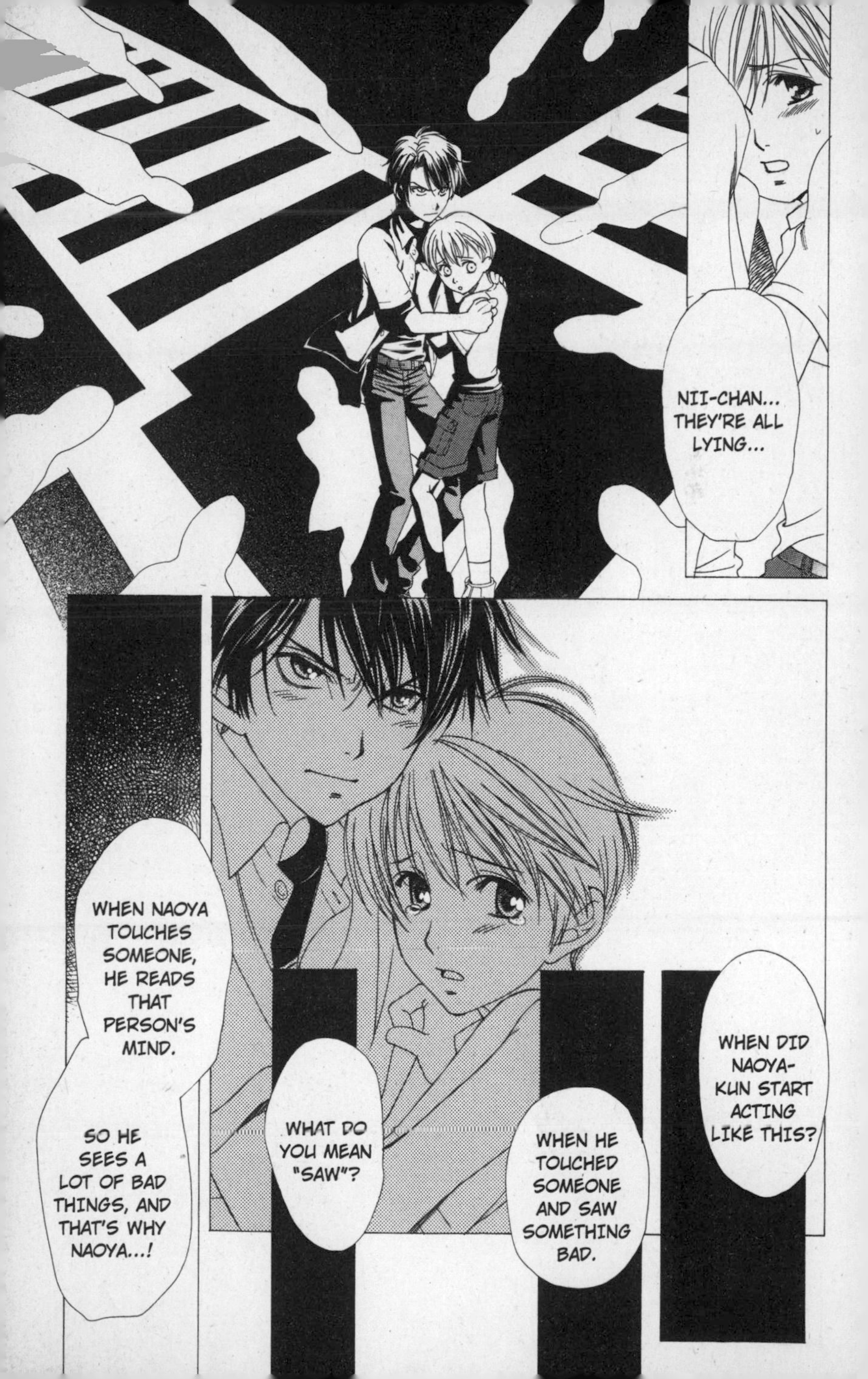
NII-CHAN... THEY'RE ALL LYING...
WHEN DID NAOYA-KUN START ACTING LIKE THIS?
WHEN HE TOUCHED SOMEONE AND SAW SOMETHING BAD.
WHAT DO YOU MEAN "SAW"?
WHEN NAOYA TOUCHES SOMEONE, HE READS THAT PERSON'S MIND.
SO HE SEES A LOT OF BAD THINGS, AND THAT'S WHY NAOYA...!

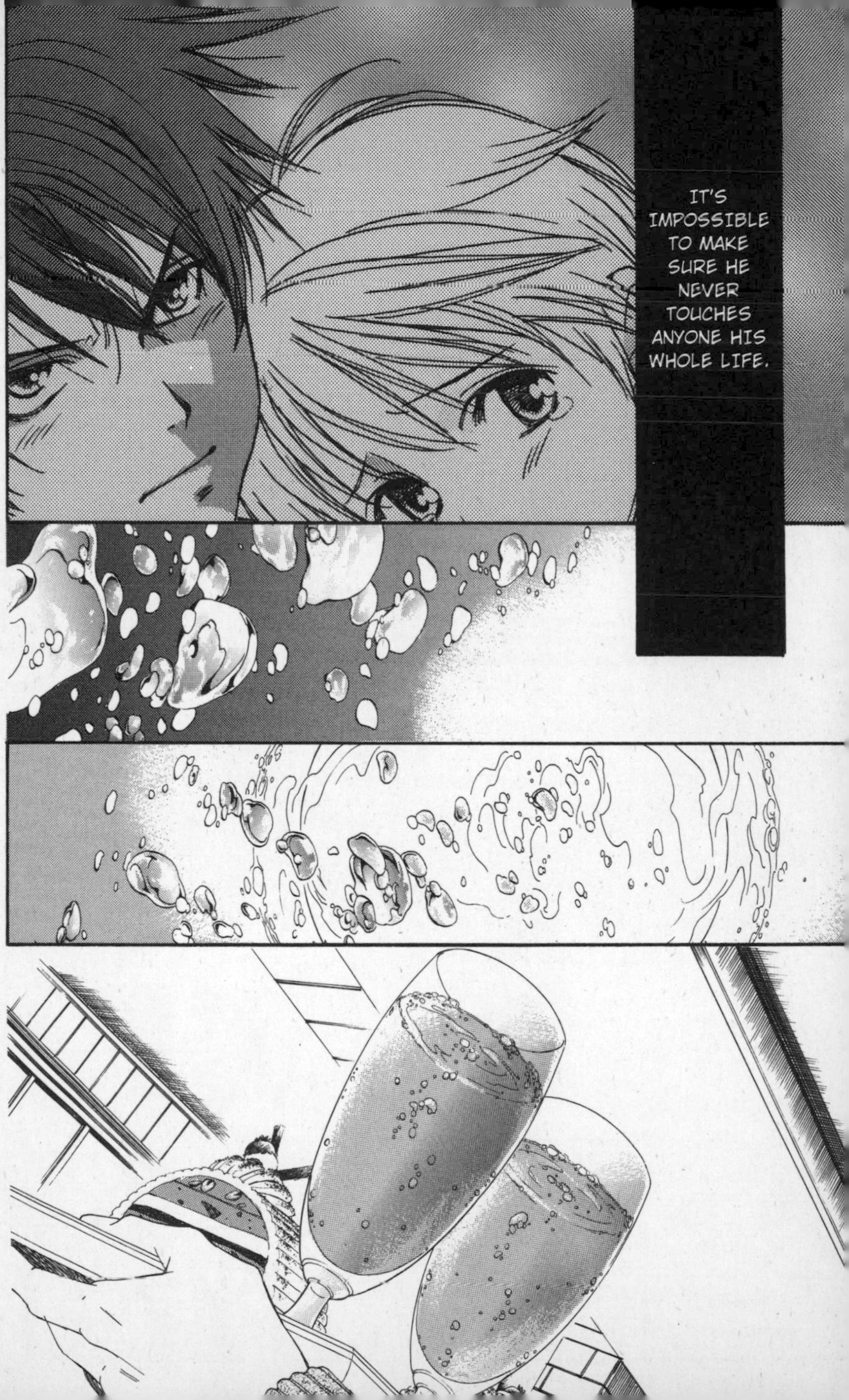
IT'S IMPOSSIBLE TO MAKE SURE HE NEVER TOUCHES ANYONE HIS WHOLE LIFE.

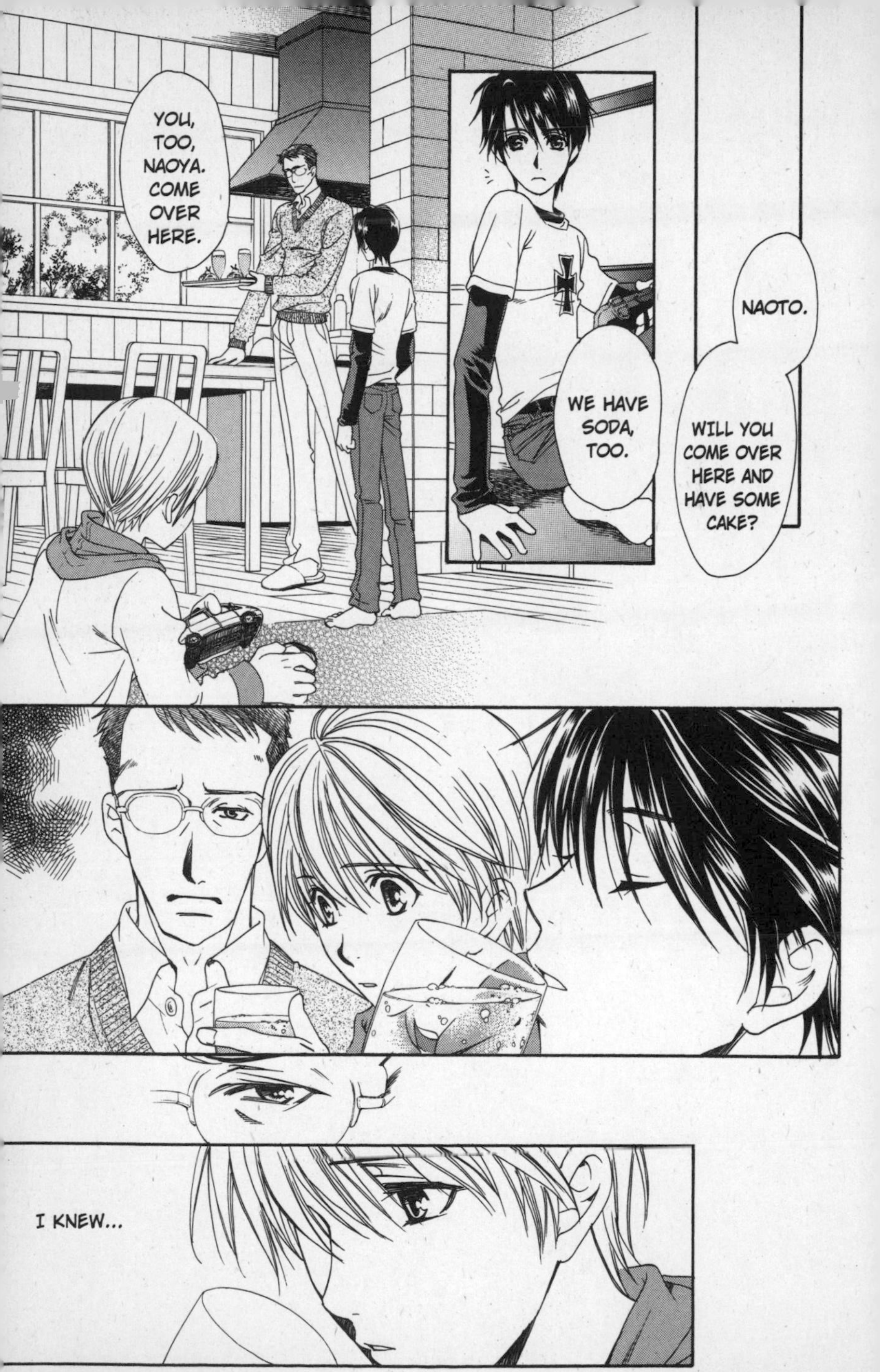
NAOTO.
WILL YOU COME OVER HERE AND HAVE SOME CAKE?
WE HAVE SODA, TOO.
YOU, TOO, NAOYA. COME OVER HERE.
I KNEW...

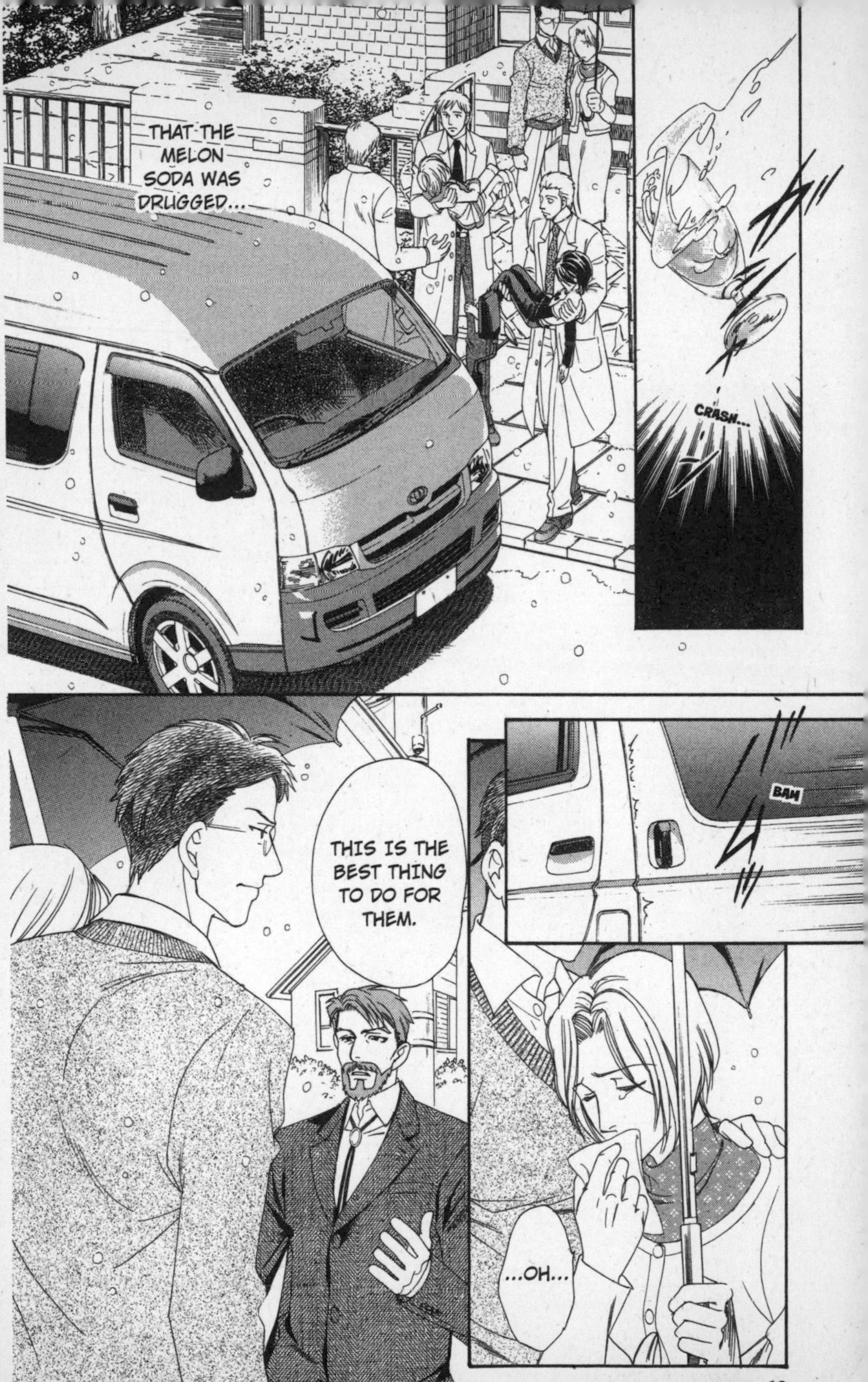
CRASH...
THAT THE MELON SODA WAS DRUGGED...
BAM
...OH...
THIS IS THE BEST THING TO DO FOR THEM.

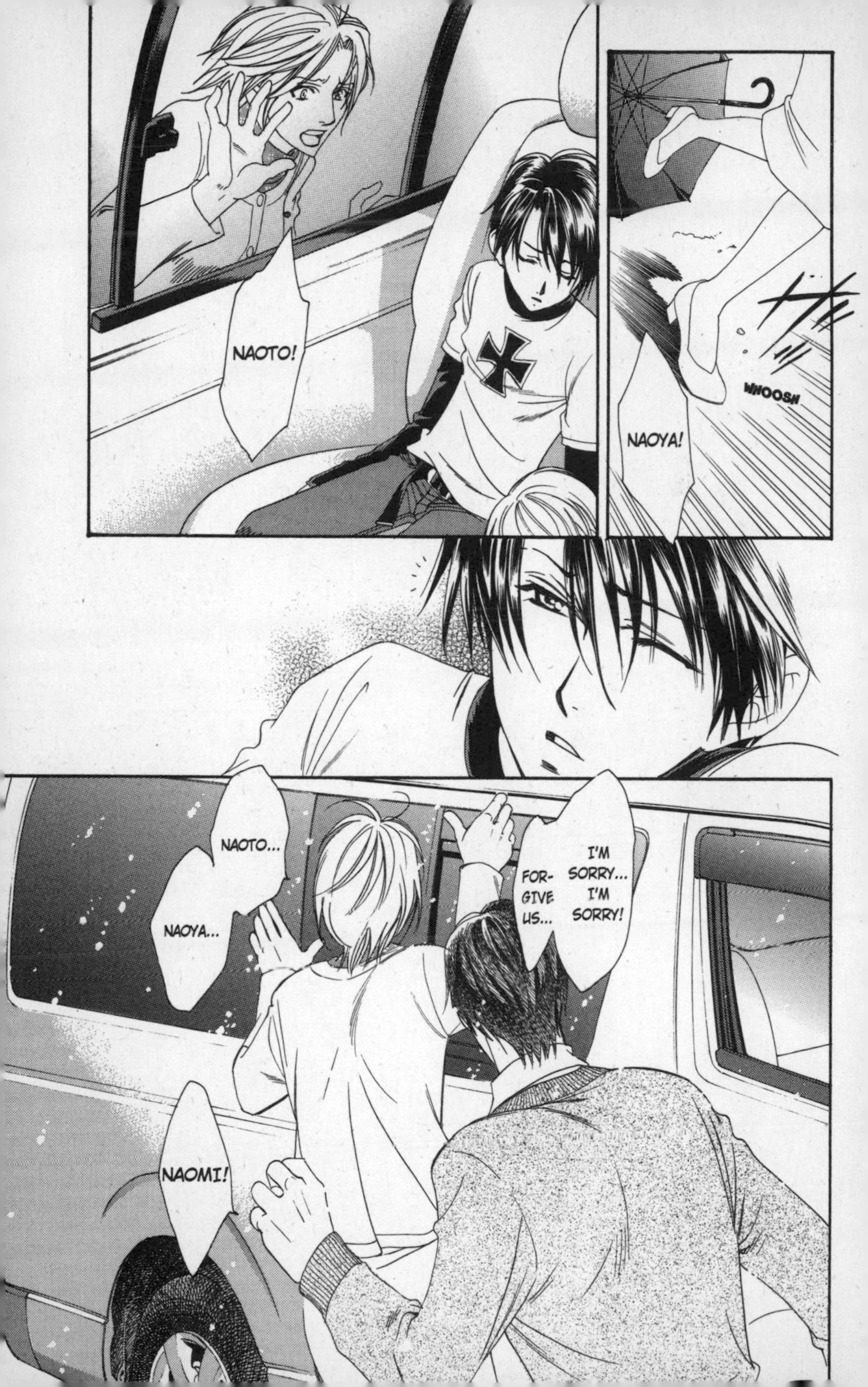
WHOOSH
NAOYA!
NAOTO!
I'M SORRY... I'M SORRY!
FOR-GIVE US...
NAOTO...
NAOYA...
NAOMI!

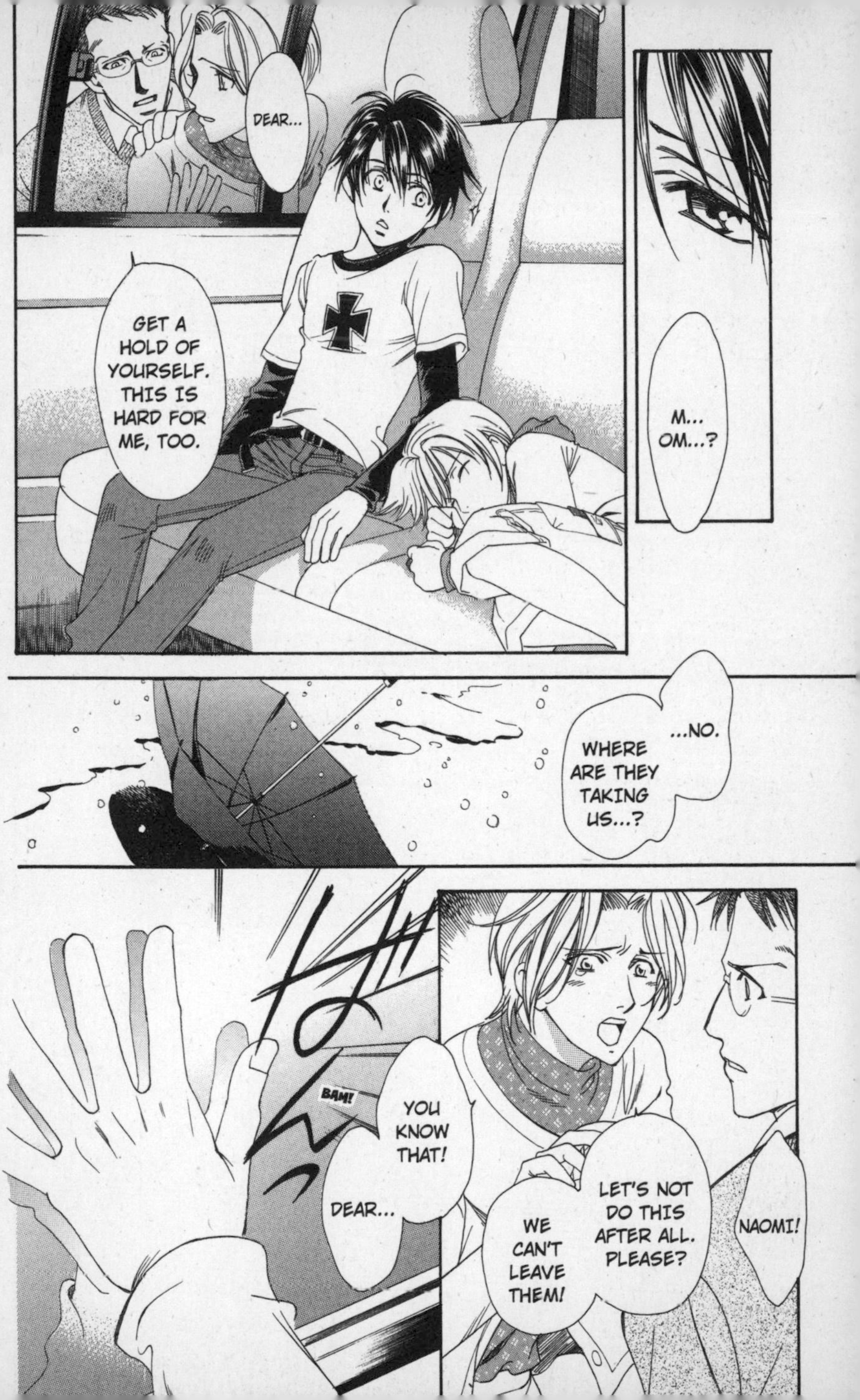
M... OM...?
DEAR...
GET A HOLD OF YOURSELF. THIS IS HARD FOR ME, TOO.
...NO.
WHERE ARE THEY TAKING US...?
NAOMI!
LET'S NOT DO THIS AFTER ALL. PLEASE?
WE CAN'T LEAVE THEM!
BAM!
YOU KNOW THAT!
DEAR...

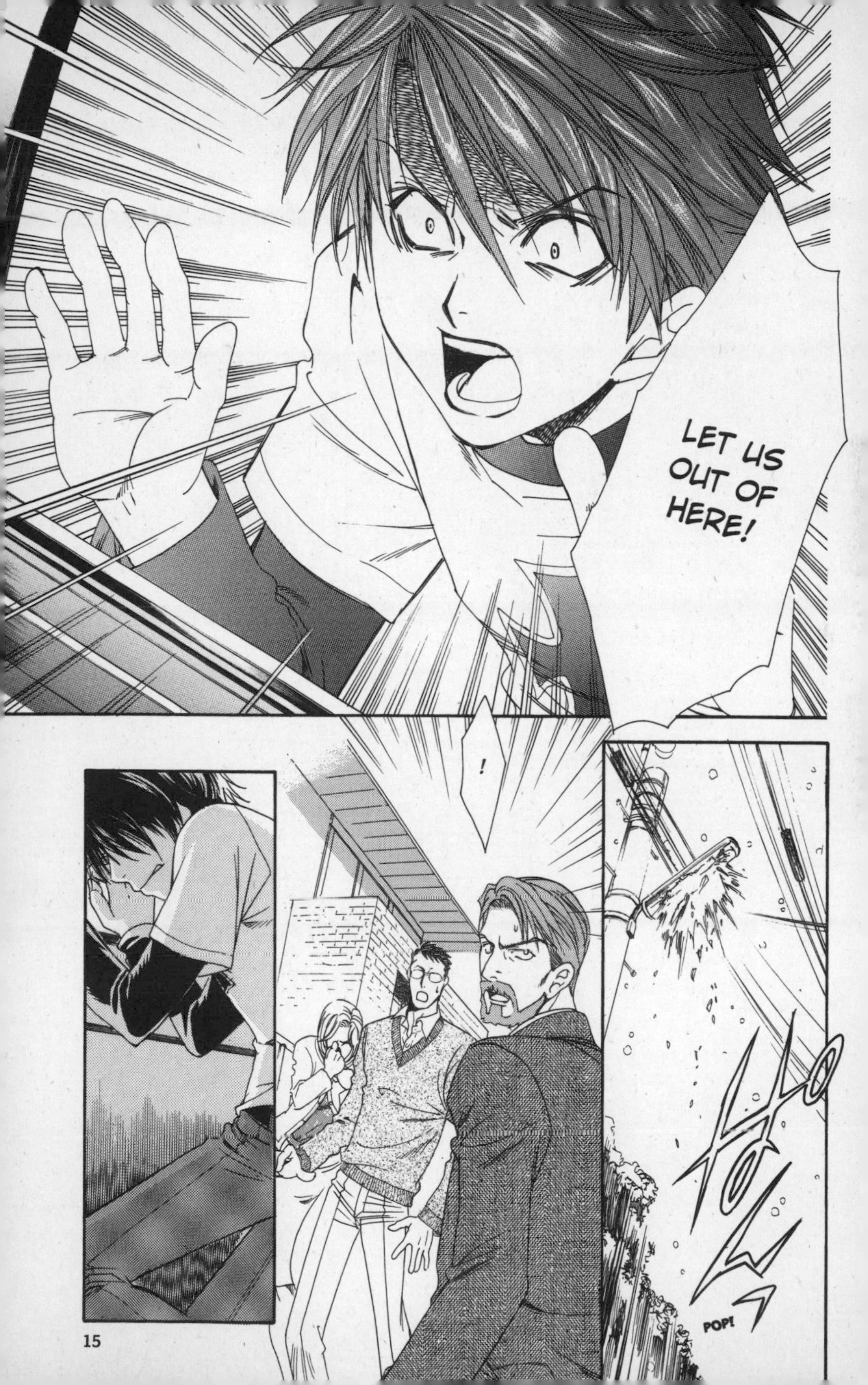
LET US OUT OF HERE!
POP!
!

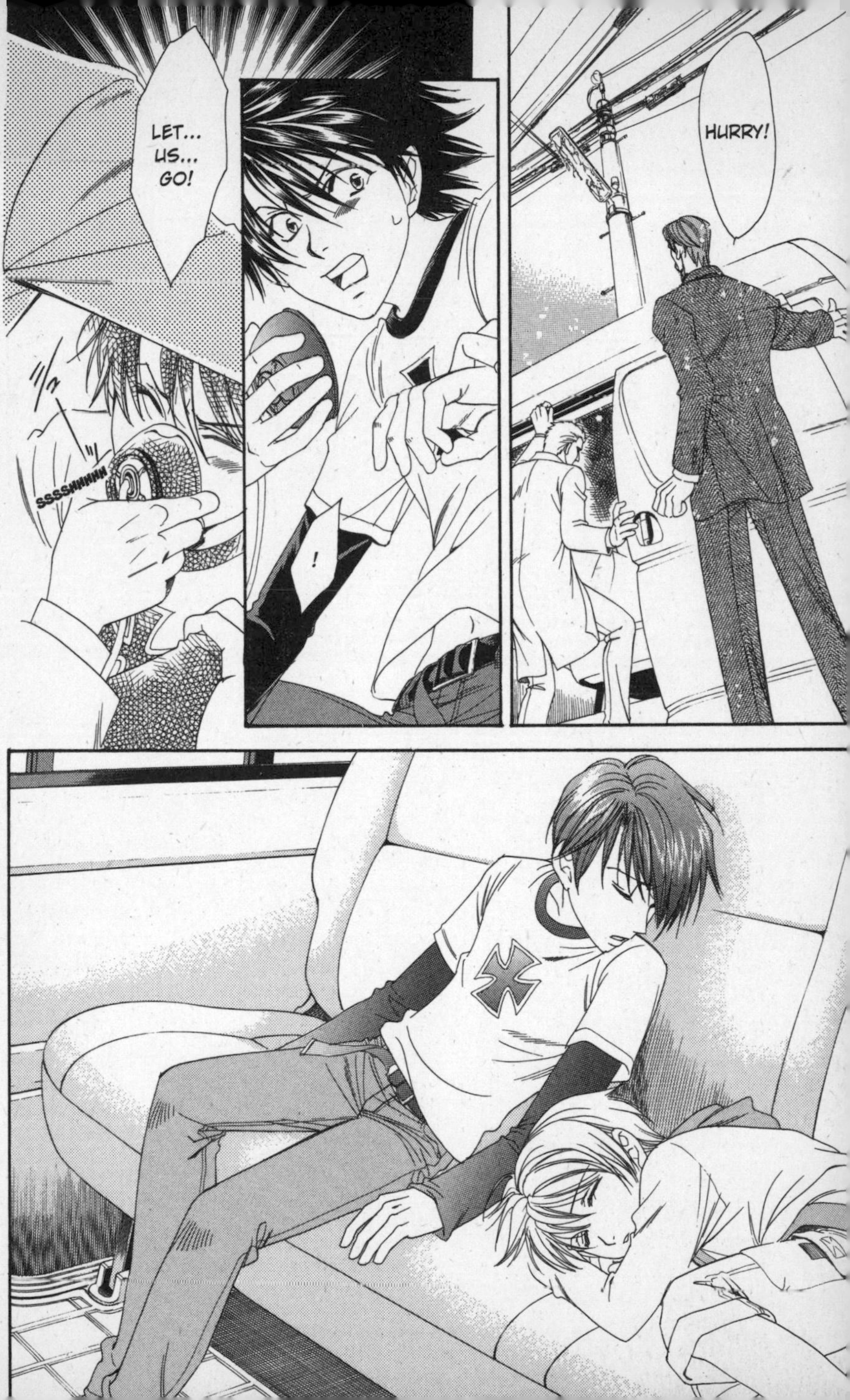
HURRY!
!
LET... US... GO!
SSSSHHHHHH

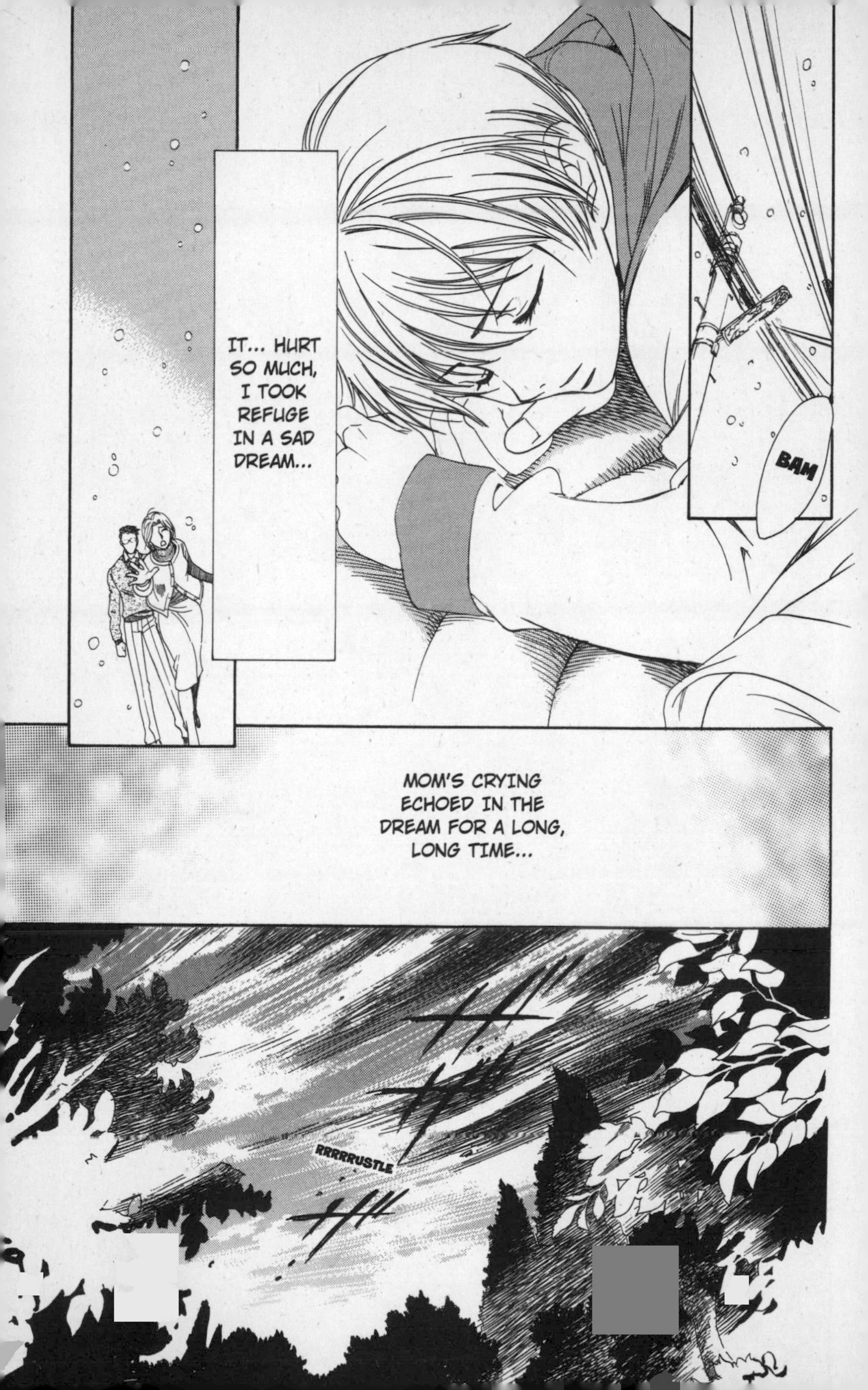
BAM
IT... HURT SO MUCH, I TOOK REFUGE IN A SAD DREAM...
MOM'S CRYING ECHOED IN THE DREAM FOR A LONG, LONG TIME...
RRRRRUSTLE

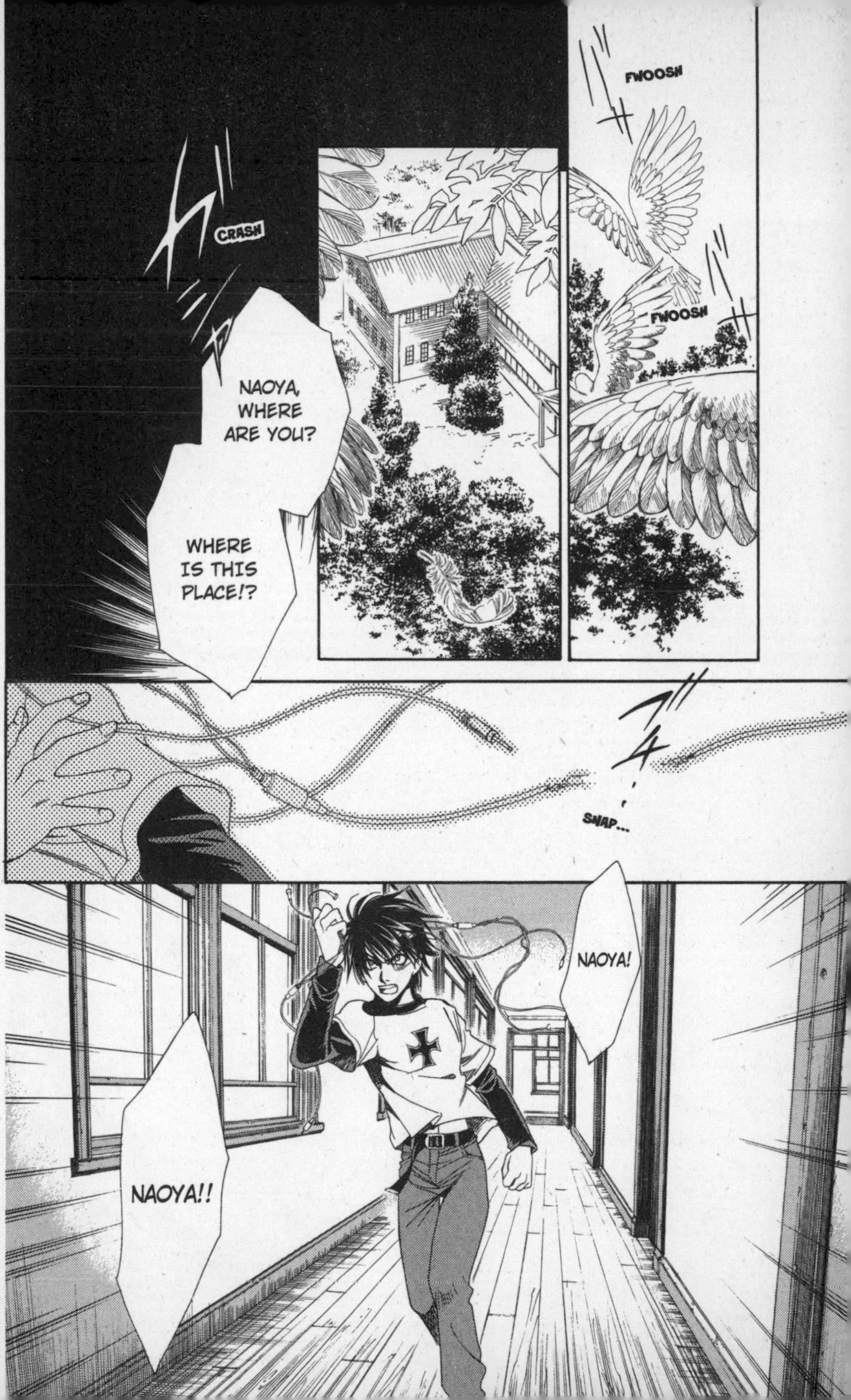
FWOOSH
FWOOSH
CRASH
NAOYA, WHERE ARE YOU?
WHERE IS THIS PLACE!?
SNAP...
NAOYA!
NAOYA!!

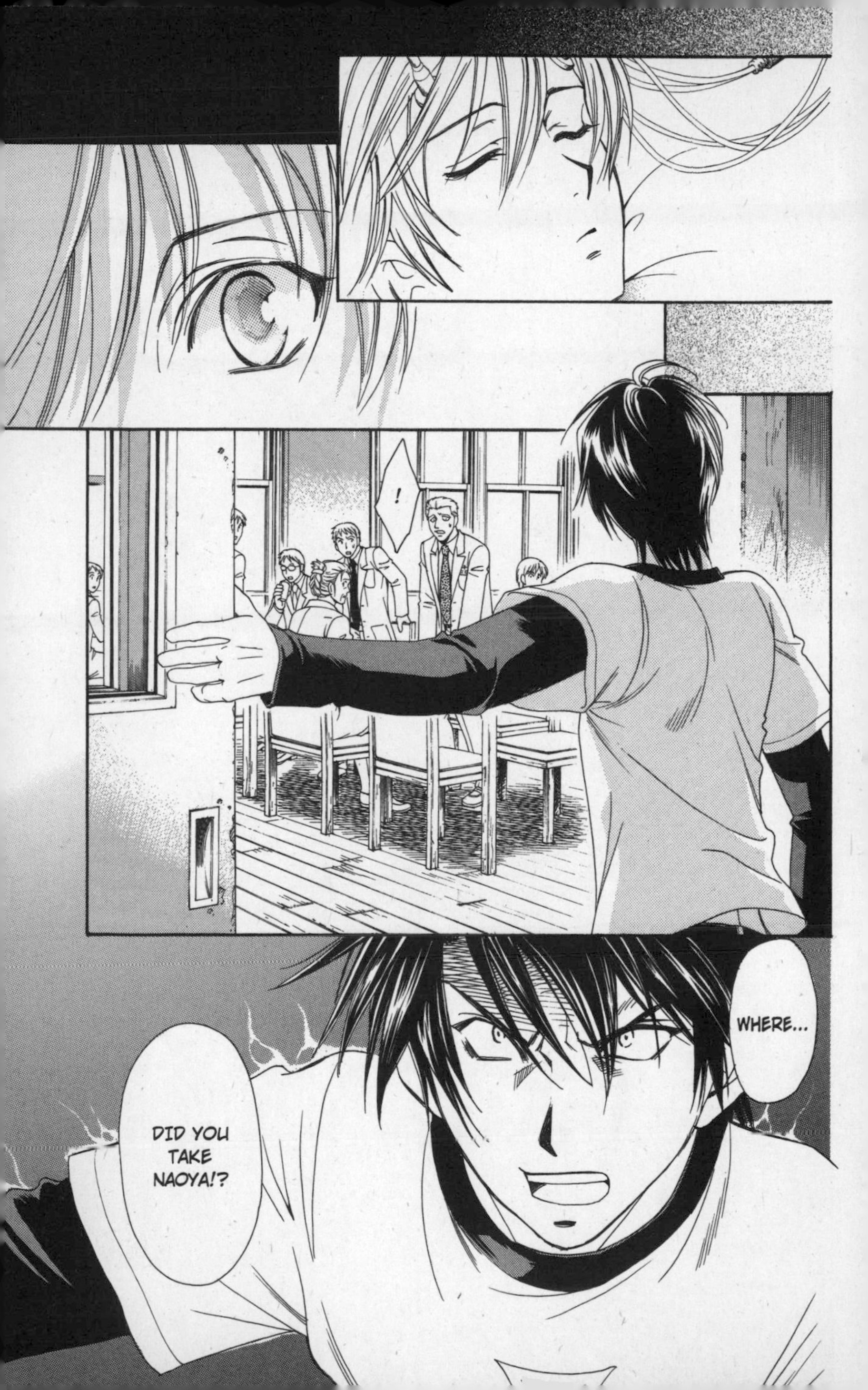
!
WHERE...
DID YOU TAKE NAOYA!?

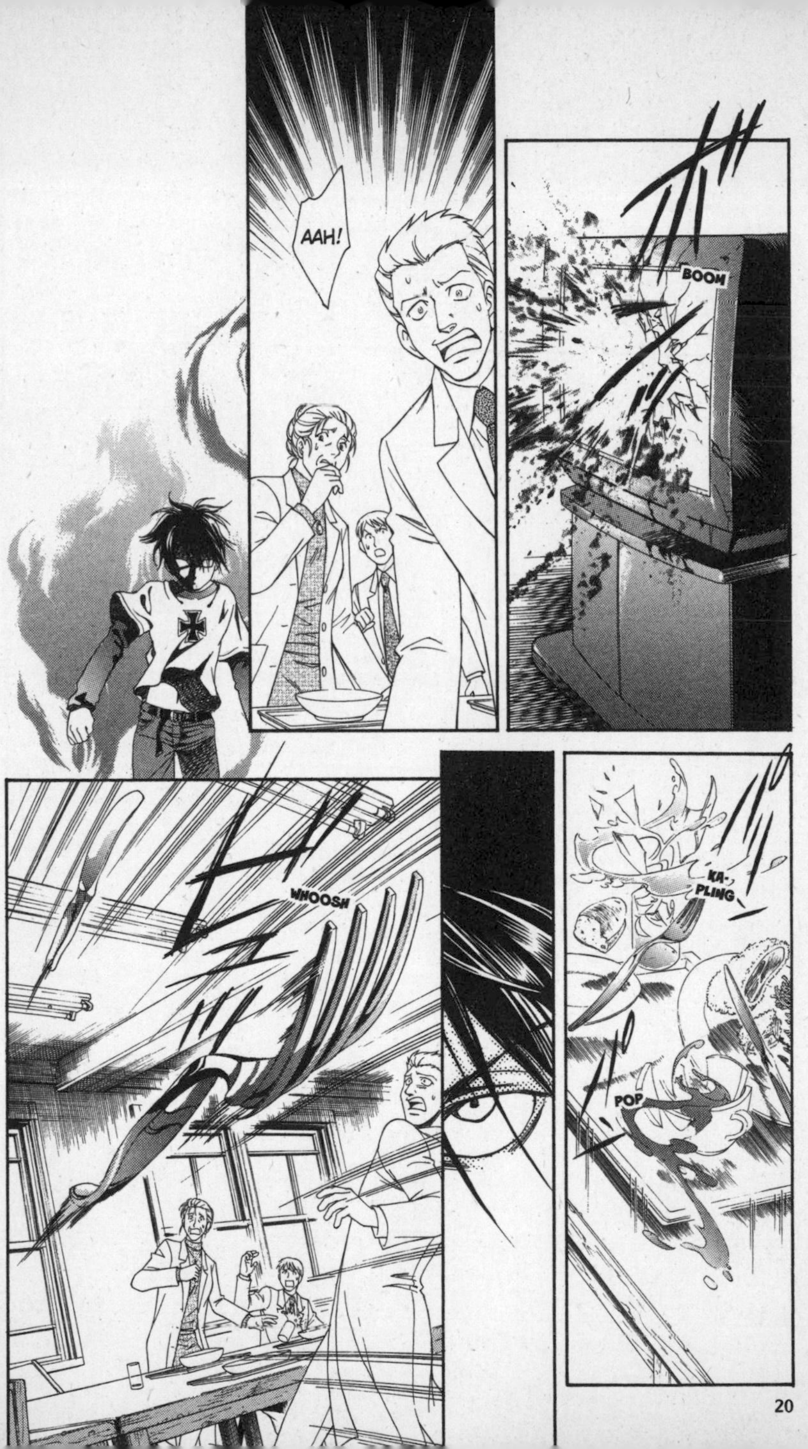
BOOM
AAH!
KA-PLING
POP
WHOOSH

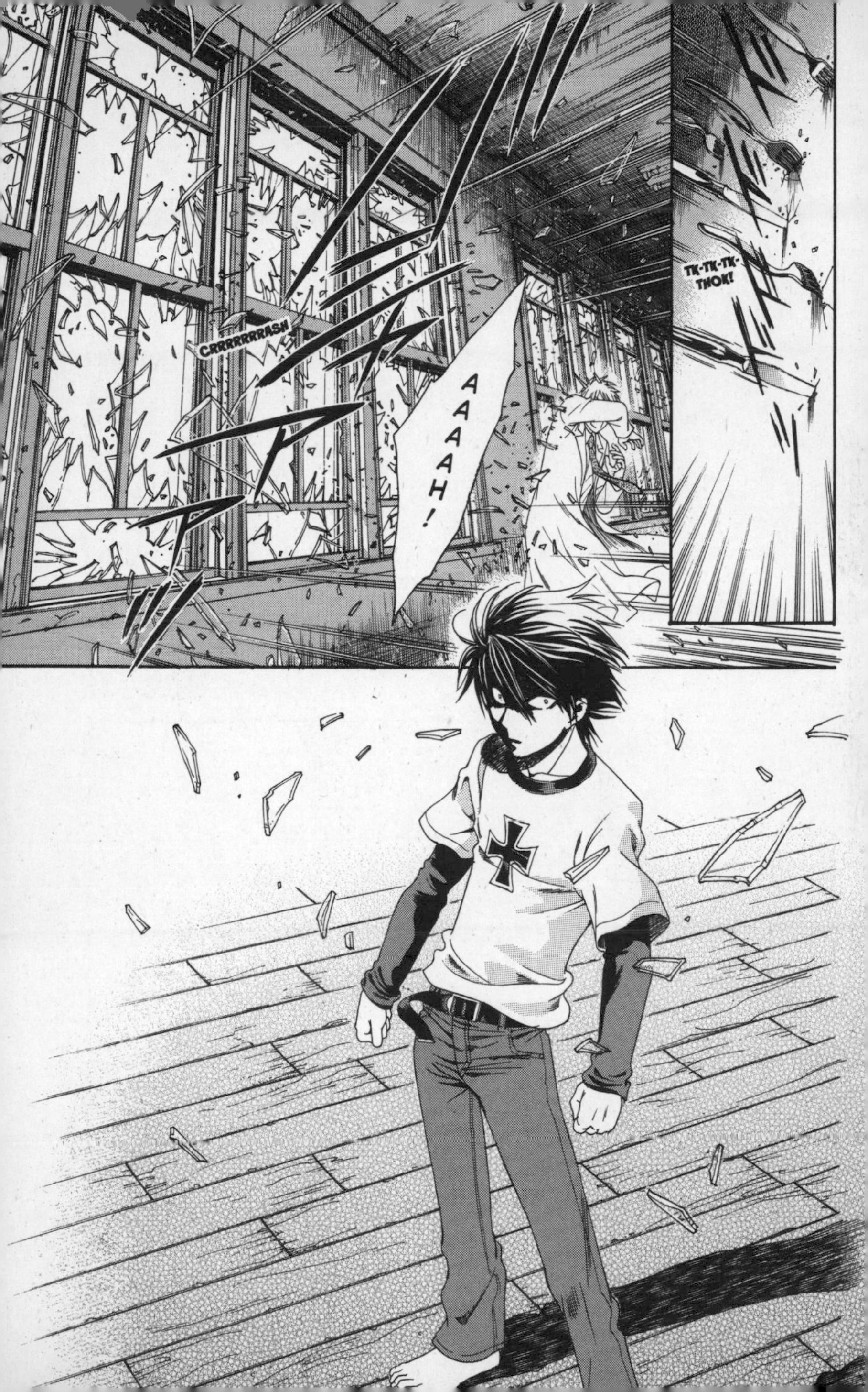
TK-TK-TK-THOK!
AAAAAH!
CRRRRRRRASH

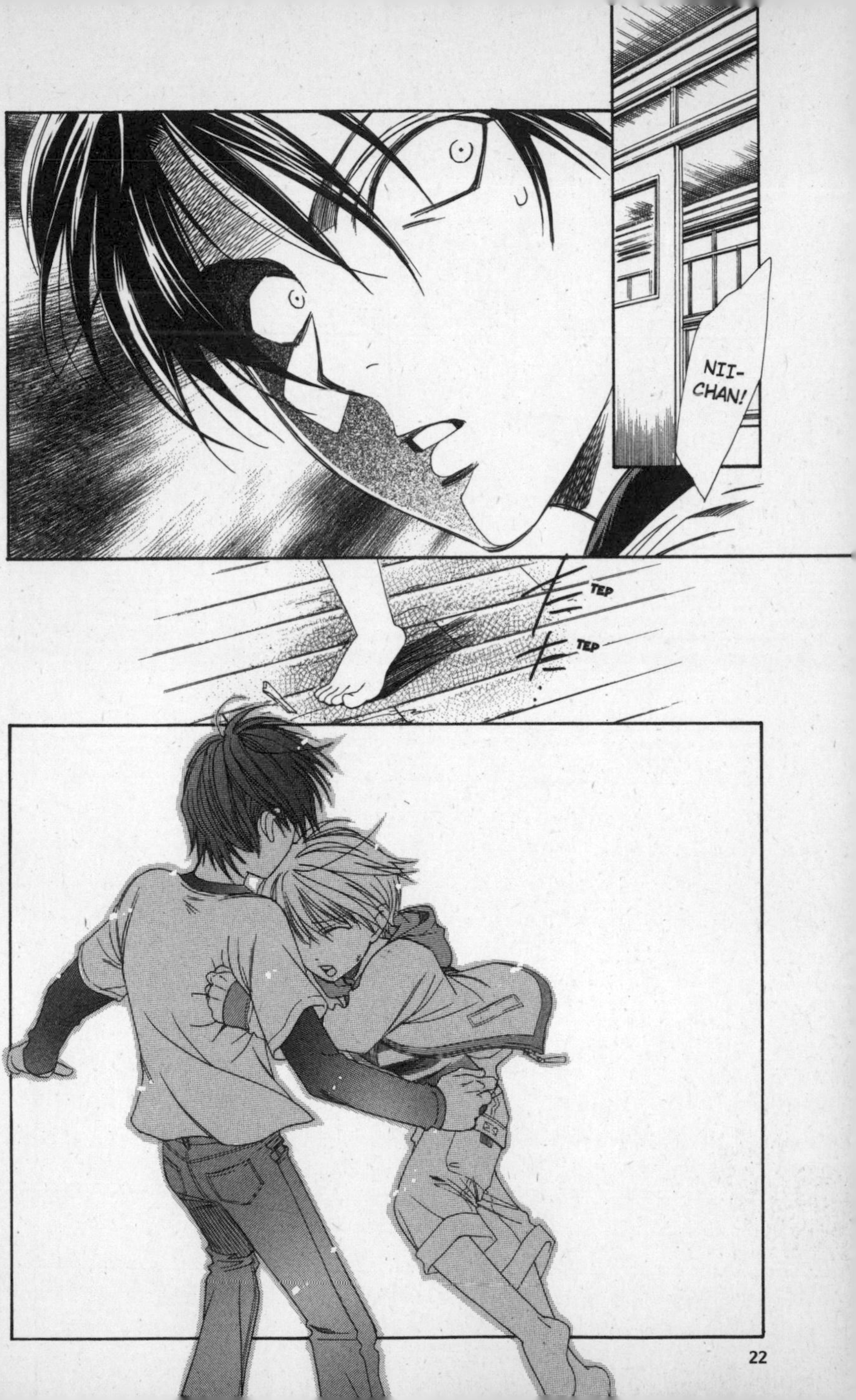
NII-
CHAN!
TEP
TEP

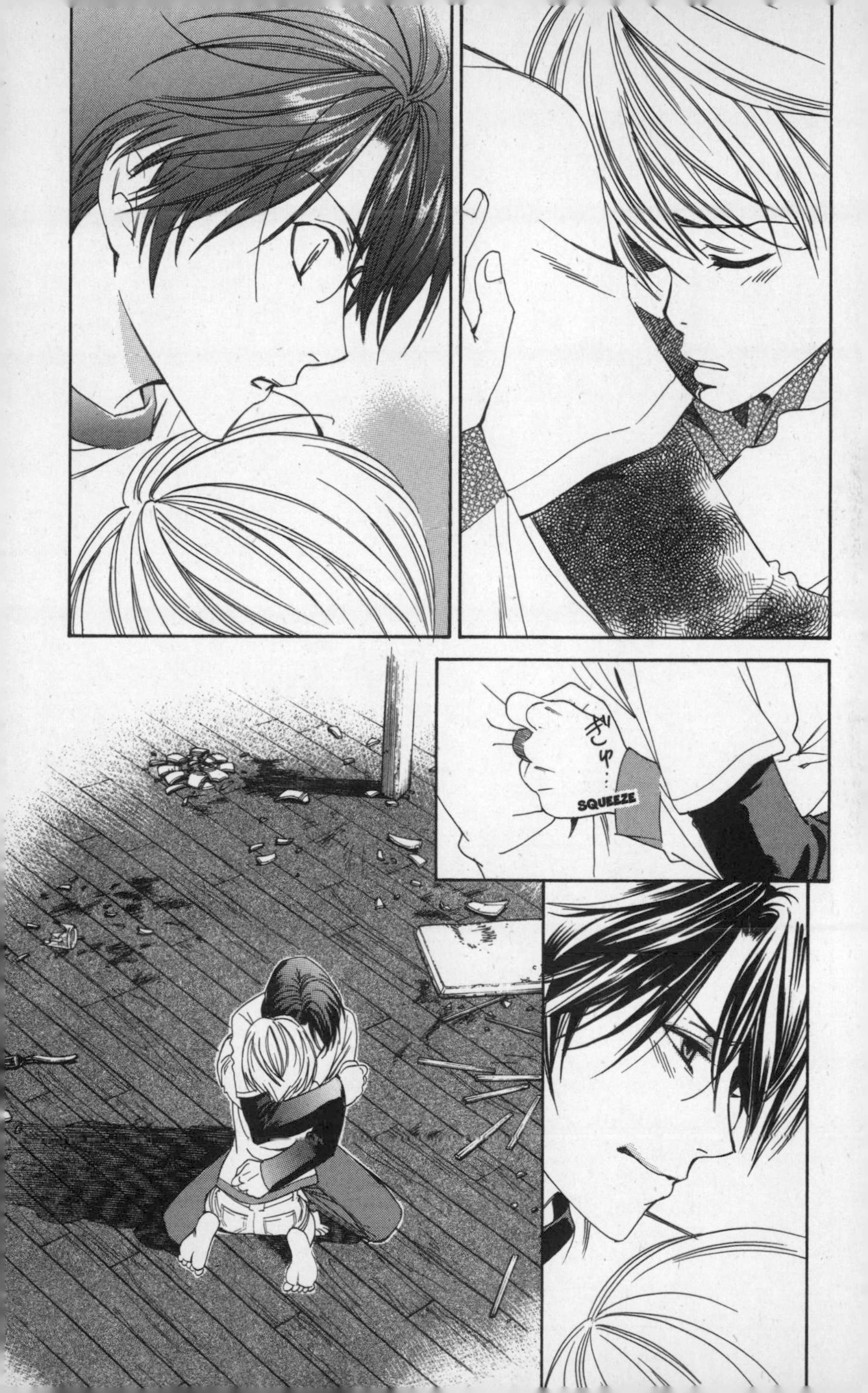
ぎゅ…
SQUEEZE

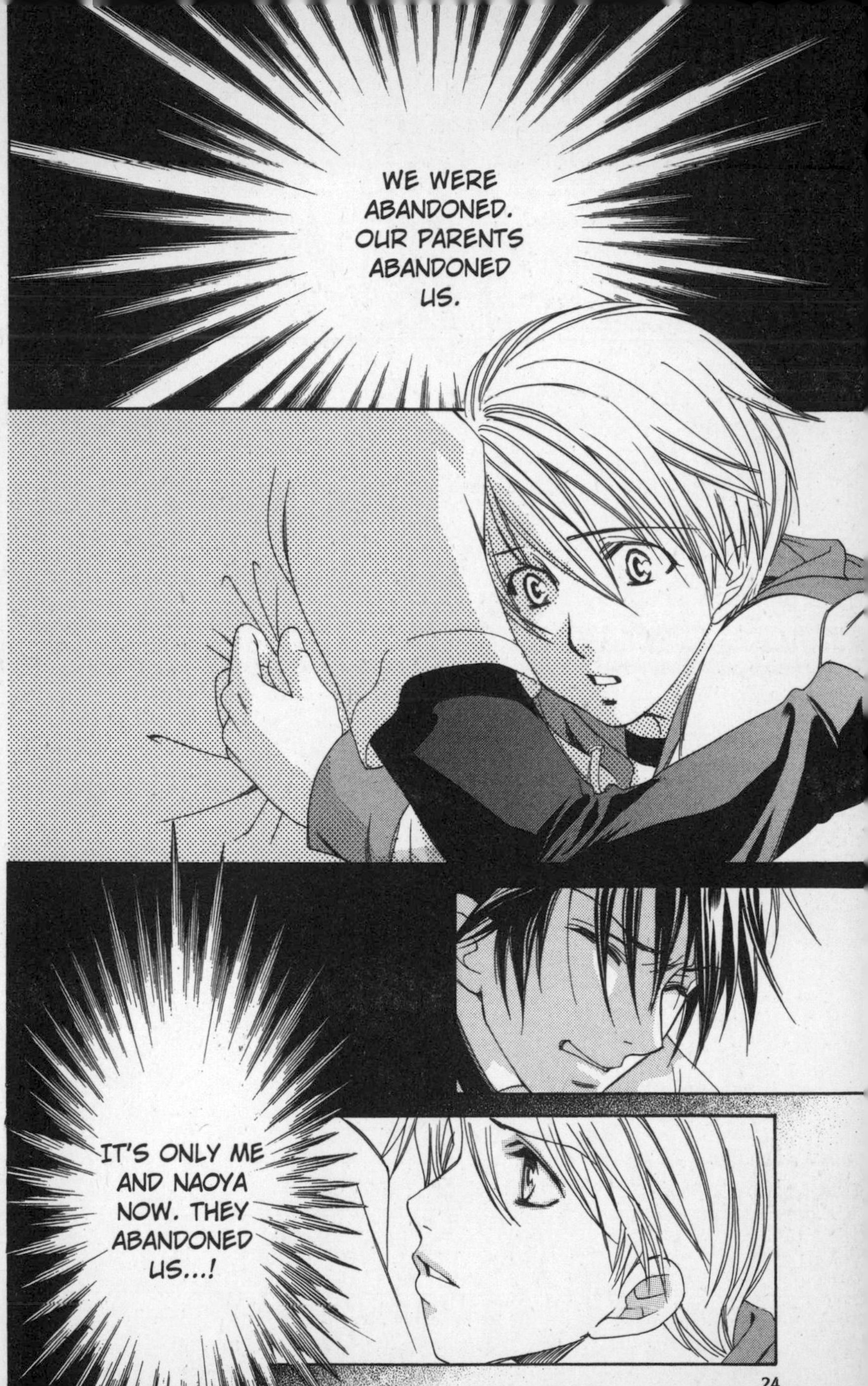
WE WERE ABANDONED. OUR PARENTS ABANDONED US.
IT'S ONLY ME AND NAOYA NOW. THEY ABANDONED US...!

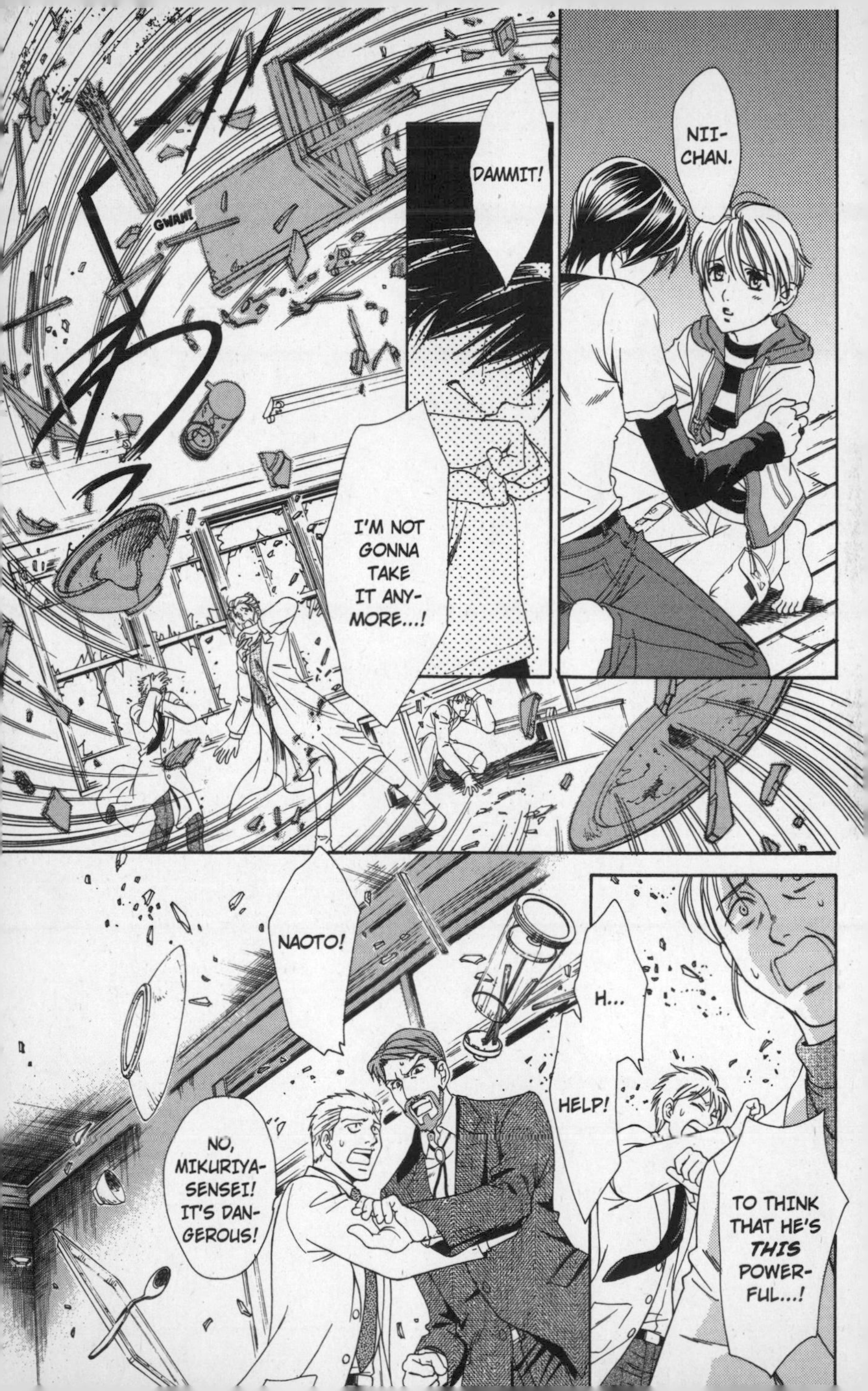
NII-CHAN.
DAMMIT!
I'M NOT GONNA TAKE IT ANY-MORE...!
GWAN!
TO THINK THAT HE'S *THIS* POWER-FUL...!
H...
HELP!
NAOTO!
NO, MIKURIYA-SENSEI! IT'S DAN-GEROUS!

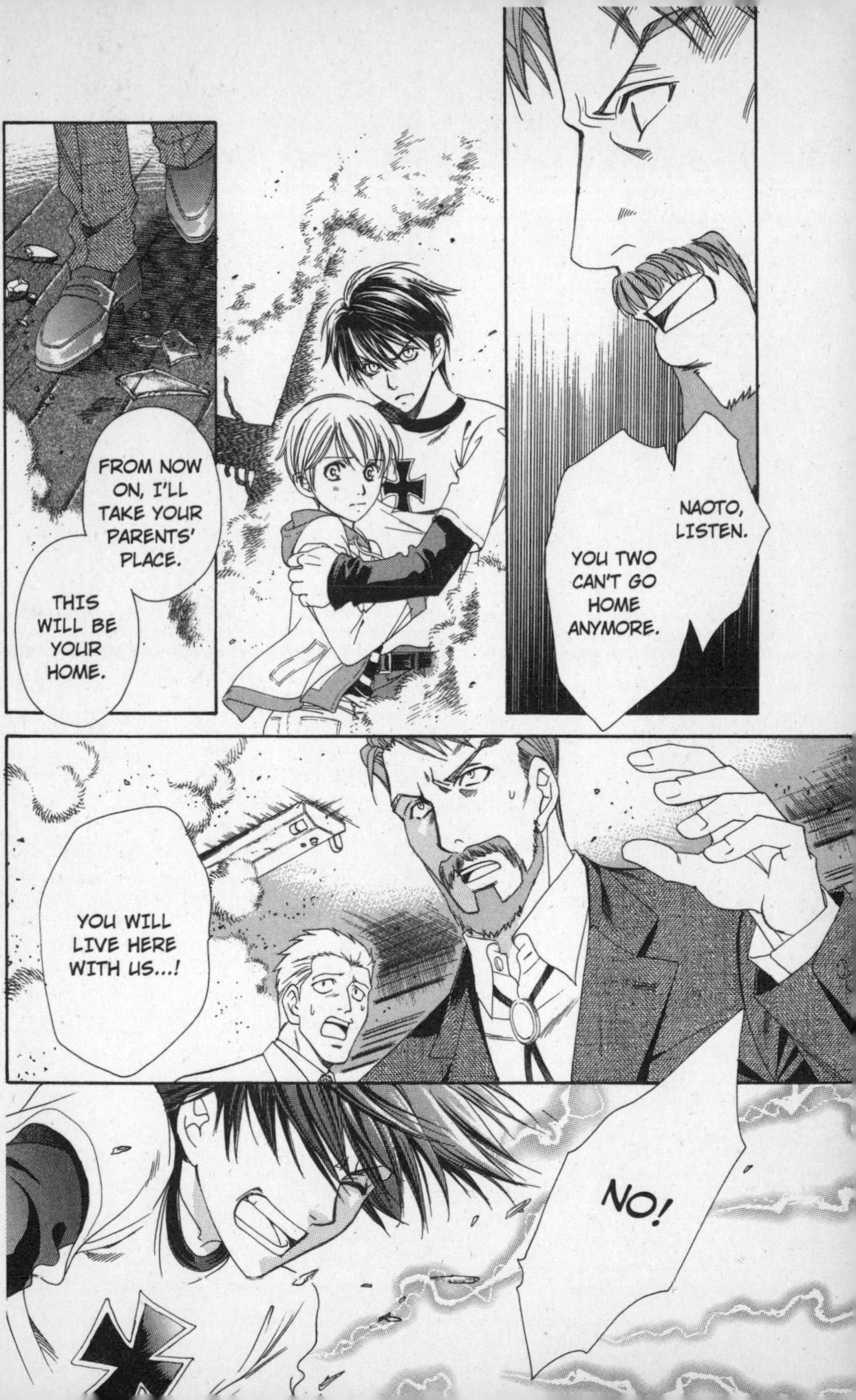
NAOTO, LISTEN.
YOU TWO CAN'T GO HOME ANYMORE.
FROM NOW ON, I'LL TAKE YOUR PARENTS' PLACE.
THIS WILL BE YOUR HOME.
YOU WILL LIVE HERE WITH US...!
NO!

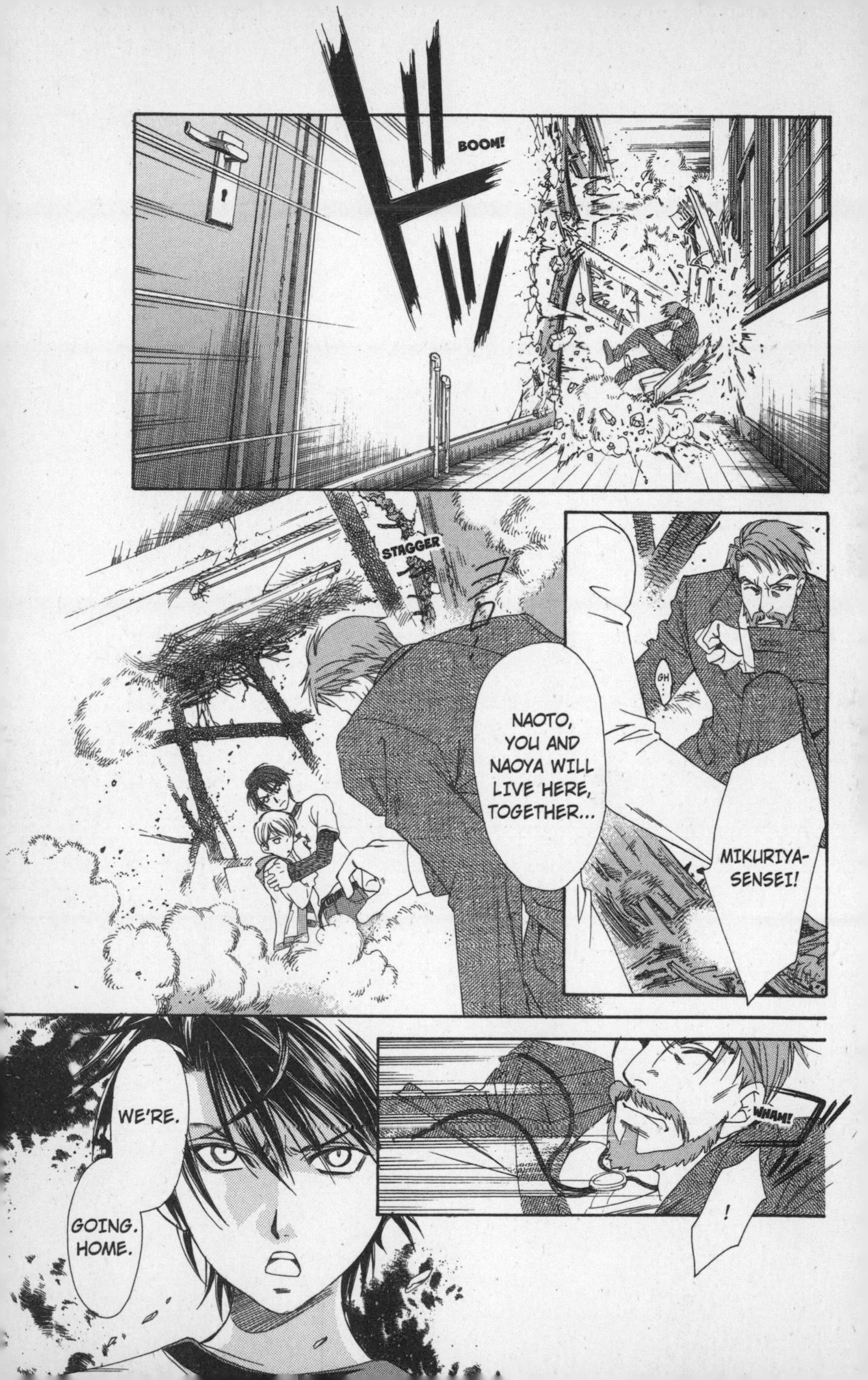
BOOM!
GH...
NAOTO, YOU AND NAOYA WILL LIVE HERE, TOGETHER...
MIKURIYA-SENSEI!
STAGGER
WHAM!
!
WE'RE.
GOING. HOME.

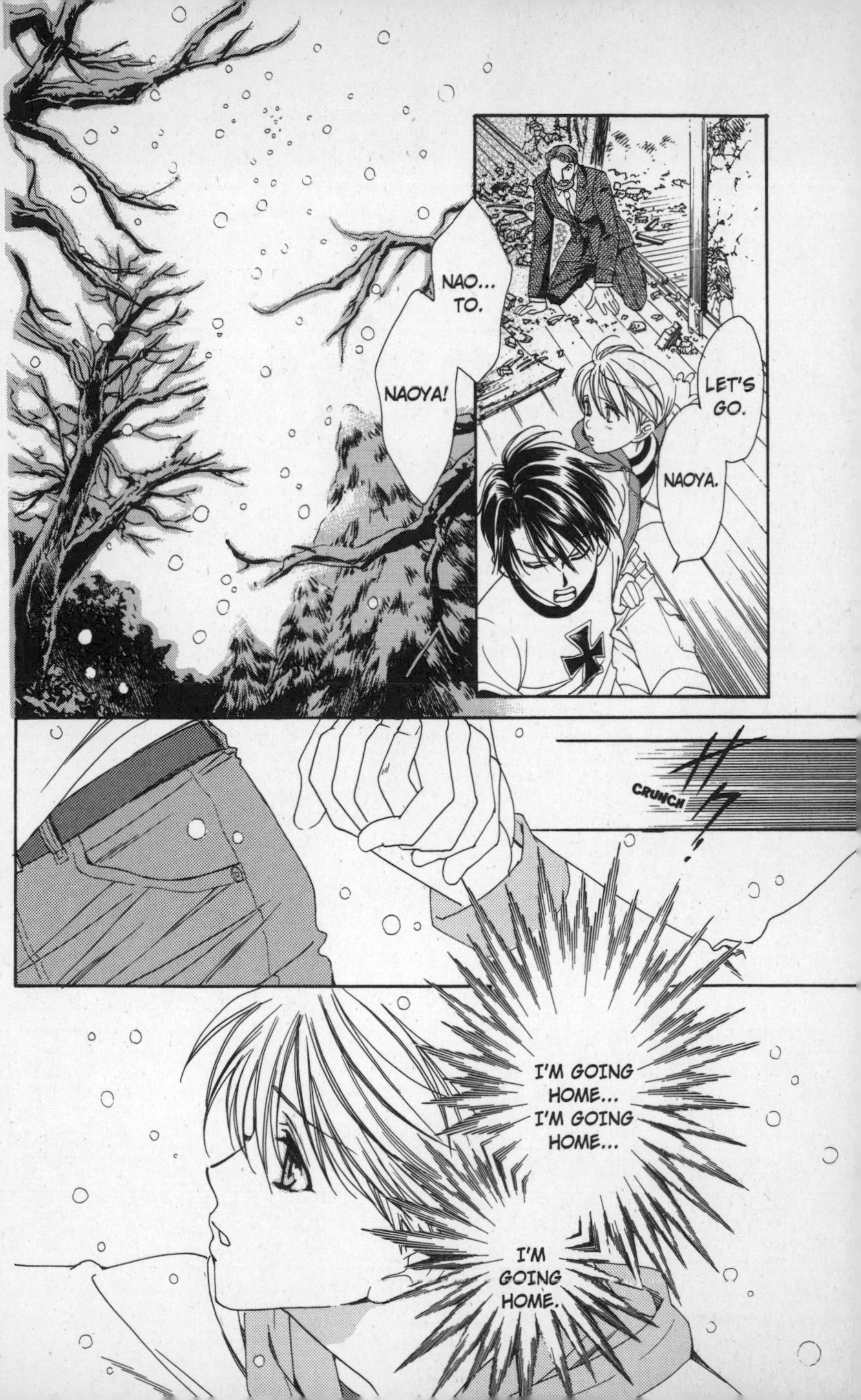
LET'S GO.
NAOYA.
NAO... TO.
NAOYA!
CRUNCH
I'M GOING HOME... I'M GOING HOME...
I'M GOING HOME.

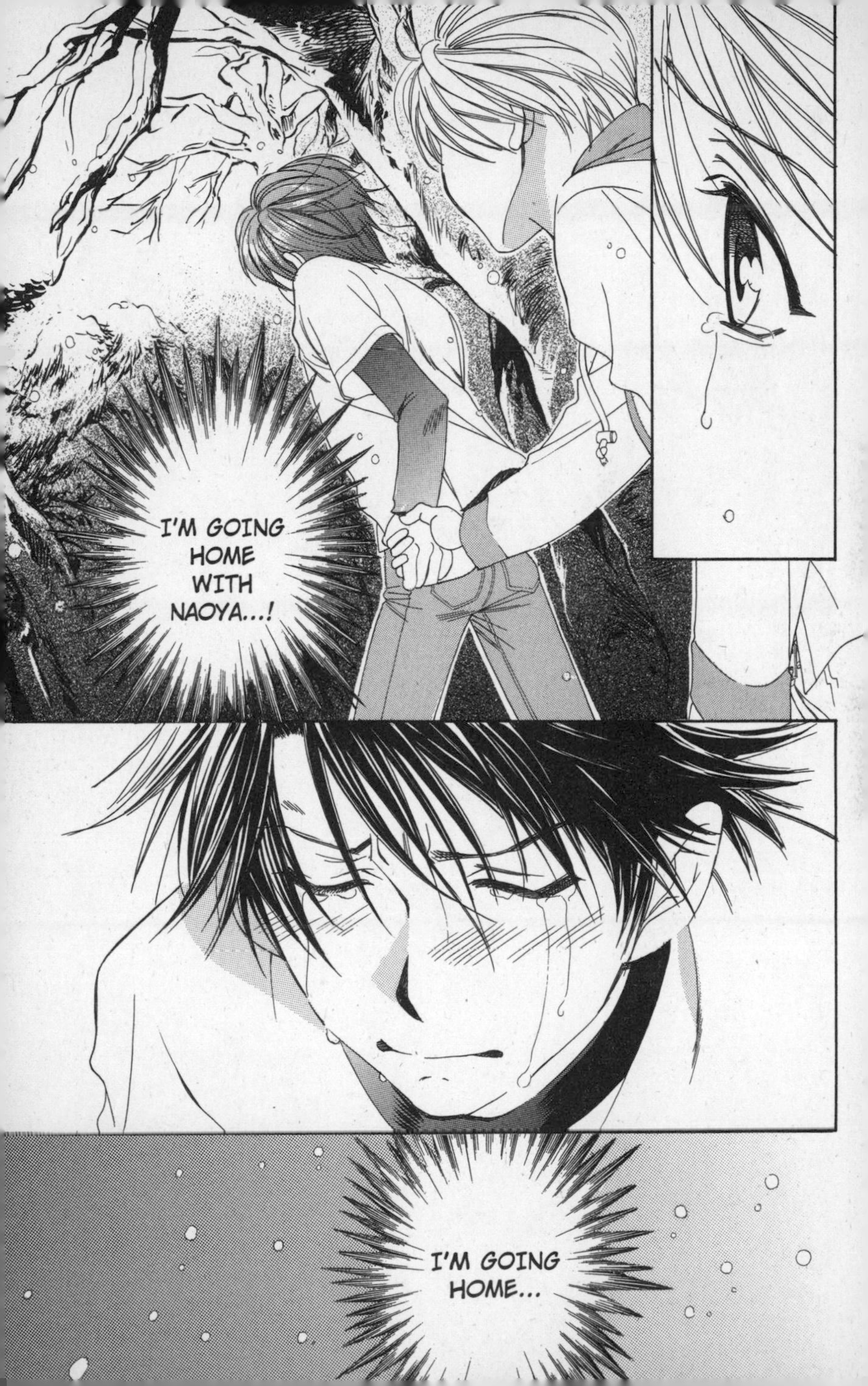
I'M GOING HOME WITH NAOYA...!
I'M GOING HOME...

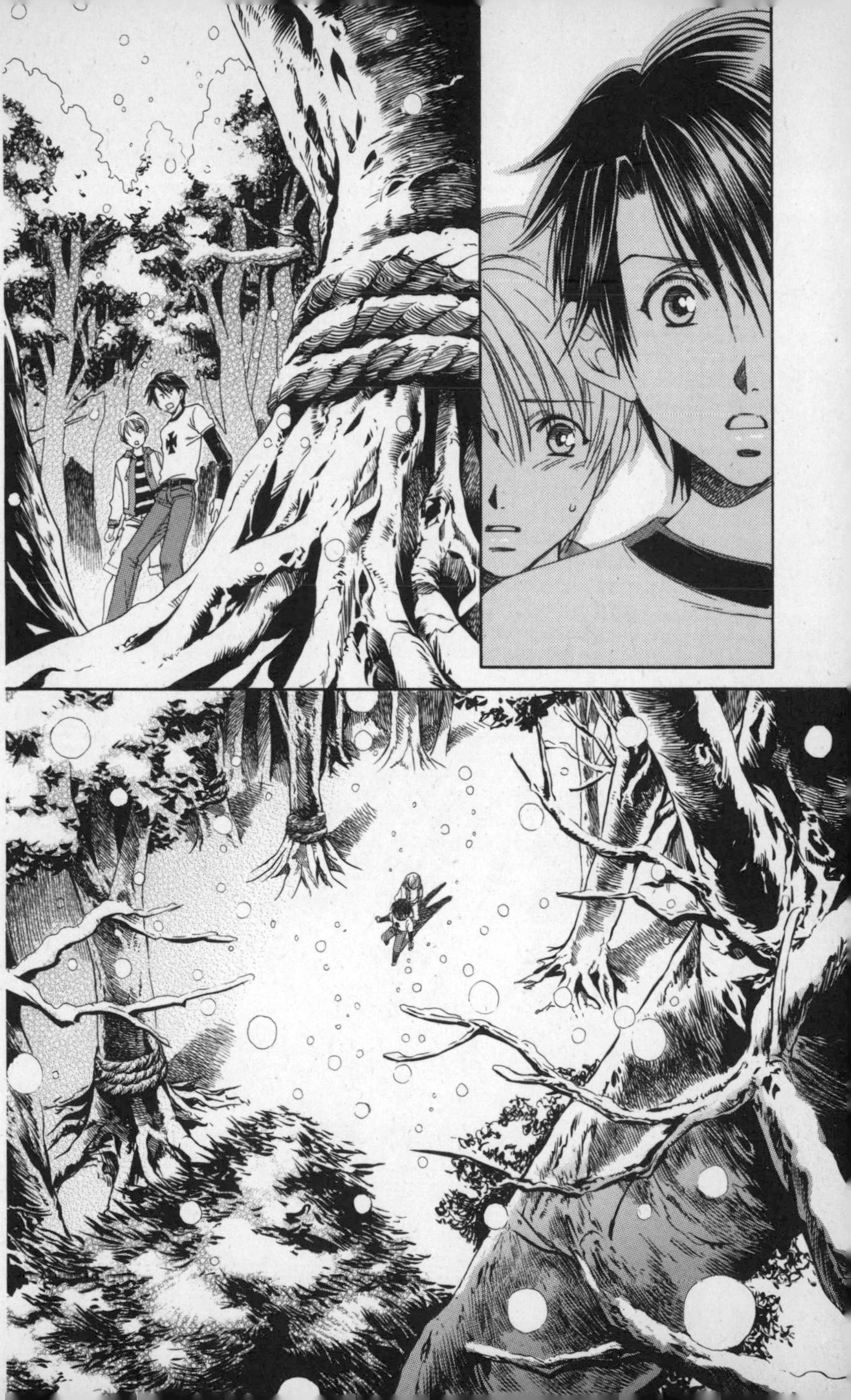

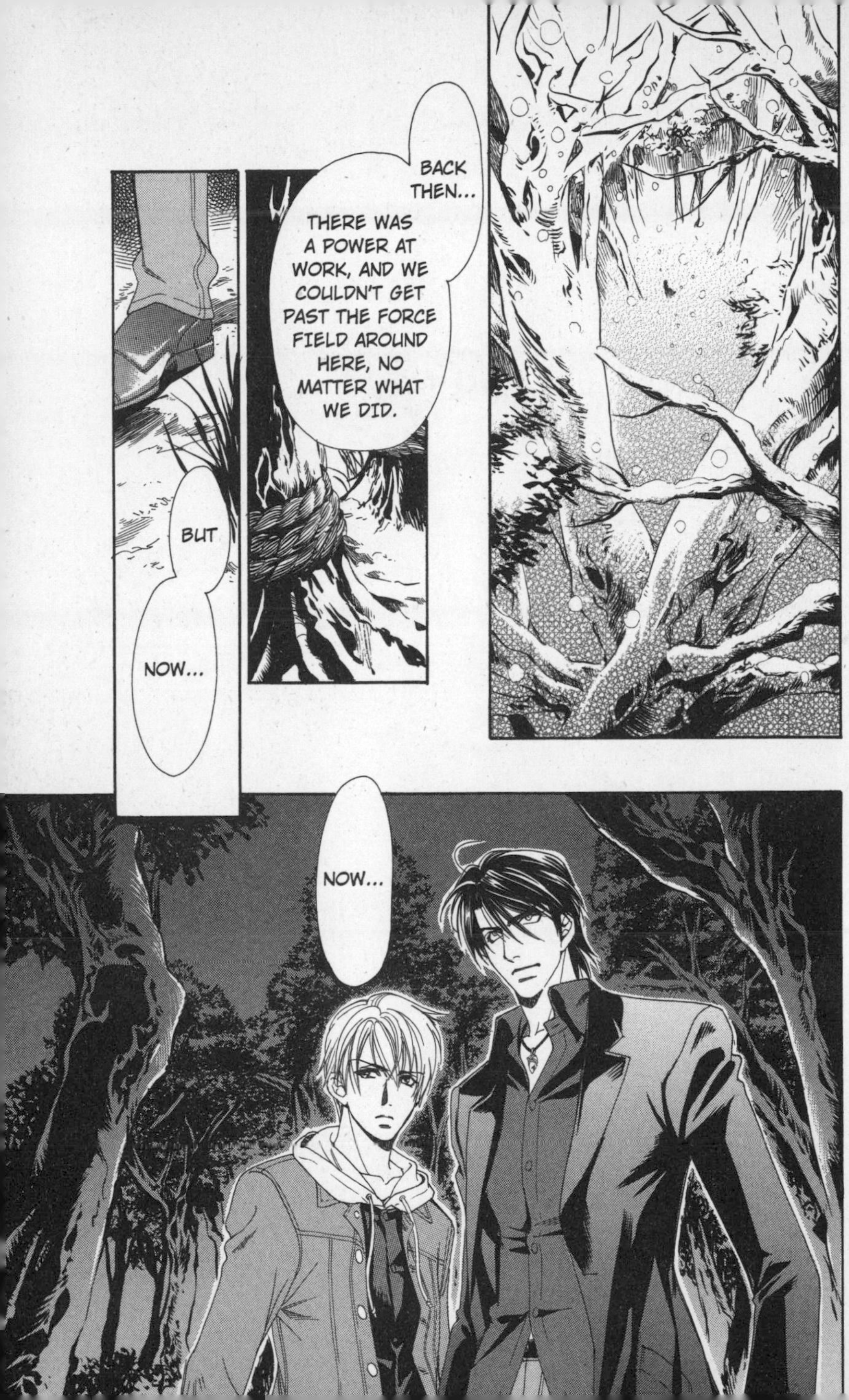
BACK THEN...
THERE WAS A POWER AT WORK, AND WE COULDN'T GET PAST THE FORCE FIELD AROUND HERE, NO MATTER WHAT WE DID.
BUT
NOW...
NOW...

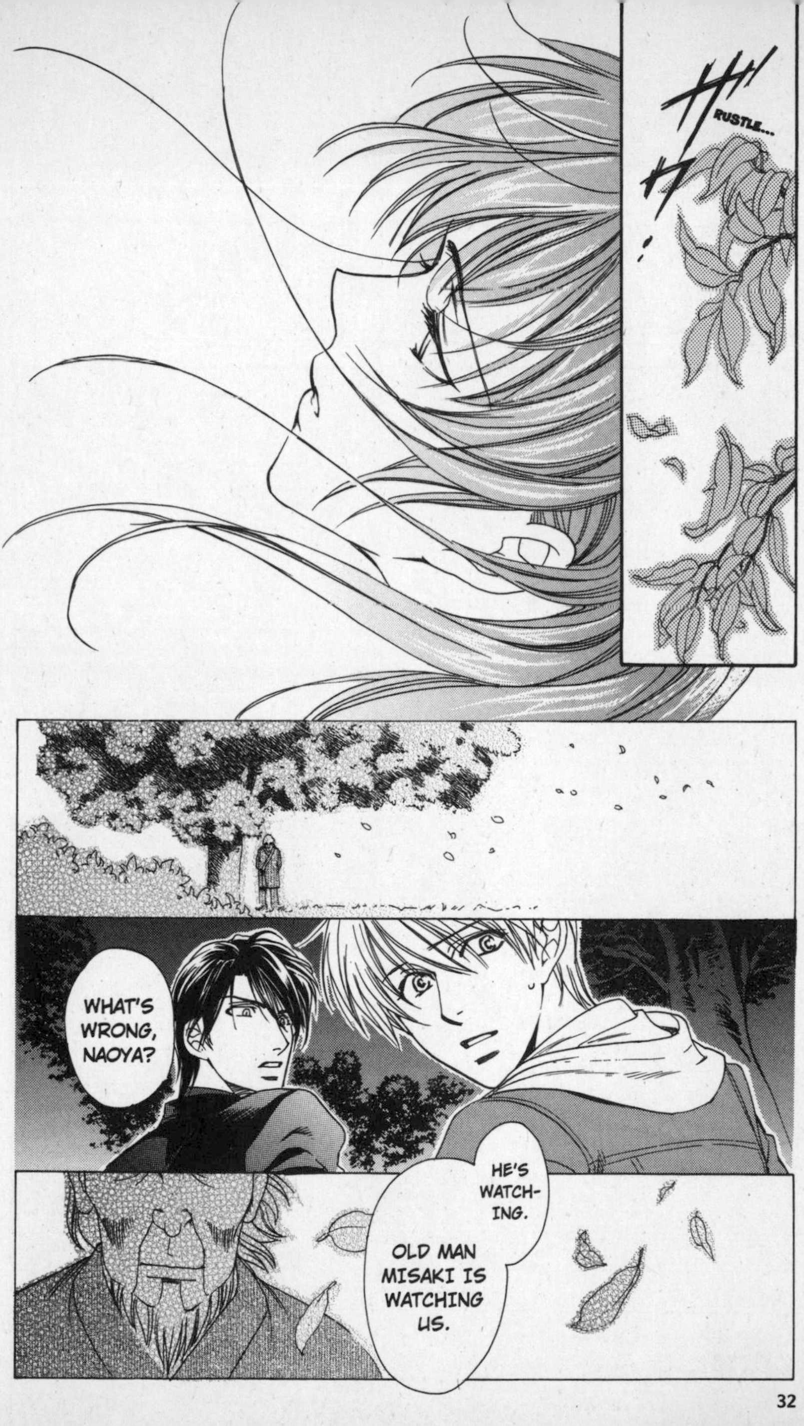
RUSTLE...
WHAT'S WRONG, NAOYA?
HE'S WATCHING.
OLD MAN MISAKI IS WATCHING US.

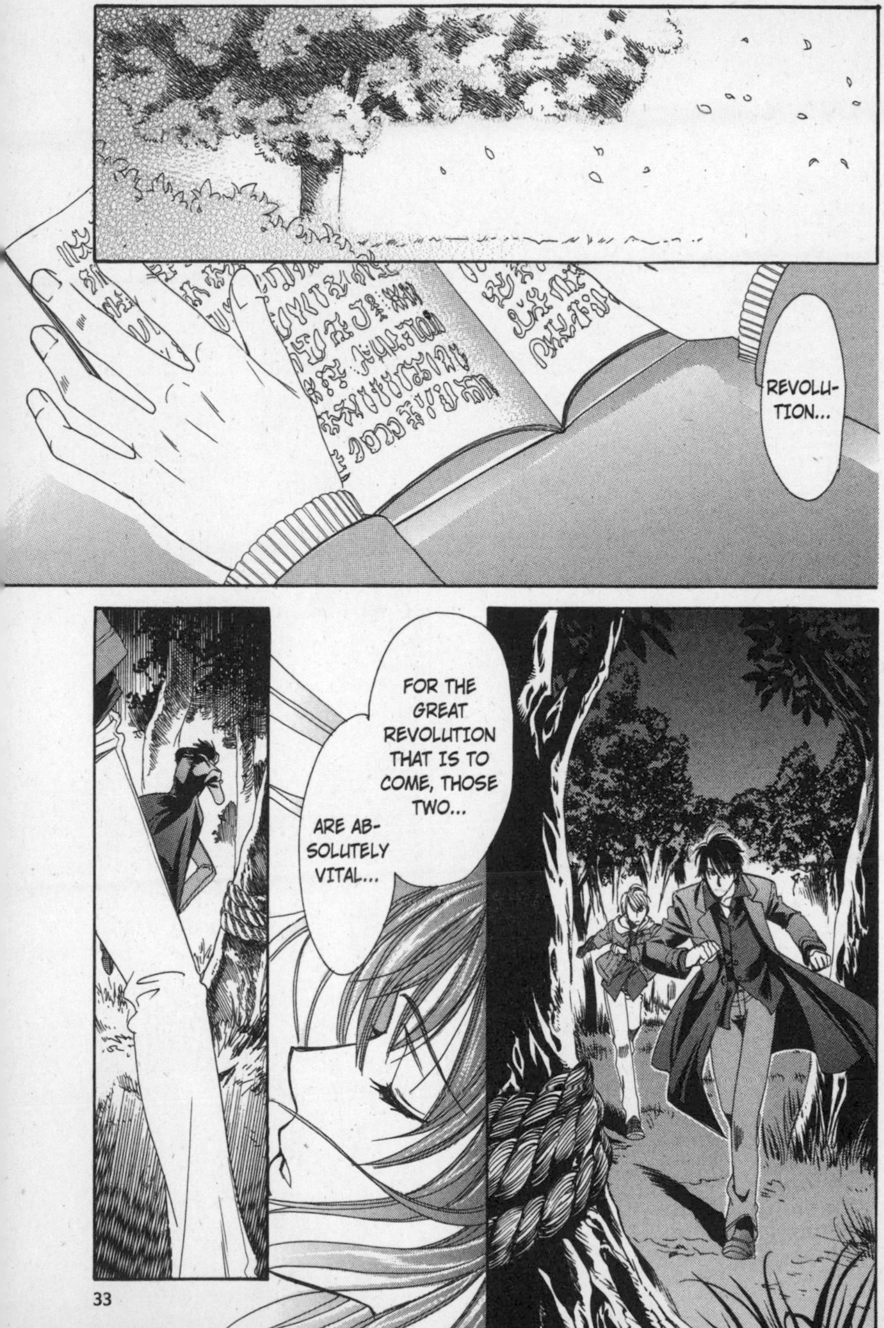
REVOLUTION...
FOR THE GREAT REVOLUTION THAT IS TO COME, THOSE TWO...
ARE ABSOLUTELY VITAL...

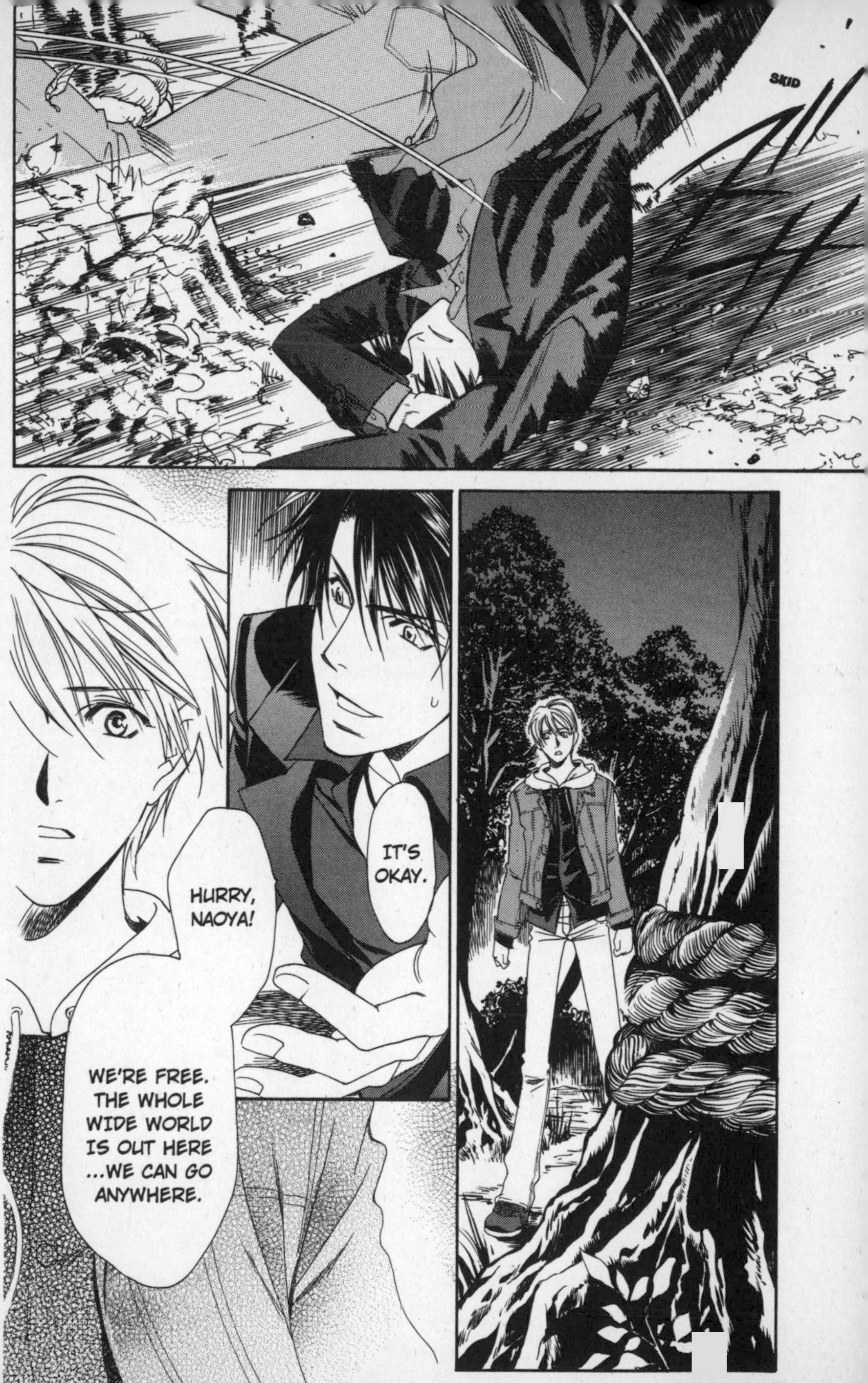
SKID
IT'S OKAY.
HURRY, NAOYA!
WE'RE FREE. THE WHOLE WIDE WORLD IS OUT HERE ...WE CAN GO ANYWHERE.

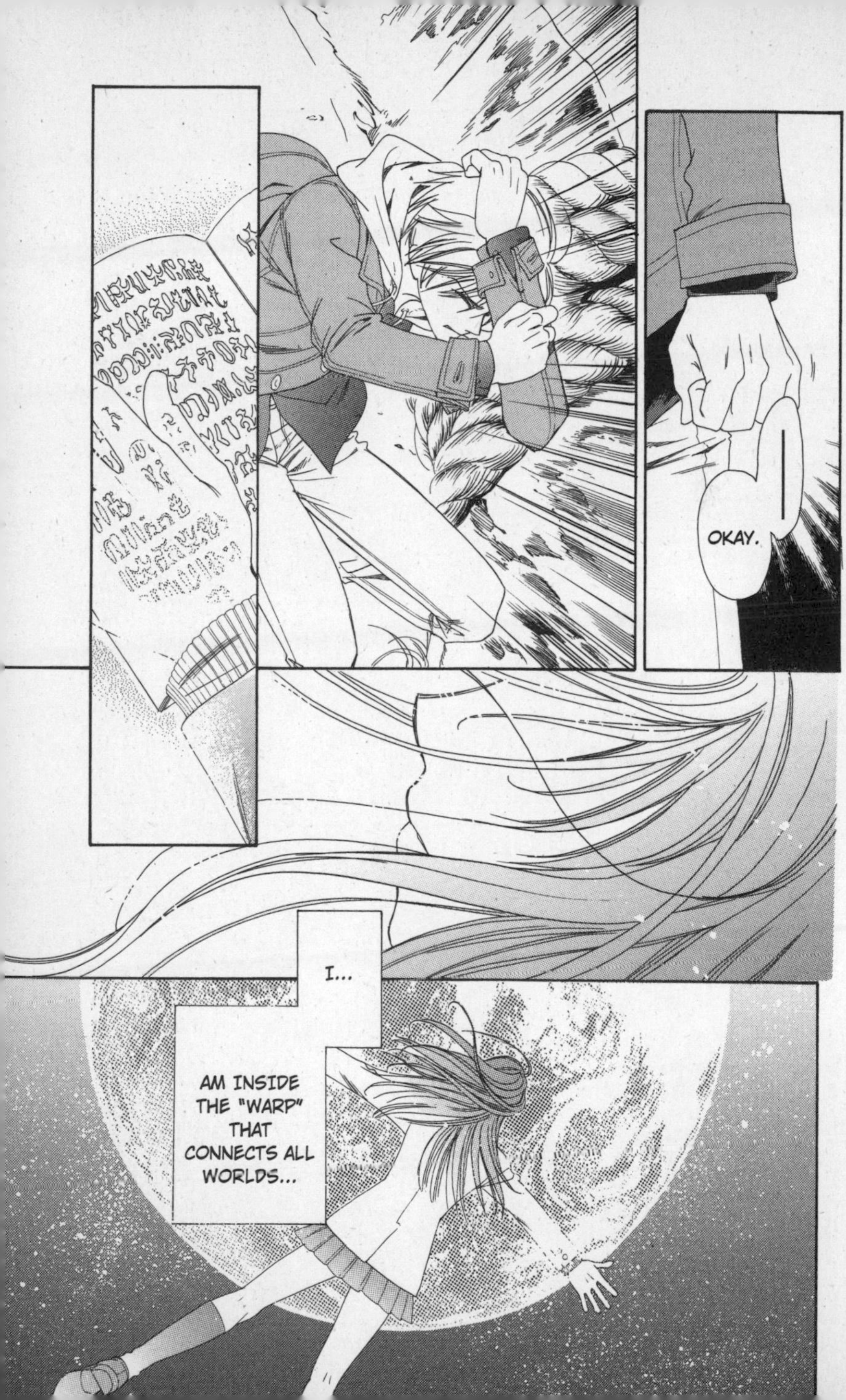
OKAY.
I...
AM INSIDE THE "WARP" THAT CONNECTS ALL WORLDS...

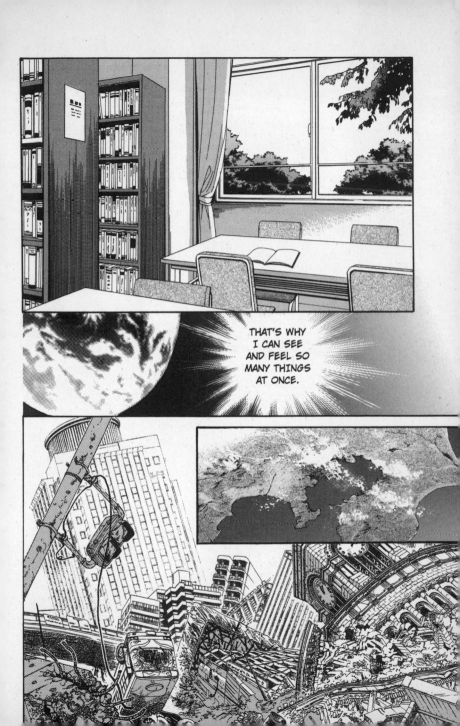

THAT'S WHY
I CAN SEE
AND FEEL SO
MANY THINGS
AT ONCE.

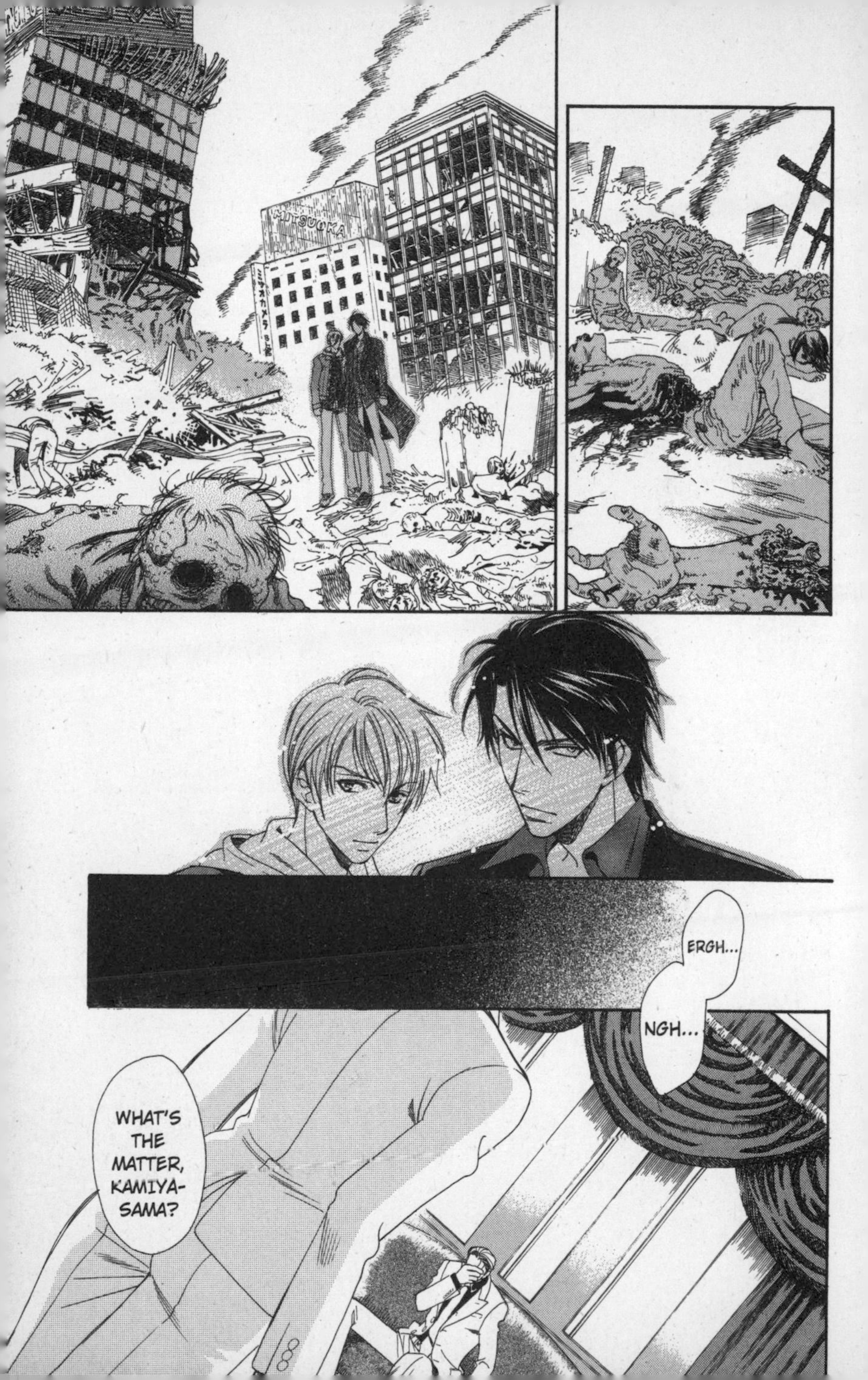
MITSUOKA
ERGH...
NGH...
WHAT'S THE MATTER, KAMIYA-SAMA?

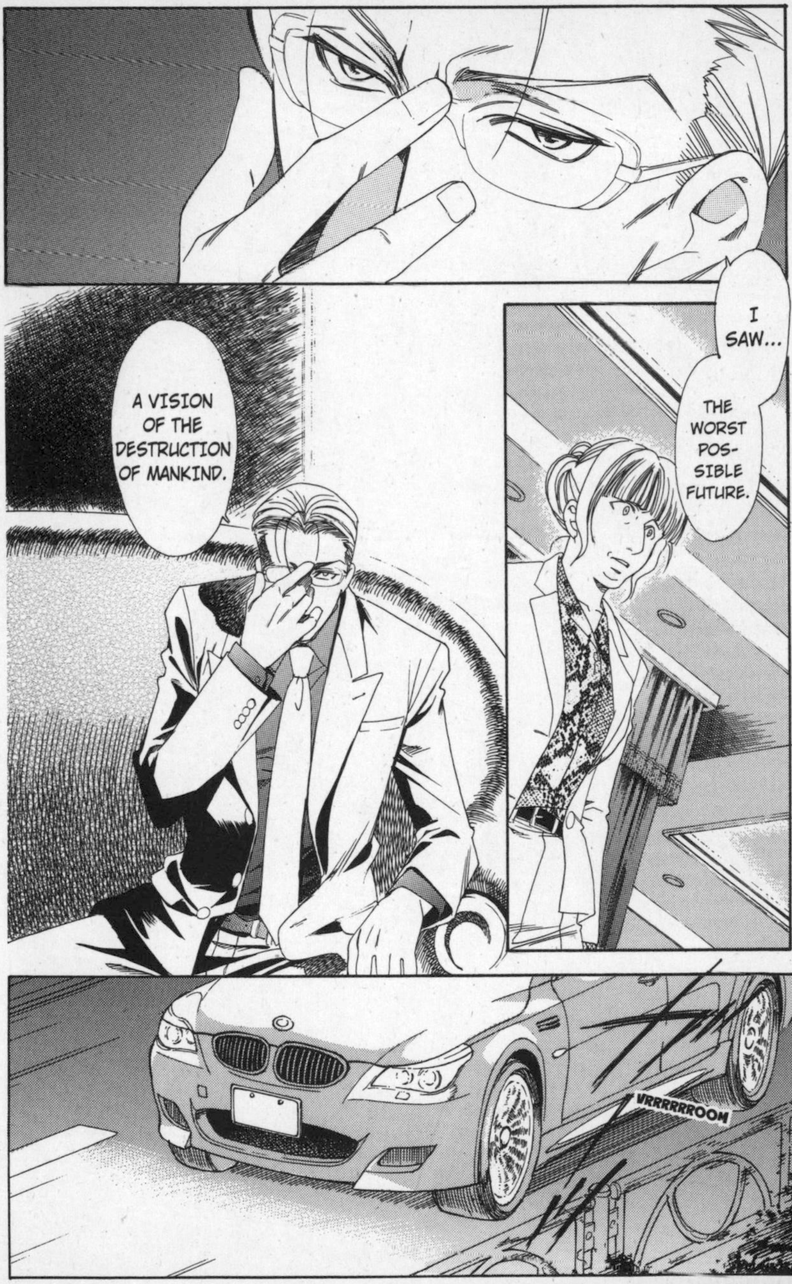
I SAW...
THE WORST POS-SIBLE FUTURE.
A VISION OF THE DESTRUCTION OF MANKIND.
VRRRRRROOM

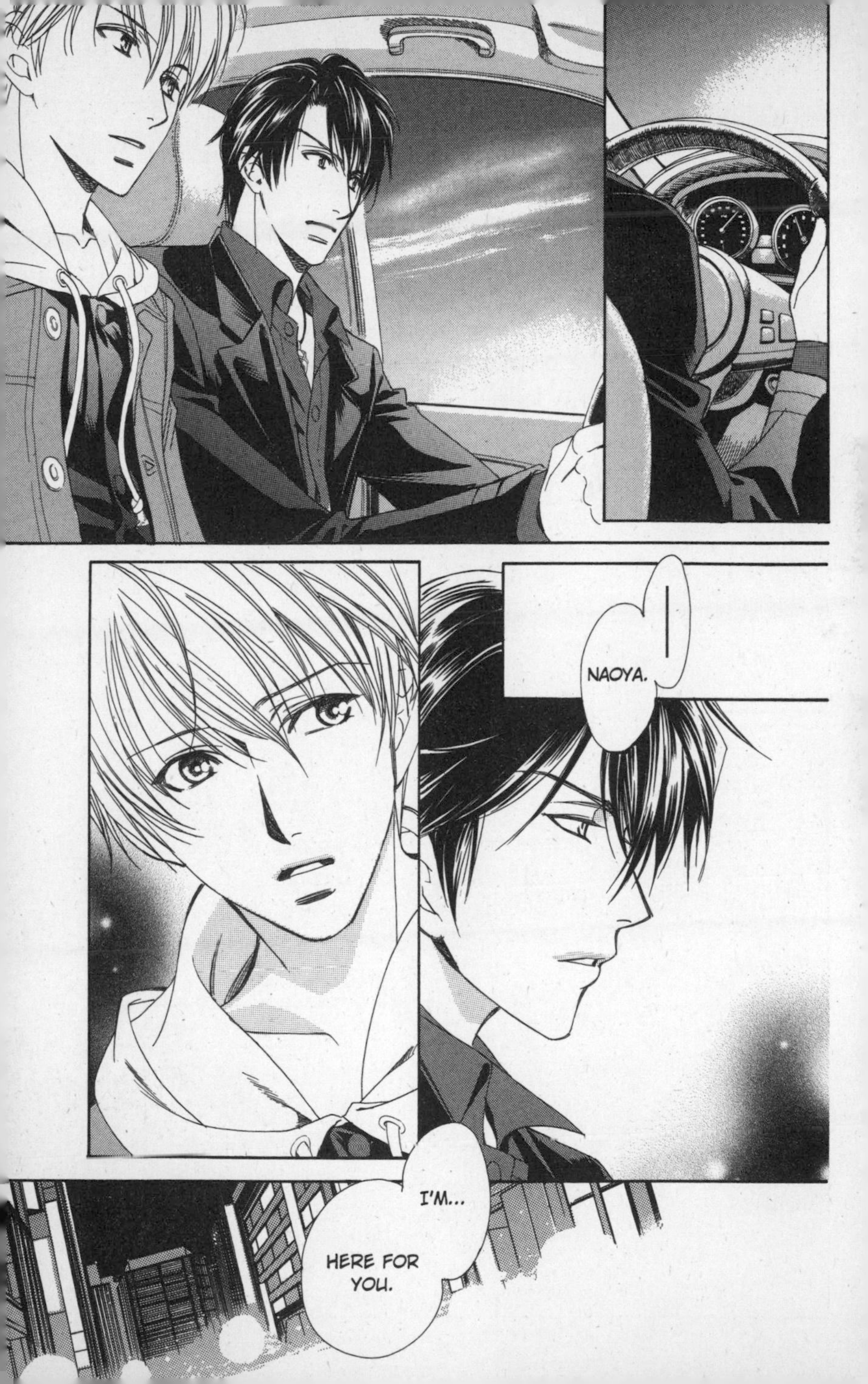
NAOYA.
I'M...
HERE FOR YOU.

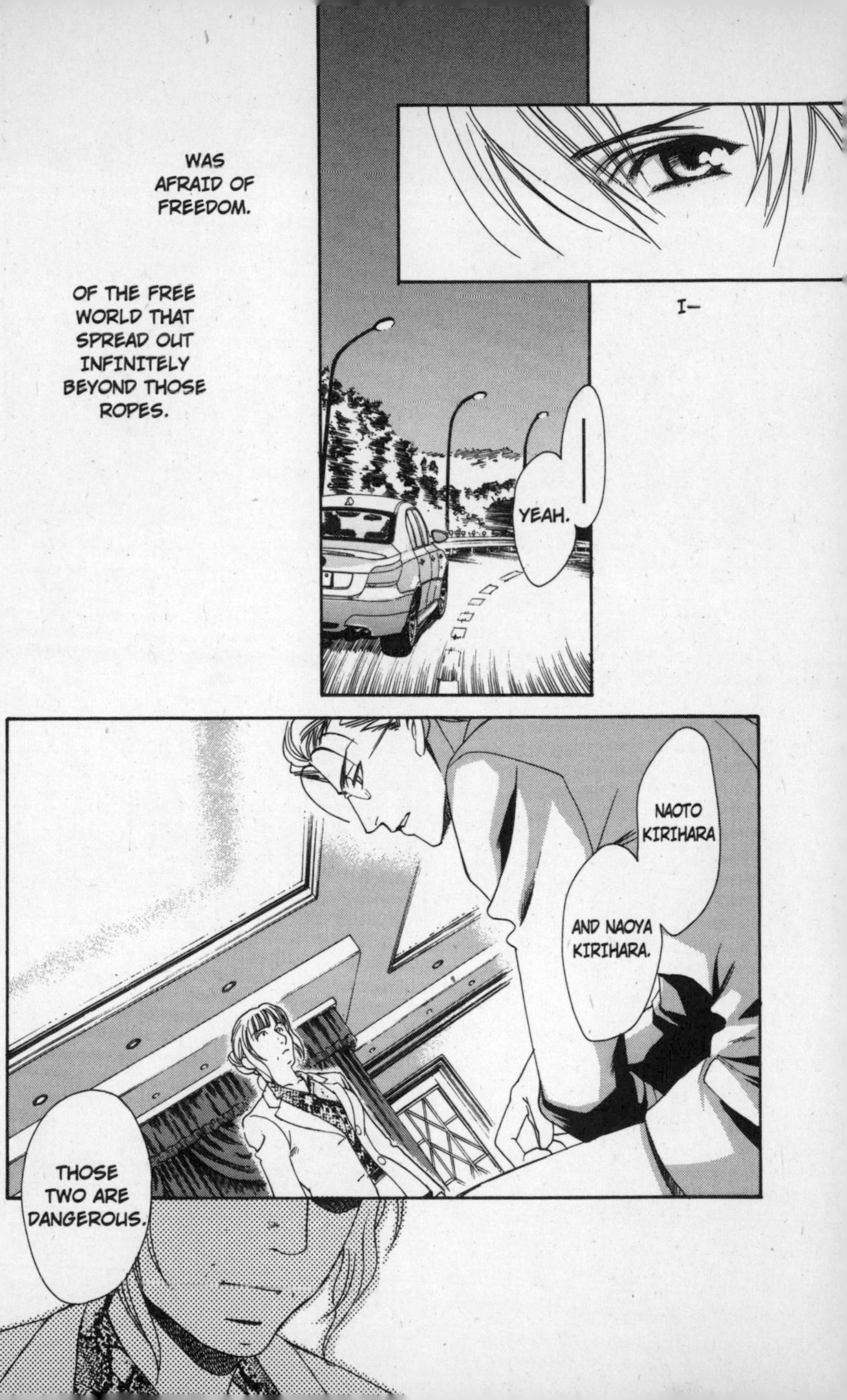
I—
YEAH.
WAS AFRAID OF FREEDOM.
OF THE FREE WORLD THAT SPREAD OUT INFINITELY BEYOND THOSE ROPES.
NAOTO KIRIHARA
AND NAOYA KIRIHARA.
THOSE TWO ARE DANGEROUS.

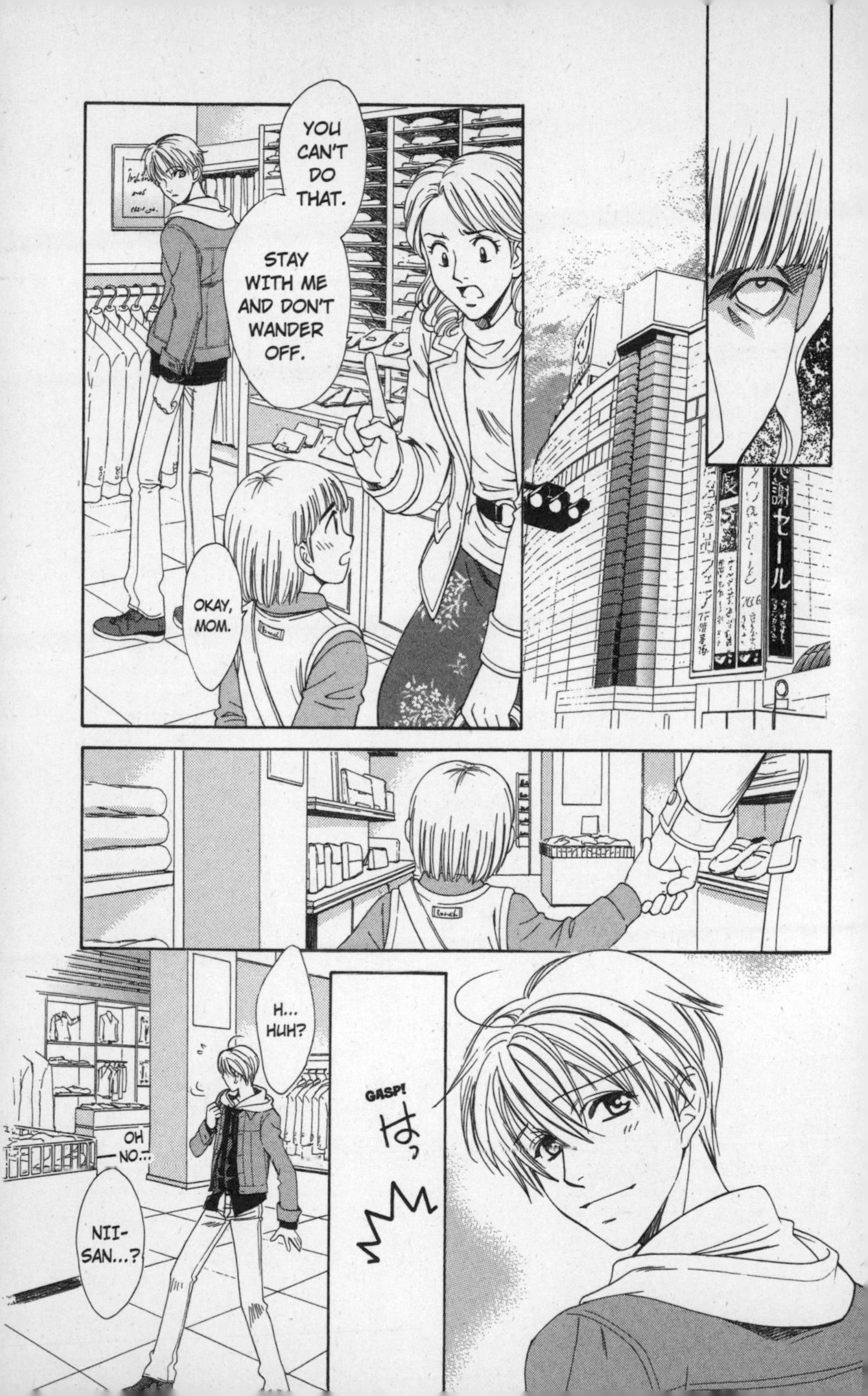
YOU CAN'T DO THAT.
STAY WITH ME AND DON'T WANDER OFF.
OKAY, MOM.
GASP!
はっ
H... HUH?
OH NO...
NII-SAN...?

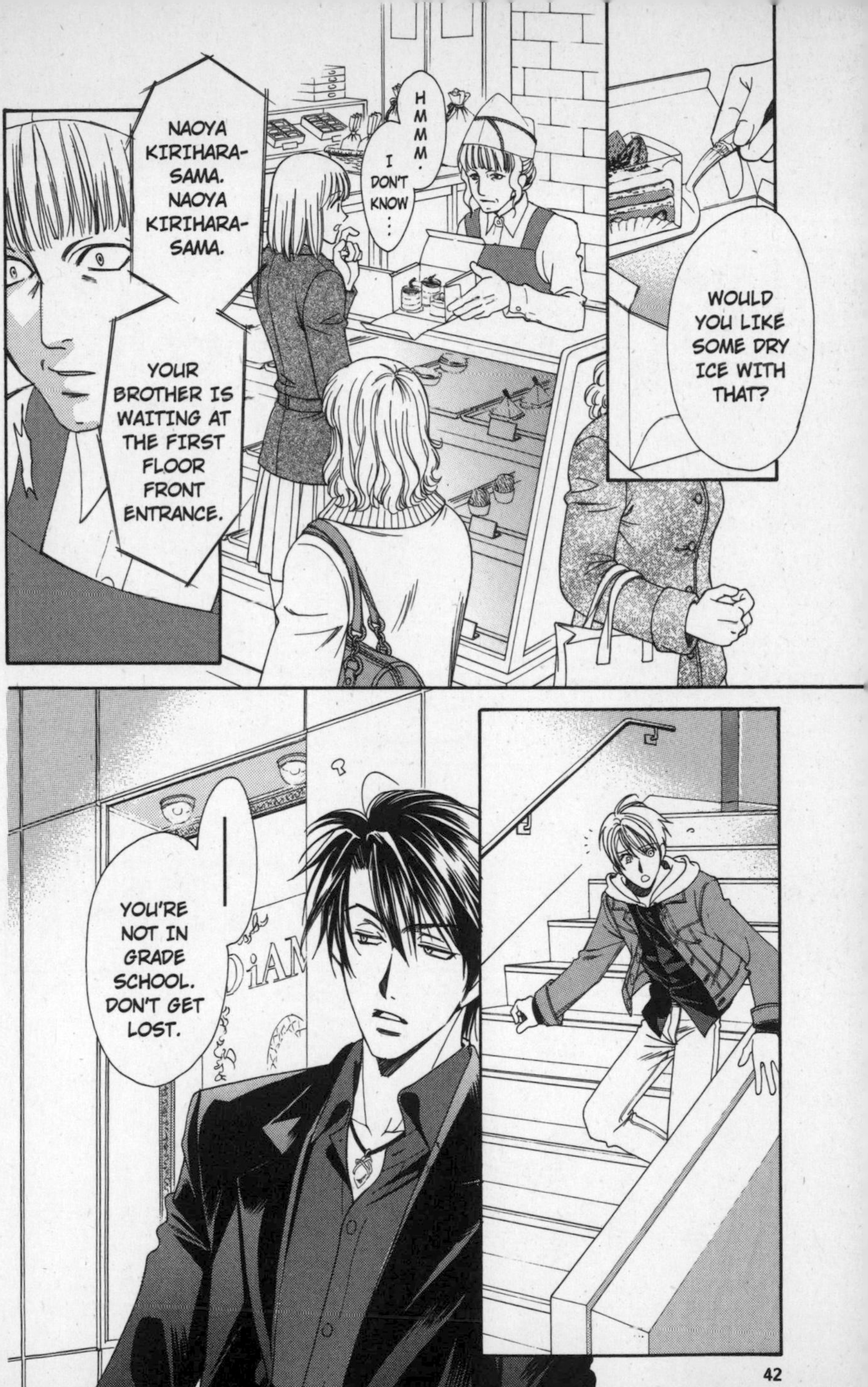
WOULD YOU LIKE SOME DRY ICE WITH THAT?
HMMM. I DON'T KNOW...
NAOYA KIRIHARA-SAMA. NAOYA KIRIHARA-SAMA.
YOUR BROTHER IS WAITING AT THE FIRST FLOOR FRONT ENTRANCE.
— YOU'RE NOT IN GRADE SCHOOL. DON'T GET LOST.

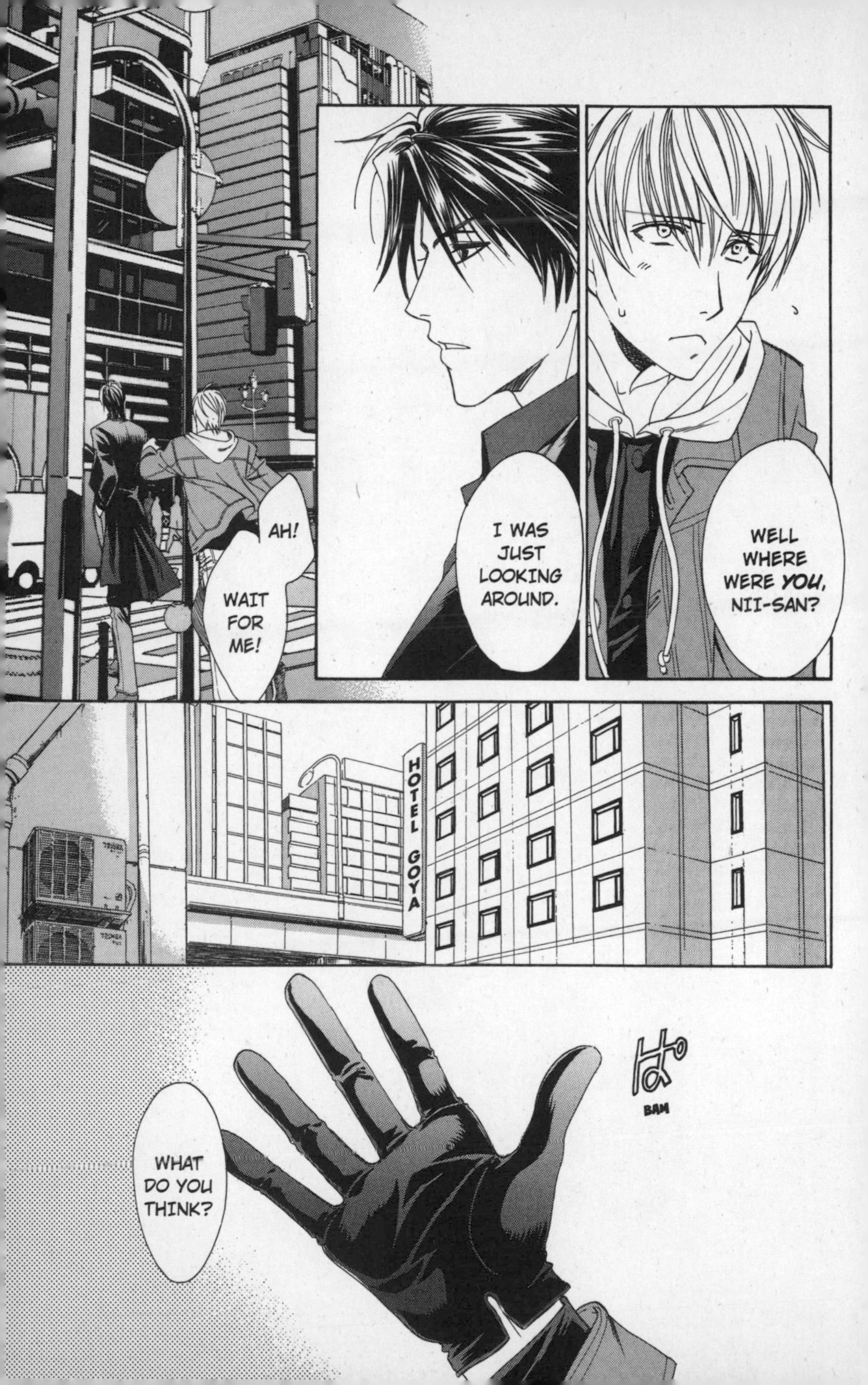
WELL WHERE WERE *YOU*, NII-SAN?
I WAS JUST LOOKING AROUND.
AH!
WAIT FOR ME!
HOTEL GOYA
BAM
WHAT DO YOU THINK?

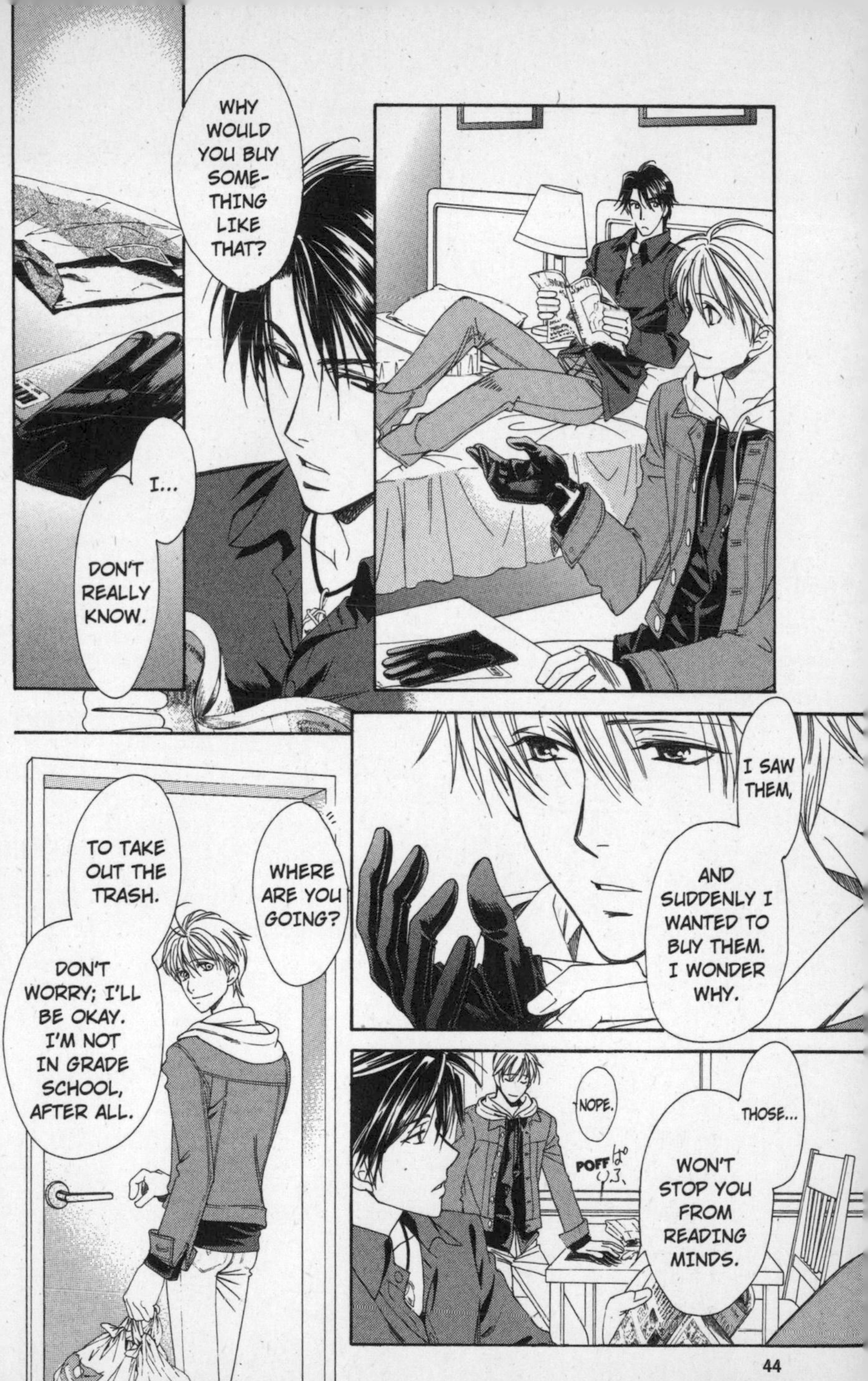
WHY WOULD YOU BUY SOME-THING LIKE THAT?
I...
DON'T REALLY KNOW.
I SAW THEM,
AND SUDDENLY I WANTED TO BUY THEM. I WONDER WHY.
THOSE...
WON'T STOP YOU FROM READING MINDS.
NOPE.
POFF
WHERE ARE YOU GOING?
TO TAKE OUT THE TRASH.
DON'T WORRY; I'LL BE OKAY. I'M NOT IN GRADE SCHOOL, AFTER ALL.

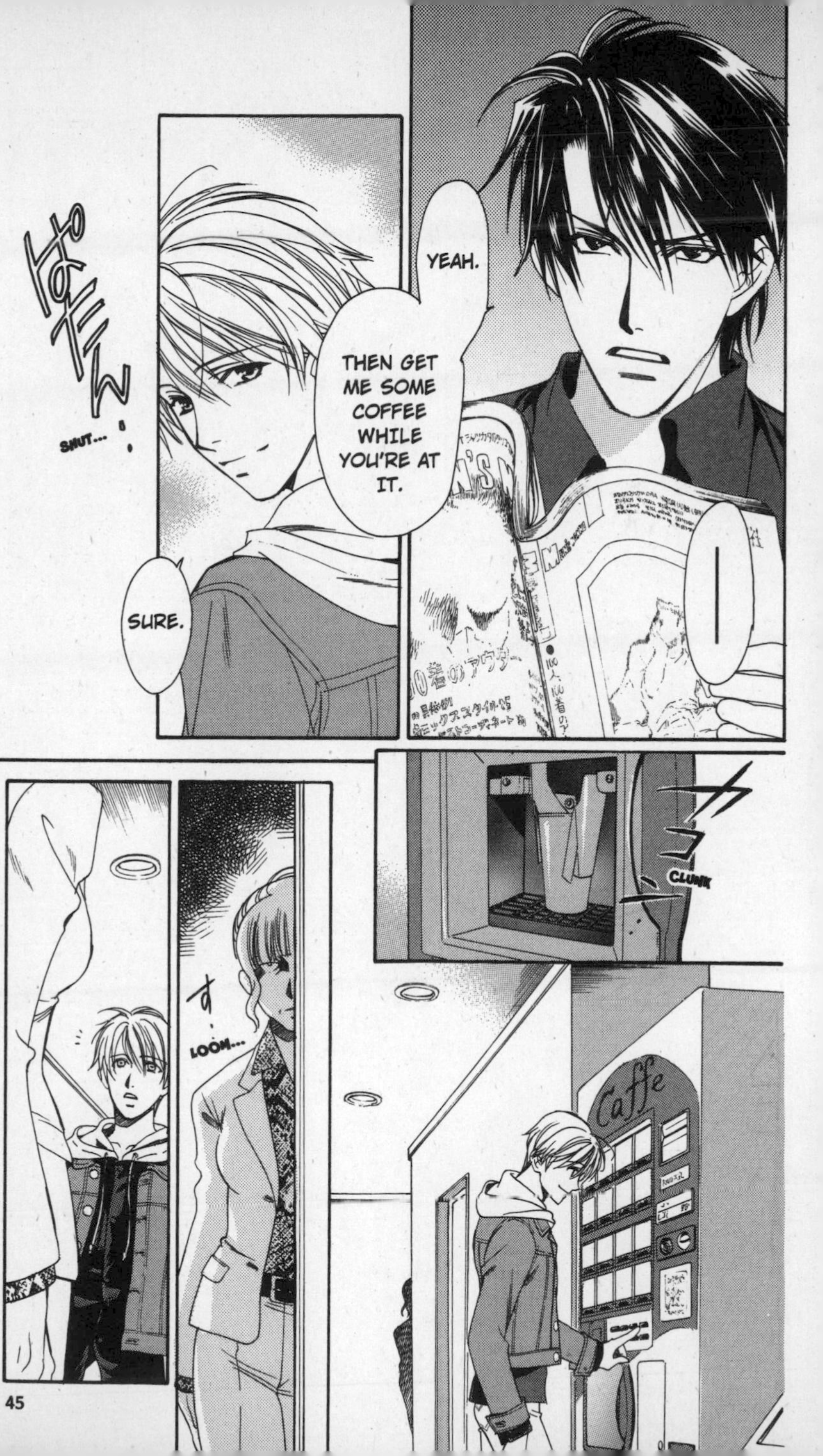
YEAH.
THEN GET ME SOME COFFEE WHILE YOU'RE AT IT.
SURE.
ぱたん
SHUT...
カコ
CLUNK
す
LOOM...

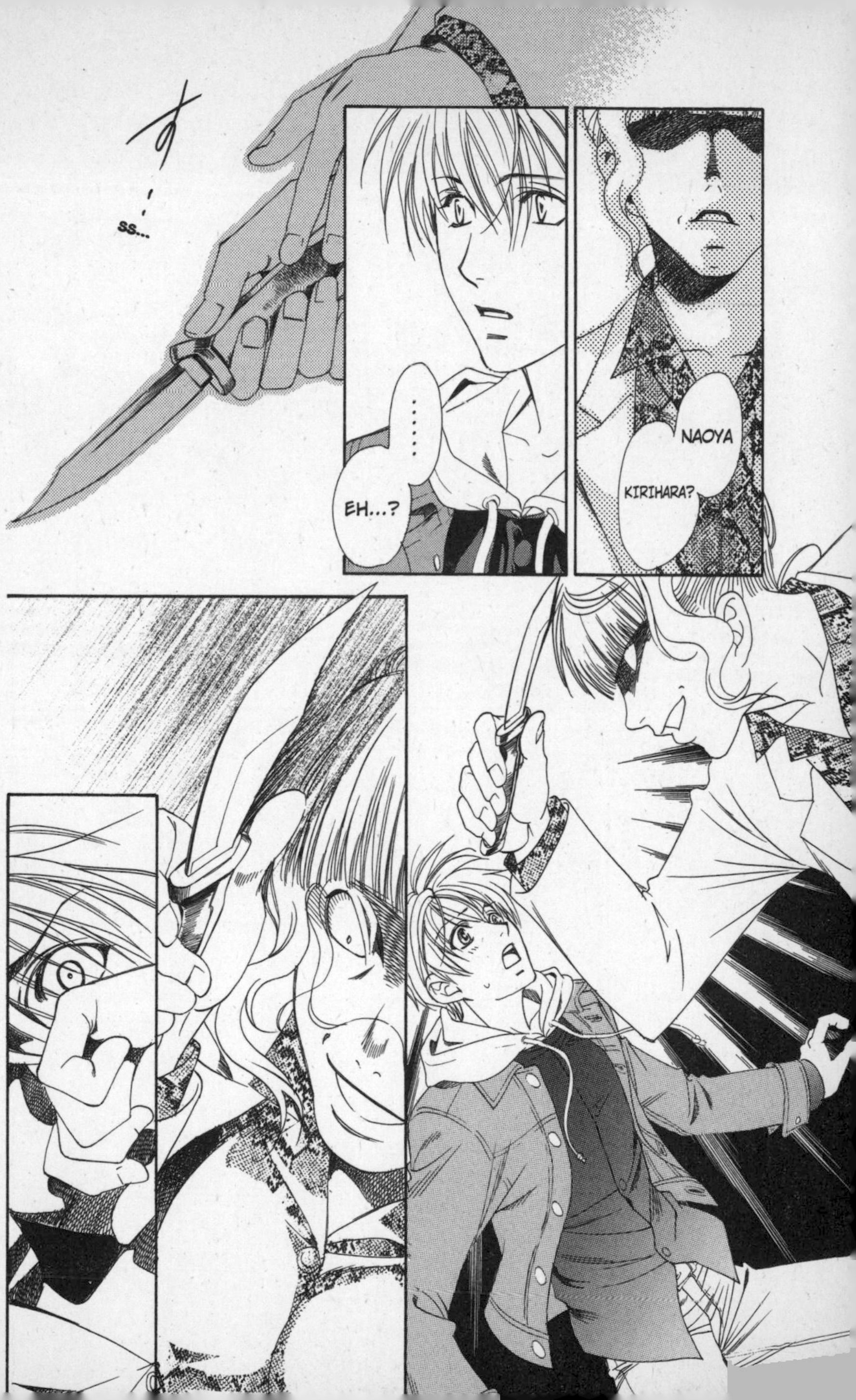

SS...
NAOYA
KIRIHARA?
......
EH...?

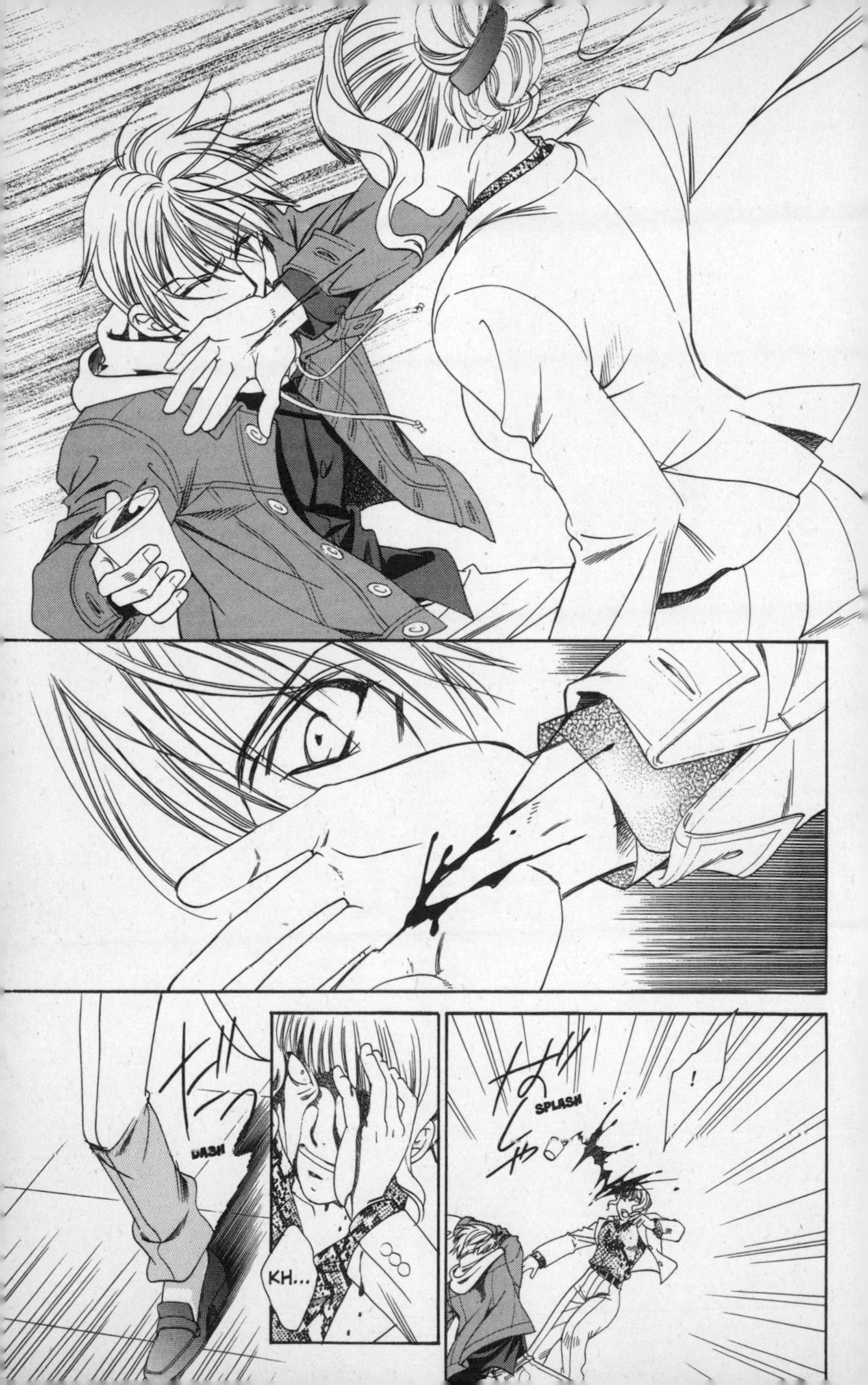

SPLASH
!
KH...
DASH

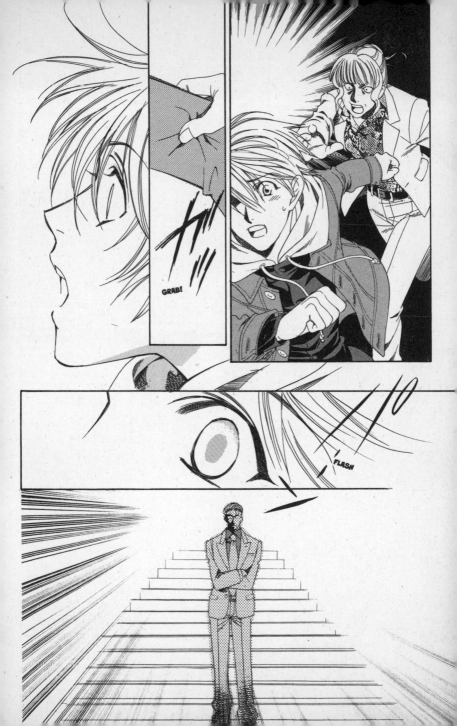

GRAB!

FLASH

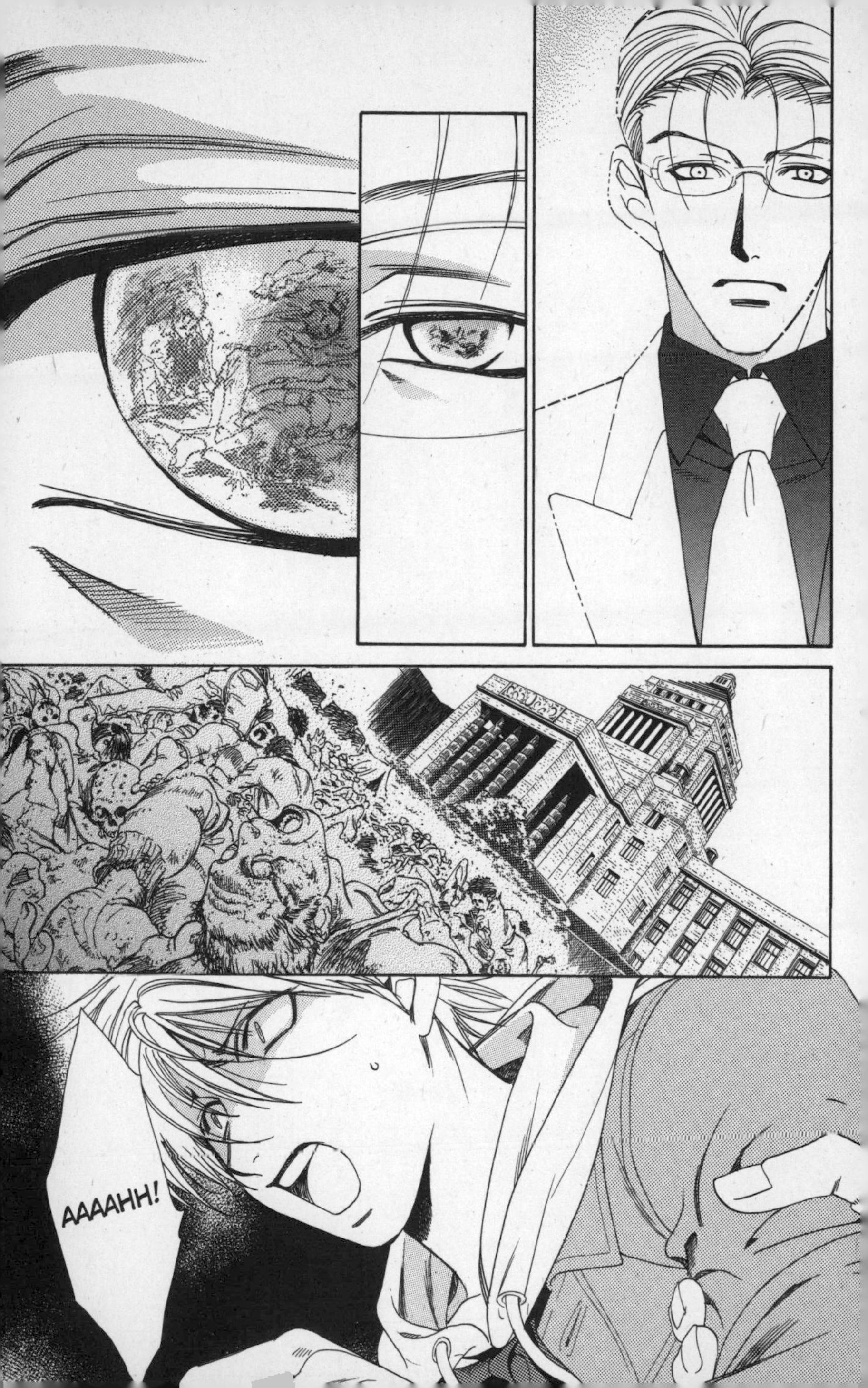
AAAAHH!

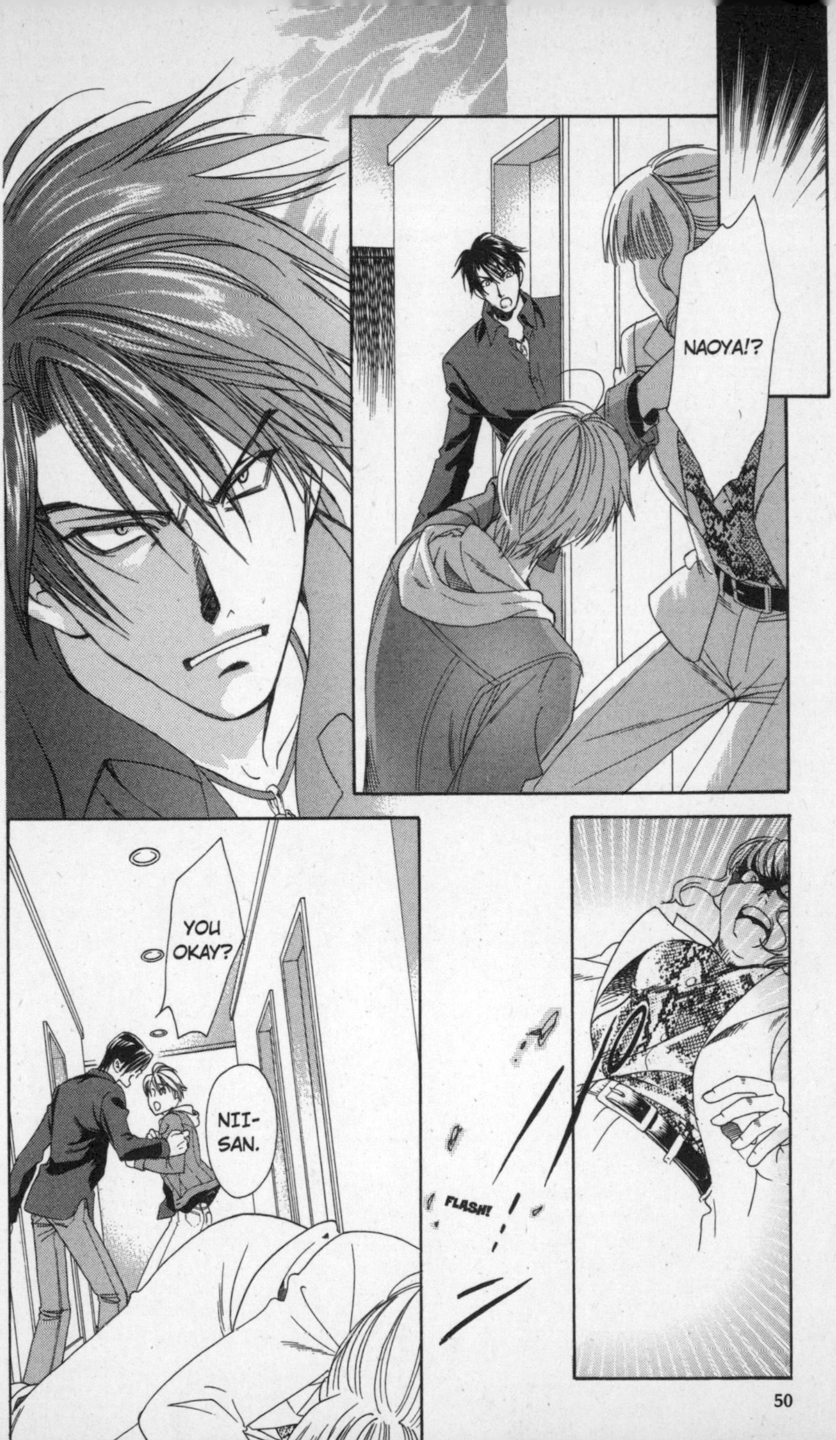
NAOYA!?
FLASH!
YOU OKAY?
NII-SAN.

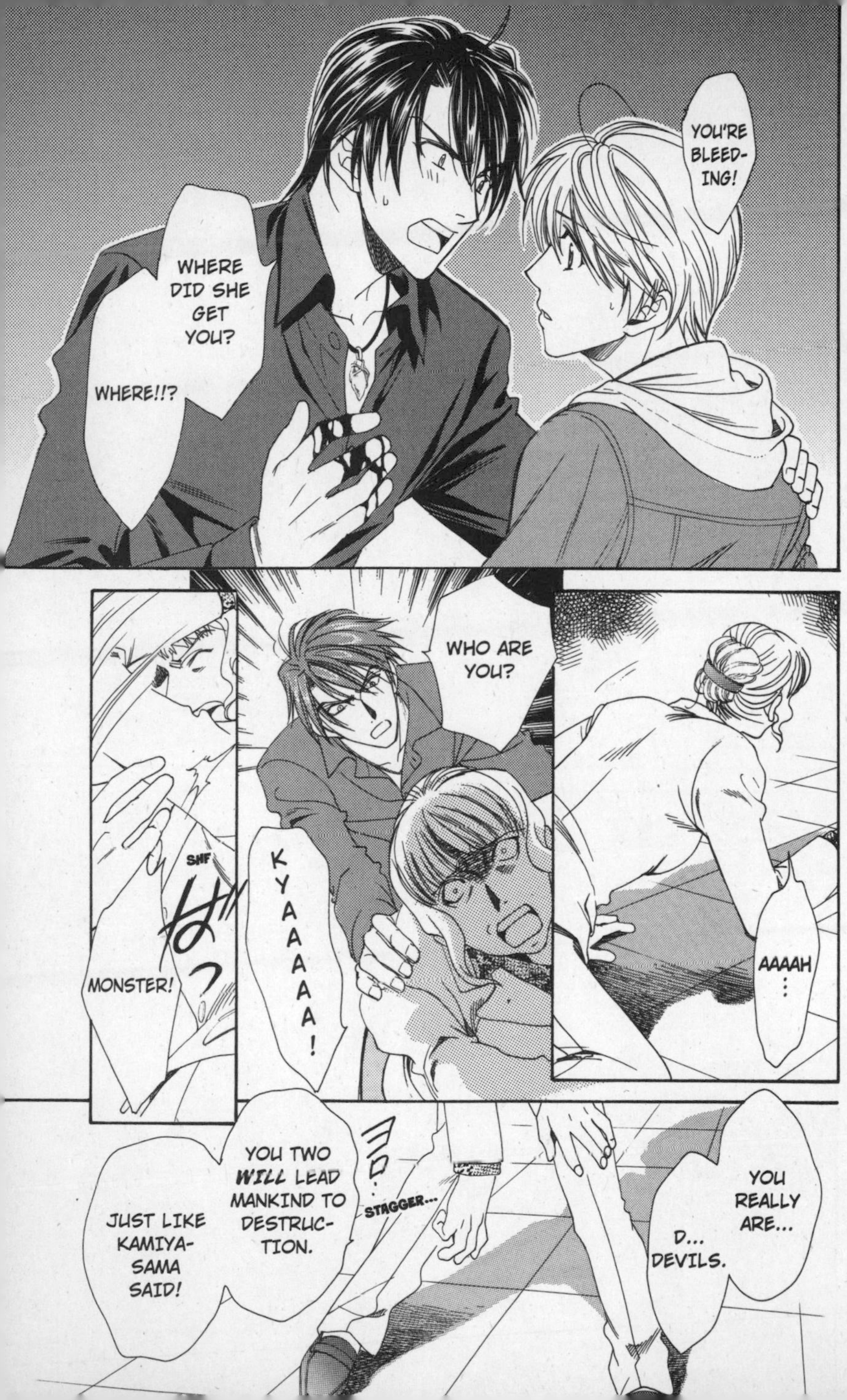
YOU'RE BLEEDING!
WHERE DID SHE GET YOU?
WHERE!!?
AAAAH...
WHO ARE YOU?
KYAAAAAA!
SHF
はっ
MONSTER!
YOU REALLY ARE...
D... DEVILS.
ヨロ
STAGGER...
YOU TWO ***WILL*** LEAD MANKIND TO DESTRUCTION.
JUST LIKE KAMIYA-SAMA SAID!

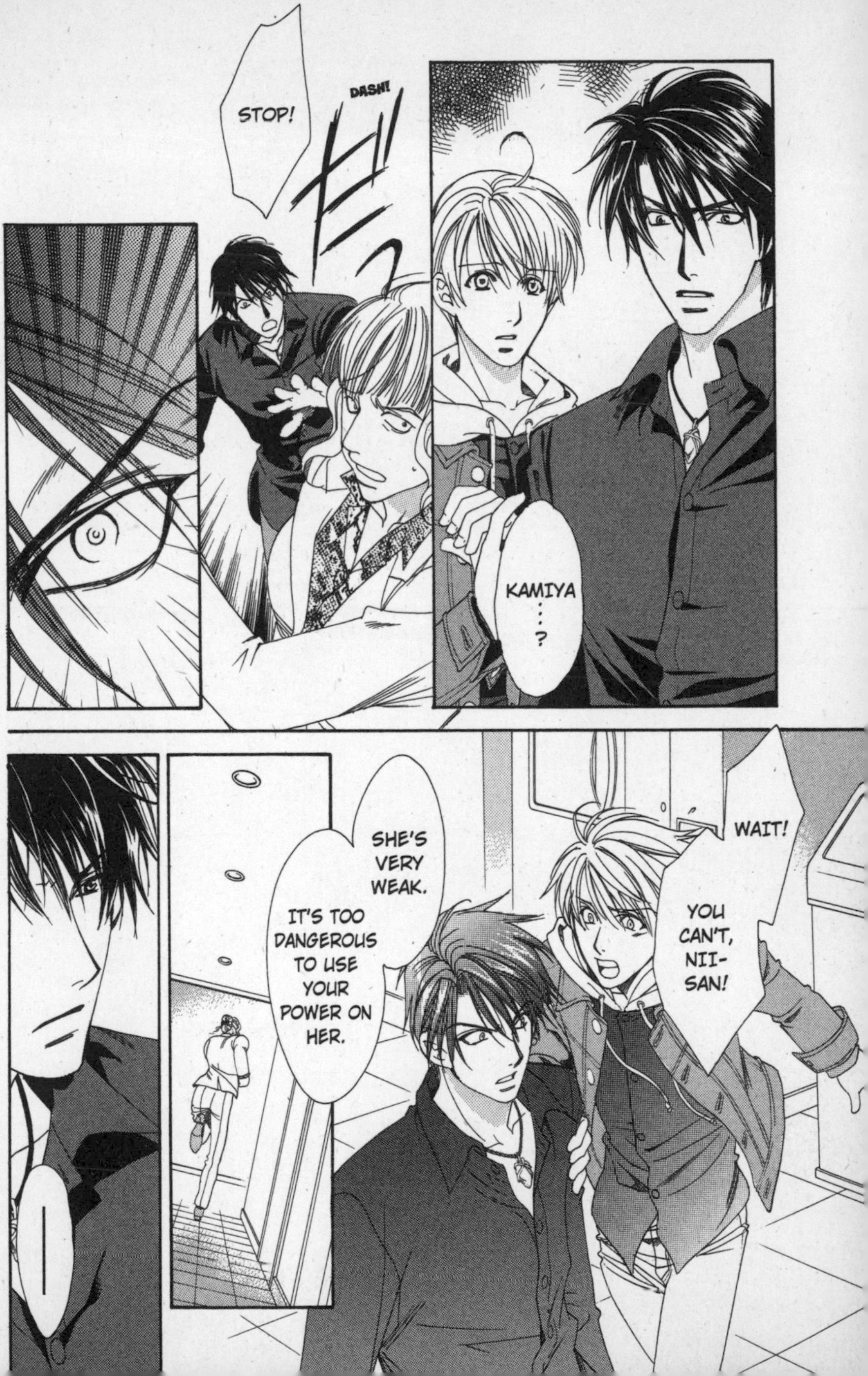
KAMIYA...?
STOP!
DASH!
WAIT!
YOU CAN'T, NII-SAN!
SHE'S VERY WEAK.
IT'S TOO DANGEROUS TO USE YOUR POWER ON HER.

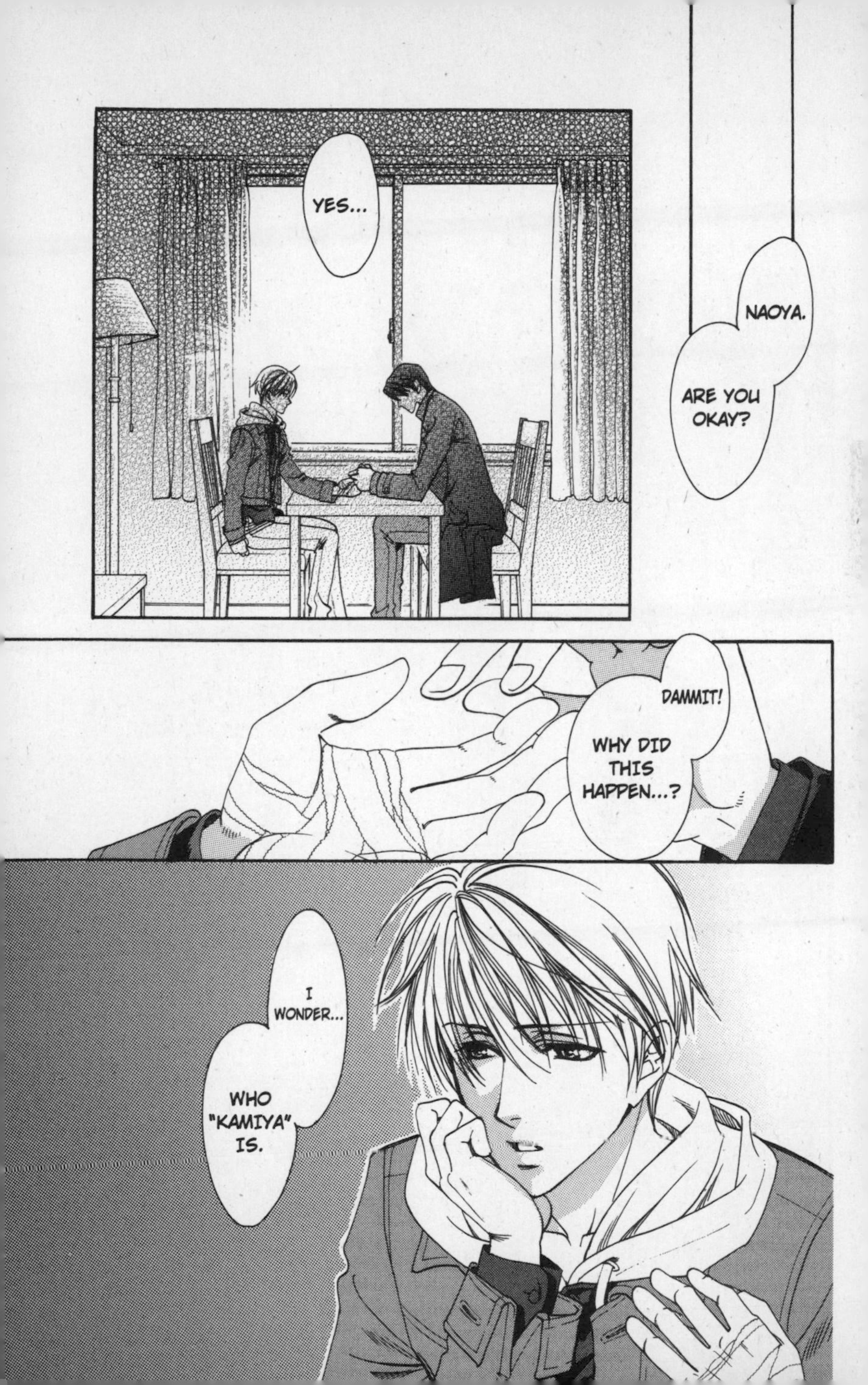
NAOYA.
ARE YOU OKAY?
YES...
DAMMIT!
WHY DID THIS HAPPEN...?
I WONDER...
WHO "KAMIYA" IS.

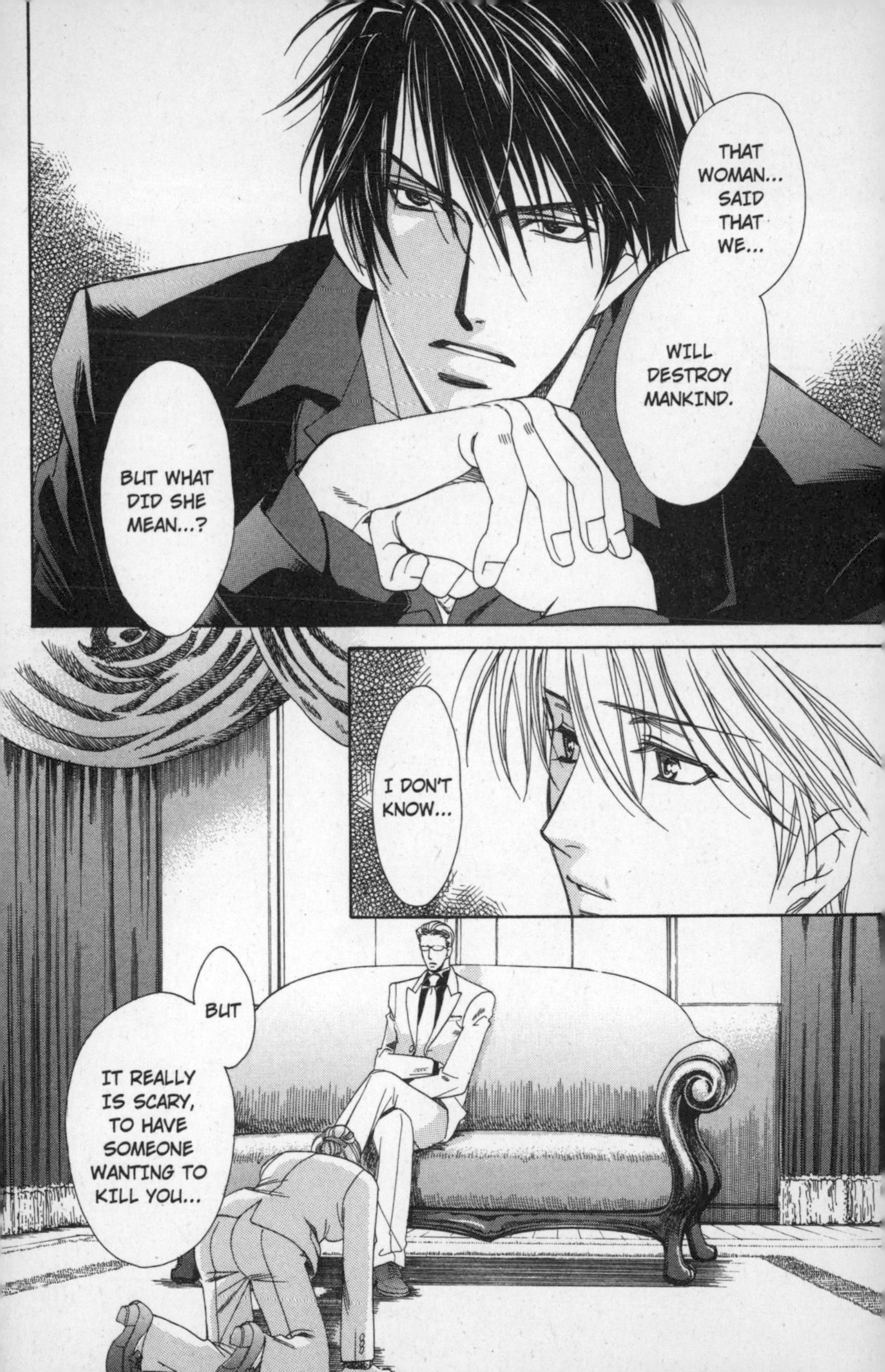
THAT WOMAN... SAID THAT WE...
WILL DESTROY MANKIND.
BUT WHAT DID SHE MEAN...?
I DON'T KNOW...
BUT
IT REALLY IS SCARY, TO HAVE SOMEONE WANTING TO KILL YOU...

Chapter 1: MEMORIES · END

Chapter 2: PROPHECY

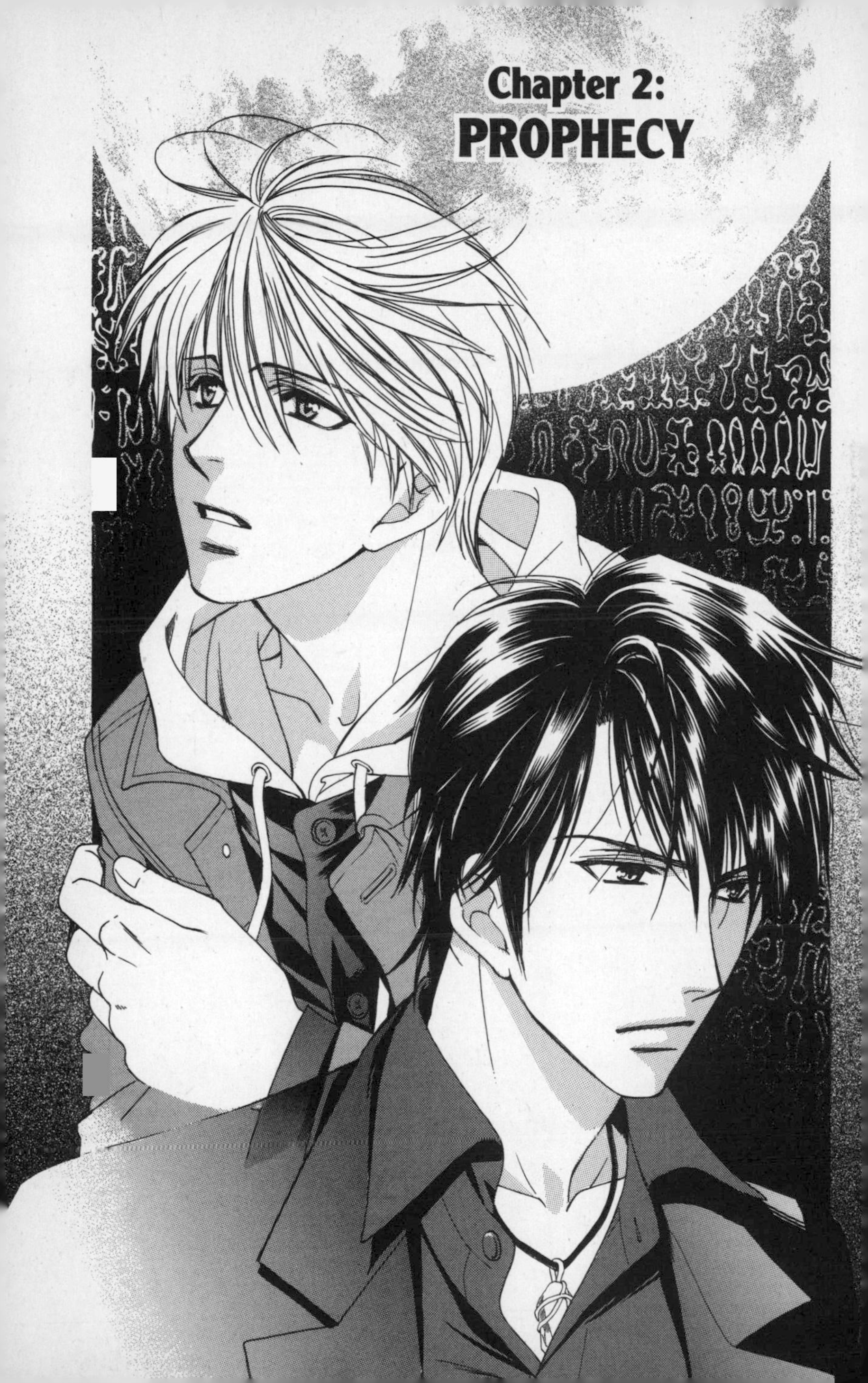

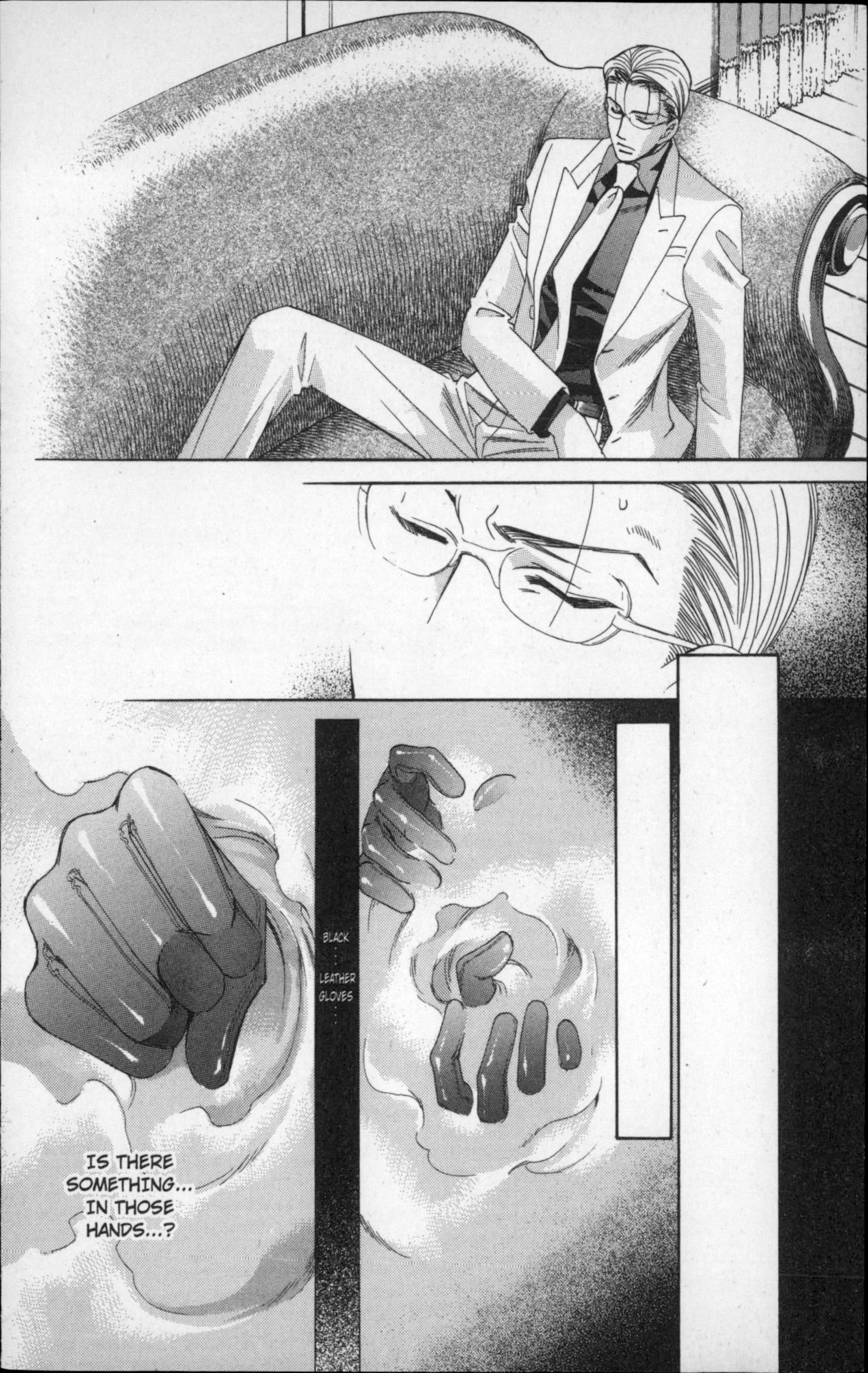
BLACK... LEATHER GLOVES...
IS THERE SOMETHING... IN THOSE HANDS...?

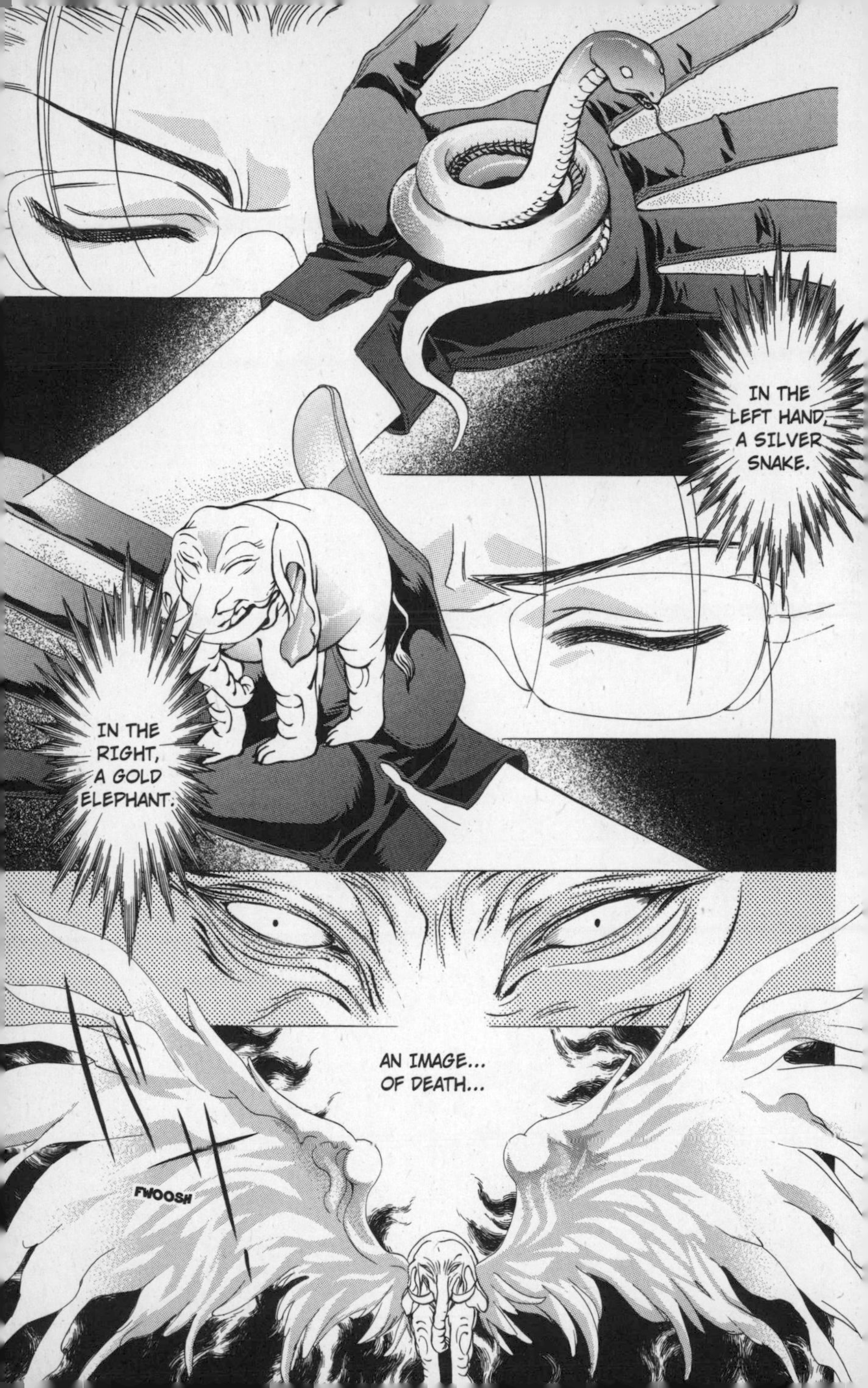
IN THE LEFT HAND, A SILVER SNAKE.
IN THE RIGHT, A GOLD ELEPHANT.
AN IMAGE... OF DEATH...
FWOOSH

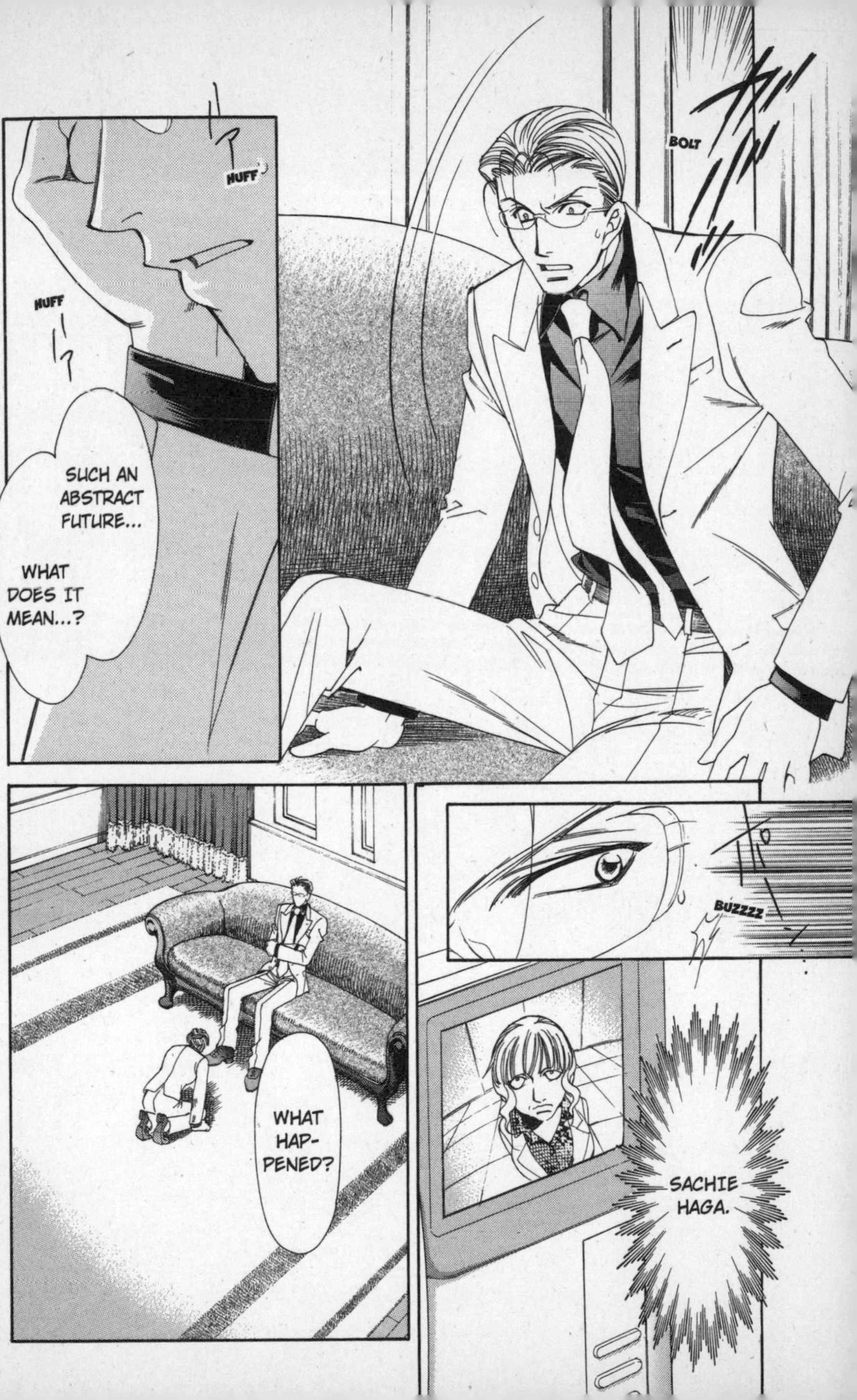
BOLT
HUFF
HUFF
SUCH AN ABSTRACT FUTURE...
WHAT DOES IT MEAN...?
BUZZZZ
SACHIE HAGA.
WHAT HAP-PENED?

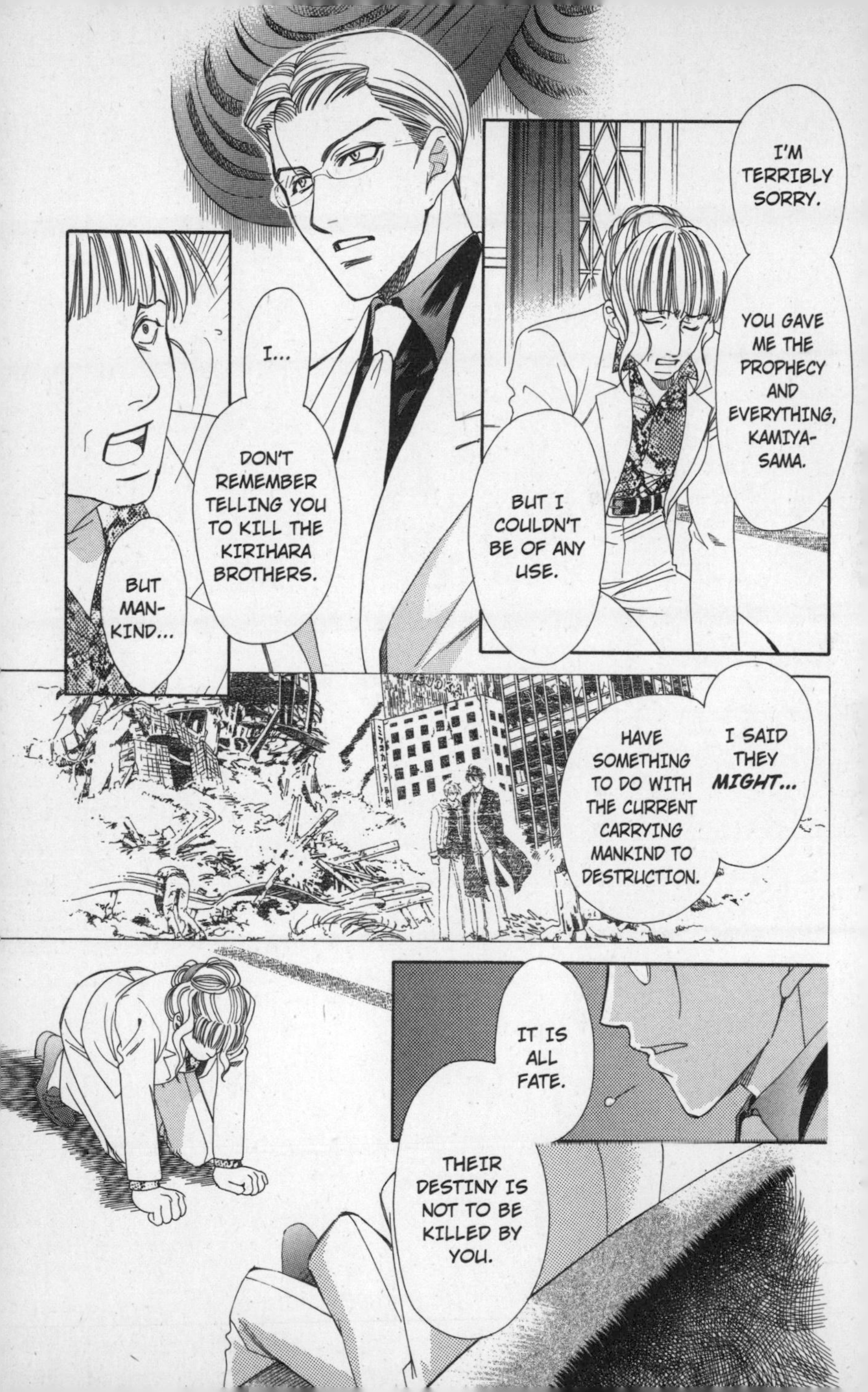
I'M TERRIBLY SORRY.
YOU GAVE ME THE PROPHECY AND EVERYTHING, KAMIYA-SAMA.
BUT I COULDN'T BE OF ANY USE.
I...
DON'T REMEMBER TELLING YOU TO KILL THE KIRIHARA BROTHERS.
BUT MAN-KIND...
I SAID THEY *MIGHT*...
HAVE SOMETHING TO DO WITH THE CURRENT CARRYING MANKIND TO DESTRUCTION.
IT IS ALL FATE.
THEIR DESTINY IS NOT TO BE KILLED BY YOU.

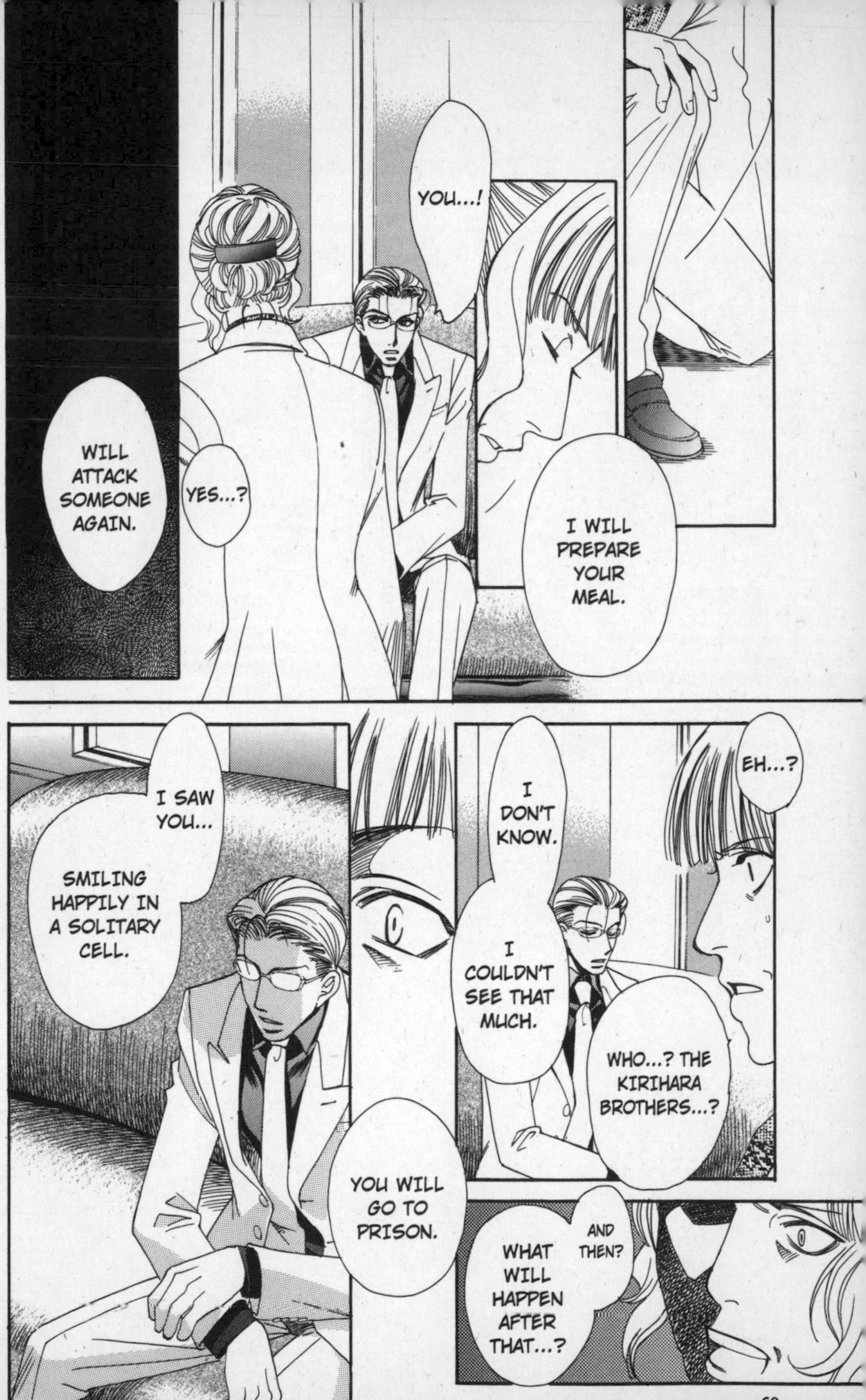
YOU...!
I WILL PREPARE YOUR MEAL.
YES...?
WILL ATTACK SOMEONE AGAIN.
EH...?
I DON'T KNOW.
I COULDN'T SEE THAT MUCH.
WHO...? THE KIRIHARA BROTHERS...?
AND THEN?
WHAT WILL HAPPEN AFTER THAT...?
YOU WILL GO TO PRISON.
I SAW YOU...
SMILING HAPPILY IN A SOLITARY CELL.

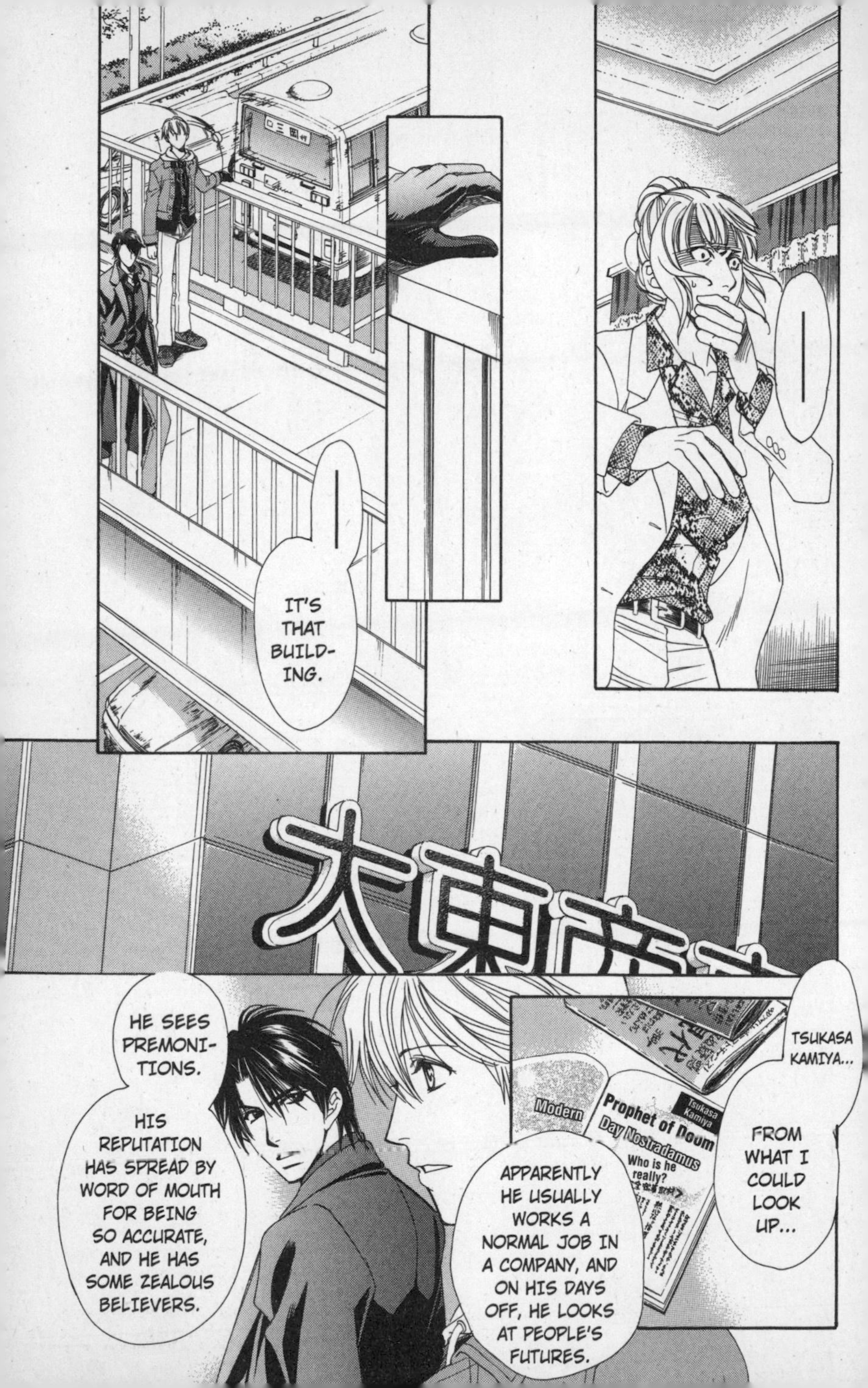
—
— IT'S THAT BUILD-ING.
TSUKASA KAMIYA...
FROM WHAT I COULD LOOK UP...
Modern Day Nostradamus
Prophet of Doom
Tsukasa Kamiya
Who is he really?
APPARENTLY HE USUALLY WORKS A NORMAL JOB IN A COMPANY, AND ON HIS DAYS OFF, HE LOOKS AT PEOPLE'S FUTURES.
HE SEES PREMONI-TIONS.
HIS REPUTATION HAS SPREAD BY WORD OF MOUTH FOR BEING SO ACCURATE, AND HE HAS SOME ZEALOUS BELIEVERS.

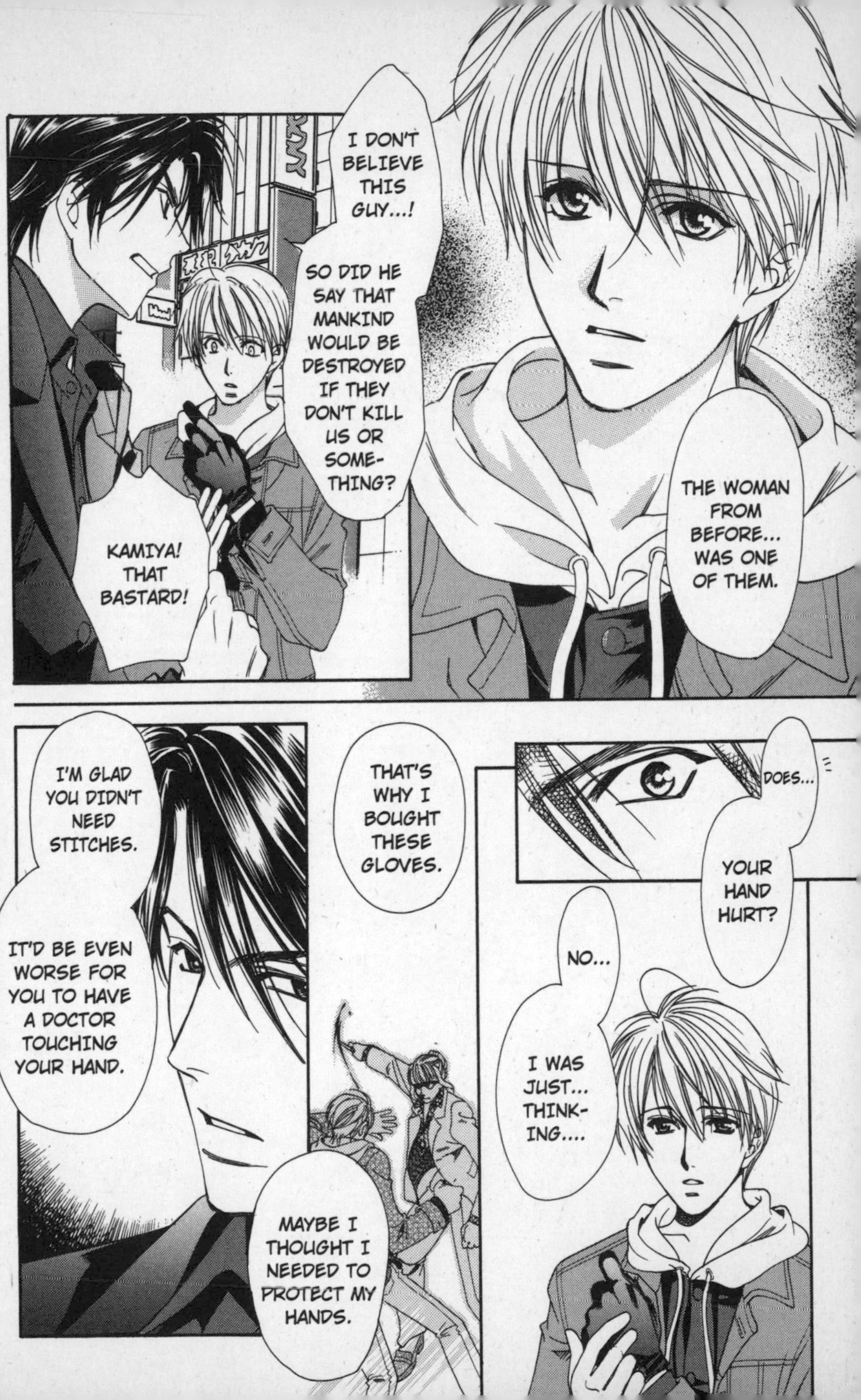
I DON'T BELIEVE THIS GUY...!
SO DID HE SAY THAT MANKIND WOULD BE DESTROYED IF THEY DON'T KILL US OR SOME-THING?
THE WOMAN FROM BEFORE... WAS ONE OF THEM.
KAMIYA! THAT BASTARD!
DOES...
YOUR HAND HURT?
NO...
I WAS JUST... THINK-ING....
MAYBE I THOUGHT I NEEDED TO PROTECT MY HANDS.
THAT'S WHY I BOUGHT THESE GLOVES.
I'M GLAD YOU DIDN'T NEED STITCHES.
IT'D BE EVEN WORSE FOR YOU TO HAVE A DOCTOR TOUCHING YOUR HAND.

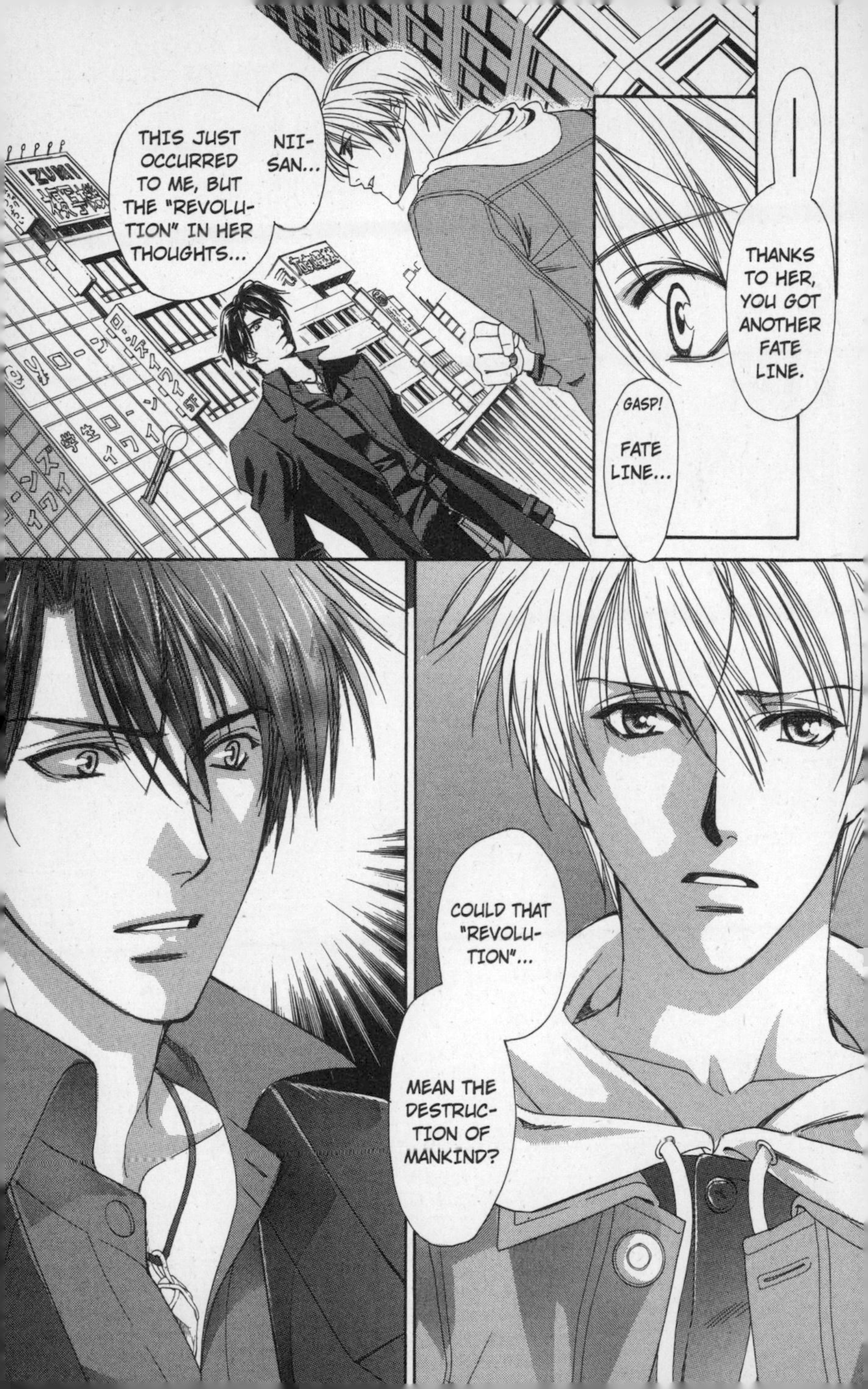
THANKS TO HER, YOU GOT ANOTHER FATE LINE.
GASP!
FATE LINE...
NII-SAN...
THIS JUST OCCURRED TO ME, BUT THE "REVOLUTION" IN HER THOUGHTS...
IZUMI
COULD THAT "REVOLUTION"...
MEAN THE DESTRUCTION OF MANKIND?

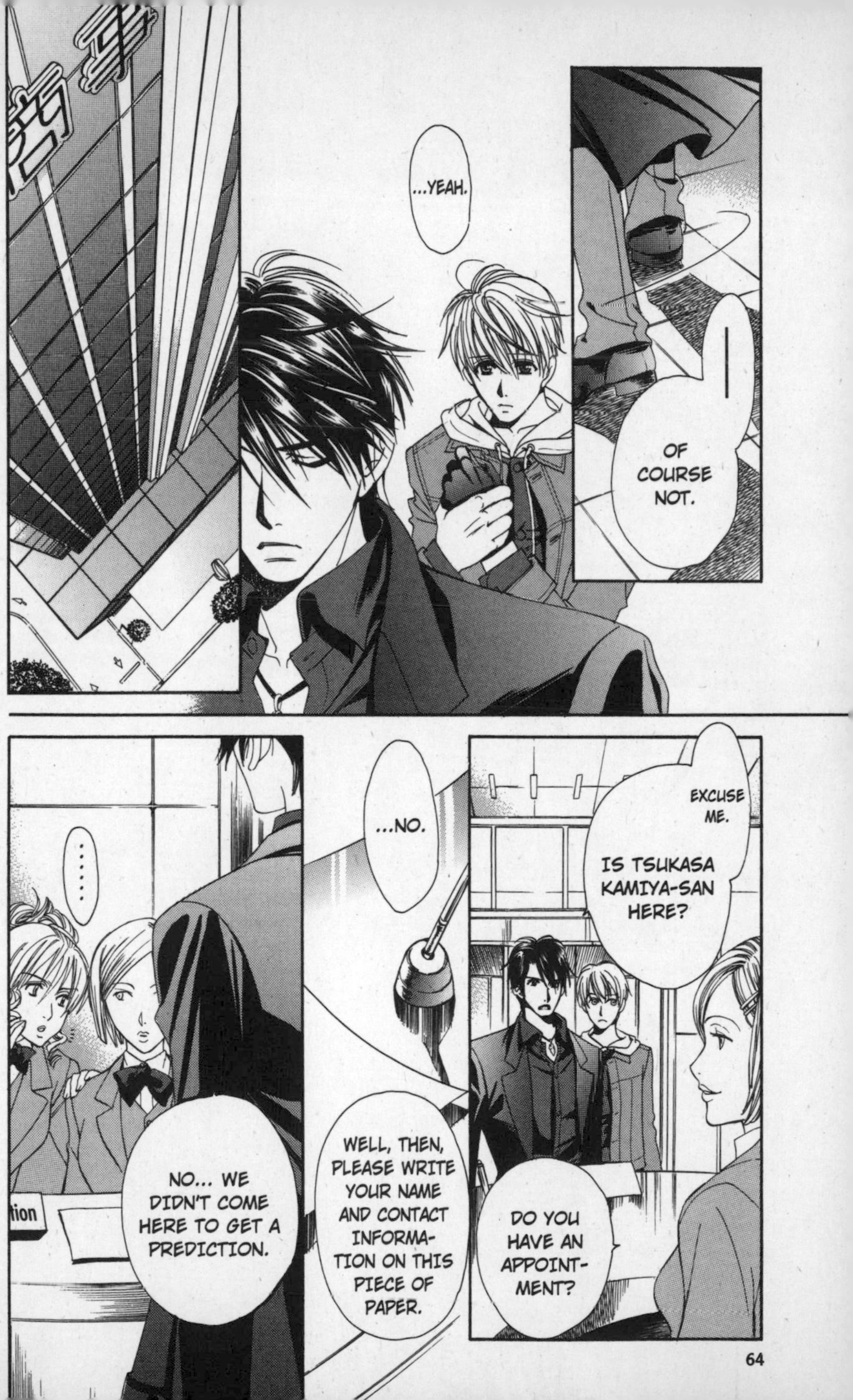
—
OF COURSE NOT.
...YEAH.
EXCUSE ME.
IS TSUKASA KAMIYA-SAN HERE?
DO YOU HAVE AN APPOINT-MENT?
...NO.
WELL, THEN, PLEASE WRITE YOUR NAME AND CONTACT INFORMA-TION ON THIS PIECE OF PAPER.
......
NO... WE DIDN'T COME HERE TO GET A PREDICTION.

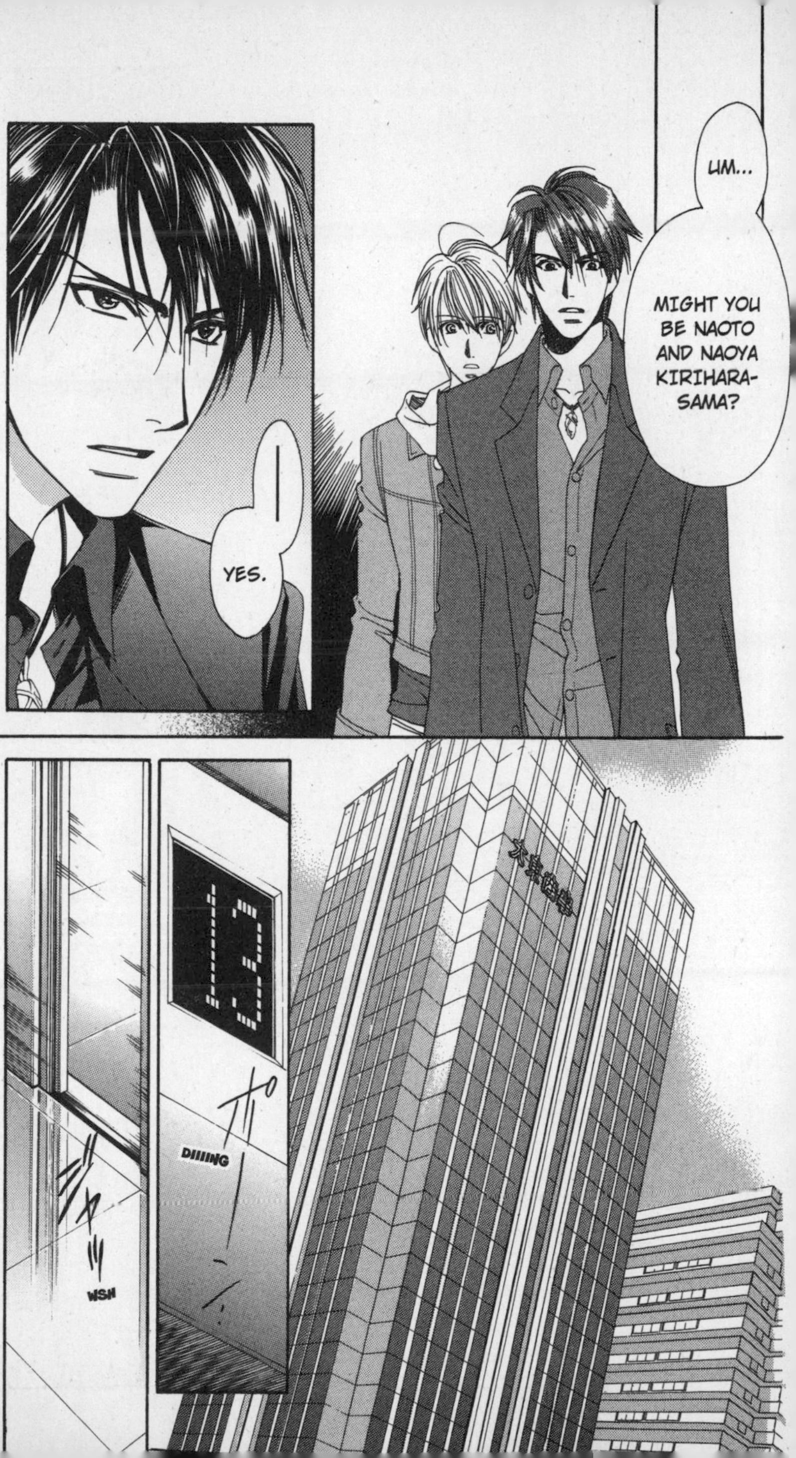
UM...
MIGHT YOU BE NAOTO AND NAOYA KIRIHARA-SAMA?
YES.
DIIIING
WSH

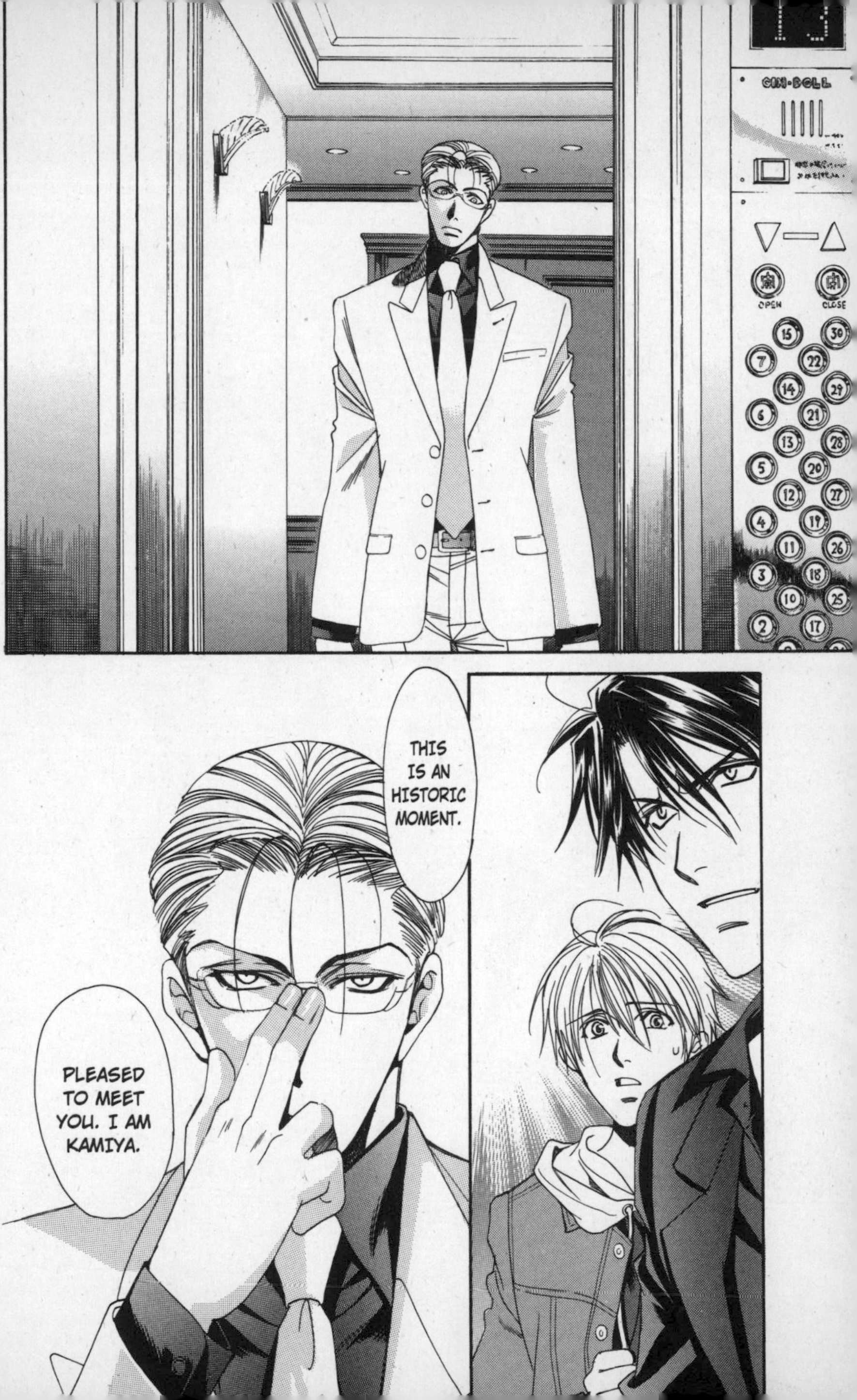
OPEN
CLOSE
THIS IS AN HISTORIC MOMENT.
PLEASED TO MEET YOU. I AM KAMIYA.

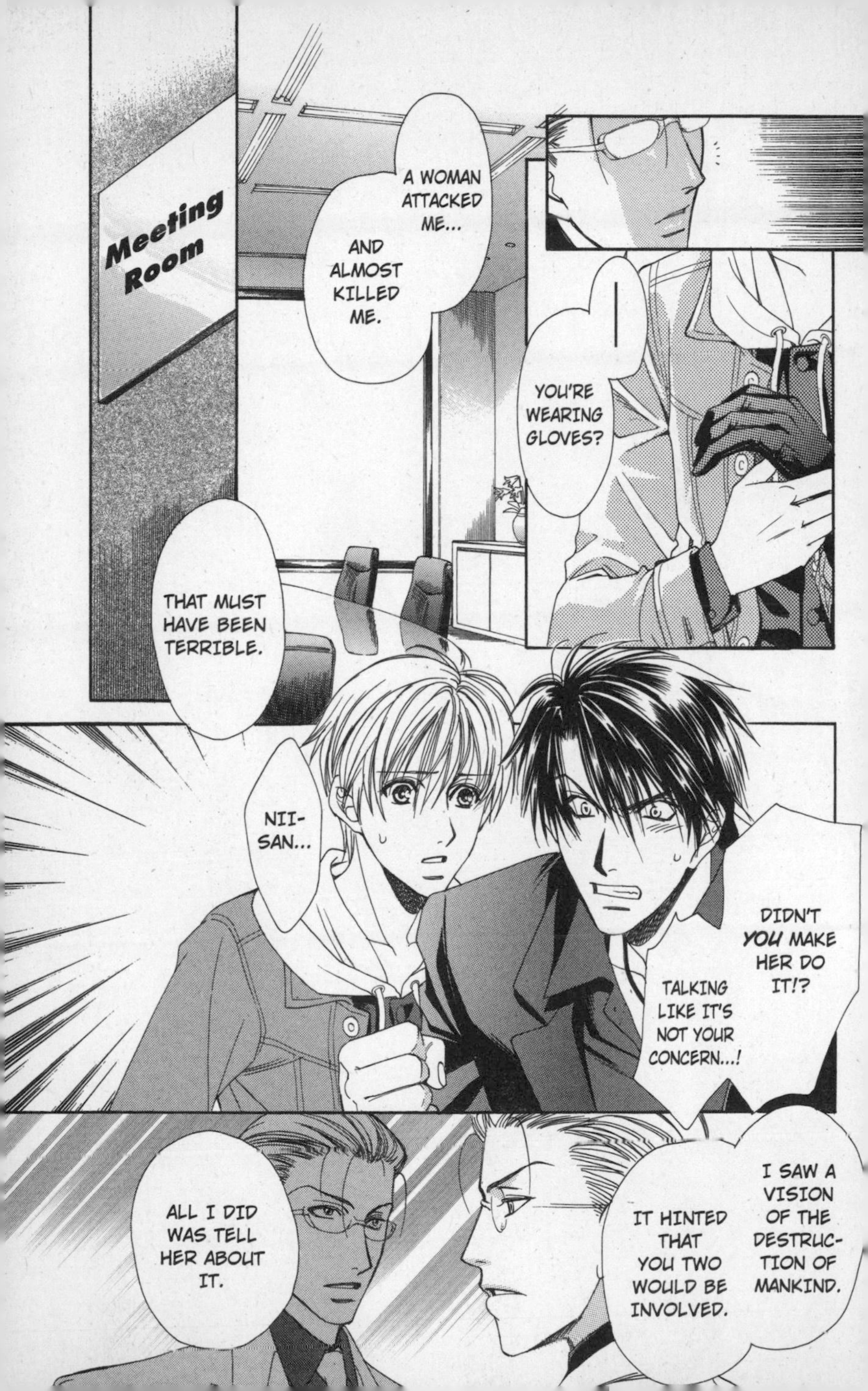
YOU'RE WEARING GLOVES?
Meeting Room
A WOMAN ATTACKED ME...
AND ALMOST KILLED ME.
THAT MUST HAVE BEEN TERRIBLE.
DIDN'T *YOU* MAKE HER DO IT!?
TALKING LIKE IT'S NOT YOUR CONCERN...!
NII-SAN...
I SAW A VISION OF THE DESTRUC-TION OF MANKIND.
IT HINTED THAT YOU TWO WOULD BE INVOLVED.
ALL I DID WAS TELL HER ABOUT IT.

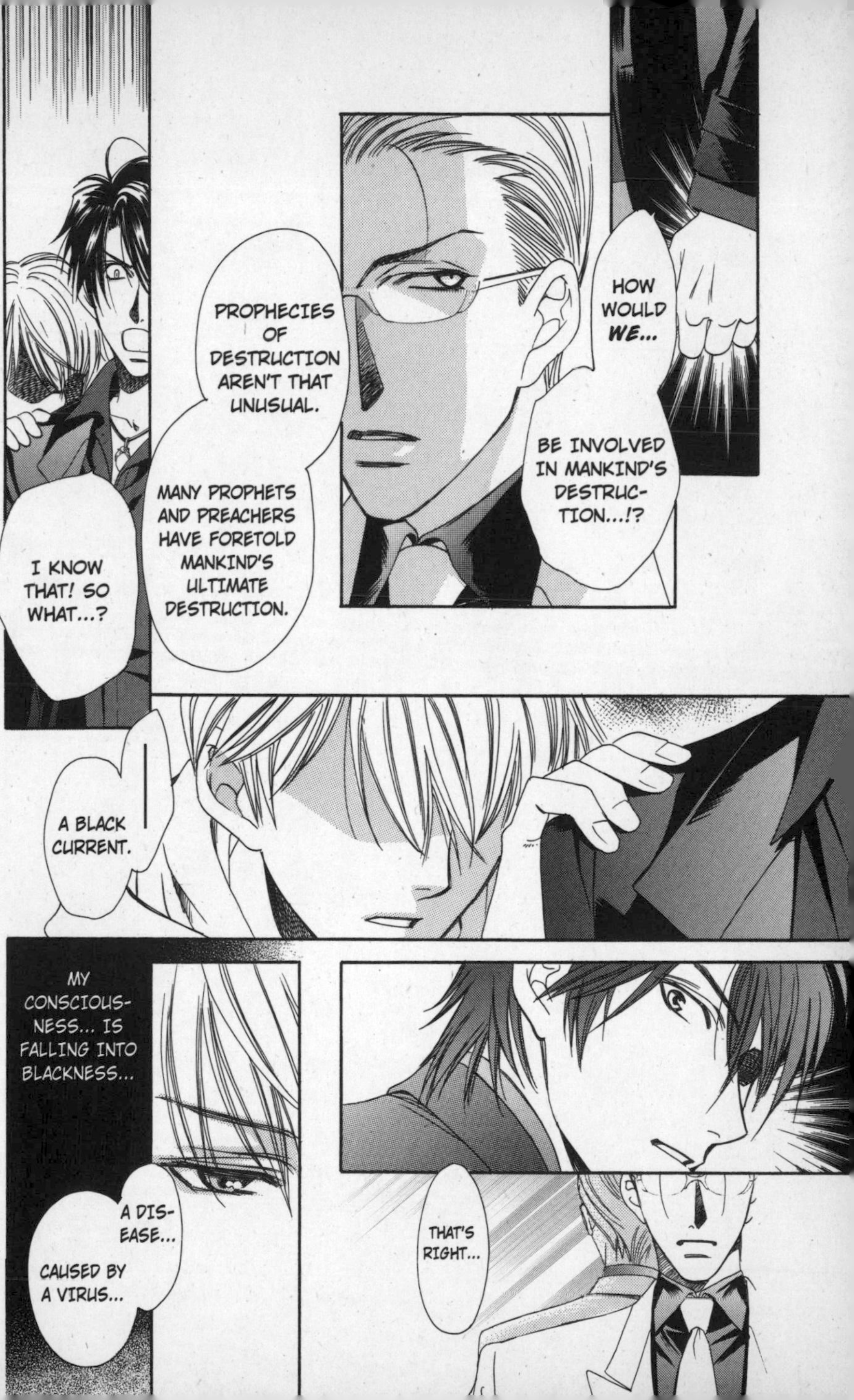
HOW WOULD WE...
BE INVOLVED IN MANKIND'S DESTRUC-TION...!?
PROPHECIES OF DESTRUCTION AREN'T THAT UNUSUAL.
MANY PROPHETS AND PREACHERS HAVE FORETOLD MANKIND'S ULTIMATE DESTRUCTION.
I KNOW THAT! SO WHAT...?
A BLACK CURRENT.
THAT'S RIGHT...
MY CONSCIOUS-NESS... IS FALLING INTO BLACKNESS...
A DIS-EASE...
CAUSED BY A VIRUS...

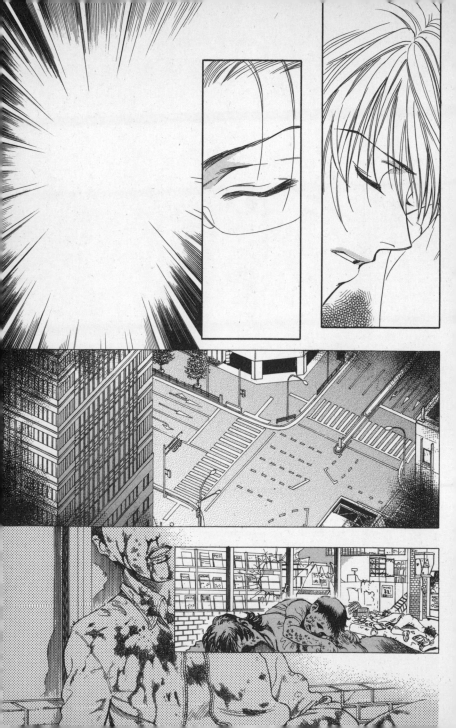

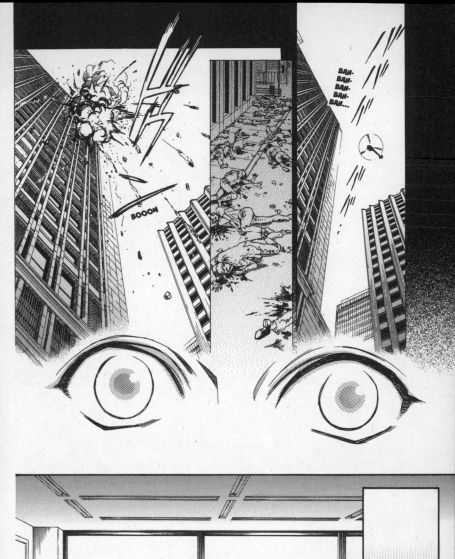

BAN-
BAN-
BAN-
BAN...

BOOOM

WHAT DID YOU SEE?

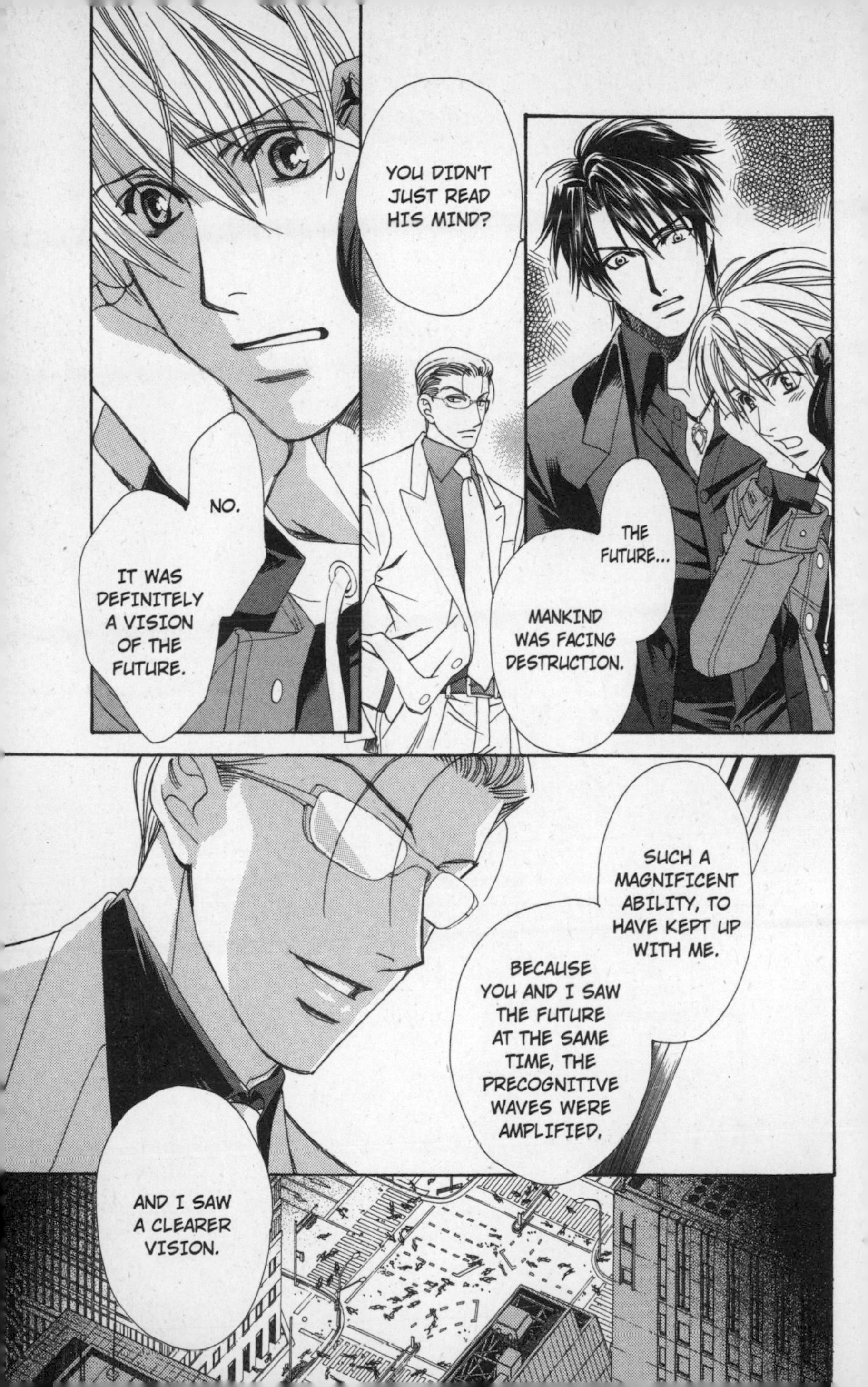
YOU DIDN'T JUST READ HIS MIND?
NO.
IT WAS DEFINITELY A VISION OF THE FUTURE.
THE FUTURE...
MANKIND WAS FACING DESTRUCTION.
SUCH A MAGNIFICENT ABILITY, TO HAVE KEPT UP WITH ME.
BECAUSE YOU AND I SAW THE FUTURE AT THE SAME TIME, THE PRECOGNITIVE WAVES WERE AMPLIFIED.
AND I SAW A CLEARER VISION.

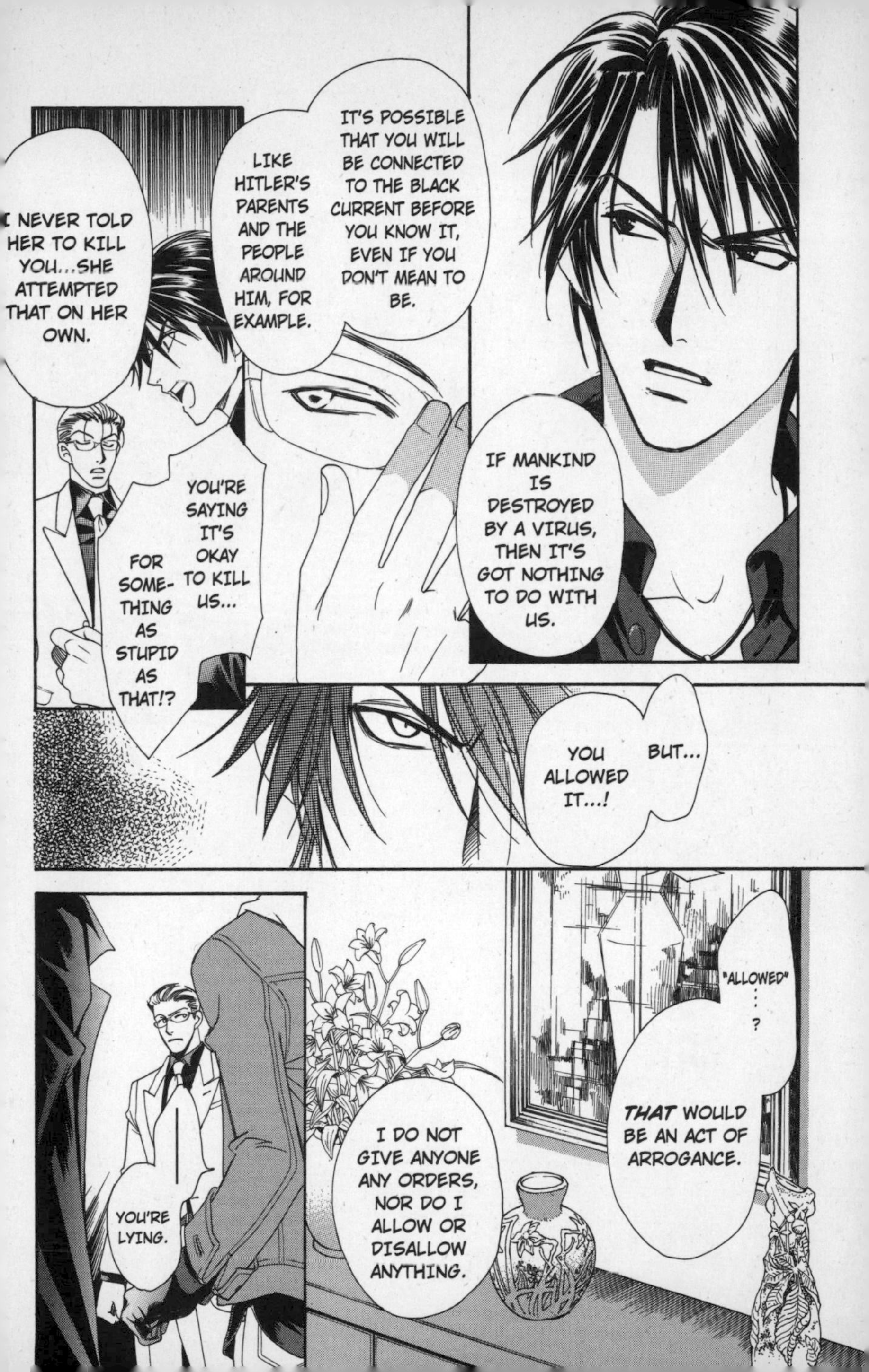
IF MANKIND IS DESTROYED BY A VIRUS, THEN IT'S GOT NOTHING TO DO WITH US.
IT'S POSSIBLE THAT YOU WILL BE CONNECTED TO THE BLACK CURRENT BEFORE YOU KNOW IT, EVEN IF YOU DON'T MEAN TO BE.
LIKE HITLER'S PARENTS AND THE PEOPLE AROUND HIM, FOR EXAMPLE.
I NEVER TOLD HER TO KILL YOU...SHE ATTEMPTED THAT ON HER OWN.
YOU'RE SAYING IT'S OKAY TO KILL US...
FOR SOME-THING AS STUPID AS THAT!?
BUT...
YOU ALLOWED IT...!
"ALLOWED" ... ?
THAT WOULD BE AN ACT OF ARROGANCE.
I DO NOT GIVE ANYONE ANY ORDERS, NOR DO I ALLOW OR DISALLOW ANYTHING.
YOU'RE LYING.

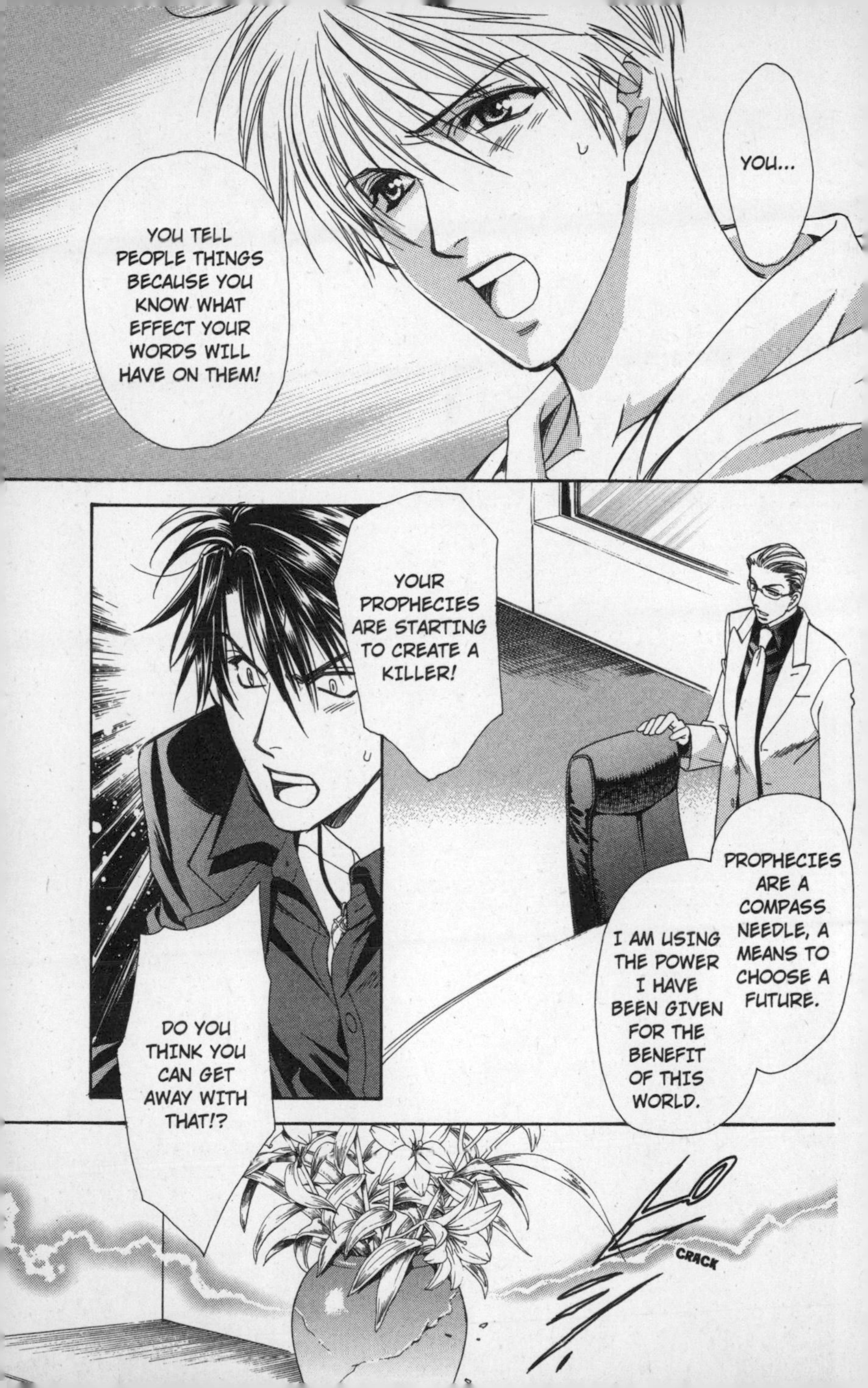
YOU...
YOU TELL PEOPLE THINGS BECAUSE YOU KNOW WHAT EFFECT YOUR WORDS WILL HAVE ON THEM!
YOUR PROPHECIES ARE STARTING TO CREATE A KILLER!
PROPHECIES ARE A COMPASS NEEDLE, A MEANS TO CHOOSE A FUTURE.
I AM USING THE POWER I HAVE BEEN GIVEN FOR THE BENEFIT OF THIS WORLD.
DO YOU THINK YOU CAN GET AWAY WITH THAT!?
CRACK

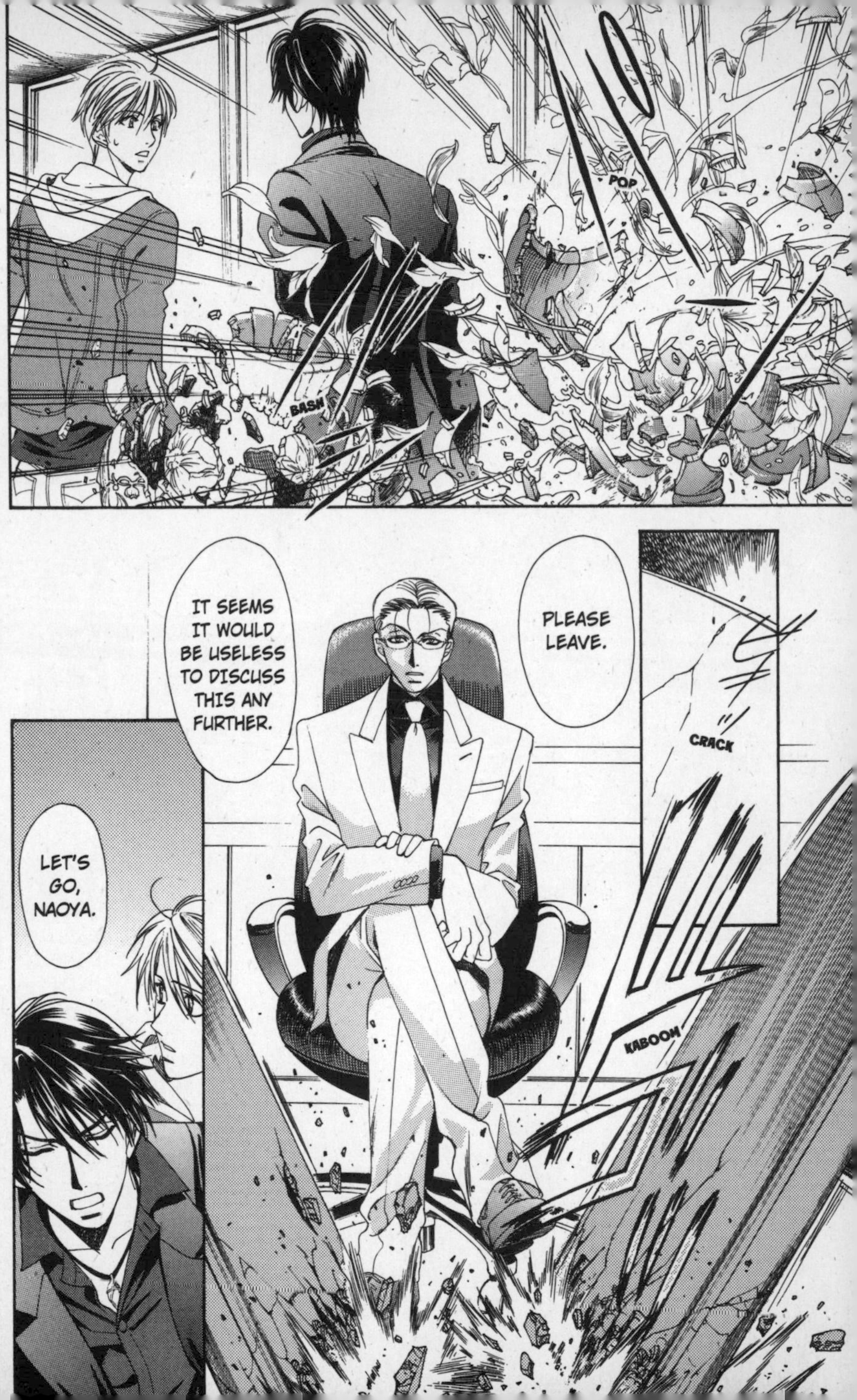

POP
BASH
CRACK
PLEASE LEAVE.
IT SEEMS IT WOULD BE USELESS TO DISCUSS THIS ANY FURTHER.
KABOOM
LET'S GO, NAOYA.

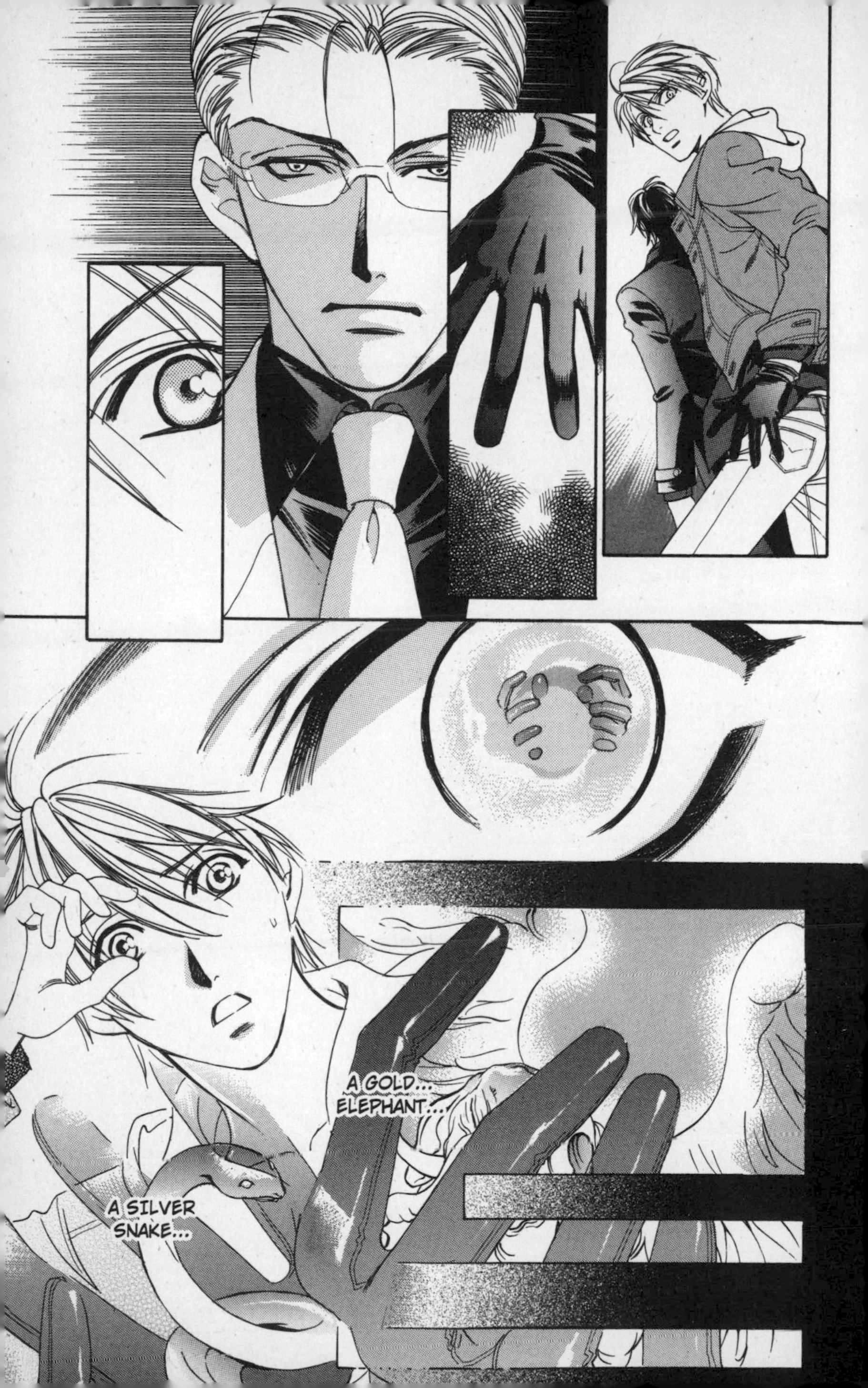
A GOLD... ELEPHANT...
A SILVER SNAKE...

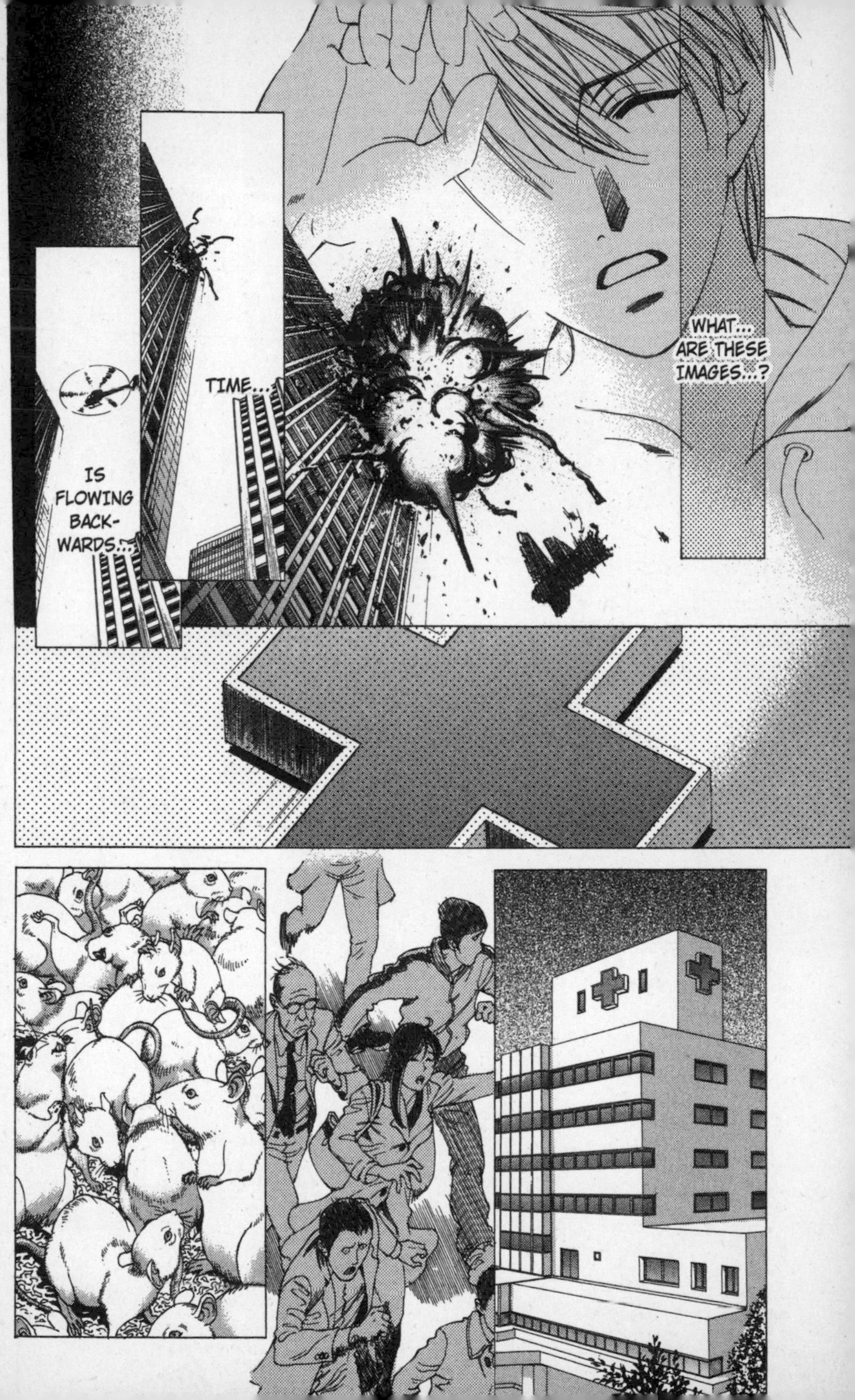
WHAT... ARE THESE IMAGES...?
TIME...
IS FLOWING BACKWARDS...

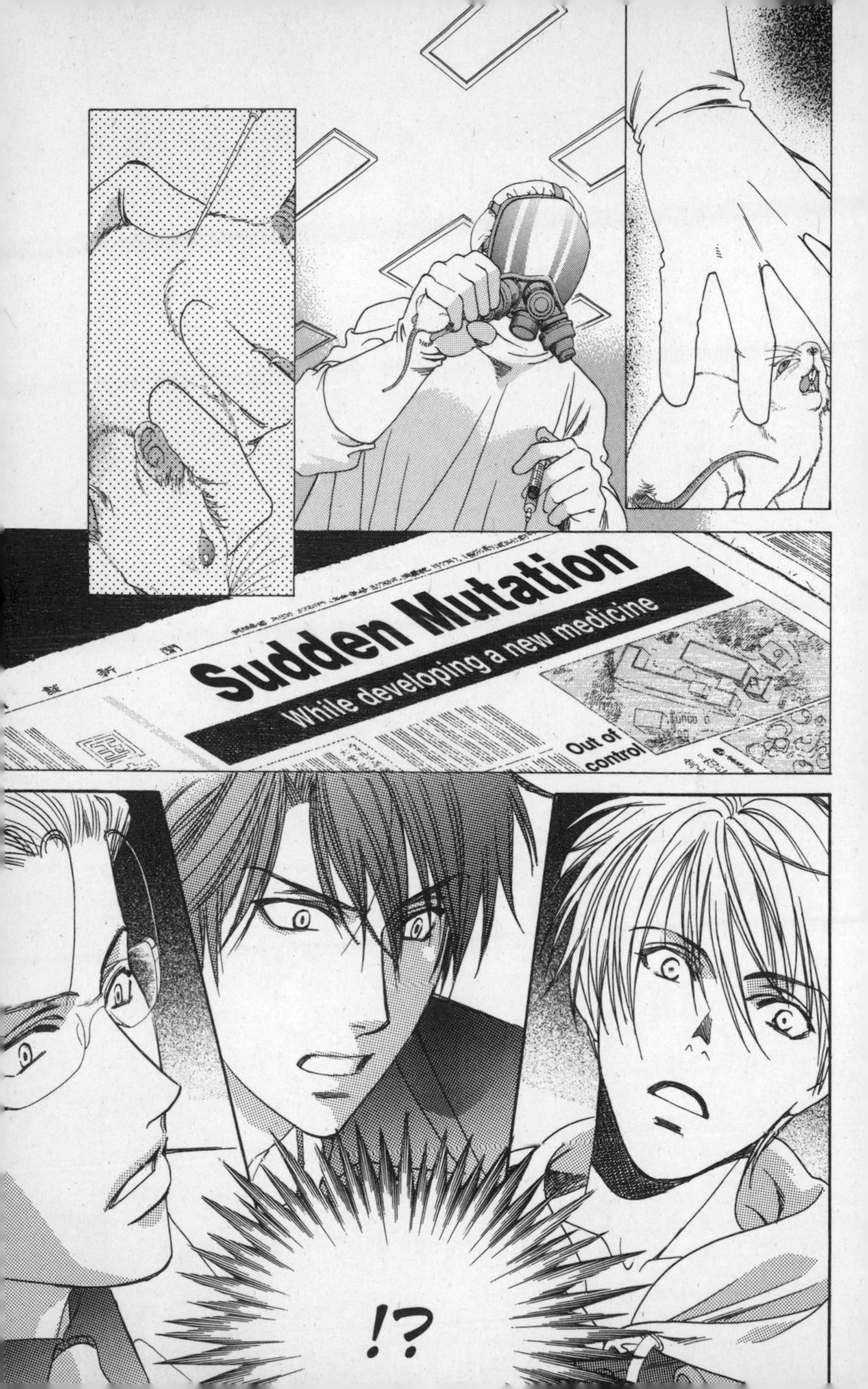
Sudden Mutation
While developing a new medicine
Out of control
!?

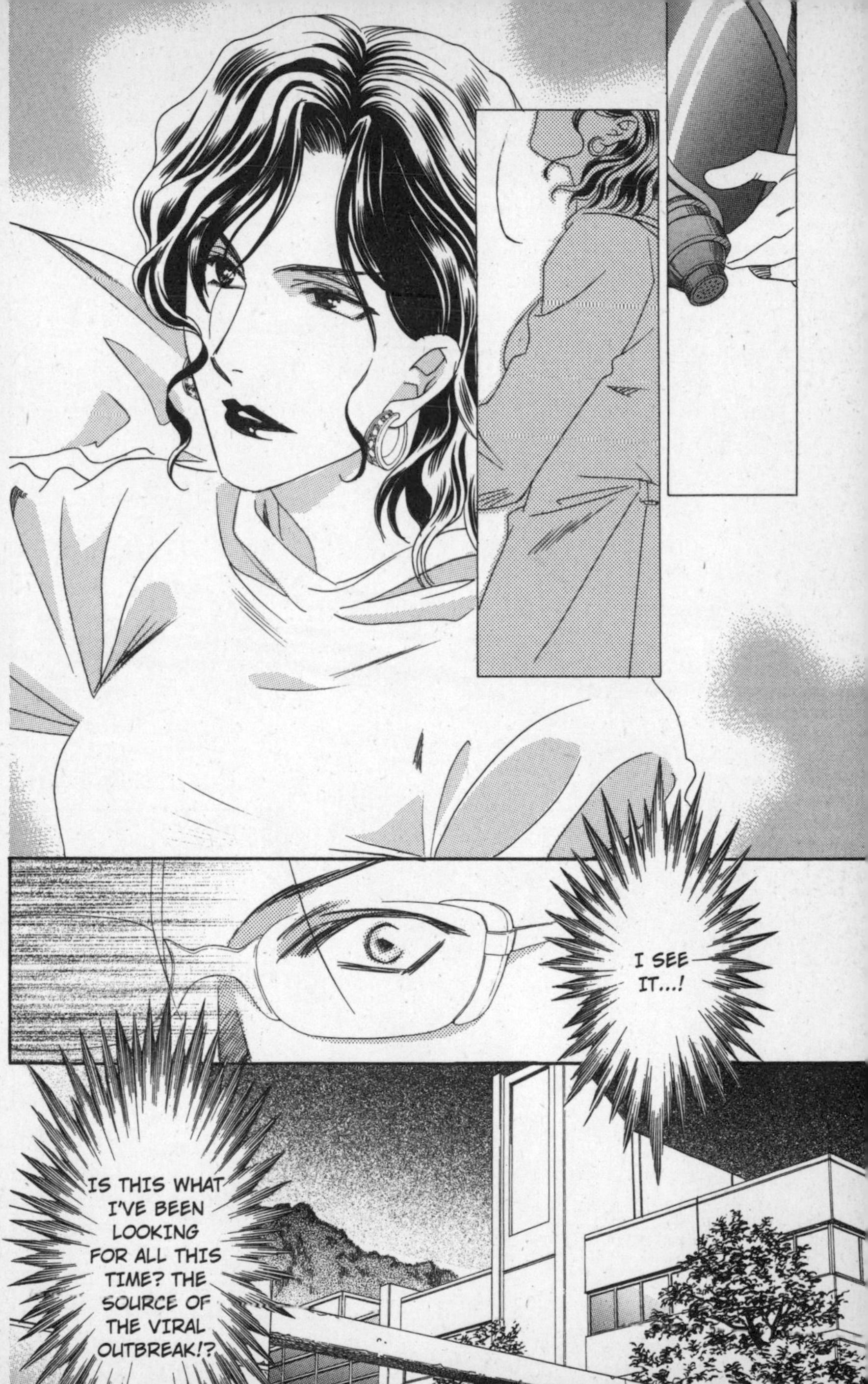
I SEE IT...!
IS THIS WHAT I'VE BEEN LOOKING FOR ALL THIS TIME? THE SOURCE OF THE VIRAL OUTBREAK!?

Chapter 2: PROPHECY · END

Chapter 3:
CHANCE ENCOUNTER

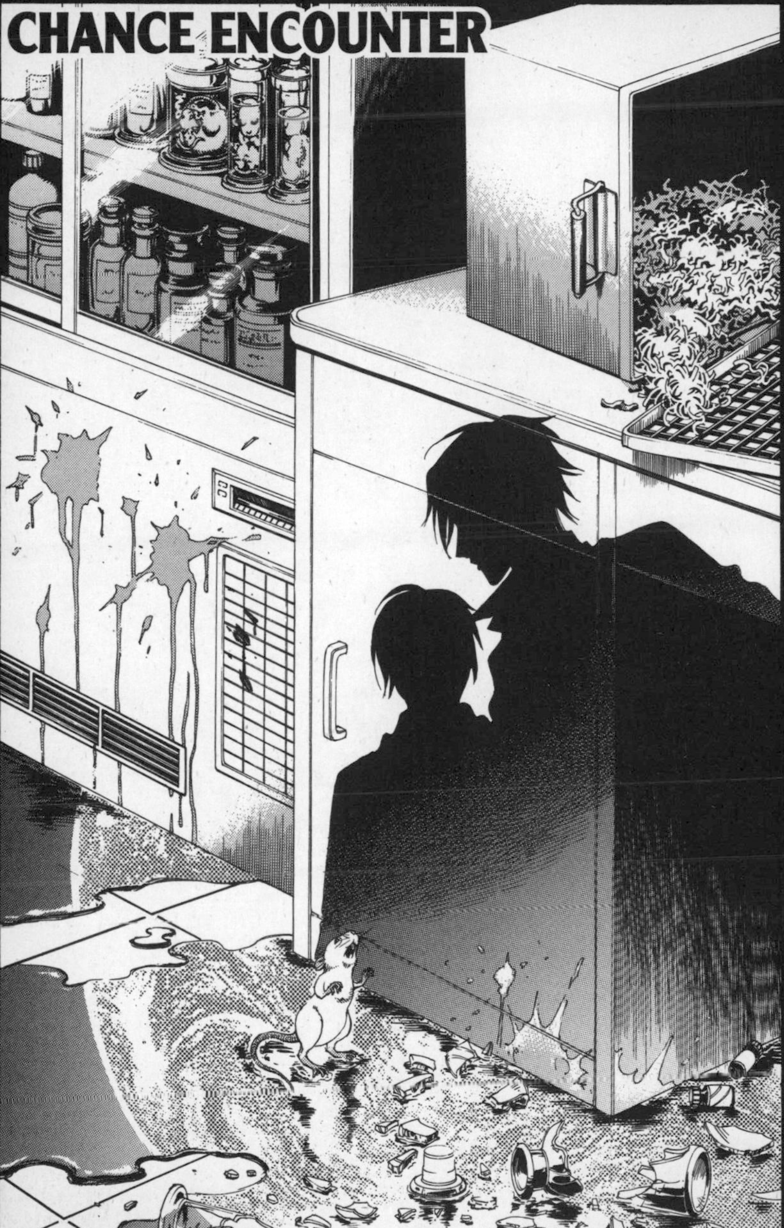

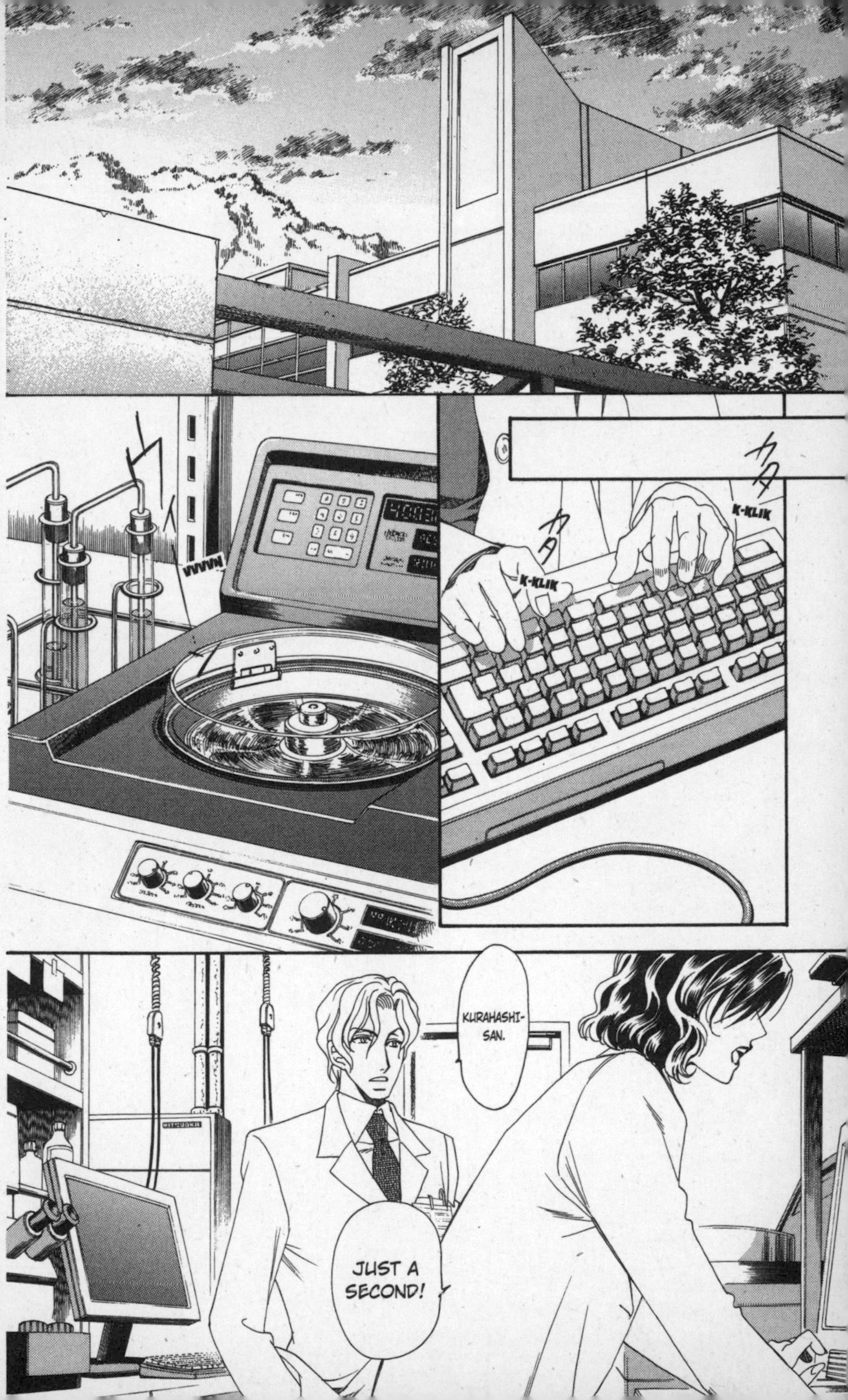

K-KLIK
K-KLIK
VVVVN
KURAHASHI-SAN.
JUST A SECOND!

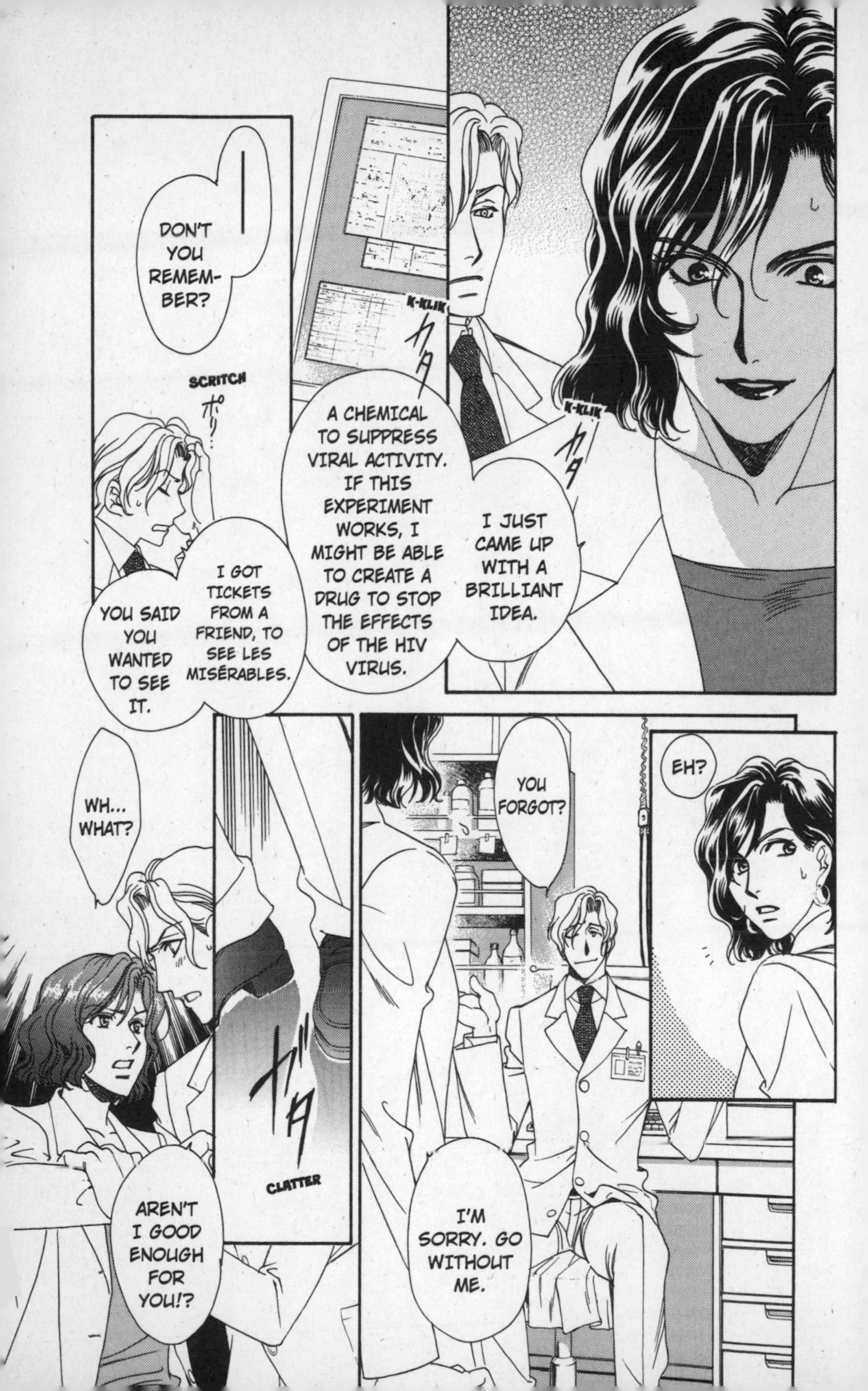
K-KLIK
K-KLIK
I JUST CAME UP WITH A BRILLIANT IDEA.
A CHEMICAL TO SUPPRESS VIRAL ACTIVITY. IF THIS EXPERIMENT WORKS, I MIGHT BE ABLE TO CREATE A DRUG TO STOP THE EFFECTS OF THE HIV VIRUS.
DON'T YOU REMEMBER?
SCRITCH
I GOT TICKETS FROM A FRIEND, TO SEE LES MISÉRABLES.
YOU SAID YOU WANTED TO SEE IT.
EH?
YOU FORGOT?
I'M SORRY. GO WITHOUT ME.
WH... WHAT?
CLATTER
AREN'T I GOOD ENOUGH FOR YOU!?

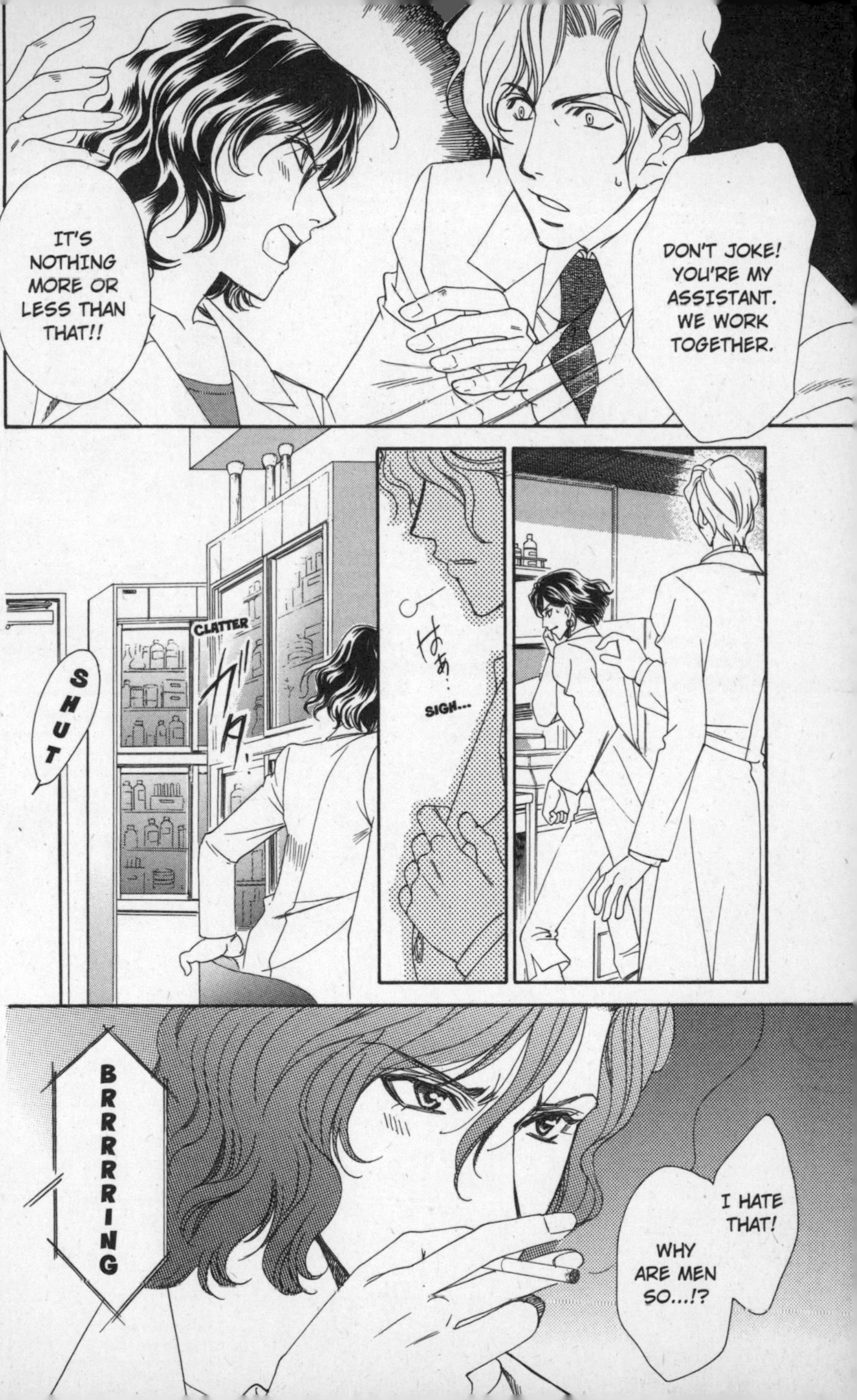
DON'T JOKE! YOU'RE MY ASSISTANT. WE WORK TOGETHER.
IT'S NOTHING MORE OR LESS THAN THAT!!
はあ
SIGH...
CLATTER
SHUT
I HATE THAT!
WHY ARE MEN SO...!?
BRRRRRING

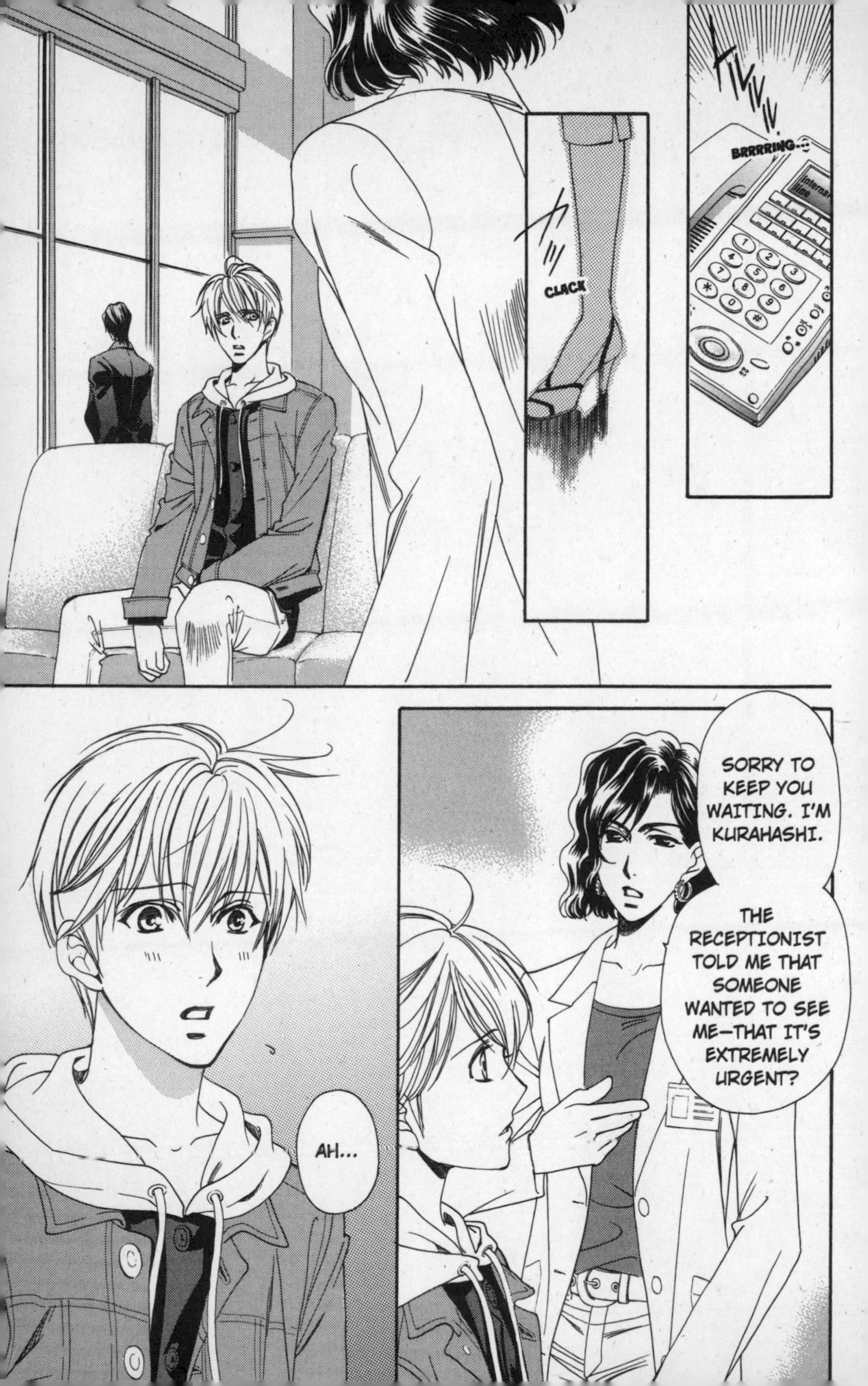
BRRRRING...
CLACK
SORRY TO KEEP YOU WAITING. I'M KURAHASHI.
THE RECEPTIONIST TOLD ME THAT SOMEONE WANTED TO SEE ME—THAT IT'S EXTREMELY URGENT?
AH...

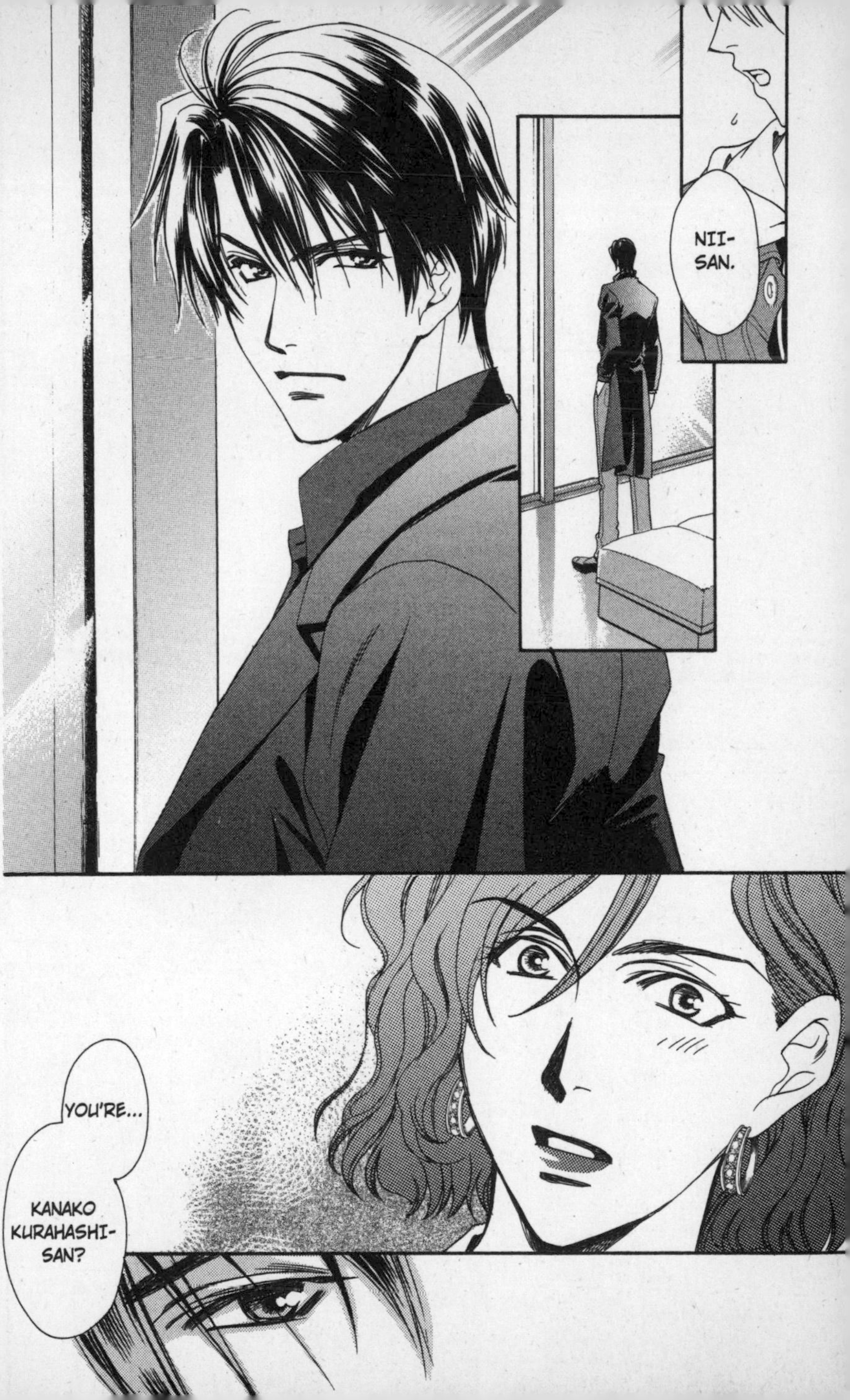
NII-SAN.
YOU'RE...
KANAKO KURAHASHI-SAN?

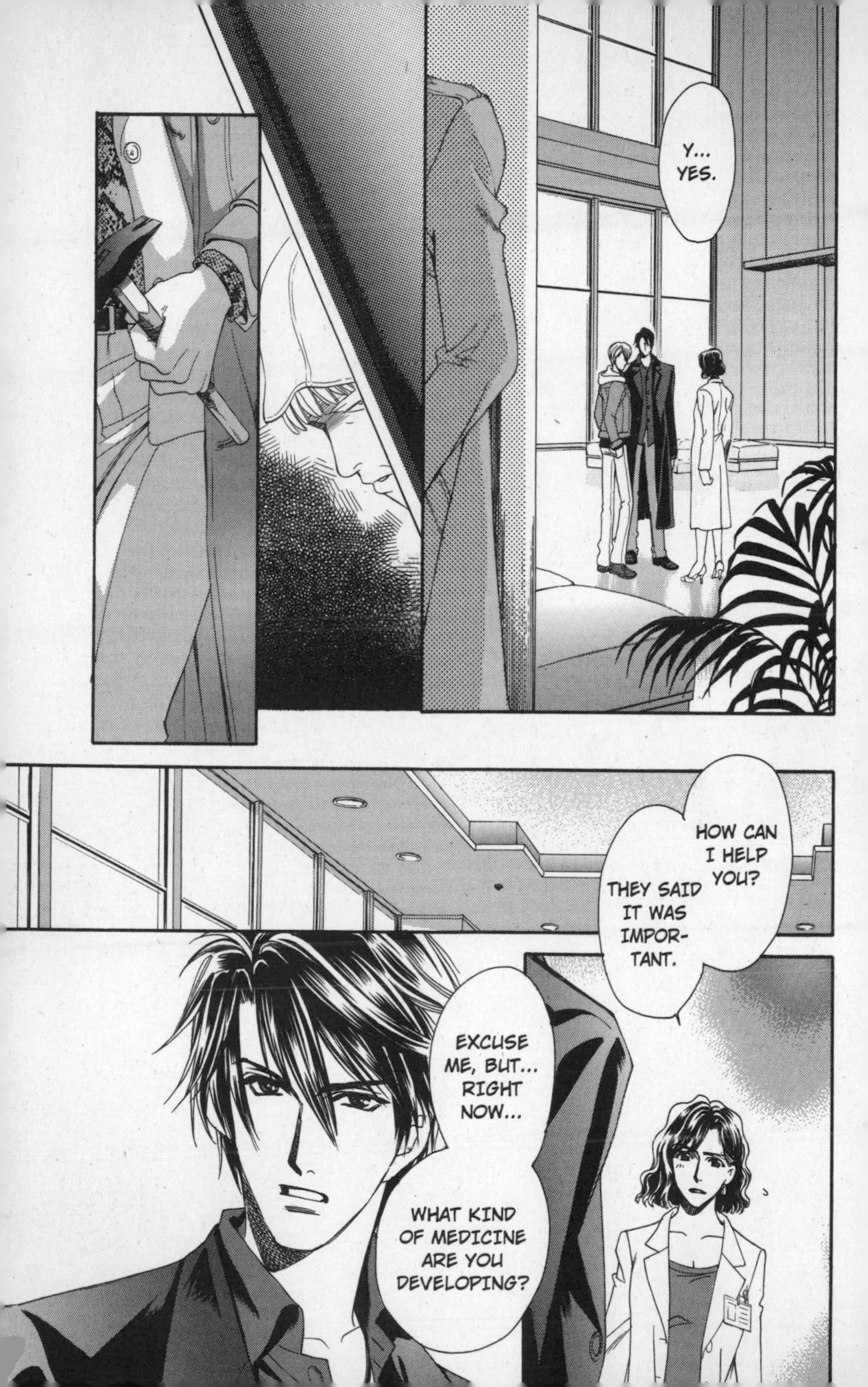

Y... YES.
HOW CAN I HELP YOU?
THEY SAID IT WAS IMPOR- TANT.
EXCUSE ME, BUT... RIGHT NOW...
WHAT KIND OF MEDICINE ARE YOU DEVELOPING?

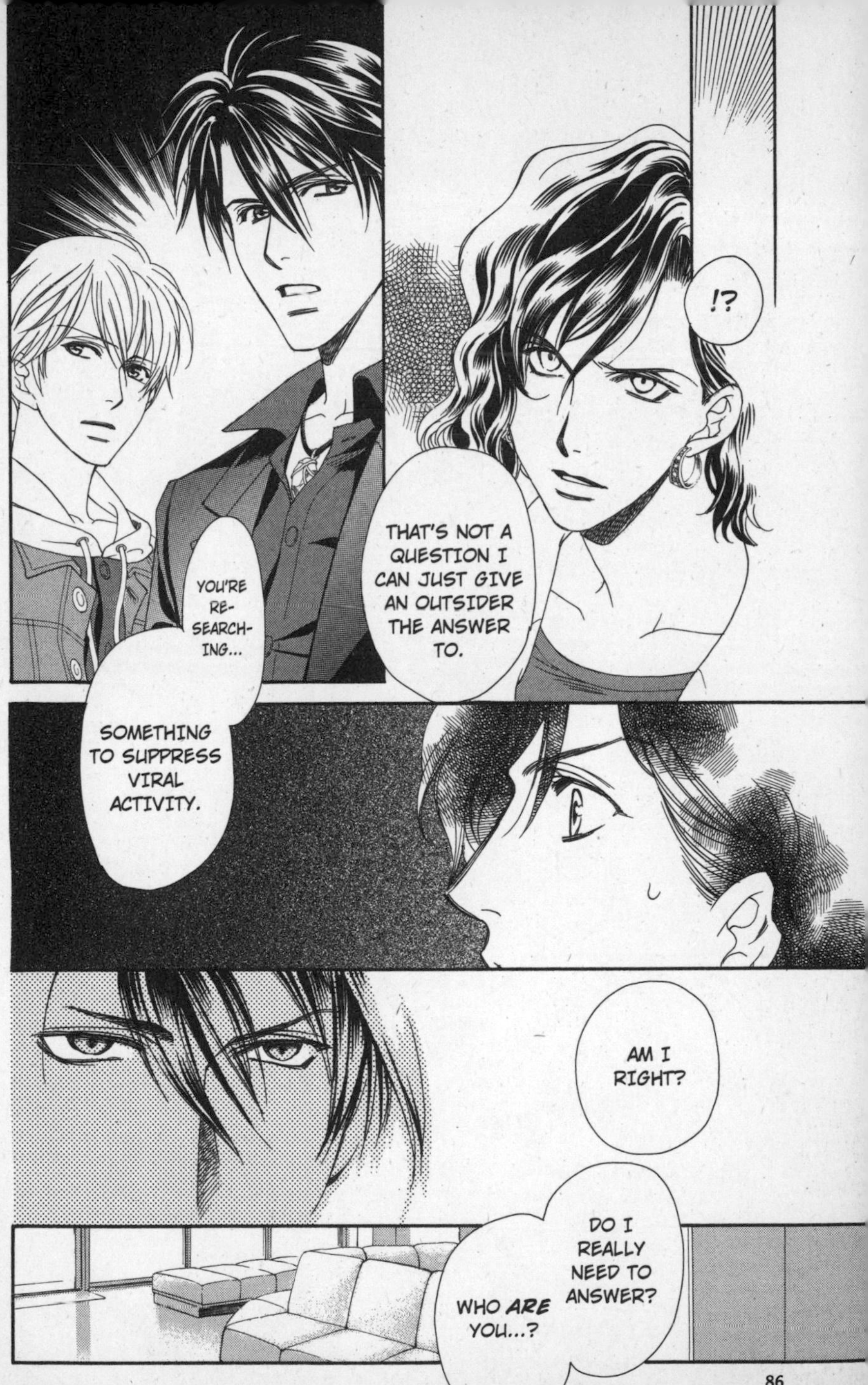
!?
THAT'S NOT A QUESTION I CAN JUST GIVE AN OUTSIDER THE ANSWER TO.
YOU'RE RE-SEARCHING-ING...
SOMETHING TO SUPPRESS VIRAL ACTIVITY.
AM I RIGHT?
DO I REALLY NEED TO ANSWER?
WHO *ARE* YOU...?

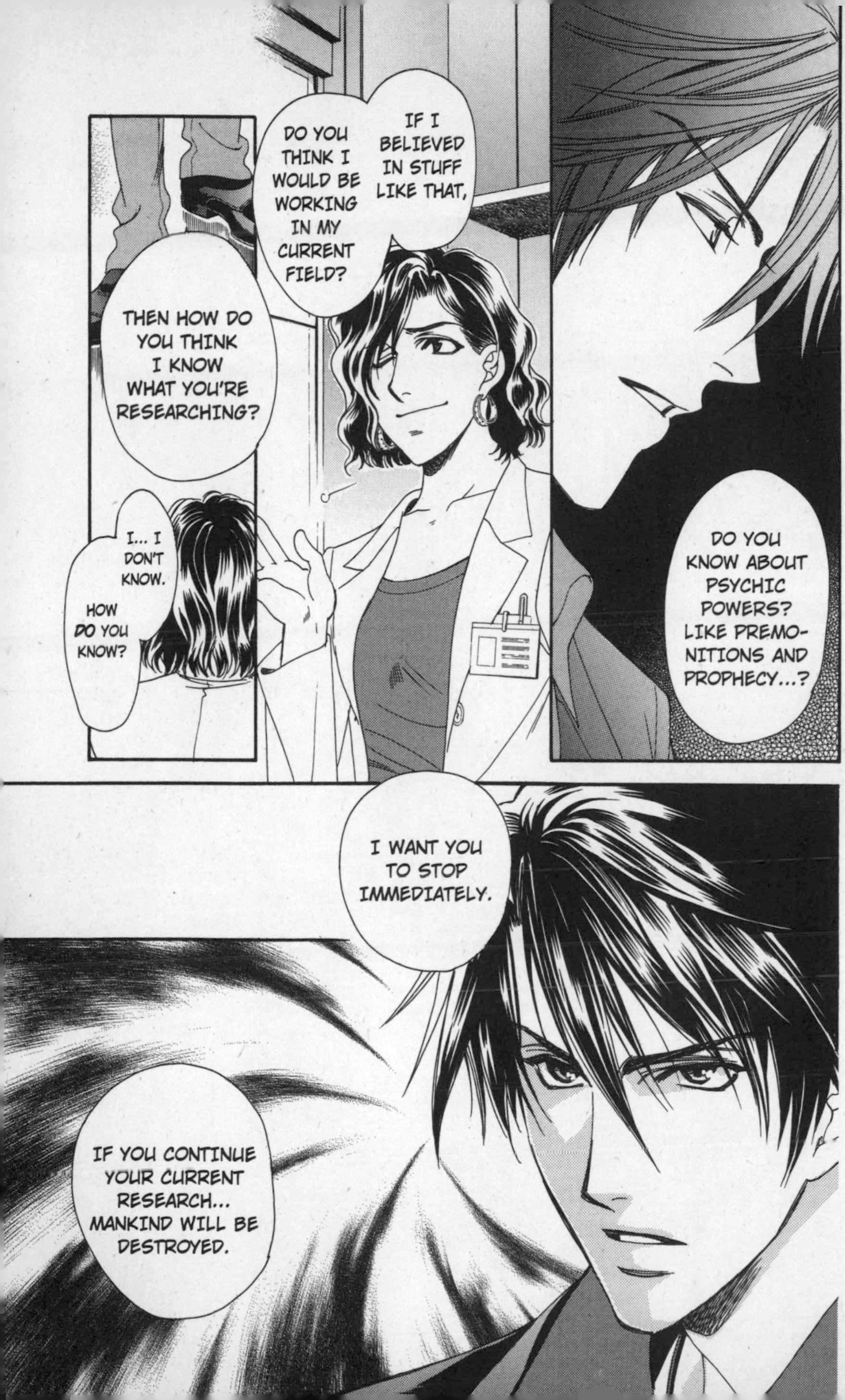
DO YOU KNOW ABOUT PSYCHIC POWERS? LIKE PREMO-NITIONS AND PROPHECY...?
IF I BELIEVED IN STUFF LIKE THAT,
DO YOU THINK I WOULD BE WORKING IN MY CURRENT FIELD?
THEN HOW DO YOU THINK I KNOW WHAT YOU'RE RESEARCHING?
I... I DON'T KNOW.
HOW DO YOU KNOW?
I WANT YOU TO STOP IMMEDIATELY.
IF YOU CONTINUE YOUR CURRENT RESEARCH... MANKIND WILL BE DESTROYED.

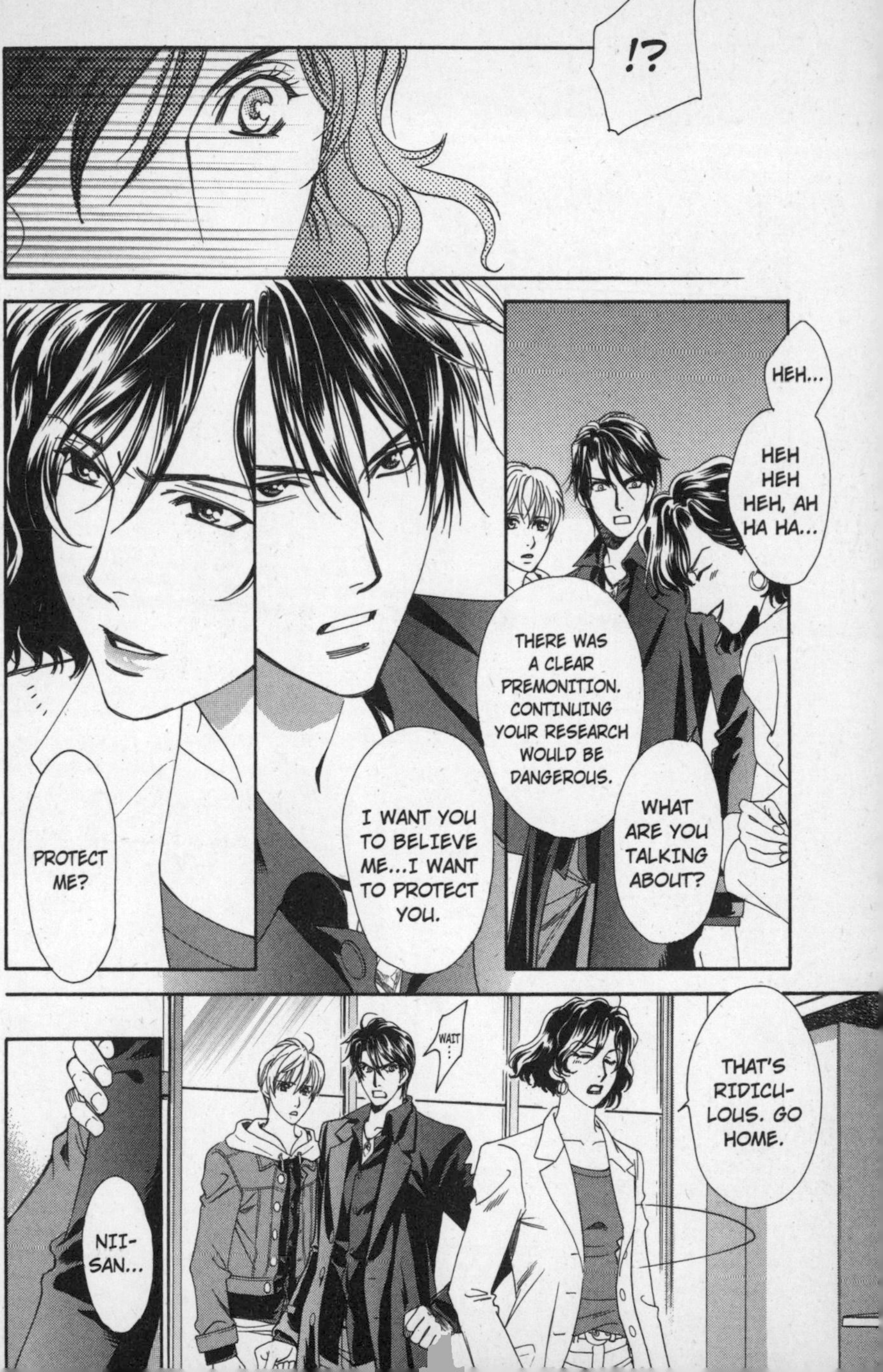
!?
HEH...
HEH HEH HEH, AH HA HA...
THERE WAS A CLEAR PREMONITION. CONTINUING YOUR RESEARCH WOULD BE DANGEROUS.
WHAT ARE YOU TALKING ABOUT?
I WANT YOU TO BELIEVE ME...I WANT TO PROTECT YOU.
PROTECT ME?
THAT'S RIDICU-LOUS. GO HOME.
WAIT...
NII-SAN...

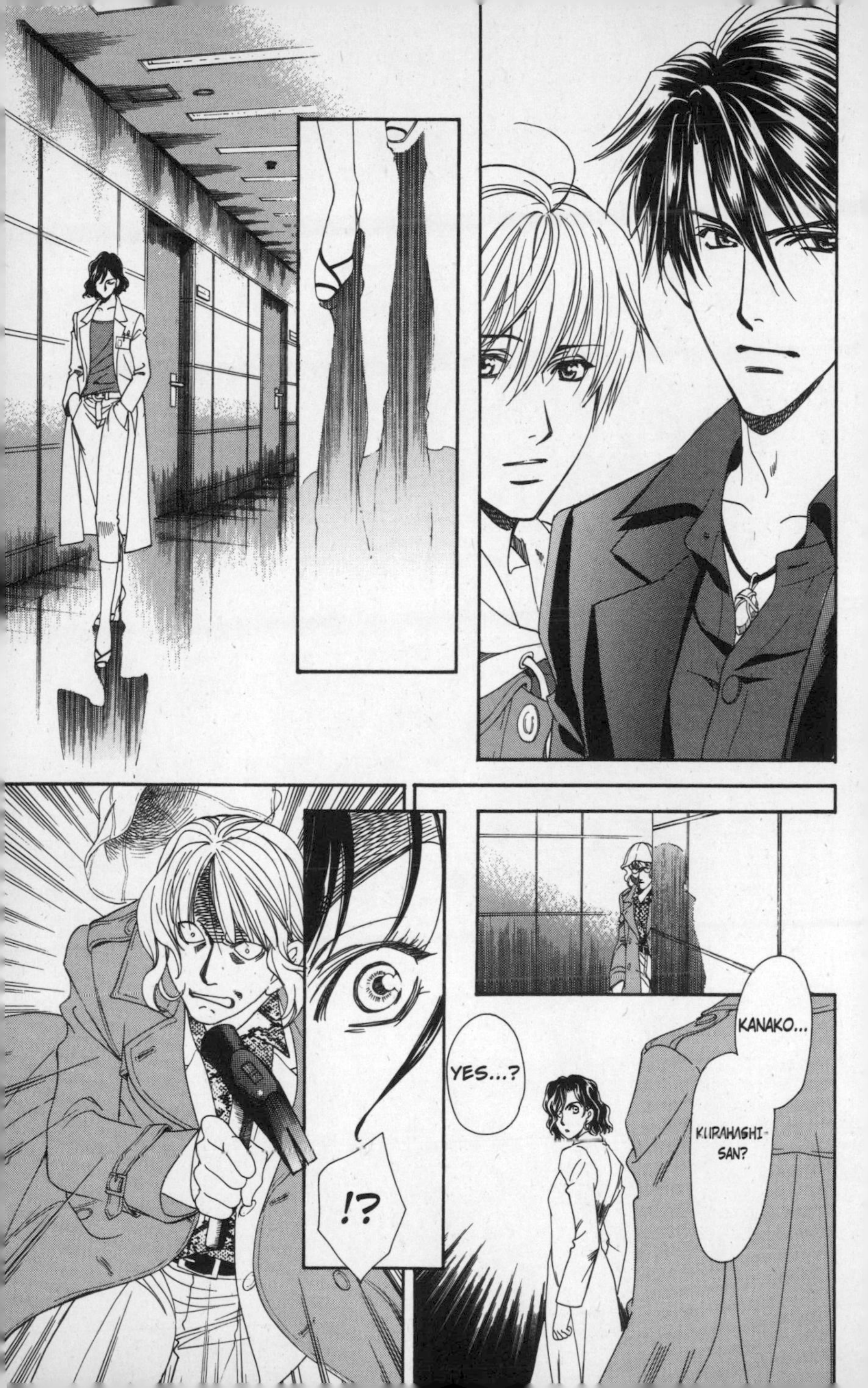
KANAKO...
KIIRAHASHI-SAN?
YES...?
!?

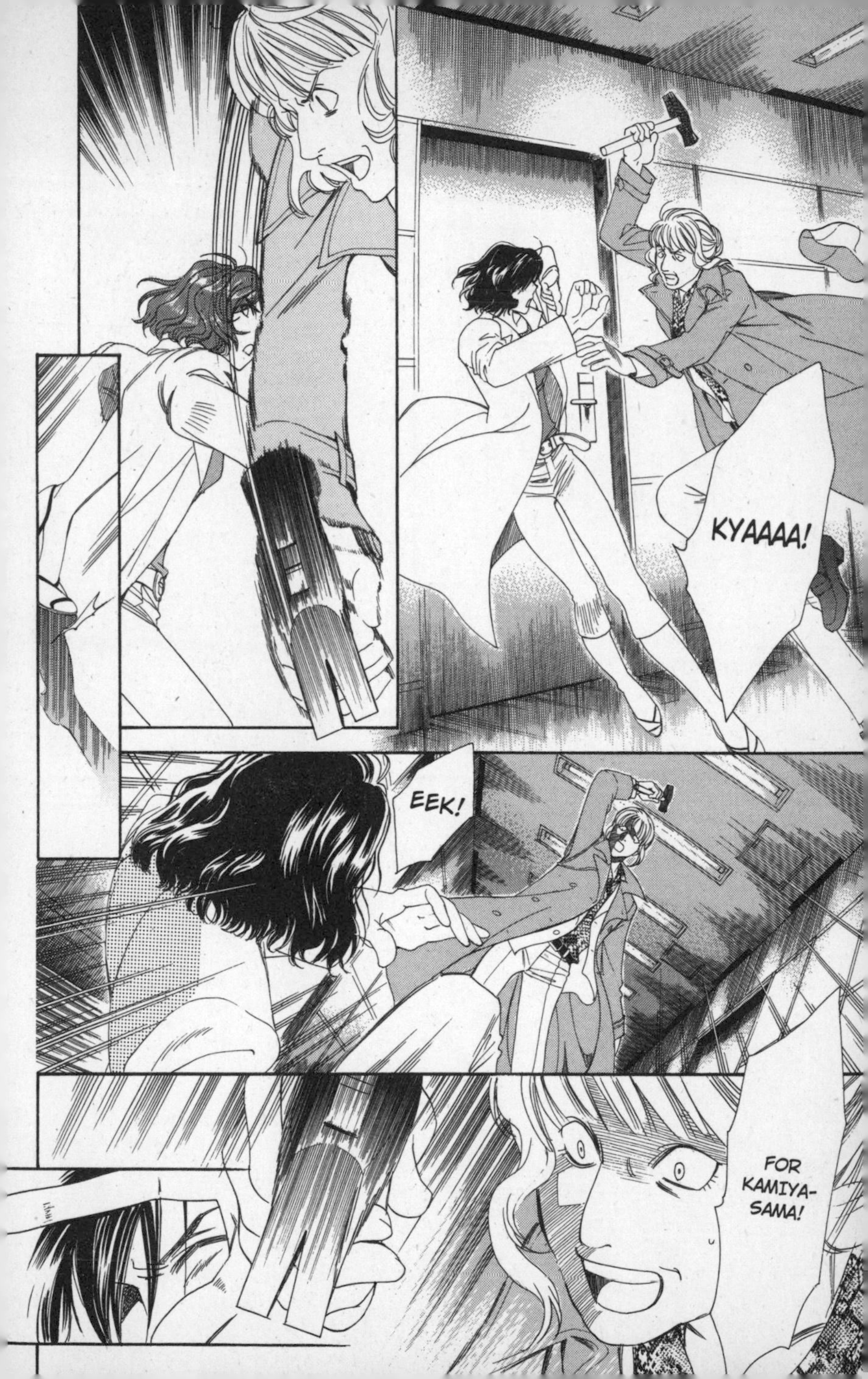
KYAAAA!
EEK!
FOR KAMIYA-SAMA!

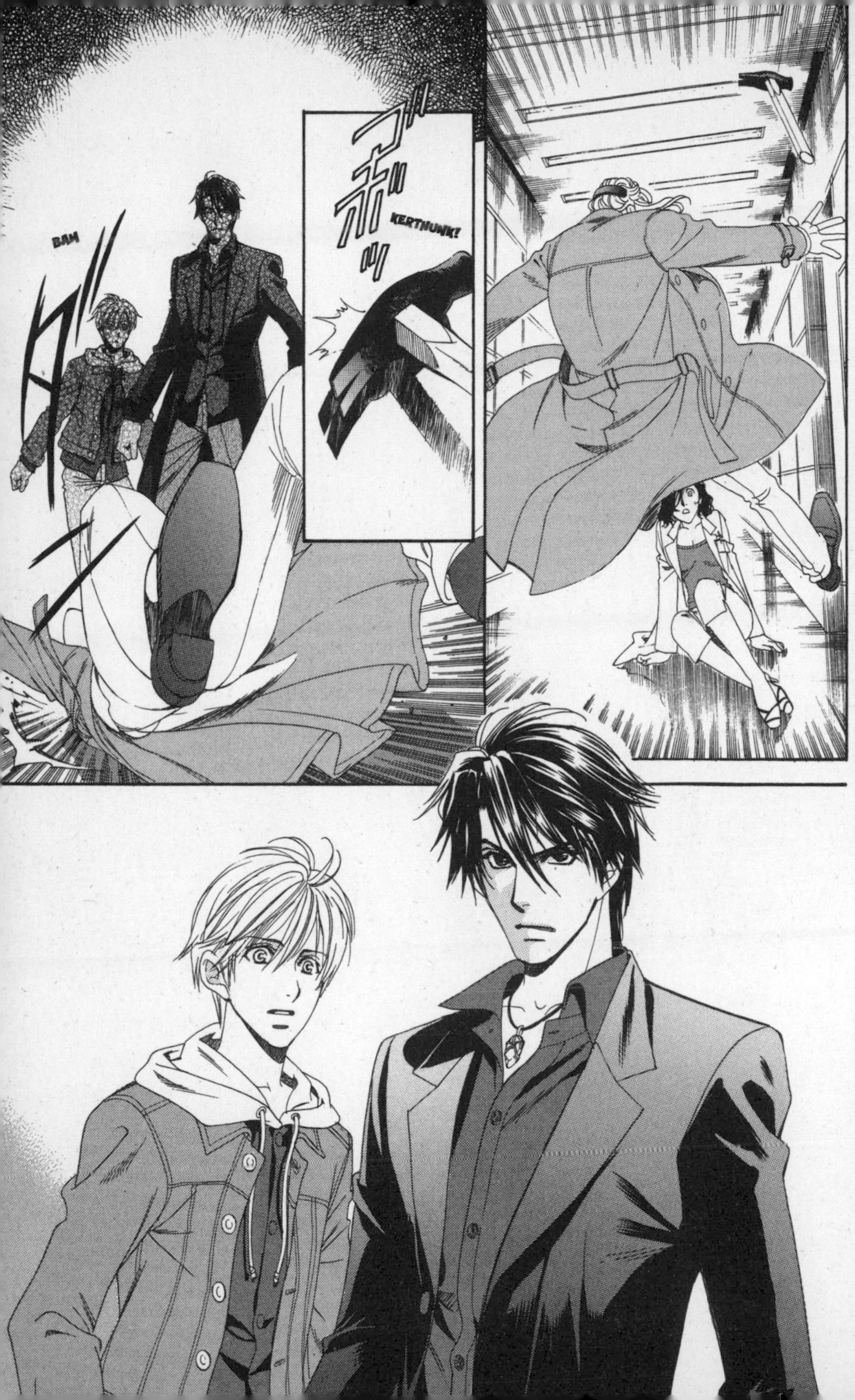

ゴボッ
KERTHUNK!
ガッ
BAM

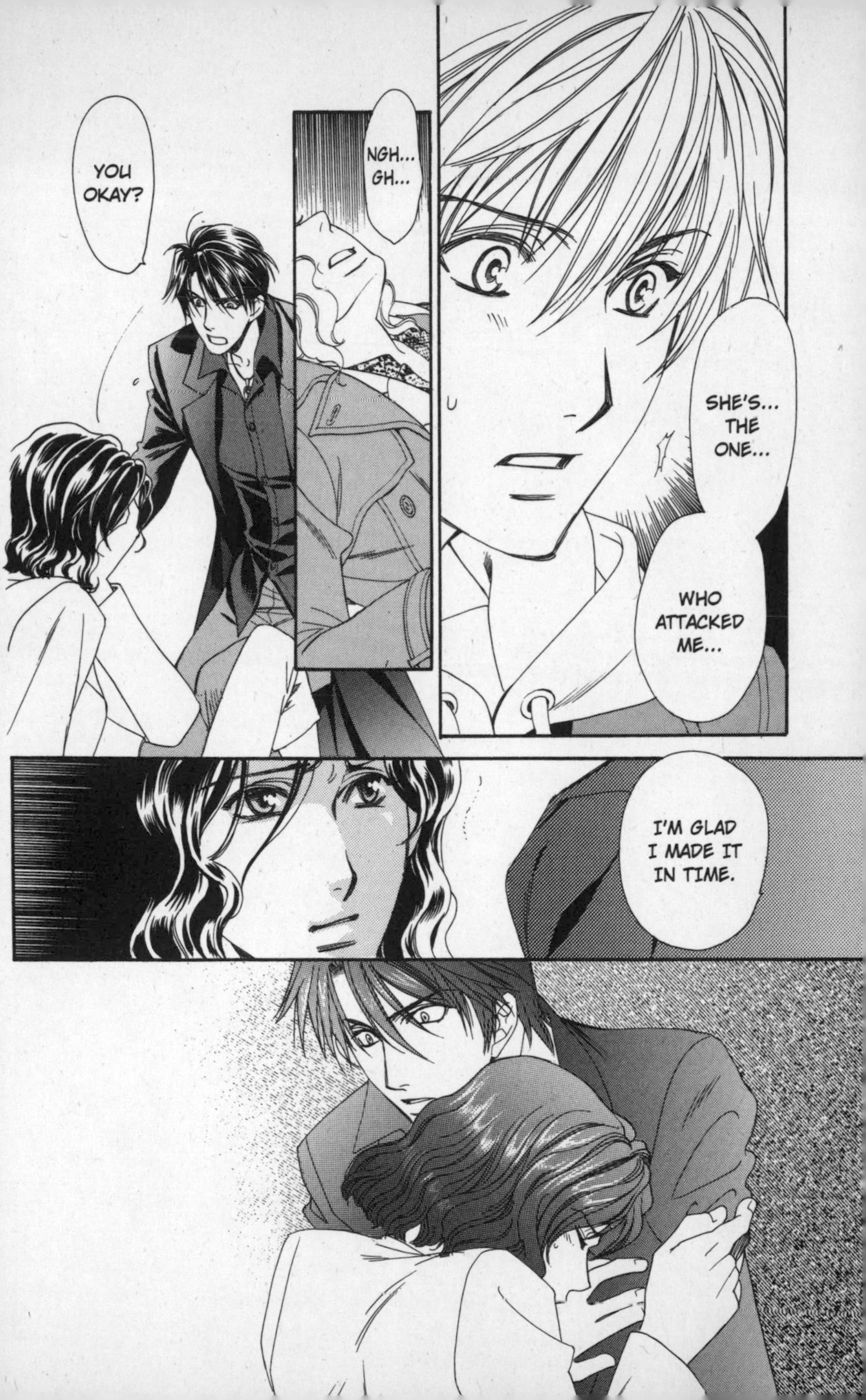
SHE'S... THE ONE...
WHO ATTACKED ME...
NGH... GH...
YOU OKAY?
I'M GLAD I MADE IT IN TIME.

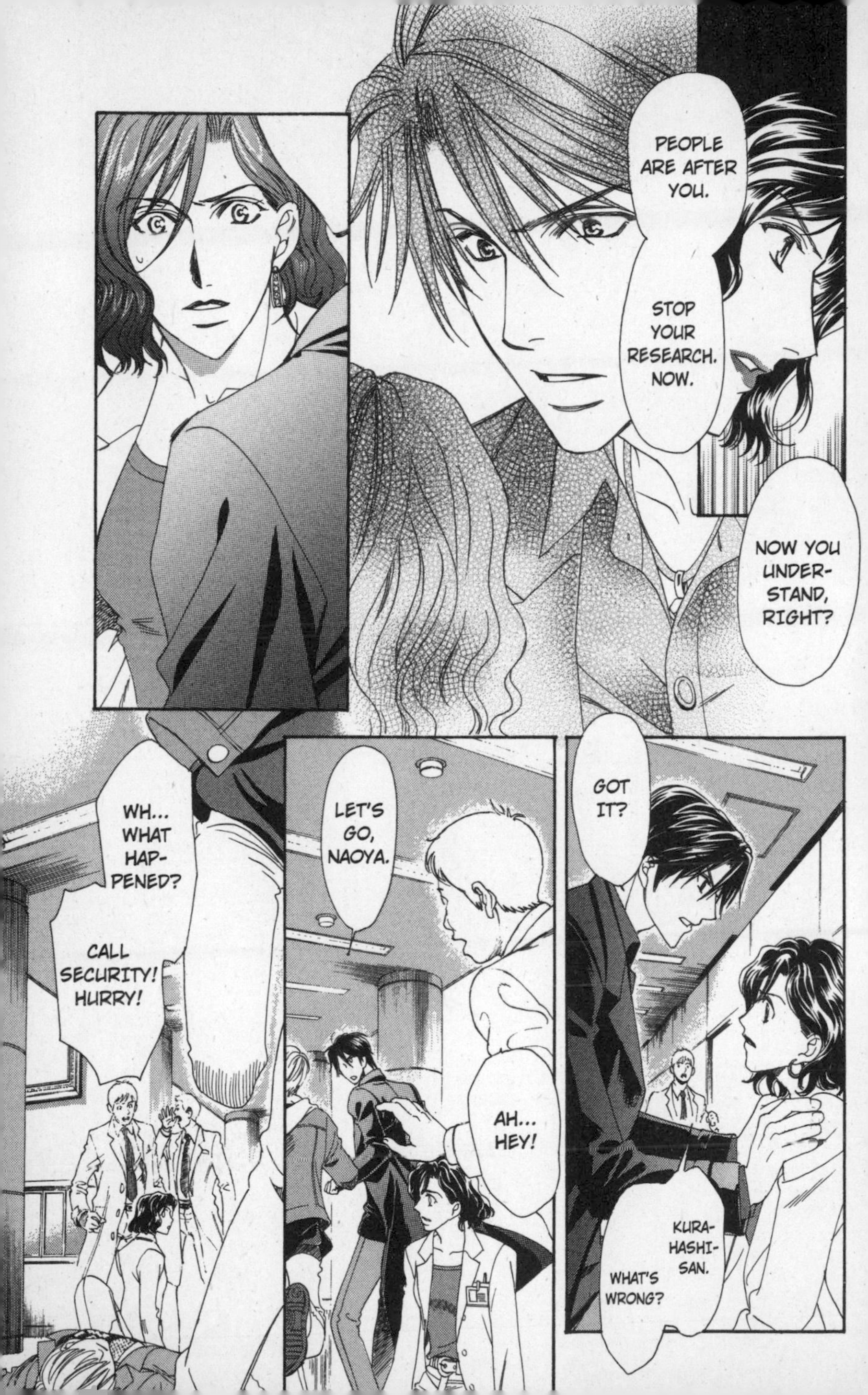
PEOPLE ARE AFTER YOU.
STOP YOUR RESEARCH. NOW.
NOW YOU UNDER-STAND, RIGHT?
GOT IT?
KURA-HASHI-SAN.
WHAT'S WRONG?
LET'S GO, NAOYA.
AH... HEY!
WH... WHAT HAP-PENED?
CALL SECURITY! HURRY!

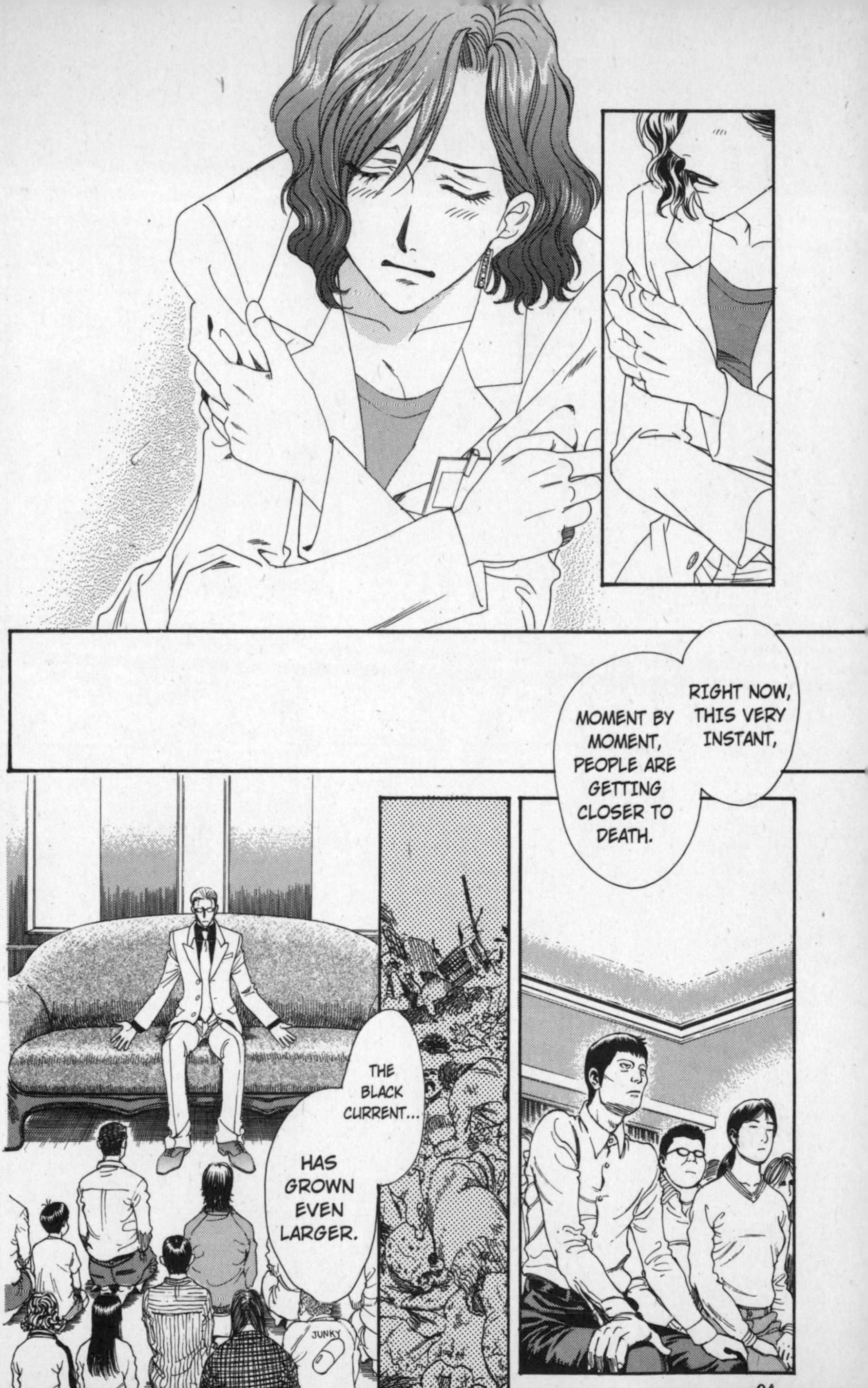
RIGHT NOW, THIS VERY INSTANT,
MOMENT BY MOMENT, PEOPLE ARE GETTING CLOSER TO DEATH.
THE BLACK CURRENT...
HAS GROWN EVEN LARGER.
JUNKY

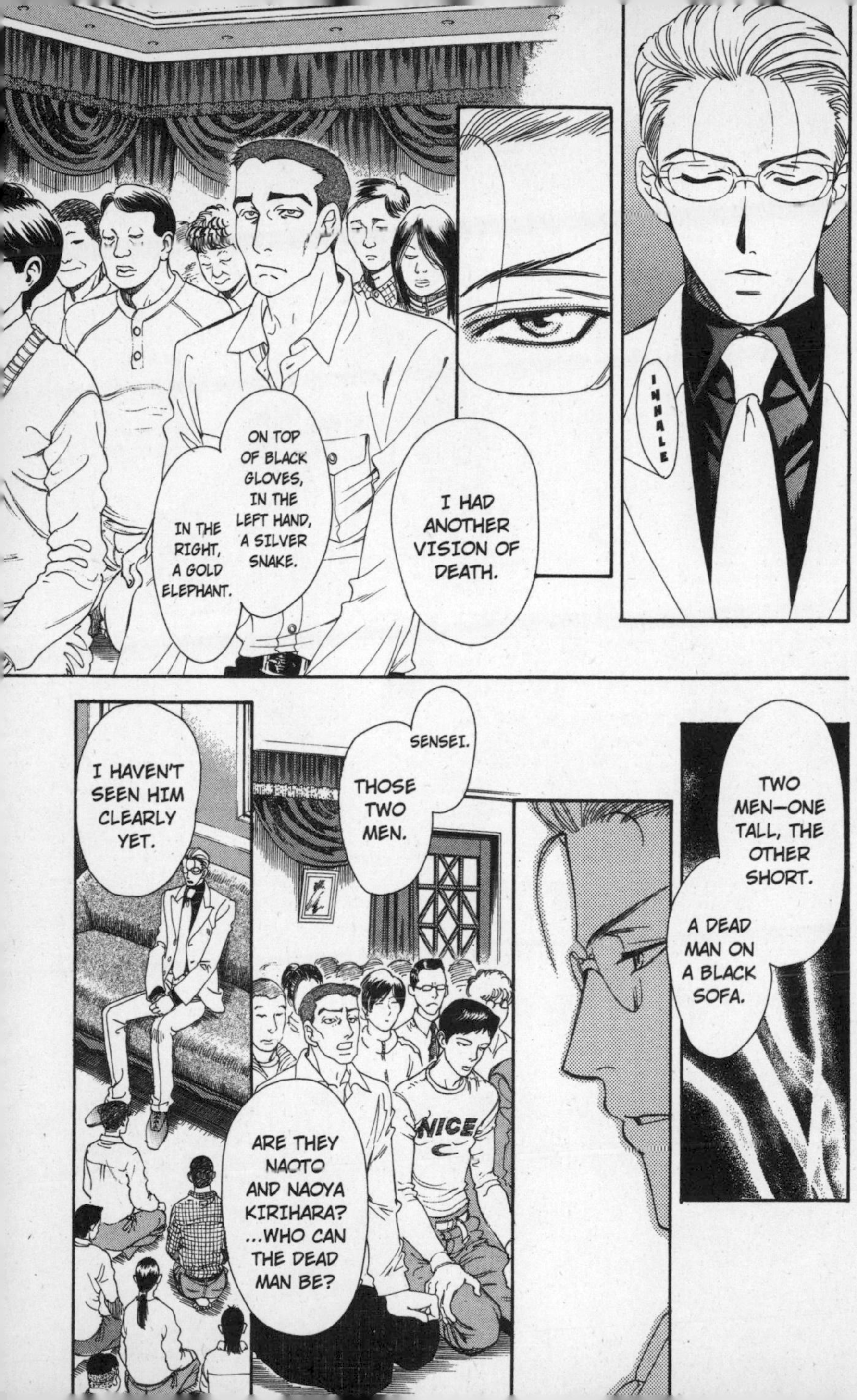
INHALE
I HAD ANOTHER VISION OF DEATH.
ON TOP OF BLACK GLOVES, IN THE LEFT HAND, A SILVER SNAKE.
IN THE RIGHT, A GOLD ELEPHANT.
TWO MEN—ONE TALL, THE OTHER SHORT.
A DEAD MAN ON A BLACK SOFA.
SENSEI.
THOSE TWO MEN.
NICE
ARE THEY NAOTO AND NAOYA KIRIHARA? ...WHO CAN THE DEAD MAN BE?
I HAVEN'T SEEN HIM CLEARLY YET.

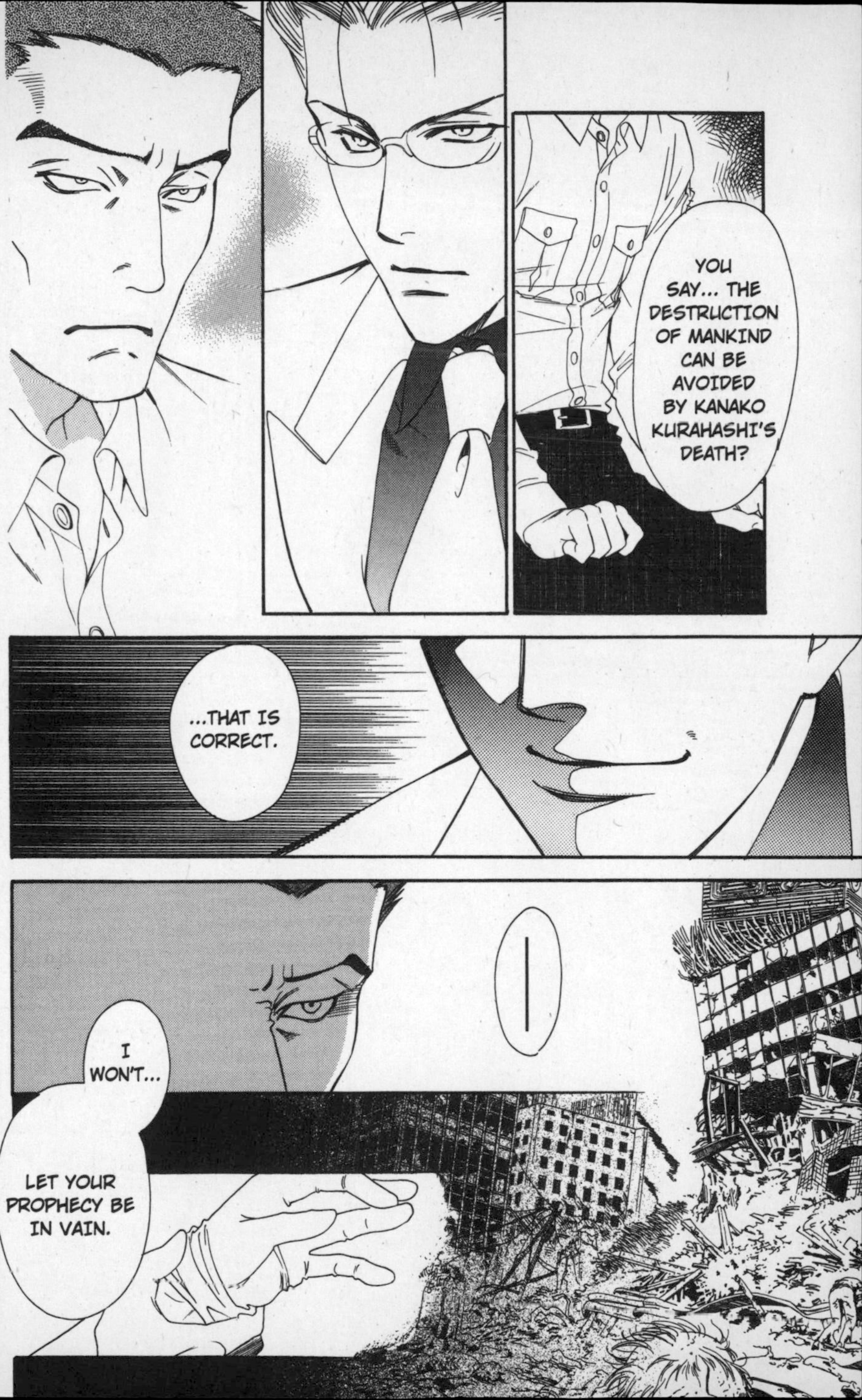
YOU SAY... THE DESTRUCTION OF MANKIND CAN BE AVOIDED BY KANAKO KURAHASHI'S DEATH?
...THAT IS CORRECT.
—
I WON'T...
LET YOUR PROPHECY BE IN VAIN.

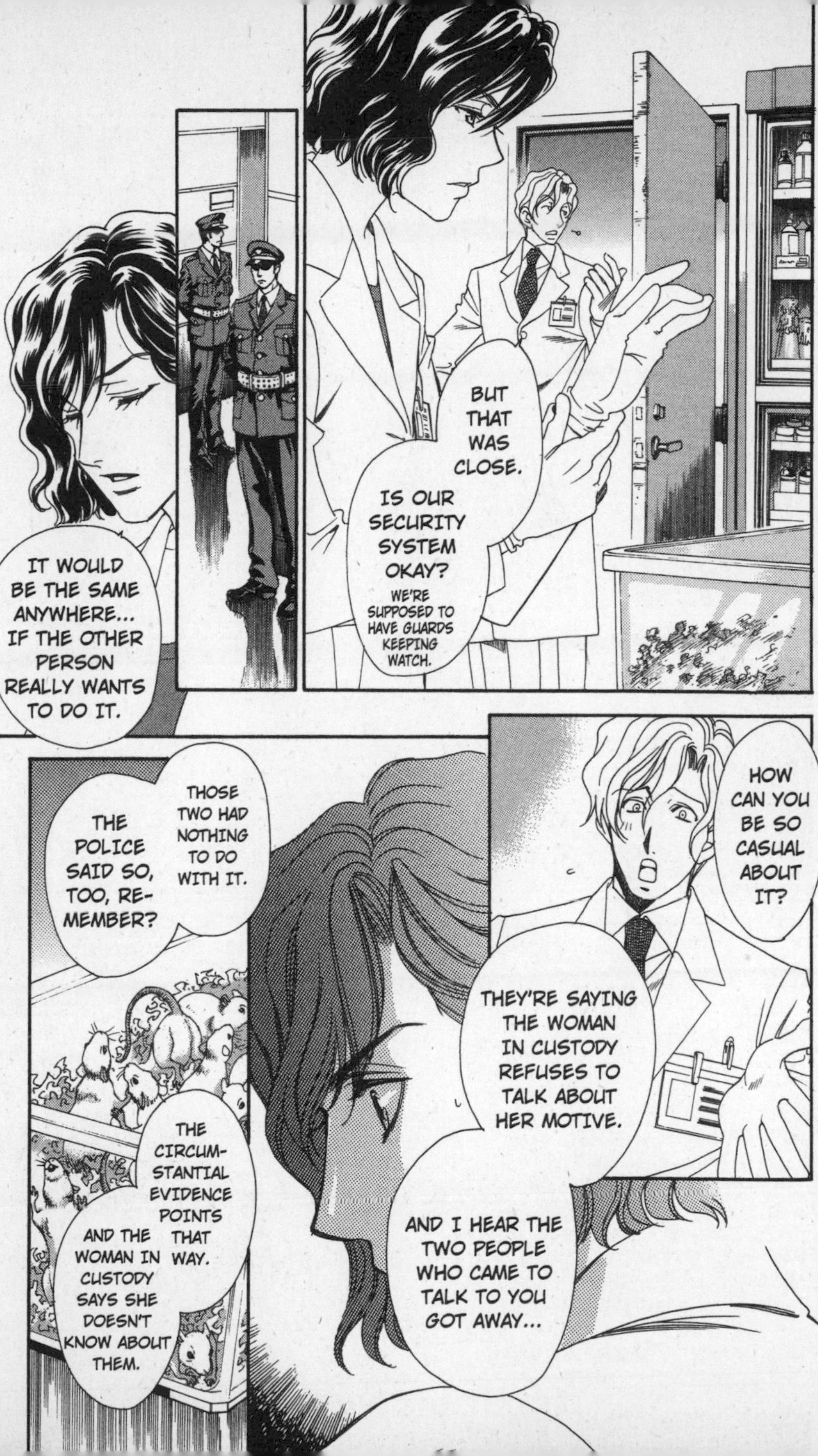
BUT THAT WAS CLOSE.
IS OUR SECURITY SYSTEM OKAY?
WE'RE SUPPOSED TO HAVE GUARDS KEEPING WATCH.
IT WOULD BE THE SAME ANYWHERE... IF THE OTHER PERSON REALLY WANTS TO DO IT.
HOW CAN YOU BE SO CASUAL ABOUT IT?
THEY'RE SAYING THE WOMAN IN CUSTODY REFUSES TO TALK ABOUT HER MOTIVE.
AND I HEAR THE TWO PEOPLE WHO CAME TO TALK TO YOU GOT AWAY...
THOSE TWO HAD NOTHING TO DO WITH IT.
THE POLICE SAID SO, TOO, RE-MEMBER?
THE CIRCUM-STANTIAL EVIDENCE POINTS THAT WAY.
AND THE WOMAN IN CUSTODY SAYS SHE DOESN'T KNOW ABOUT THEM.

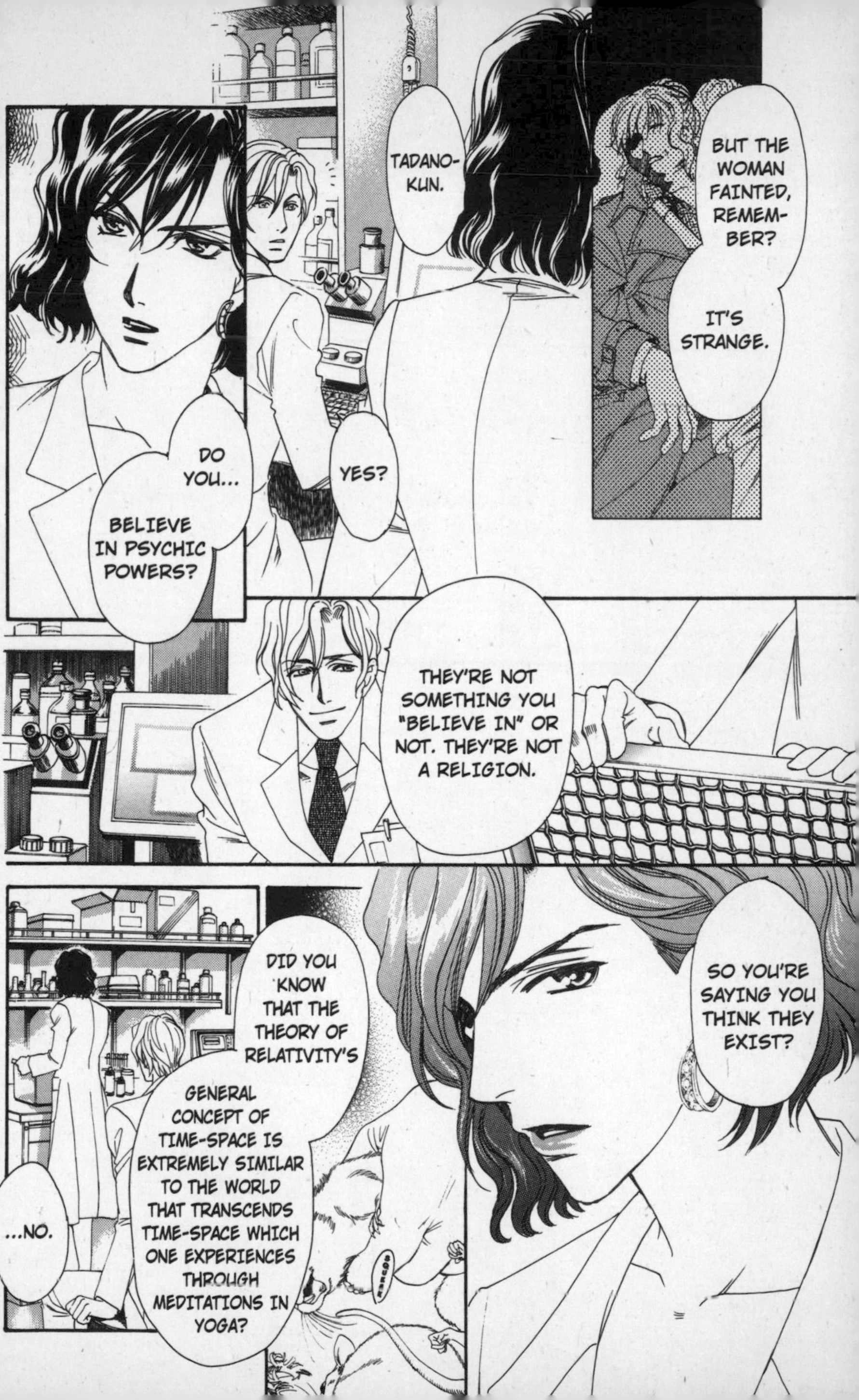
BUT THE WOMAN FAINTED, REMEMBER?
IT'S STRANGE.
TADANO-KUN.
YES?
DO YOU...
BELIEVE IN PSYCHIC POWERS?
THEY'RE NOT SOMETHING YOU "BELIEVE IN" OR NOT. THEY'RE NOT A RELIGION.
SO YOU'RE SAYING YOU THINK THEY EXIST?
DID YOU KNOW THAT THE THEORY OF RELATIVITY'S
GENERAL CONCEPT OF TIME-SPACE IS EXTREMELY SIMILAR TO THE WORLD THAT TRANSCENDS TIME-SPACE WHICH ONE EXPERIENCES THROUGH MEDITATIONS IN YOGA?
...NO.

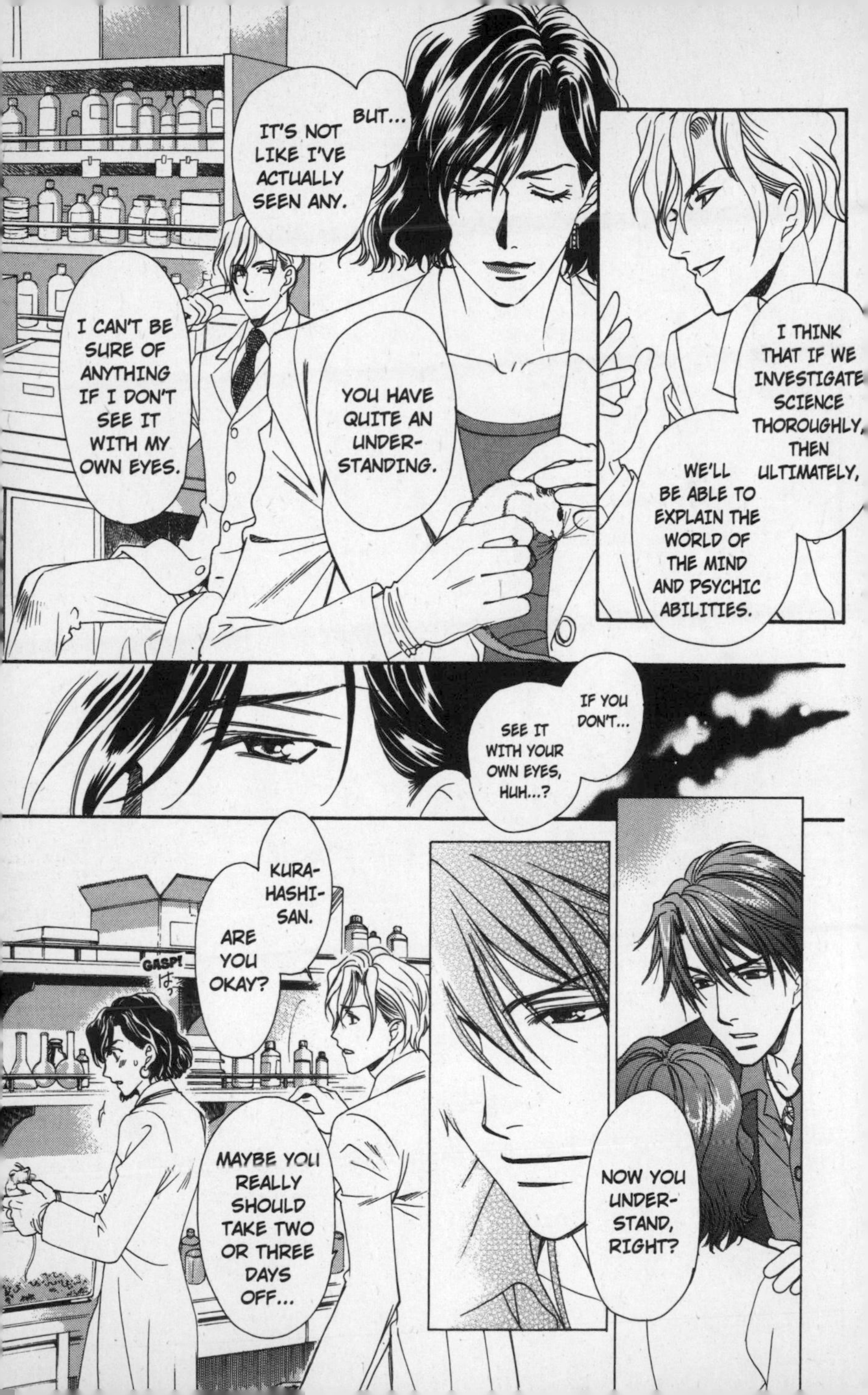
I THINK THAT IF WE INVESTIGATE SCIENCE THOROUGHLY, THEN ULTIMATELY,
WE'LL BE ABLE TO EXPLAIN THE WORLD OF THE MIND AND PSYCHIC ABILITIES.
YOU HAVE QUITE AN UNDER-STANDING.
BUT... IT'S NOT LIKE I'VE ACTUALLY SEEN ANY.
I CAN'T BE SURE OF ANYTHING IF I DON'T SEE IT WITH MY OWN EYES.
IF YOU DON'T...
SEE IT WITH YOUR OWN EYES, HUH...?
NOW YOU UNDER-STAND, RIGHT?
GASP! はっ
KURA-HASHI-SAN.
ARE YOU OKAY?
MAYBE YOU REALLY SHOULD TAKE TWO OR THREE DAYS OFF...

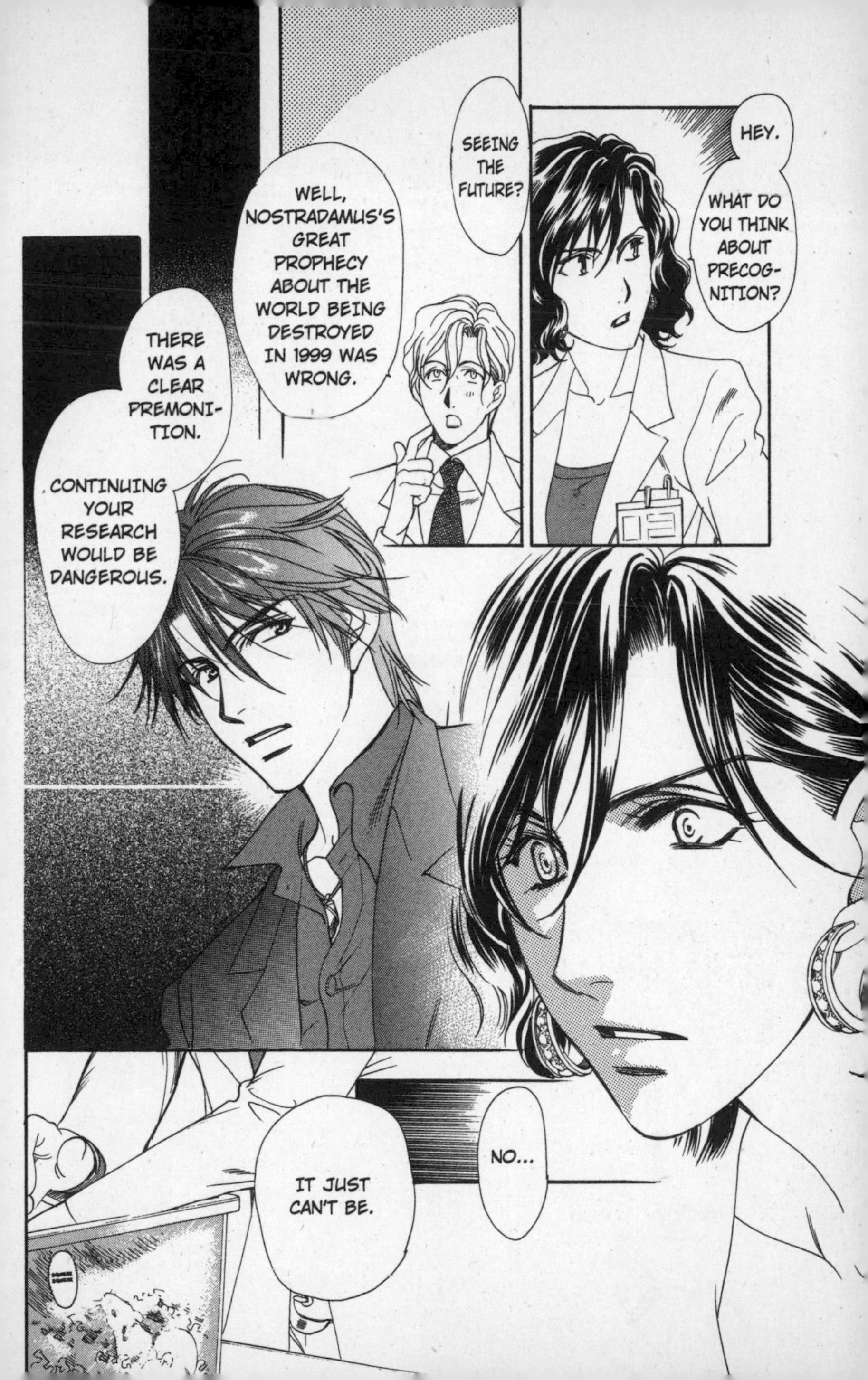
HEY.
WHAT DO YOU THINK ABOUT PRECOG-NITION?
SEEING THE FUTURE?
WELL, NOSTRADAMUS'S GREAT PROPHECY ABOUT THE WORLD BEING DESTROYED IN 1999 WAS WRONG.
THERE WAS A CLEAR PREMONI-TION.
CONTINUING YOUR RESEARCH WOULD BE DANGEROUS.
NO...
IT JUST CAN'T BE.

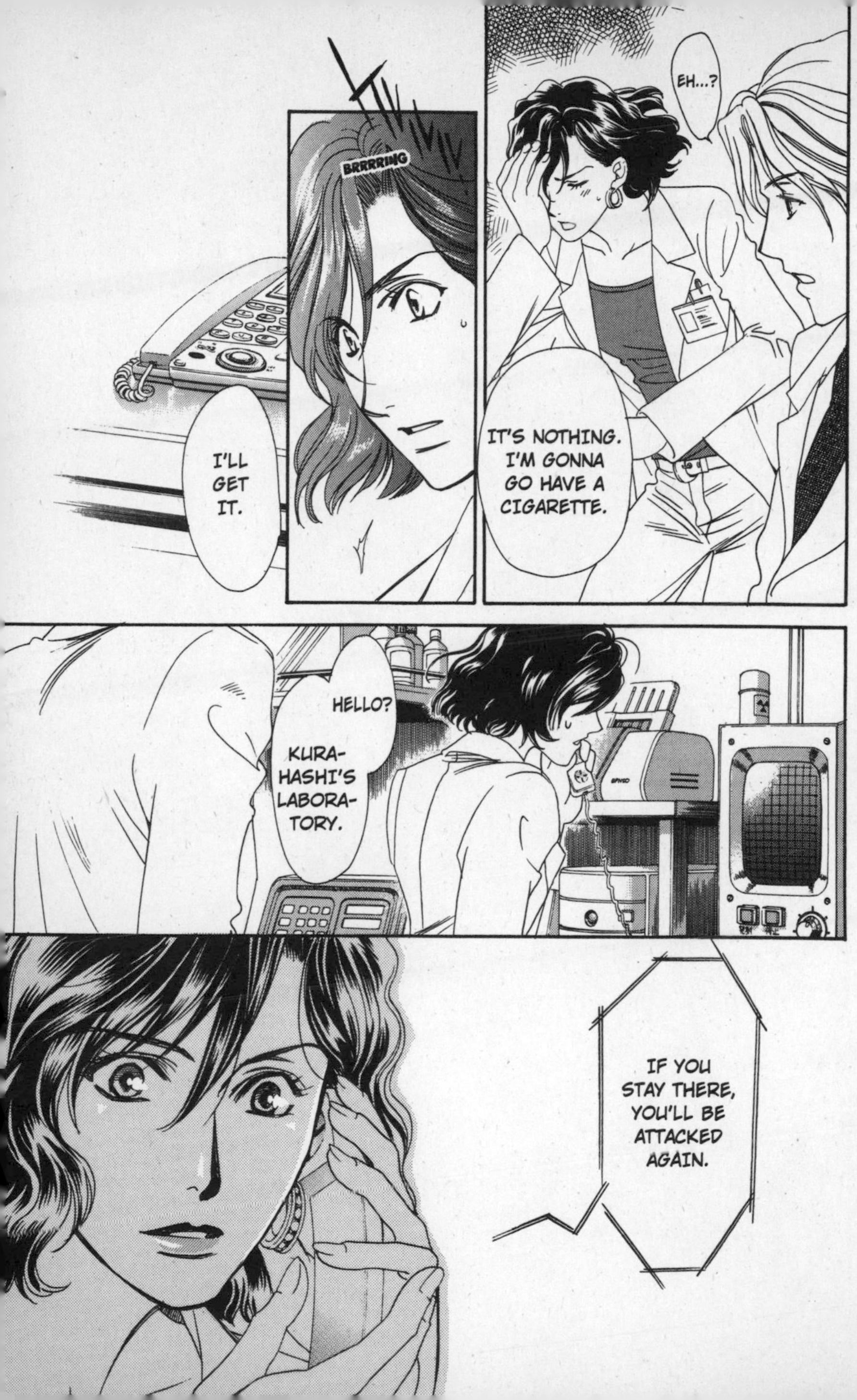
EH...?
IT'S NOTHING. I'M GONNA GO HAVE A CIGARETTE.
BRRRRING
I'LL GET IT.
HELLO?
KURA-HASHI'S LABORA-TORY.
IF YOU STAY THERE, YOU'LL BE ATTACKED AGAIN.

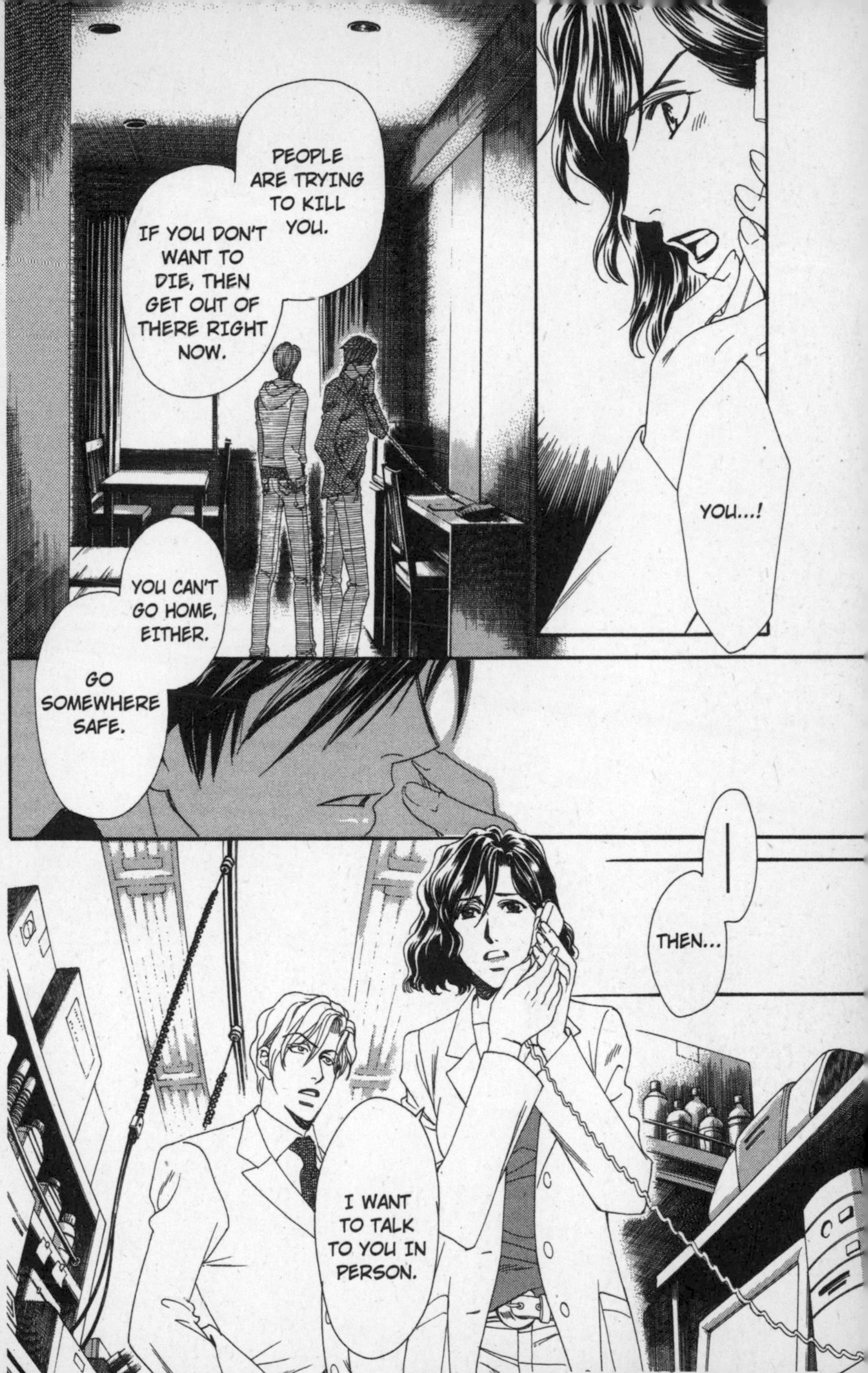
YOU...!
PEOPLE ARE TRYING TO KILL YOU.
IF YOU DON'T WANT TO DIE, THEN GET OUT OF THERE RIGHT NOW.
YOU CAN'T GO HOME, EITHER.
GO SOMEWHERE SAFE.
—
THEN...
I WANT TO TALK TO YOU IN PERSON.

Chapter 3: CHANCE ENCOUNTER · END

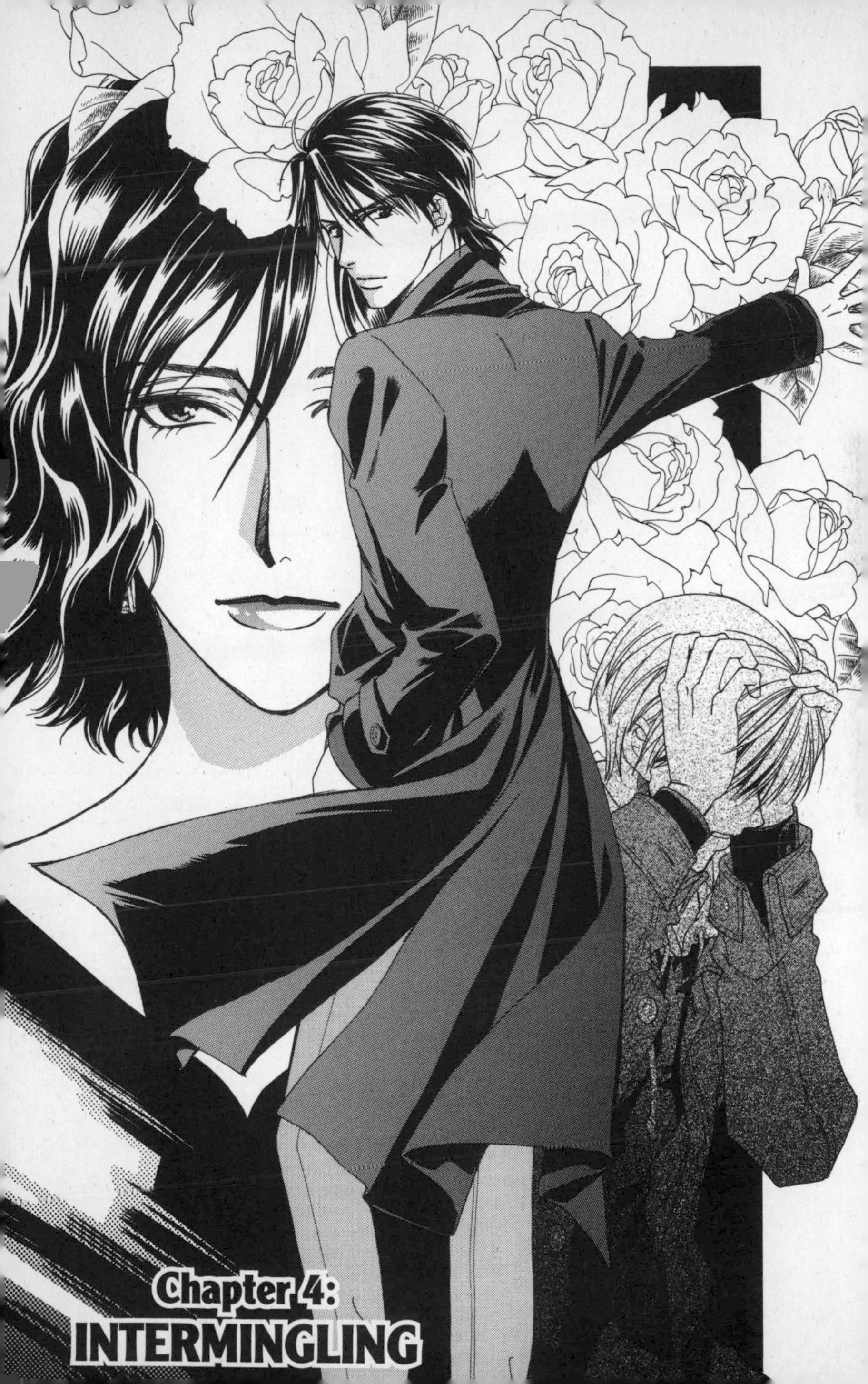
Chapter 4:
INTERMINGLING

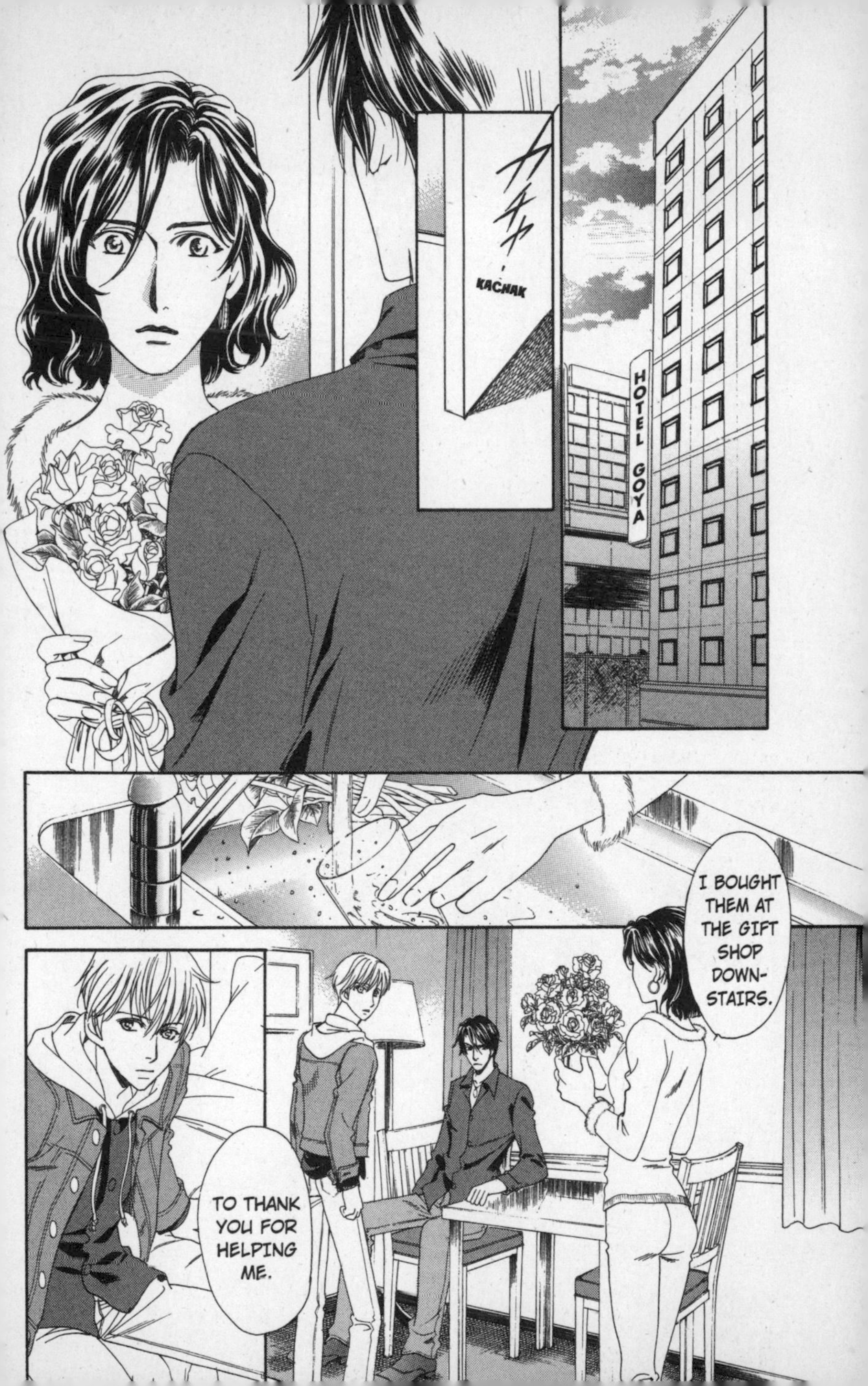
KACHAK
HOTEL GOYA
I BOUGHT THEM AT THE GIFT SHOP DOWN-STAIRS.
TO THANK YOU FOR HELPING ME.

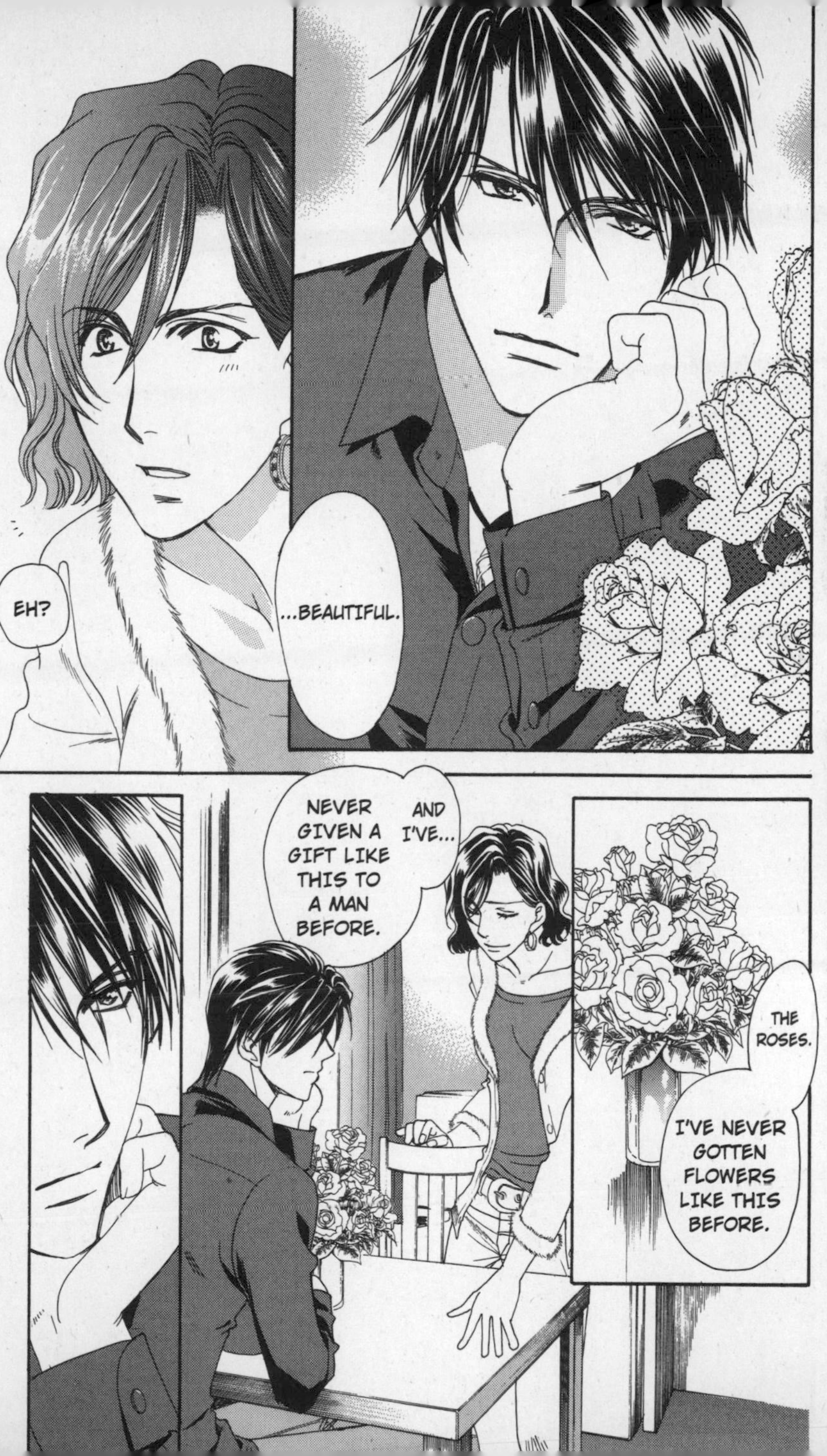
...BEAUTIFUL.
EH?
THE ROSES.
I'VE NEVER GOTTEN FLOWERS LIKE THIS BEFORE.
AND I'VE...
NEVER GIVEN A GIFT LIKE THIS TO A MAN BEFORE.

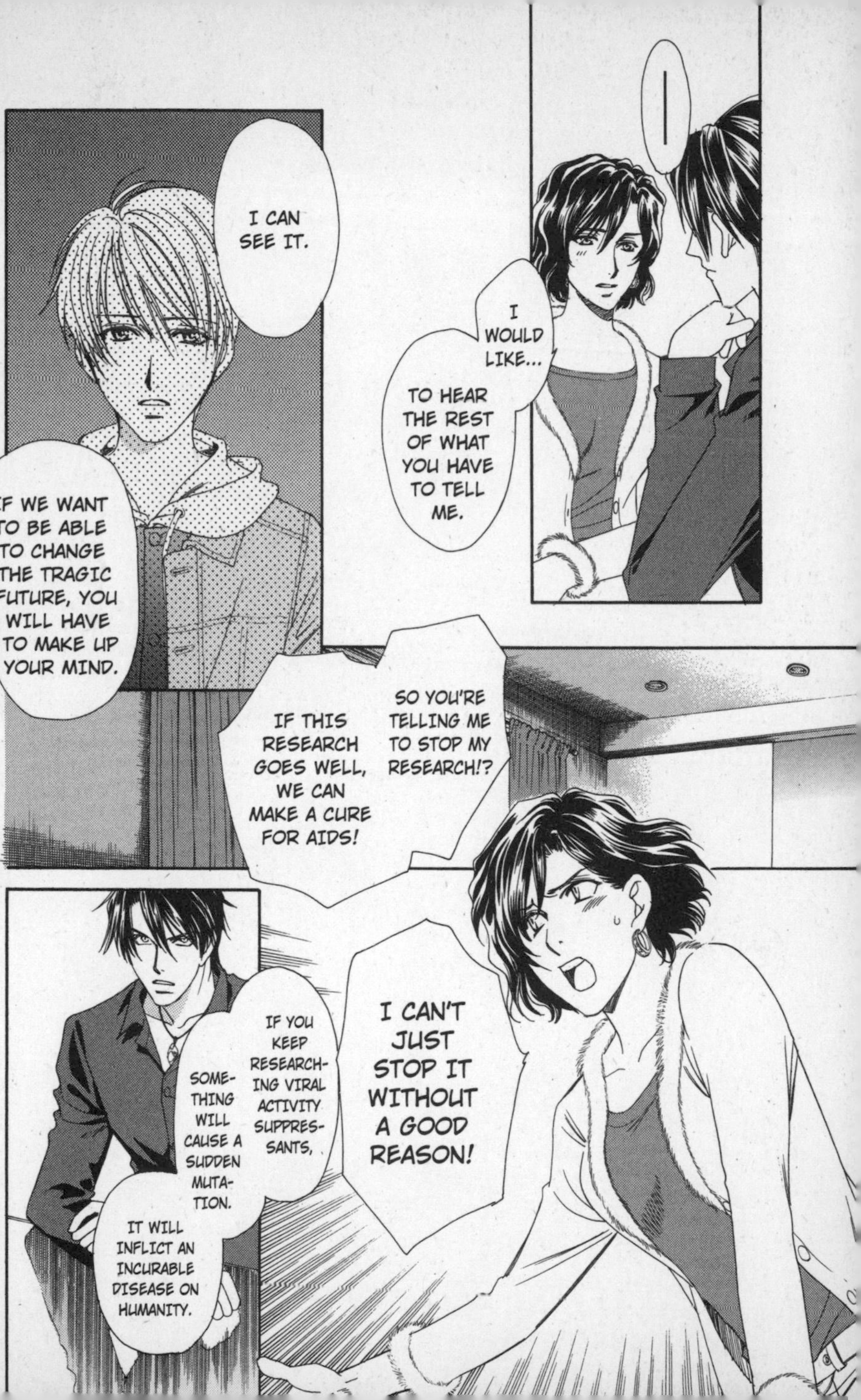
—
I WOULD LIKE...
TO HEAR THE REST OF WHAT YOU HAVE TO TELL ME.
I CAN SEE IT.
IF WE WANT TO BE ABLE TO CHANGE THE TRAGIC FUTURE, YOU WILL HAVE TO MAKE UP YOUR MIND.
SO YOU'RE TELLING ME TO STOP MY RESEARCH!?
IF THIS RESEARCH GOES WELL, WE CAN MAKE A CURE FOR AIDS!
I CAN'T JUST STOP IT WITHOUT A GOOD REASON!
IF YOU KEEP RESEARCHING VIRAL ACTIVITY SUPPRESSANTS,
SOMETHING WILL CAUSE A SUDDEN MUTATION.
IT WILL INFLICT AN INCURABLE DISEASE ON HUMANITY.

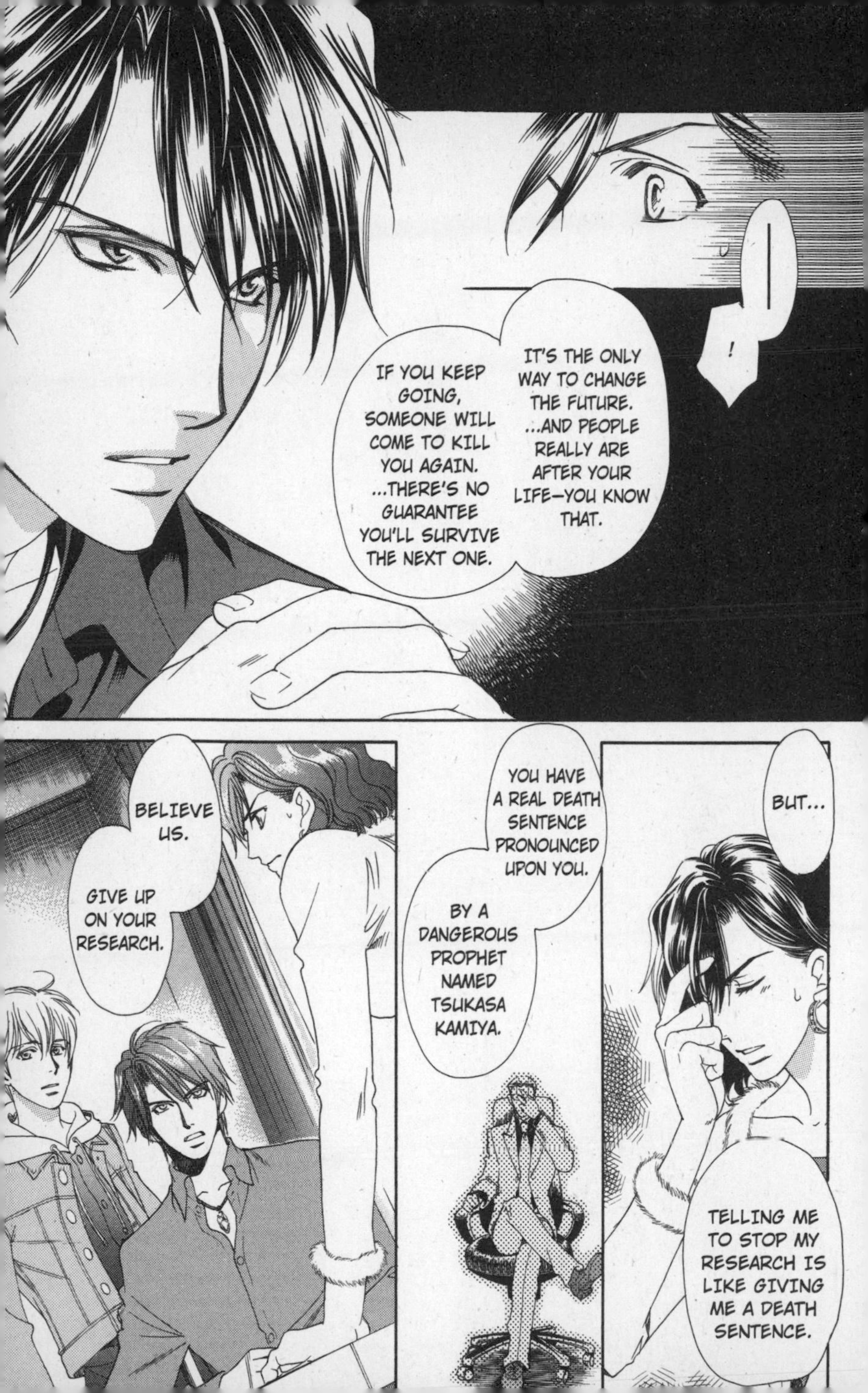
!
IT'S THE ONLY WAY TO CHANGE THE FUTURE. ...AND PEOPLE REALLY ARE AFTER YOUR LIFE—YOU KNOW THAT.
IF YOU KEEP GOING, SOMEONE WILL COME TO KILL YOU AGAIN. ...THERE'S NO GUARANTEE YOU'LL SURVIVE THE NEXT ONE.
BUT...
TELLING ME TO STOP MY RESEARCH IS LIKE GIVING ME A DEATH SENTENCE.
YOU HAVE A REAL DEATH SENTENCE PRONOUNCED UPON YOU.
BY A DANGEROUS PROPHET NAMED TSUKASA KAMIYA.
BELIEVE US.
GIVE UP ON YOUR RESEARCH.

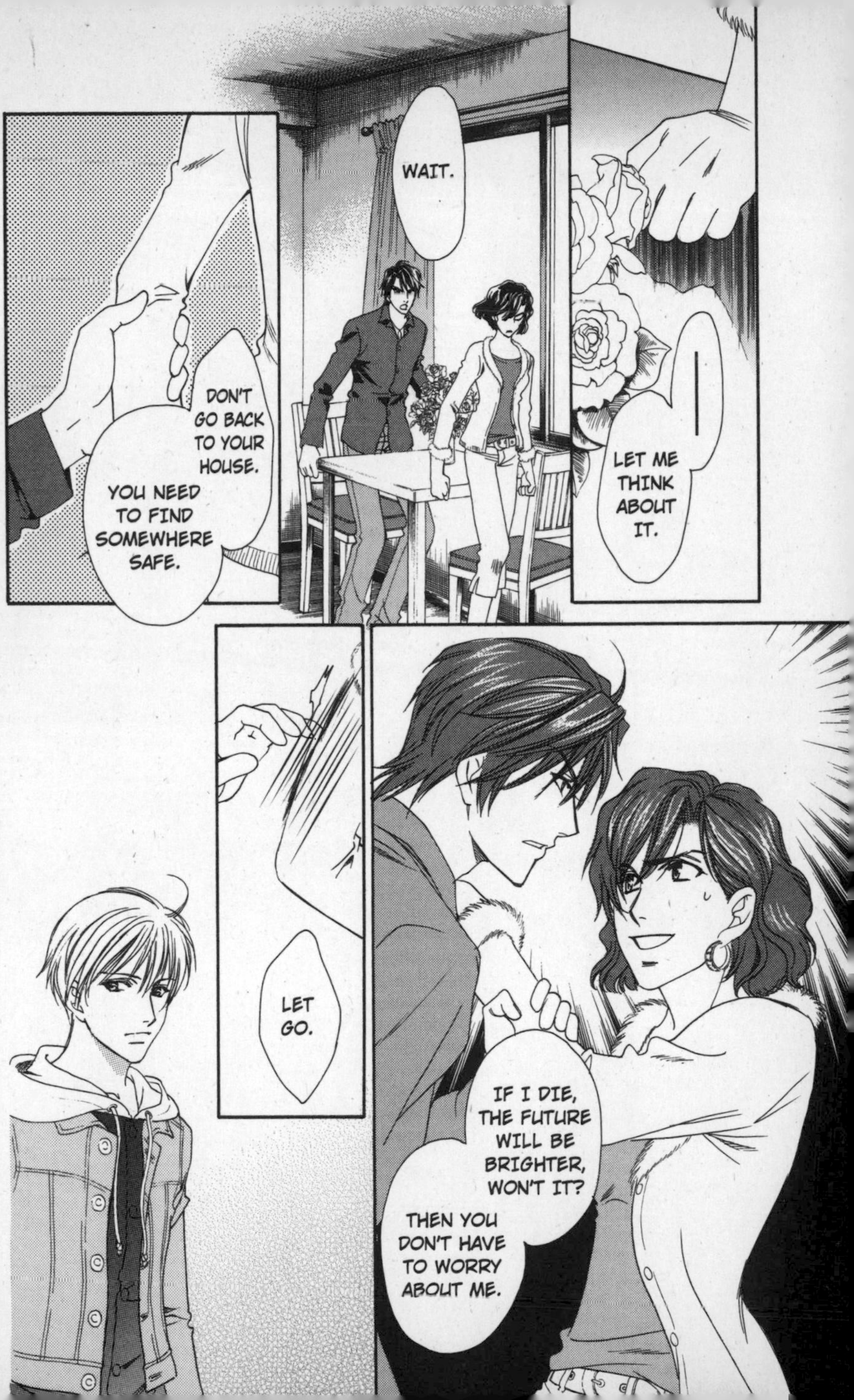
—
LET ME THINK ABOUT IT.
WAIT.
DON'T GO BACK TO YOUR HOUSE.
YOU NEED TO FIND SOMEWHERE SAFE.
IF I DIE, THE FUTURE WILL BE BRIGHTER, WON'T IT?
THEN YOU DON'T HAVE TO WORRY ABOUT ME.
LET GO.

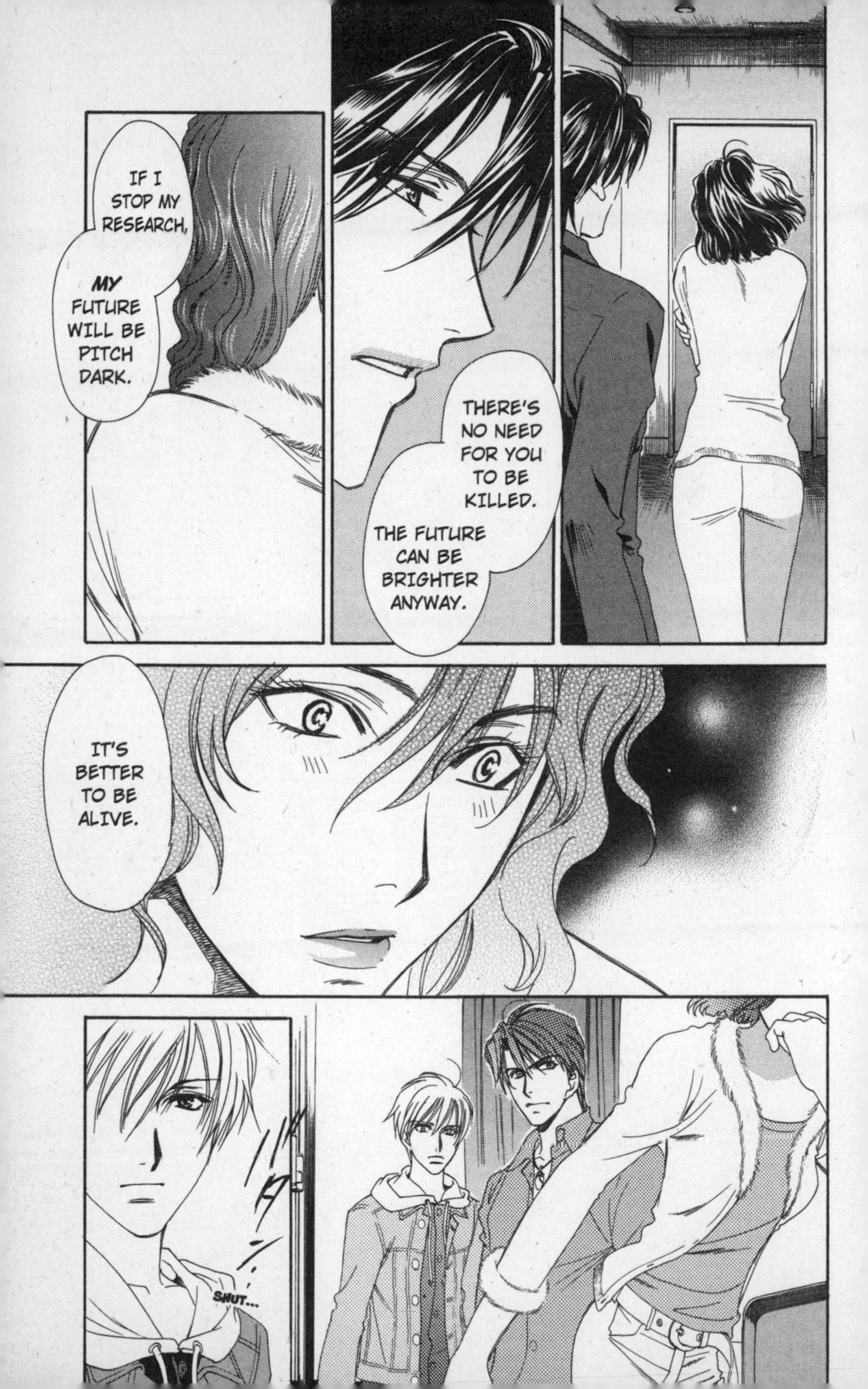

THERE'S NO NEED FOR YOU TO BE KILLED.
THE FUTURE CAN BE BRIGHTER ANYWAY.
IF I STOP MY RESEARCH,
MY FUTURE WILL BE PITCH DARK.
IT'S BETTER TO BE ALIVE.
SHUT...

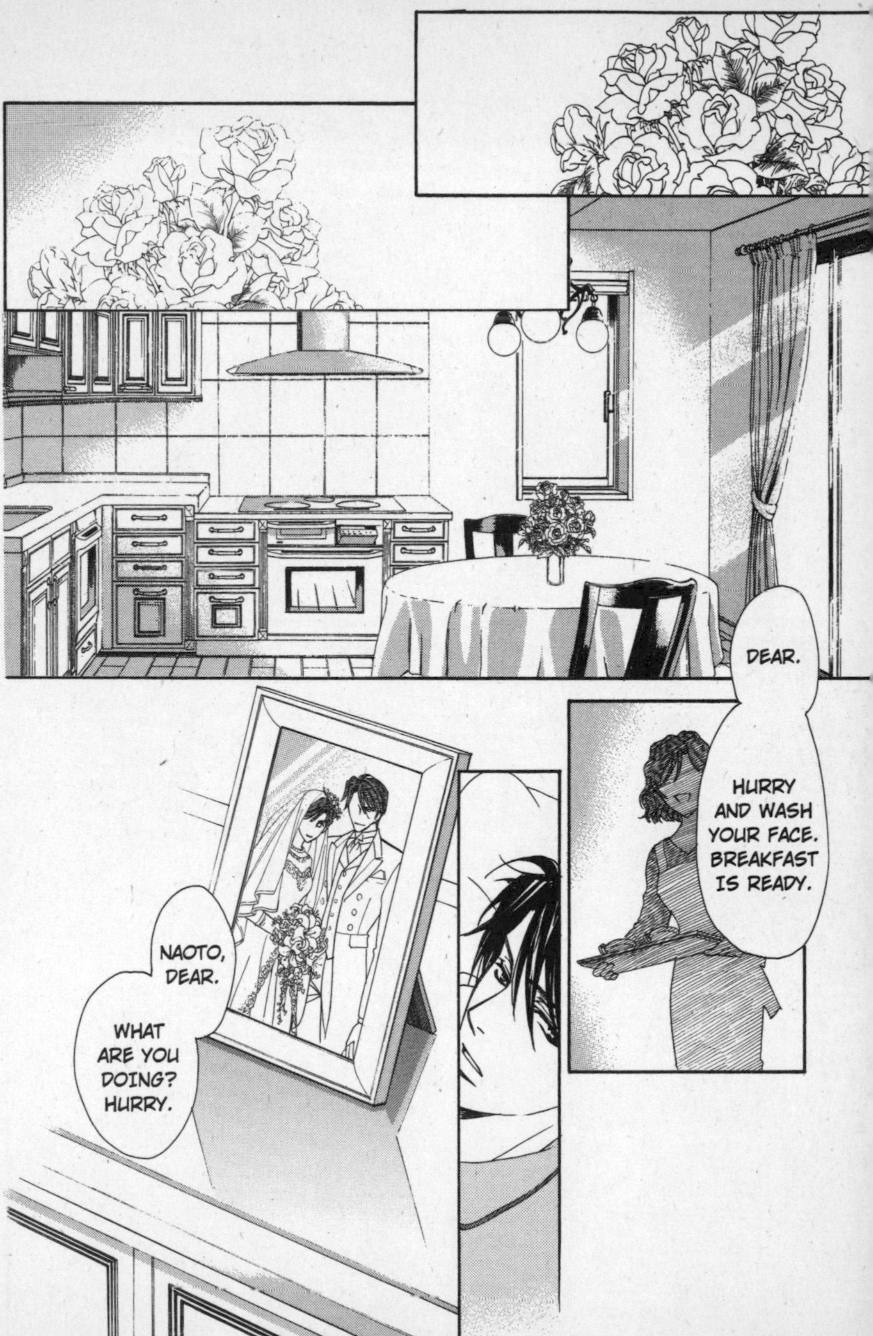
DEAR.
HURRY AND WASH YOUR FACE. BREAKFAST IS READY.
NAOTO, DEAR.
WHAT ARE YOU DOING? HURRY.

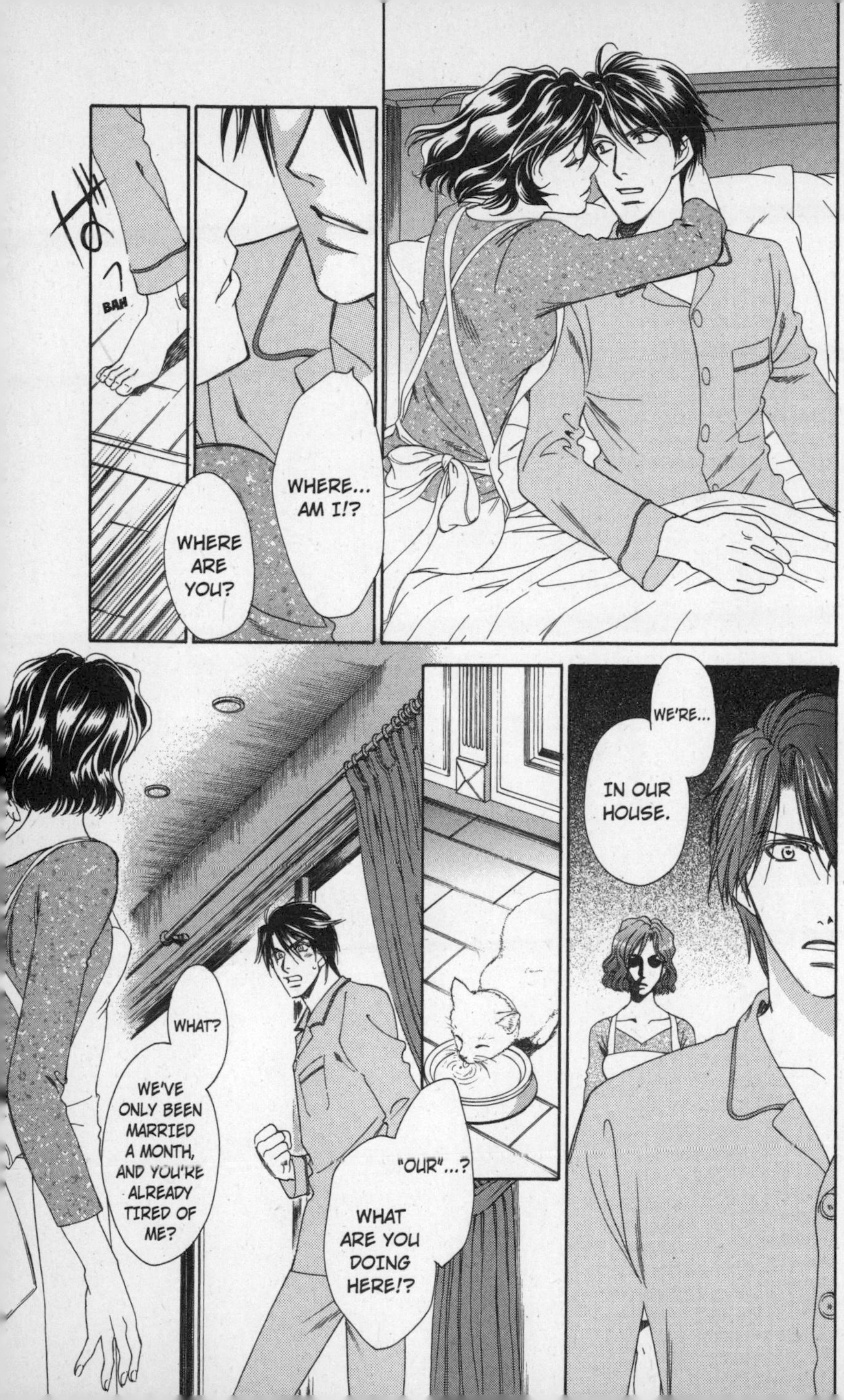
WHERE... AM I!?
WHERE ARE YOU?
BAH
WE'RE...
IN OUR HOUSE.
"OUR"...?
WHAT ARE YOU DOING HERE!?
WHAT?
WE'VE ONLY BEEN MARRIED A MONTH, AND YOU'RE ALREADY TIRED OF ME?

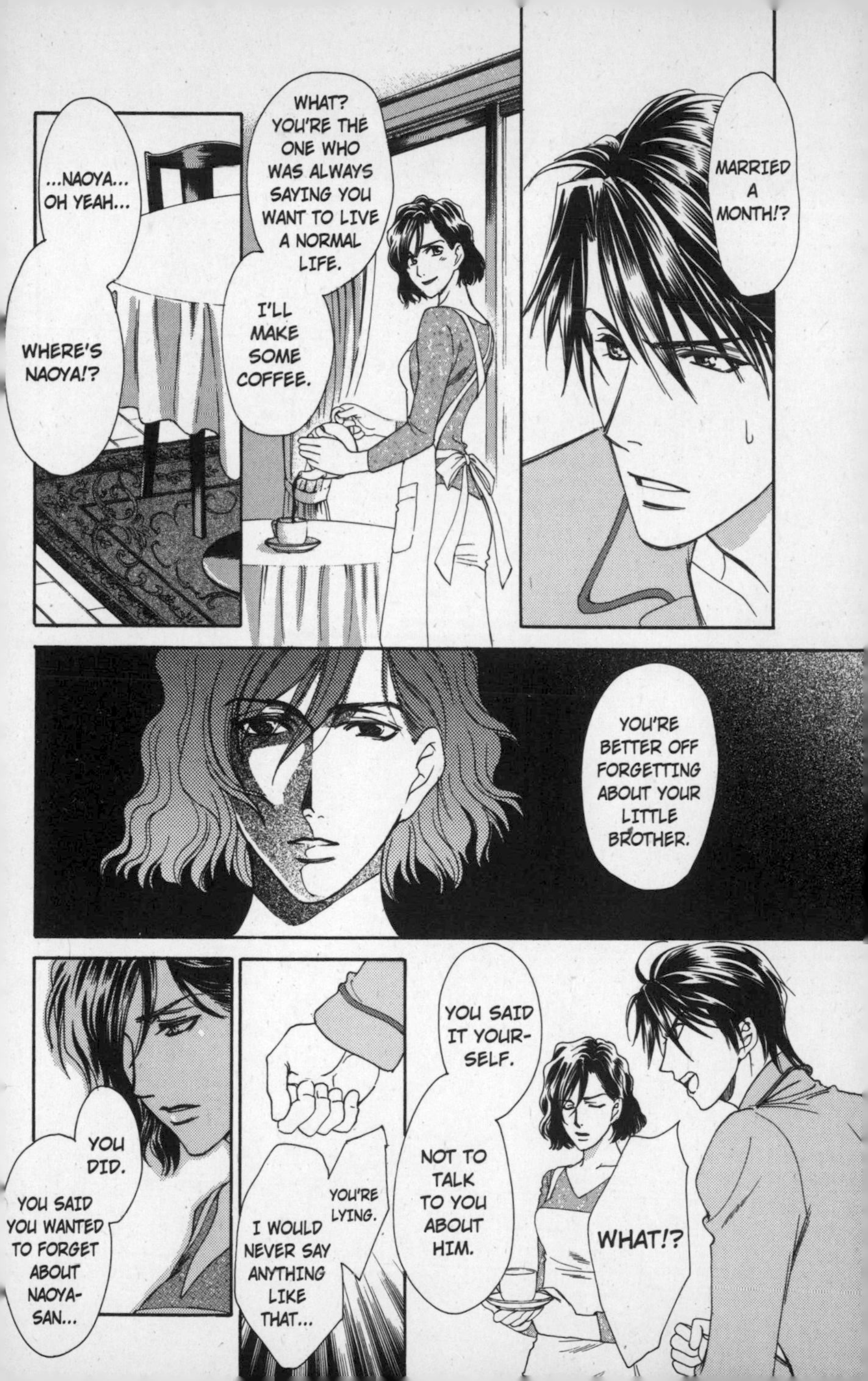
MARRIED A MONTH!?
WHAT? YOU'RE THE ONE WHO WAS ALWAYS SAYING YOU WANT TO LIVE A NORMAL LIFE.
I'LL MAKE SOME COFFEE.
...NAOYA... OH YEAH...
WHERE'S NAOYA!?
YOU'RE BETTER OFF FORGETTING ABOUT YOUR LITTLE BROTHER.
YOU SAID IT YOUR-SELF.
NOT TO TALK TO YOU ABOUT HIM.
WHAT!?
YOU'RE LYING.
I WOULD NEVER SAY ANYTHING LIKE THAT...
YOU DID.
YOU SAID YOU WANTED TO FORGET ABOUT NAOYA-SAN...

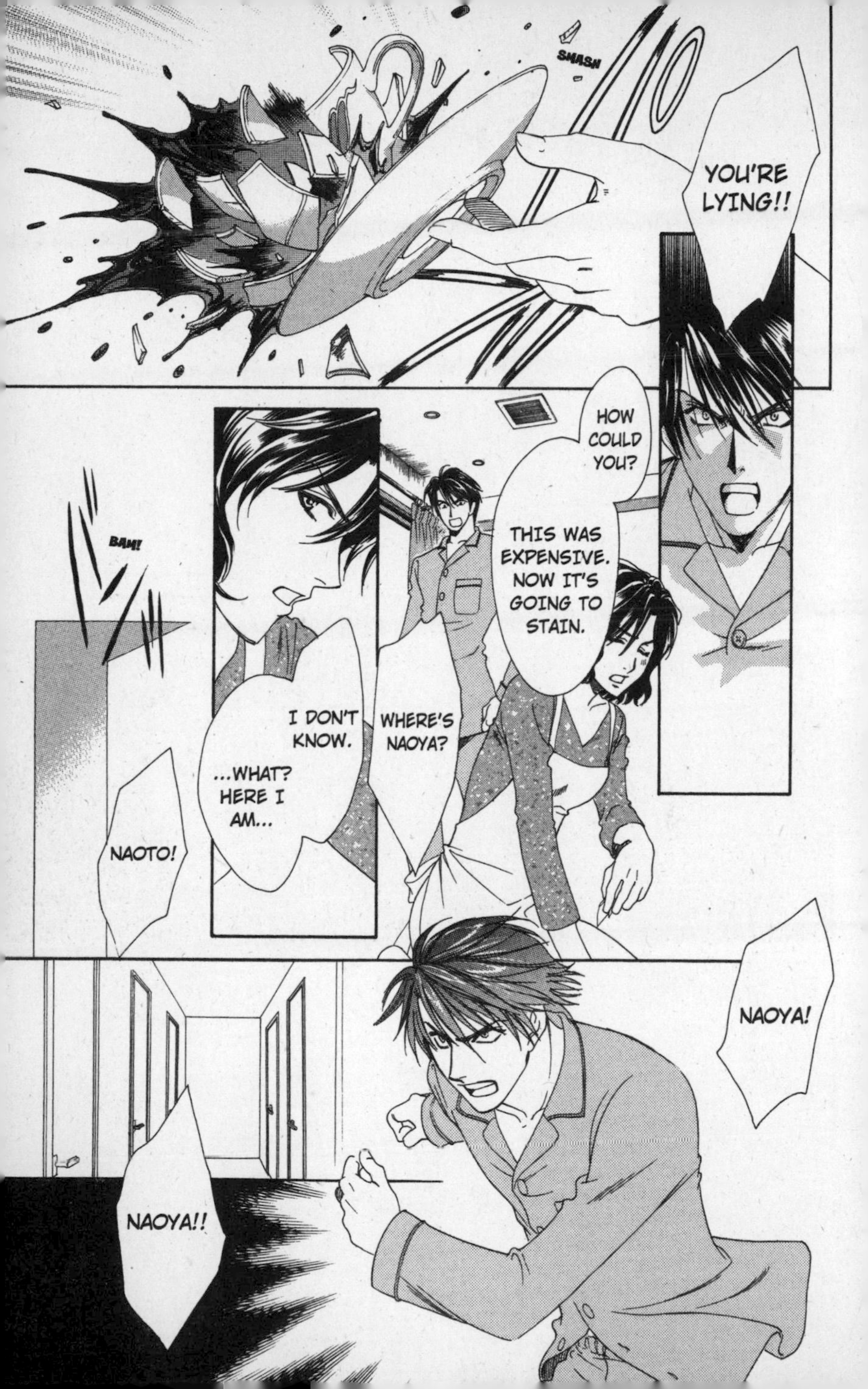
SMASH
YOU'RE LYING!!
HOW COULD YOU?
THIS WAS EXPENSIVE. NOW IT'S GOING TO STAIN.
WHERE'S NAOYA?
I DON'T KNOW.
...WHAT? HERE I AM...
BAM!
NAOTO!
NAOYA!
NAOYA!!

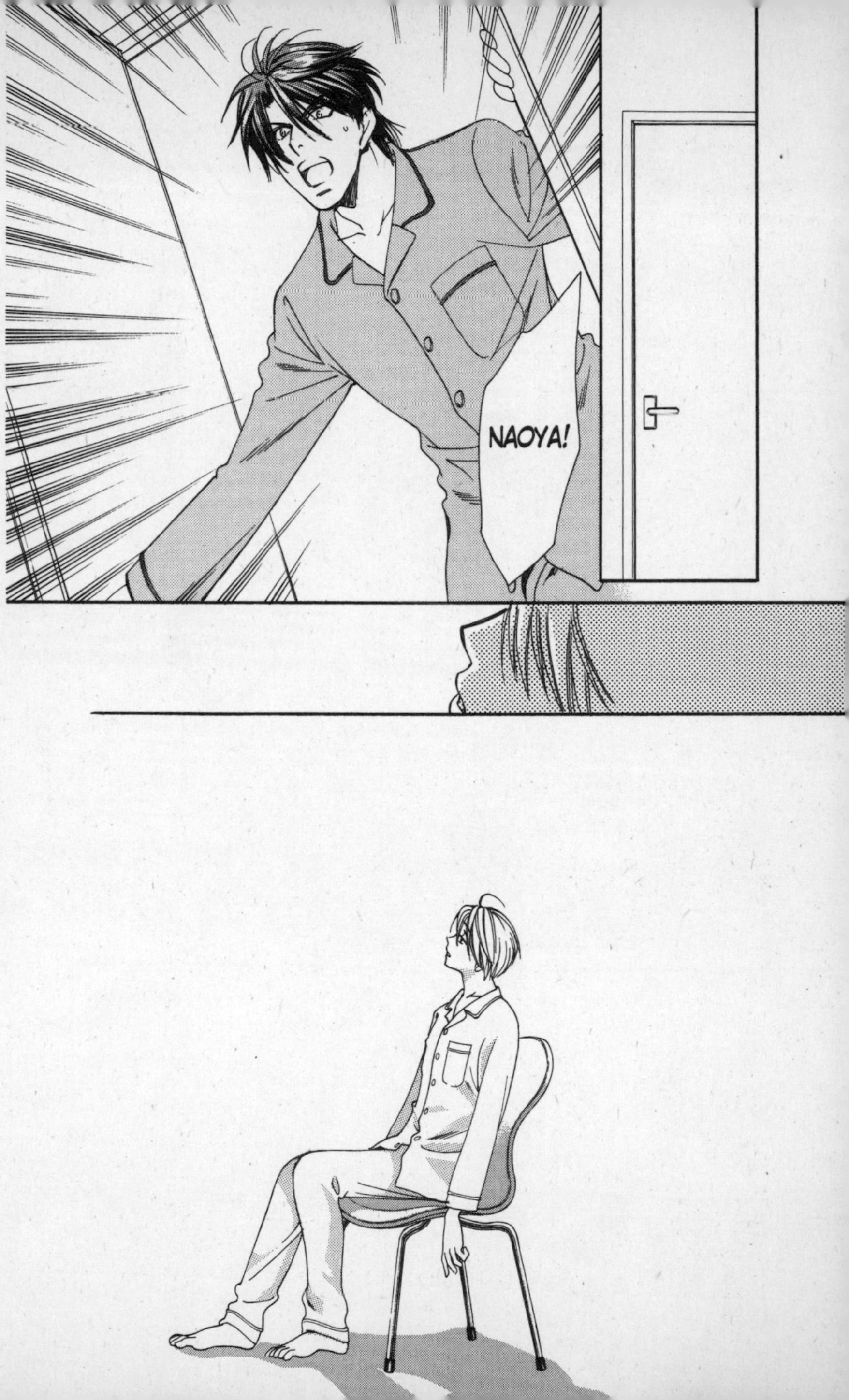
NAOYA!

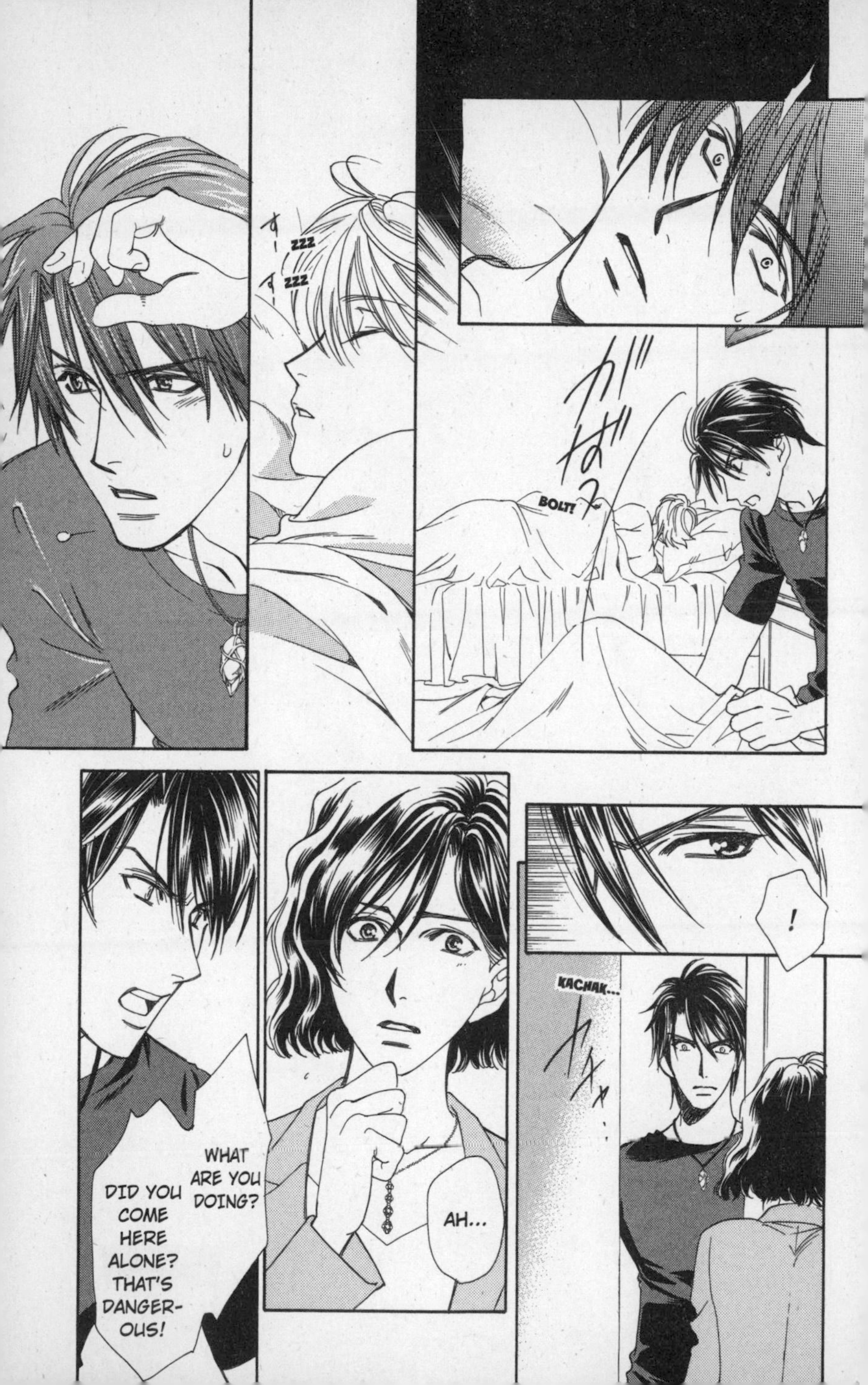
BOLT!
ZZZ
ZZZ
!
KACHAK...
WHAT ARE YOU DOING?
AH...
DID YOU COME HERE ALONE? THAT'S DANGER-OUS!

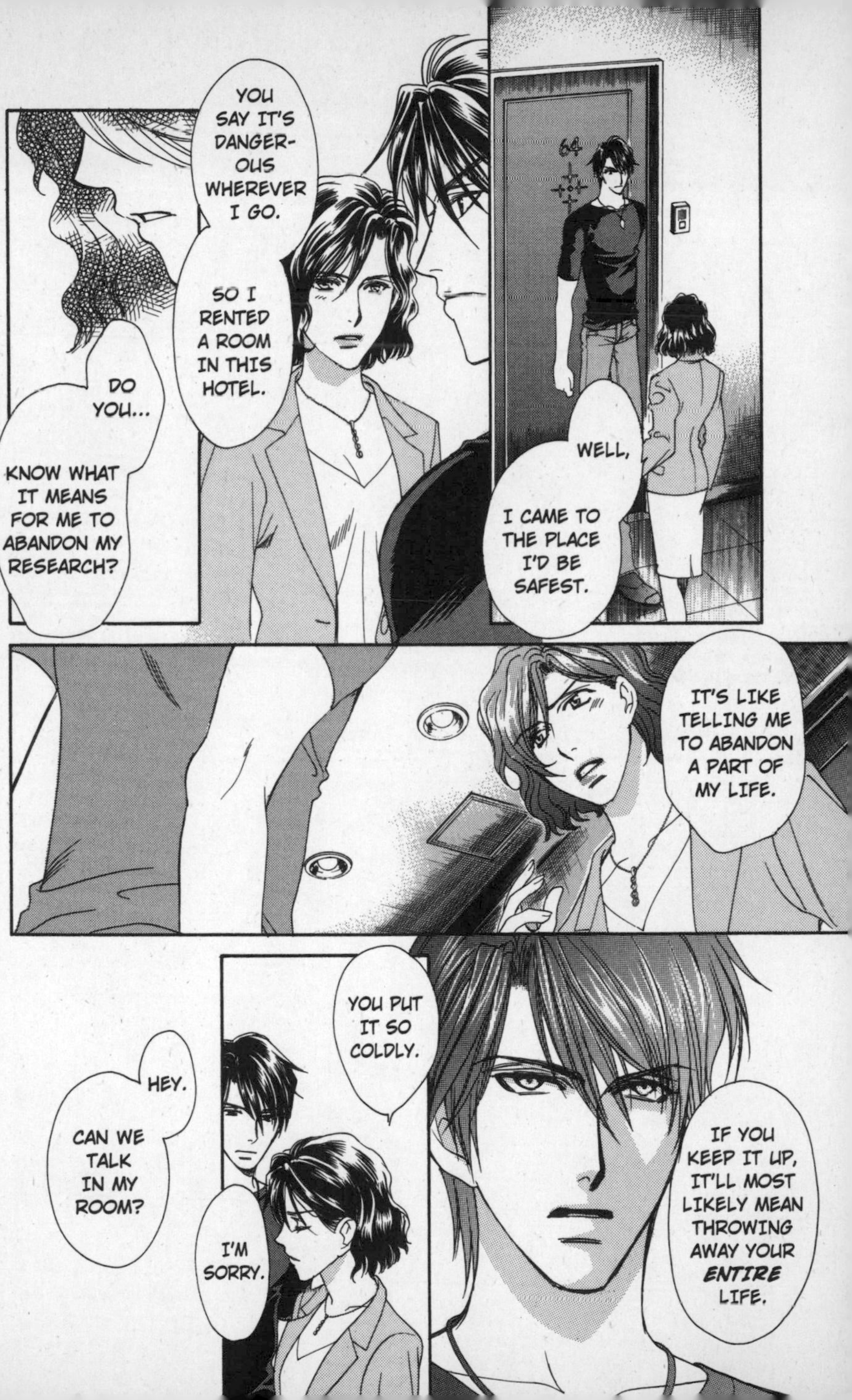
WELL,
I CAME TO THE PLACE I'D BE SAFEST.
YOU SAY IT'S DANGER-OUS WHEREVER I GO.
SO I RENTED A ROOM IN THIS HOTEL.
DO YOU...
KNOW WHAT IT MEANS FOR ME TO ABANDON MY RESEARCH?
IT'S LIKE TELLING ME TO ABANDON A PART OF MY LIFE.
IF YOU KEEP IT UP, IT'LL MOST LIKELY MEAN THROWING AWAY YOUR *ENTIRE* LIFE.
YOU PUT IT SO COLDLY.
HEY.
CAN WE TALK IN MY ROOM?
I'M SORRY.

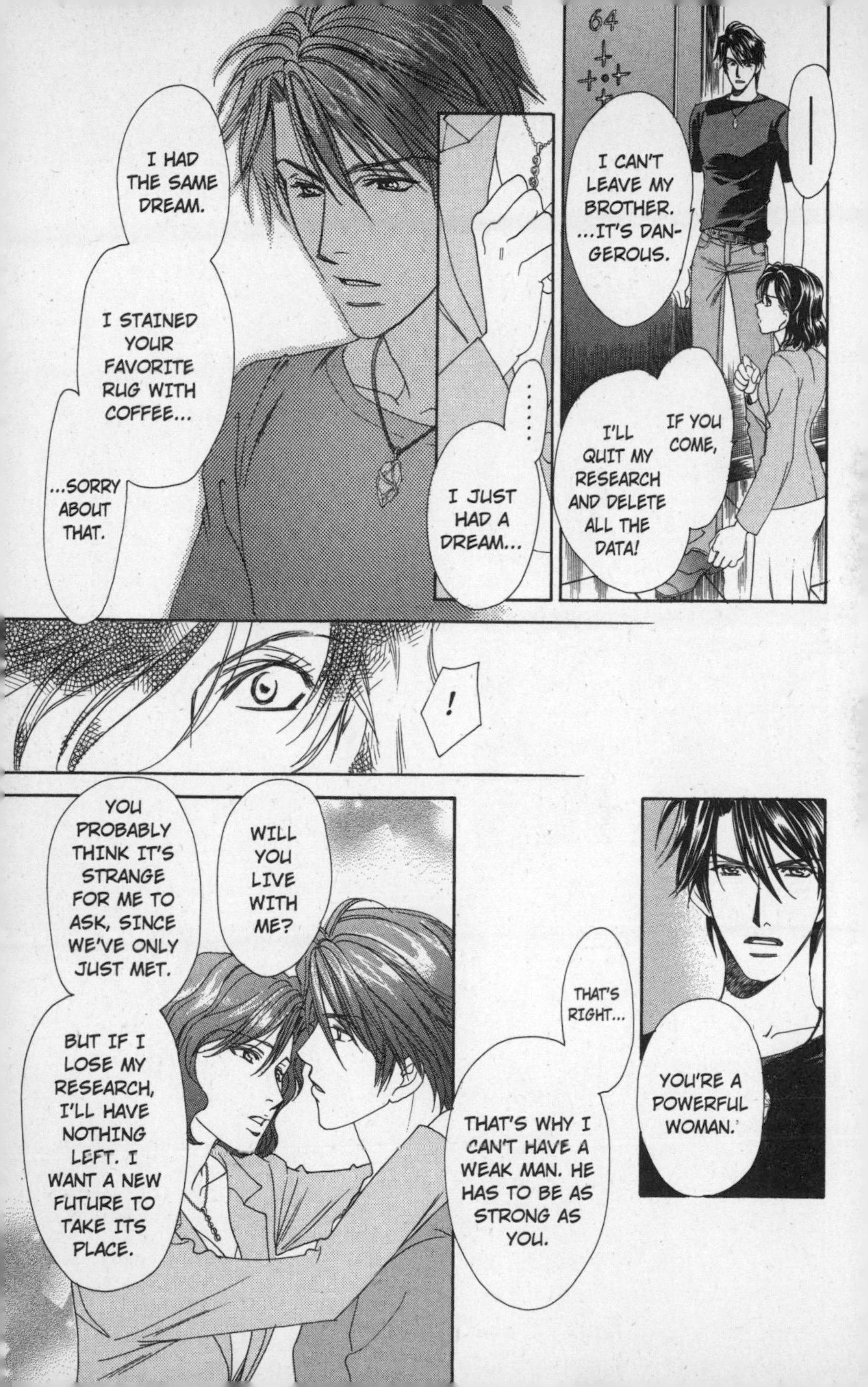
64
I CAN'T LEAVE MY BROTHER. ...IT'S DANGEROUS.
IF YOU COME,
I'LL QUIT MY RESEARCH AND DELETE ALL THE DATA!
......
I JUST HAD A DREAM...
I HAD THE SAME DREAM.
I STAINED YOUR FAVORITE RUG WITH COFFEE...
...SORRY ABOUT THAT.
!
YOU'RE A POWERFUL WOMAN.
THAT'S RIGHT...
THAT'S WHY I CAN'T HAVE A WEAK MAN. HE HAS TO BE AS STRONG AS YOU.
WILL YOU LIVE WITH ME?
YOU PROBABLY THINK IT'S STRANGE FOR ME TO ASK, SINCE WE'VE ONLY JUST MET.
BUT IF I LOSE MY RESEARCH, I'LL HAVE NOTHING LEFT. I WANT A NEW FUTURE TO TAKE ITS PLACE.

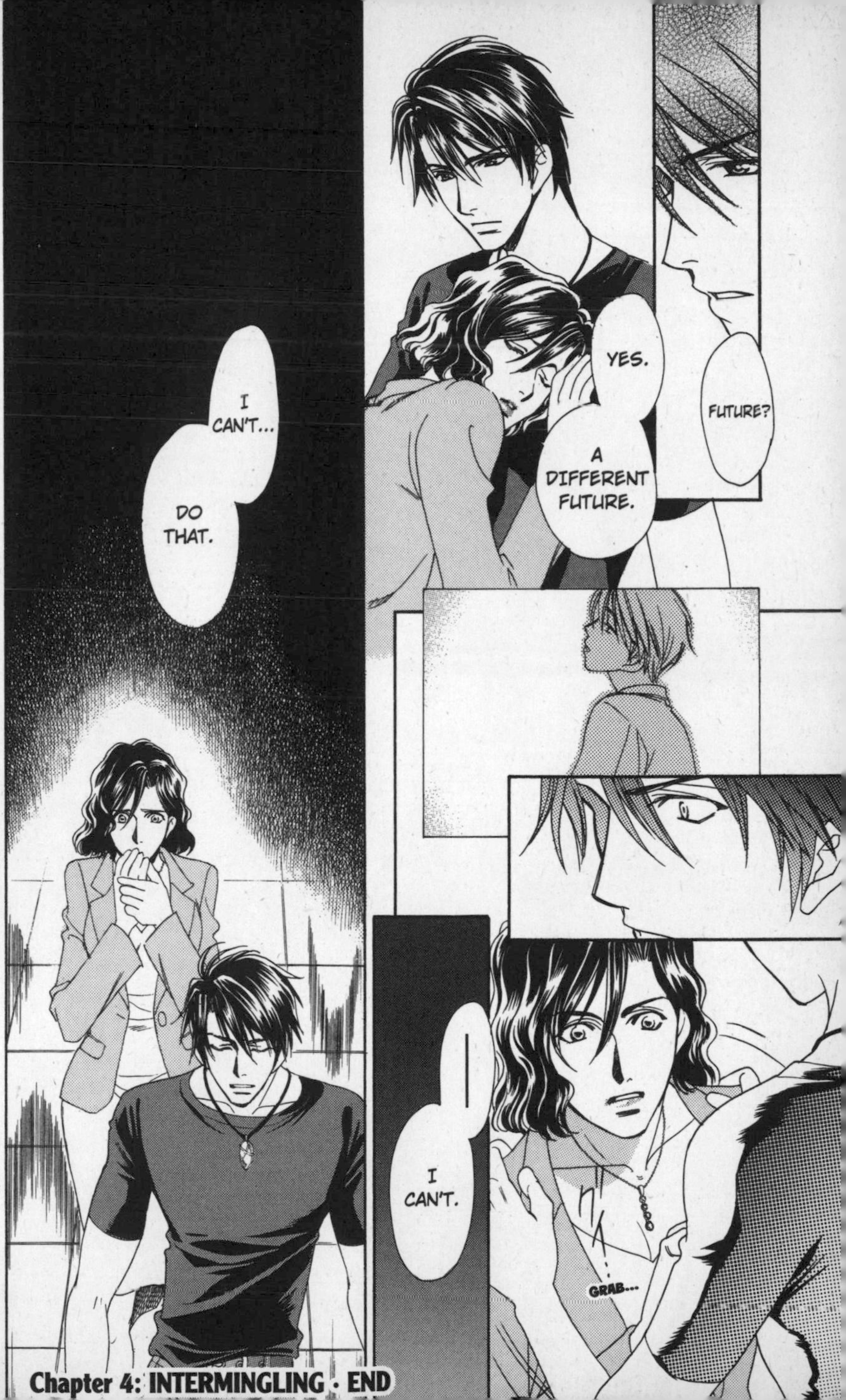
FUTURE?
YES.
A DIFFERENT FUTURE.
I CAN'T.
GRAB...
I CAN'T...
DO THAT.

Chapter 4: INTERMINGLING · END

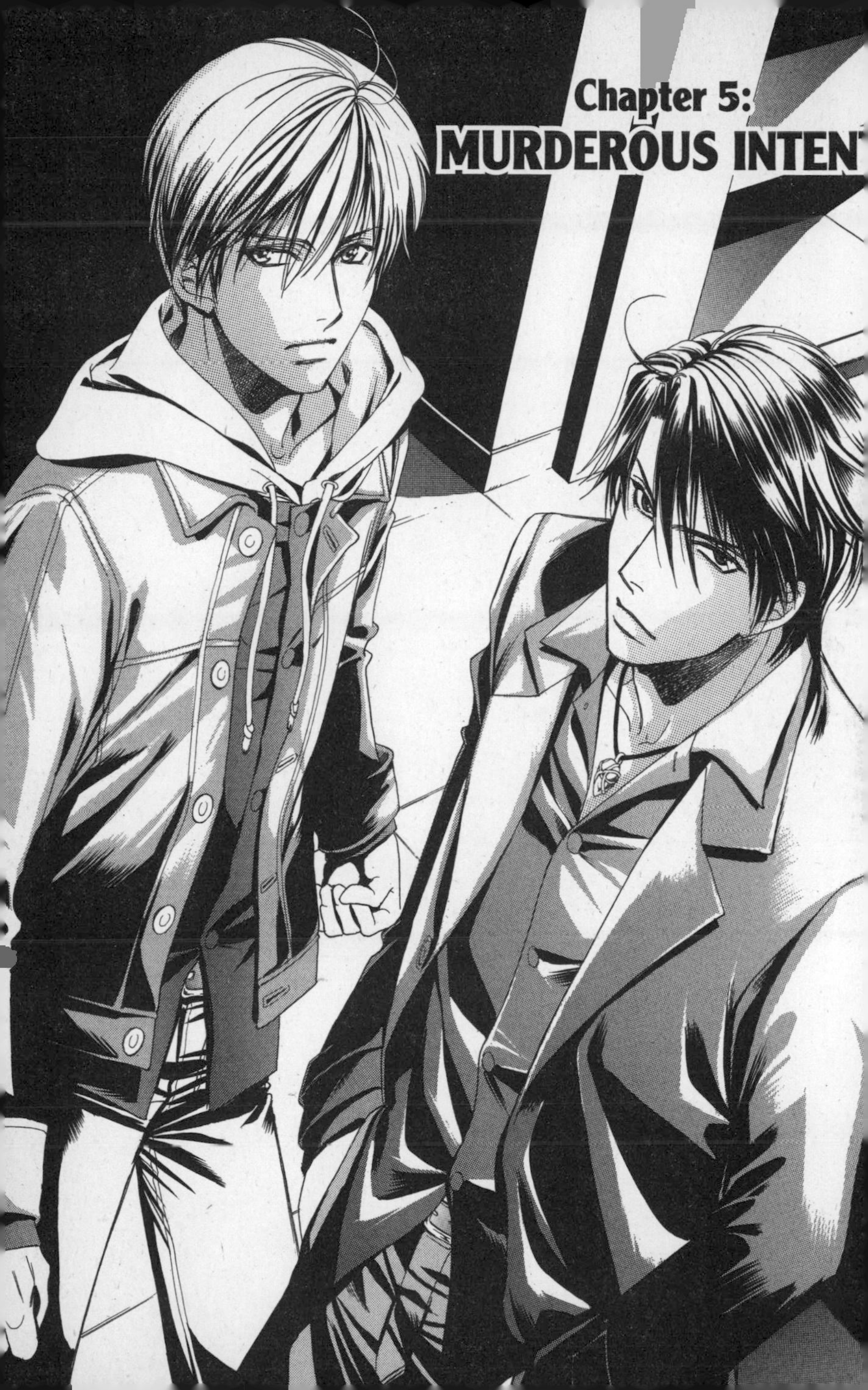
Chapter 5:
MURDEROUS INTENT

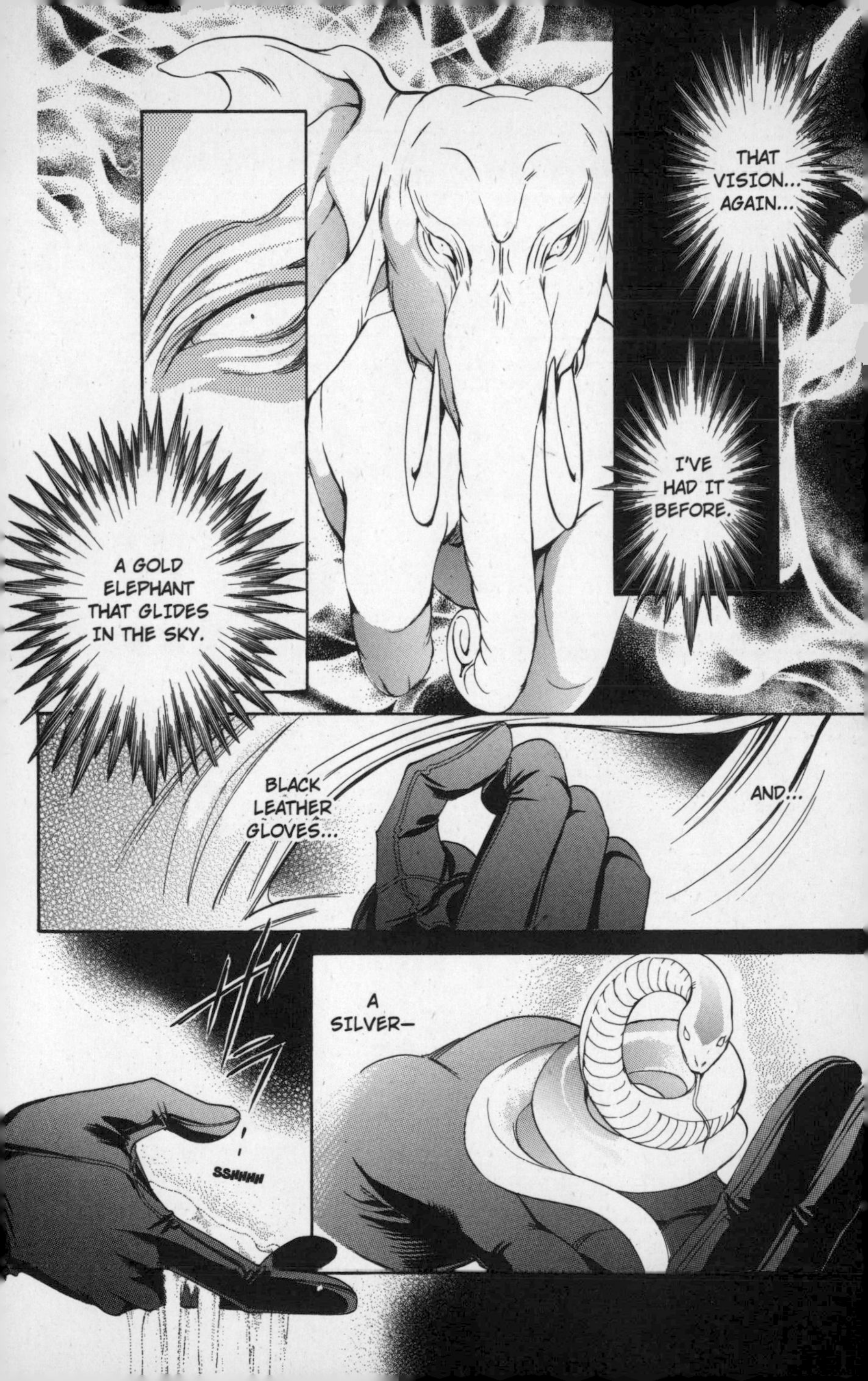
THAT VISION... AGAIN...
I'VE HAD IT BEFORE.
A GOLD ELEPHANT THAT GLIDES IN THE SKY.
AND...
BLACK LEATHER GLOVES...
A SILVER—
!
SSHHHN

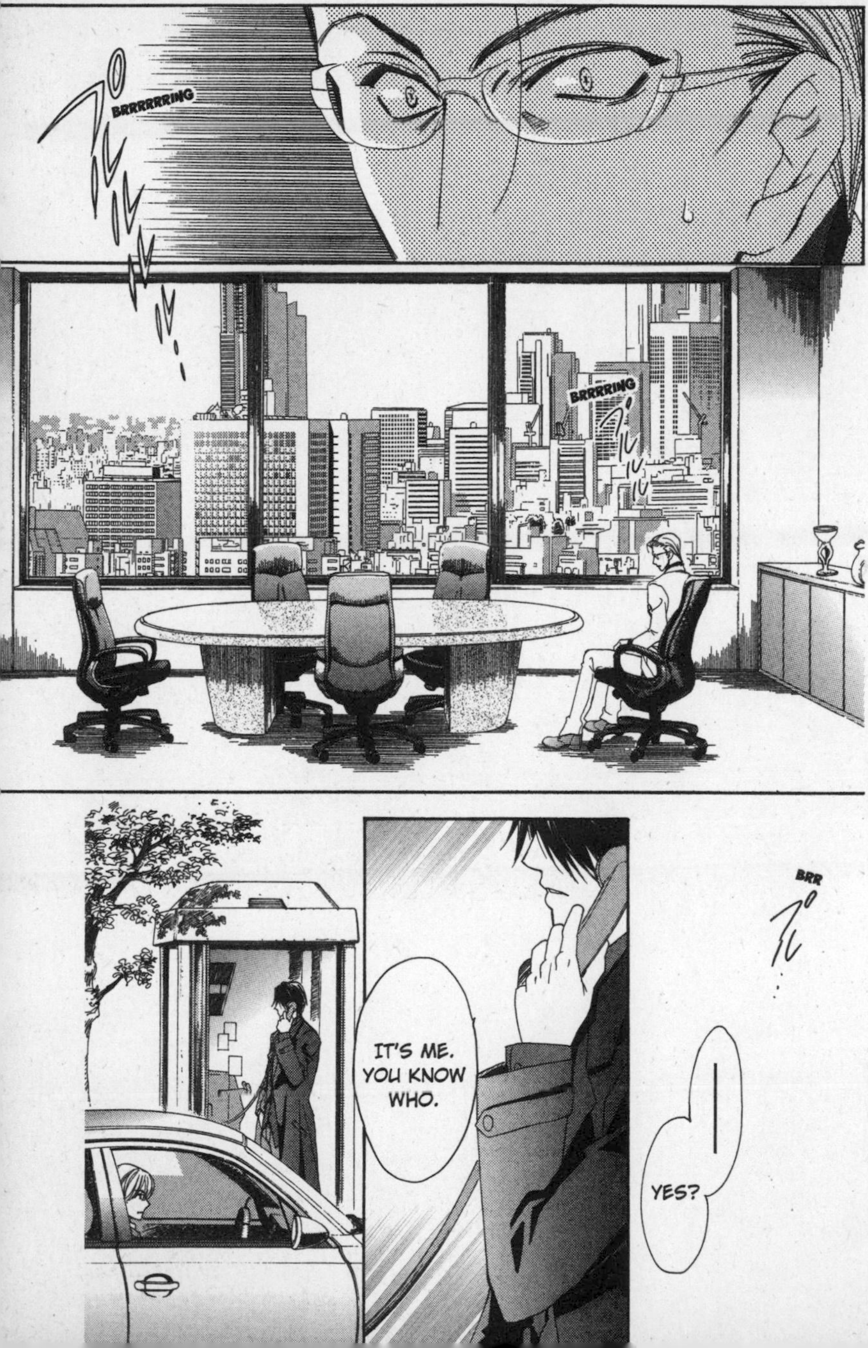
BRRRRRRING
BRRRRING
BRR
—
YES?
IT'S ME. YOU KNOW WHO.

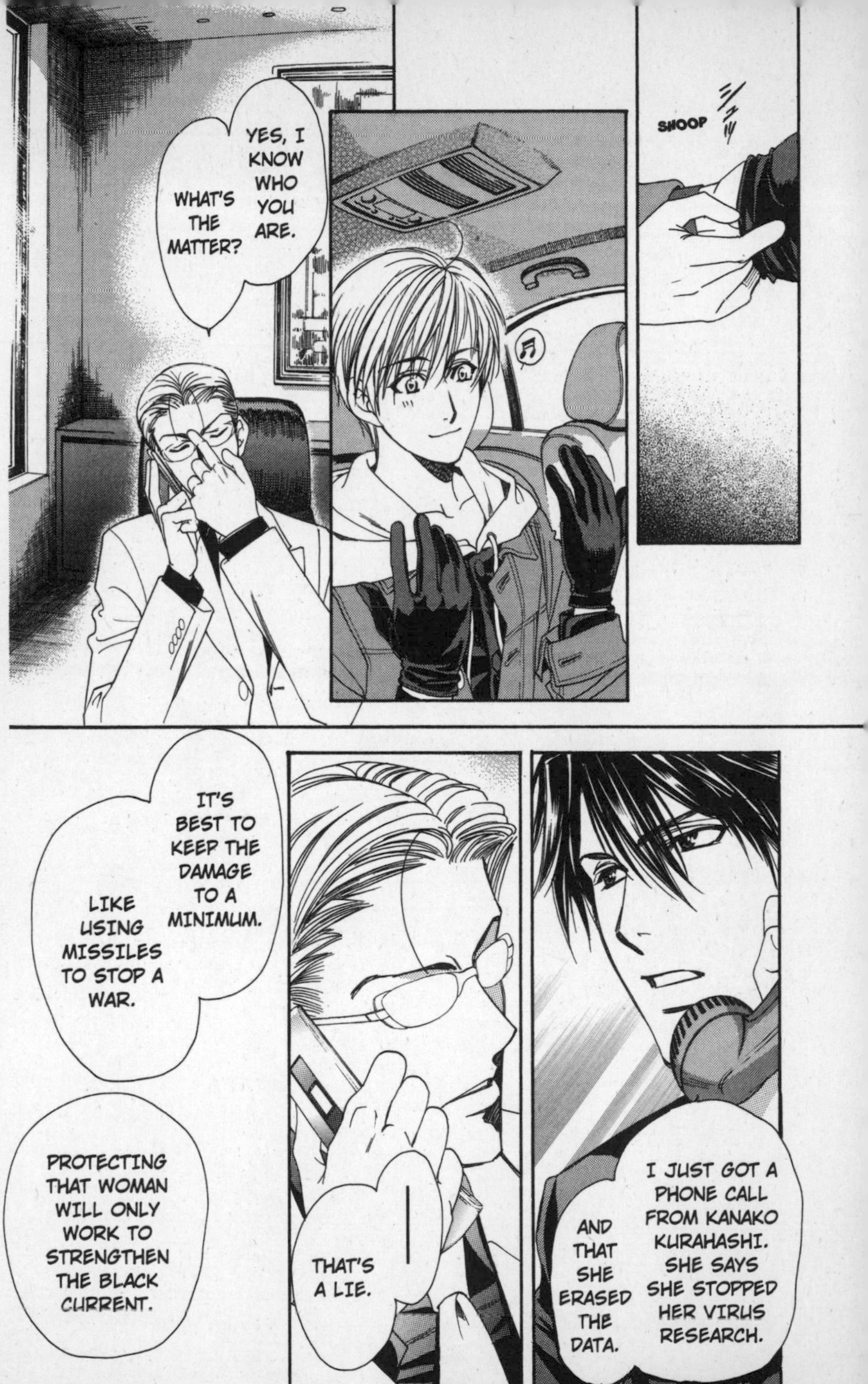
SHOOP
YES, I KNOW WHO YOU ARE.
WHAT'S THE MATTER?
I JUST GOT A PHONE CALL FROM KANAKO KURAHASHI. SHE SAYS SHE STOPPED HER VIRUS RESEARCH.
AND THAT SHE ERASED THE DATA.
THAT'S A LIE.
IT'S BEST TO KEEP THE DAMAGE TO A MINIMUM.
LIKE USING MISSILES TO STOP A WAR.
PROTECTING THAT WOMAN WILL ONLY WORK TO STRENGTHEN THE BLACK CURRENT.

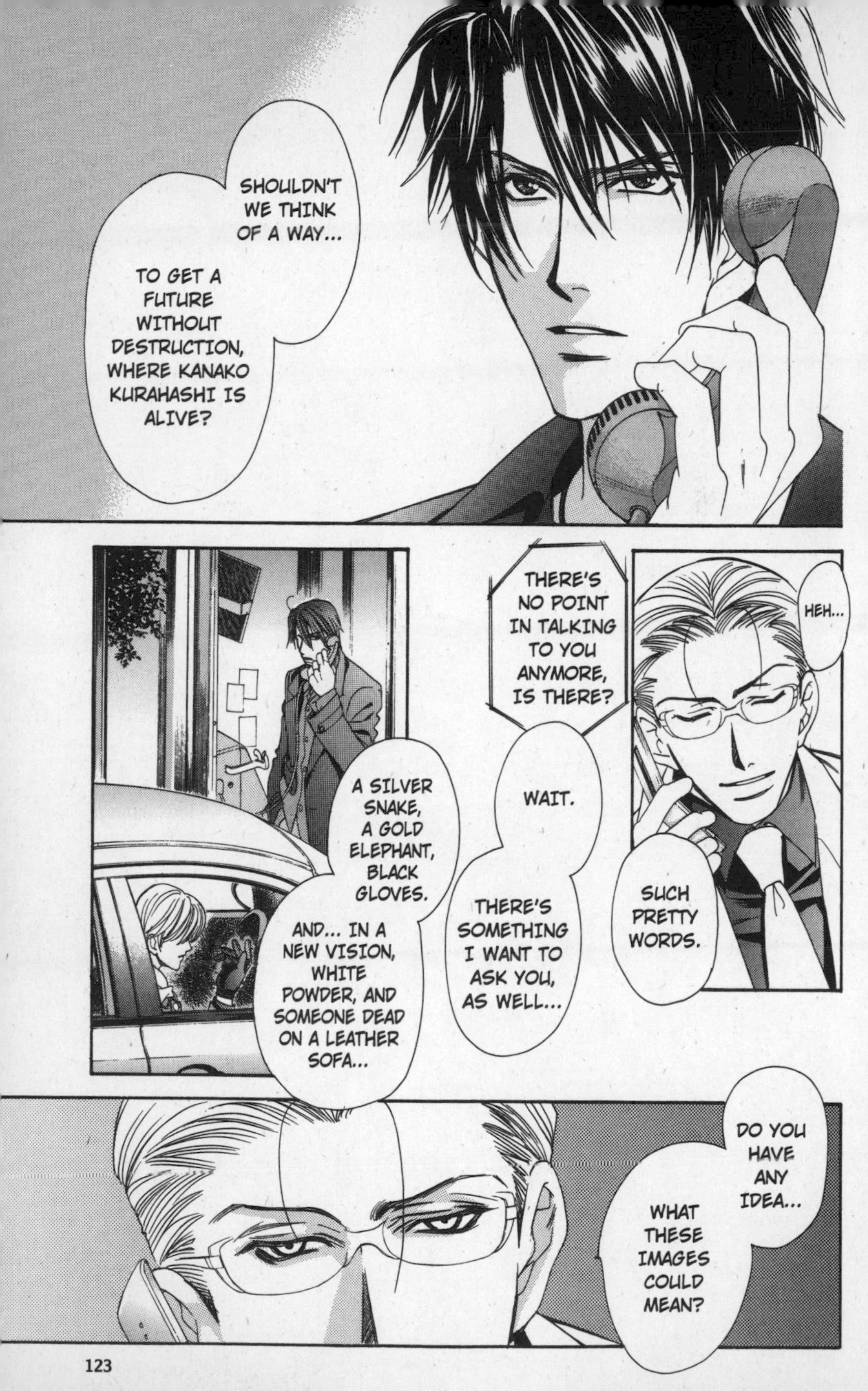
SHOULDN'T WE THINK OF A WAY...
TO GET A FUTURE WITHOUT DESTRUCTION, WHERE KANAKO KURAHASHI IS ALIVE?
HEH...
SUCH PRETTY WORDS.
THERE'S NO POINT IN TALKING TO YOU ANYMORE, IS THERE?
WAIT.
THERE'S SOMETHING I WANT TO ASK YOU, AS WELL...
A SILVER SNAKE, A GOLD ELEPHANT, BLACK GLOVES.
AND... IN A NEW VISION, WHITE POWDER, AND SOMEONE DEAD ON A LEATHER SOFA...
DO YOU HAVE ANY IDEA...
WHAT THESE IMAGES COULD MEAN?

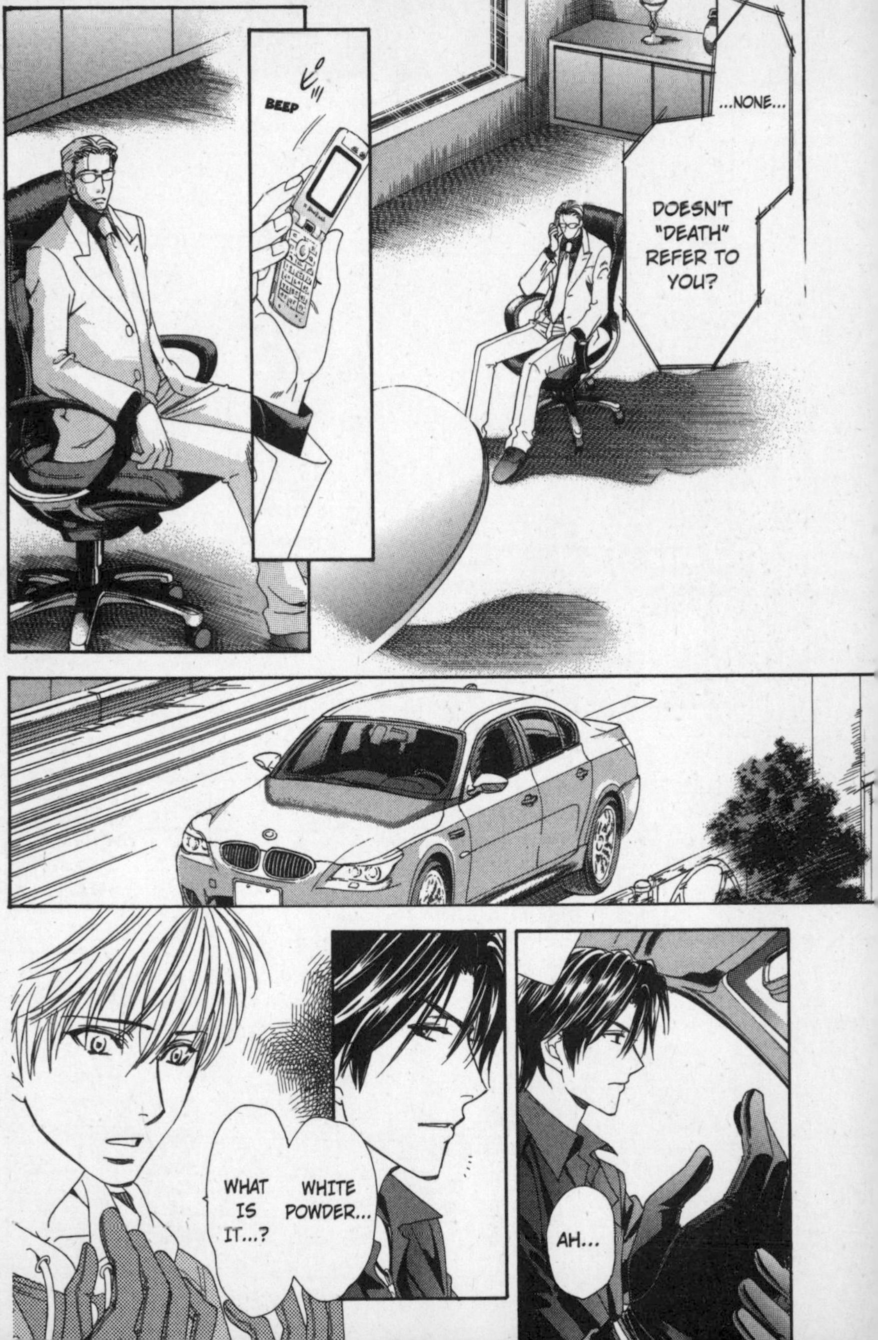
...NONE...
DOESN'T "DEATH" REFER TO YOU?
BEEP
AH...
WHITE POWDER...
WHAT IS IT...?

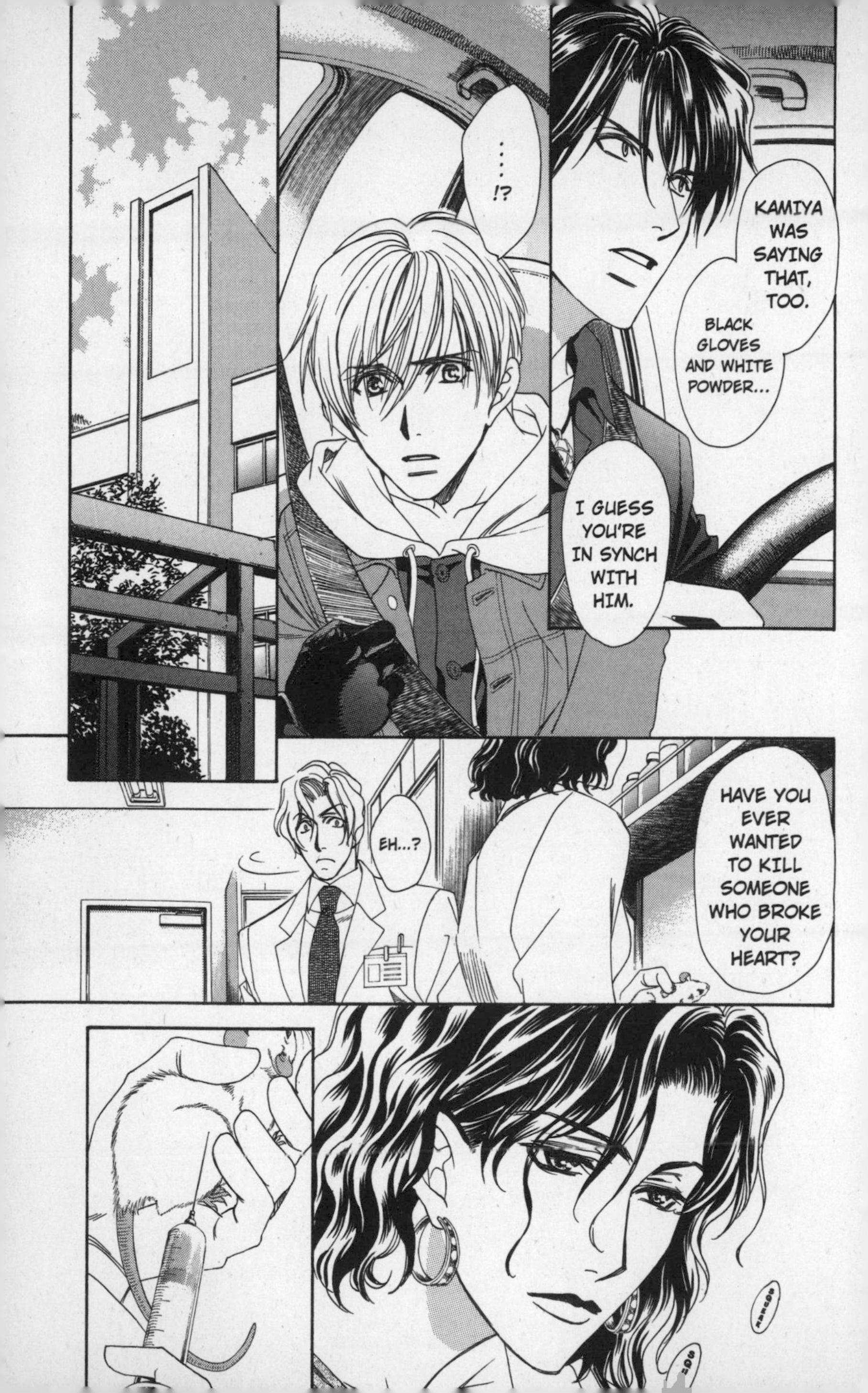
KAMIYA WAS SAYING THAT, TOO.
BLACK GLOVES AND WHITE POWDER...
I GUESS YOU'RE IN SYNCH WITH HIM.
....!?
HAVE YOU EVER WANTED TO KILL SOMEONE WHO BROKE YOUR HEART?
EH...?
SQUEAK

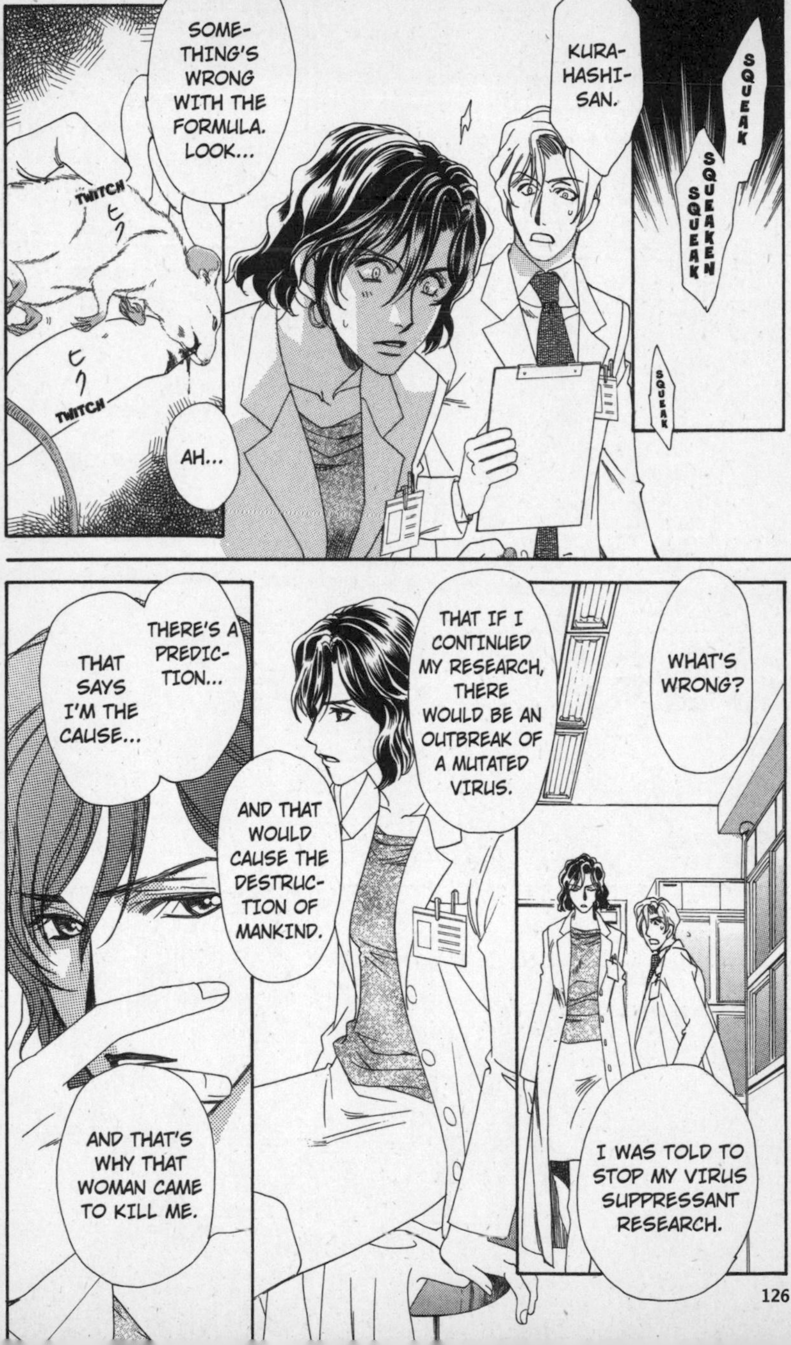
SQUEAK
SQUEAKEN
SQUEAK
SQUEAK
KURA-HASHI-SAN.
SOME-THING'S WRONG WITH THE FORMULA. LOOK...
TWITCH
ヒク
ヒク
TWITCH
AH...
WHAT'S WRONG?
I WAS TOLD TO STOP MY VIRUS SUPPRESSANT RESEARCH.
THAT IF I CONTINUED MY RESEARCH, THERE WOULD BE AN OUTBREAK OF A MUTATED VIRUS.
AND THAT WOULD CAUSE THE DESTRUC-TION OF MANKIND.
THERE'S A PREDIC-TION...
THAT SAYS I'M THE CAUSE...
AND THAT'S WHY THAT WOMAN CAME TO KILL ME.

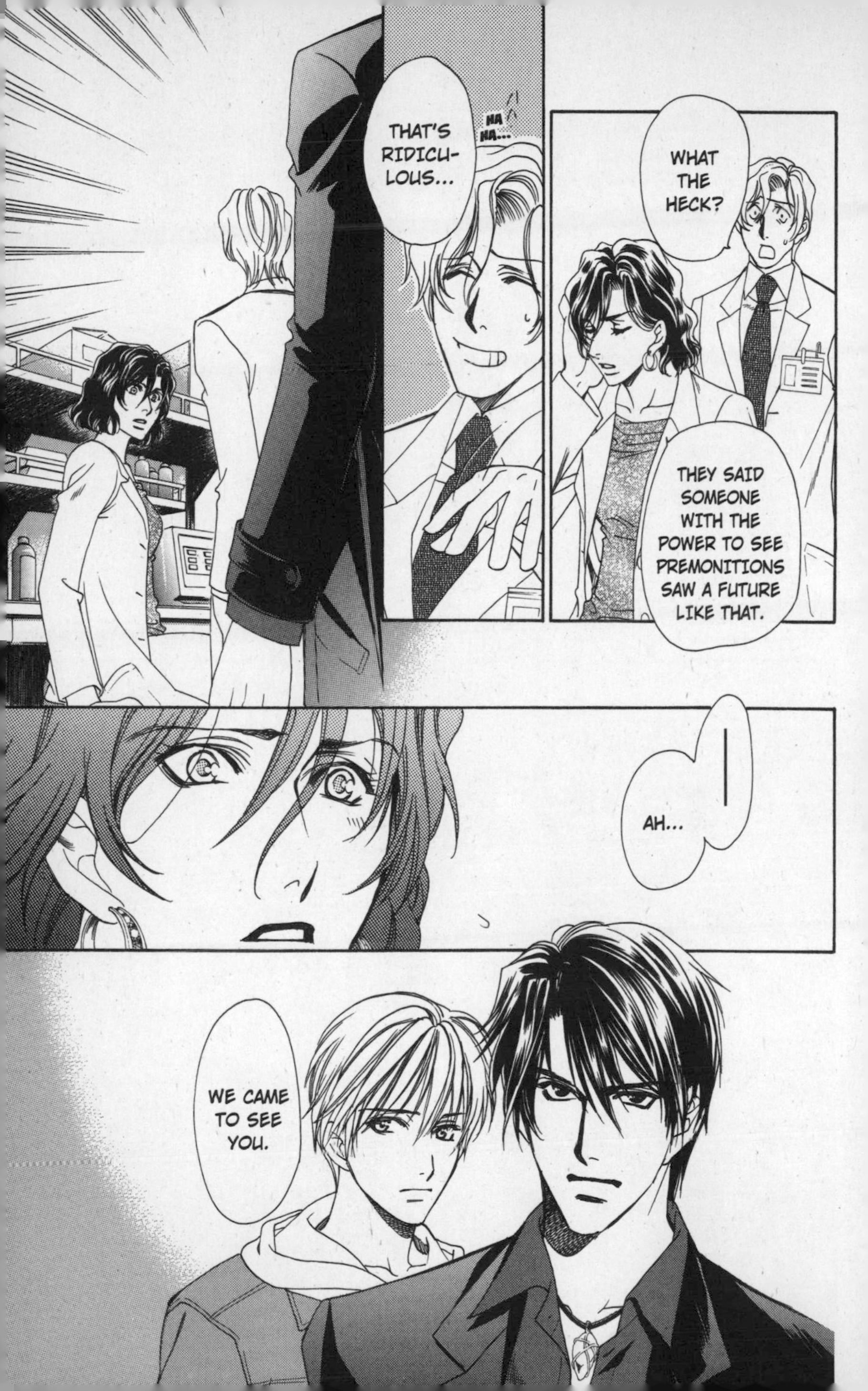
WHAT THE HECK?
THEY SAID SOMEONE WITH THE POWER TO SEE PREMONITIONS SAW A FUTURE LIKE THAT.
THAT'S RIDICU-LOUS...
HA HA...
AH...
WE CAME TO SEE YOU.

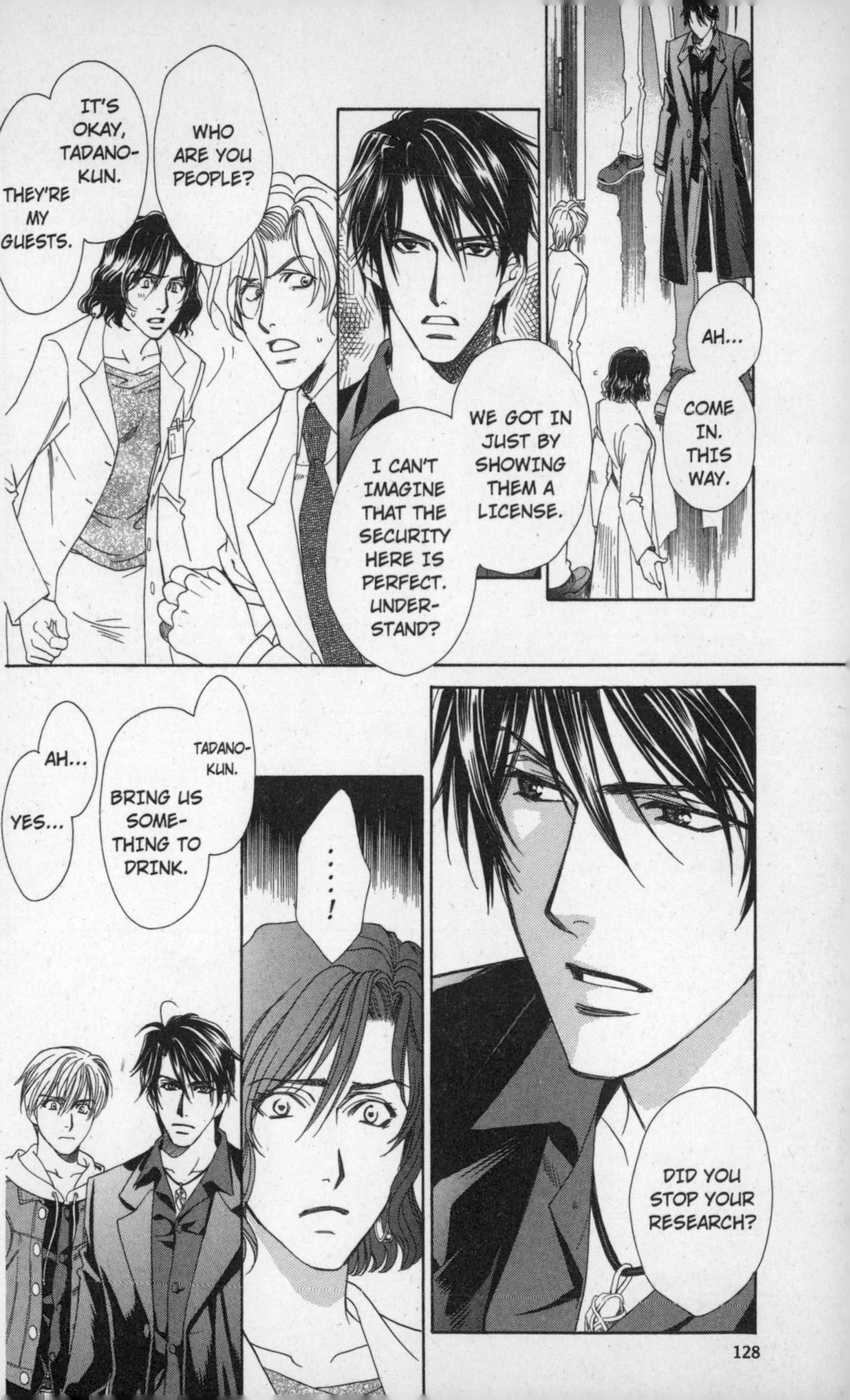
AH...
COME IN. THIS WAY.
WE GOT IN JUST BY SHOWING THEM A LICENSE.
I CAN'T IMAGINE THAT THE SECURITY HERE IS PERFECT. UNDER-STAND?
WHO ARE YOU PEOPLE?
IT'S OKAY, TADANO-KUN.
THEY'RE MY GUESTS.
DID YOU STOP YOUR RESEARCH?
....!
TADANO-KUN.
BRING US SOME-THING TO DRINK.
AH...
YES...

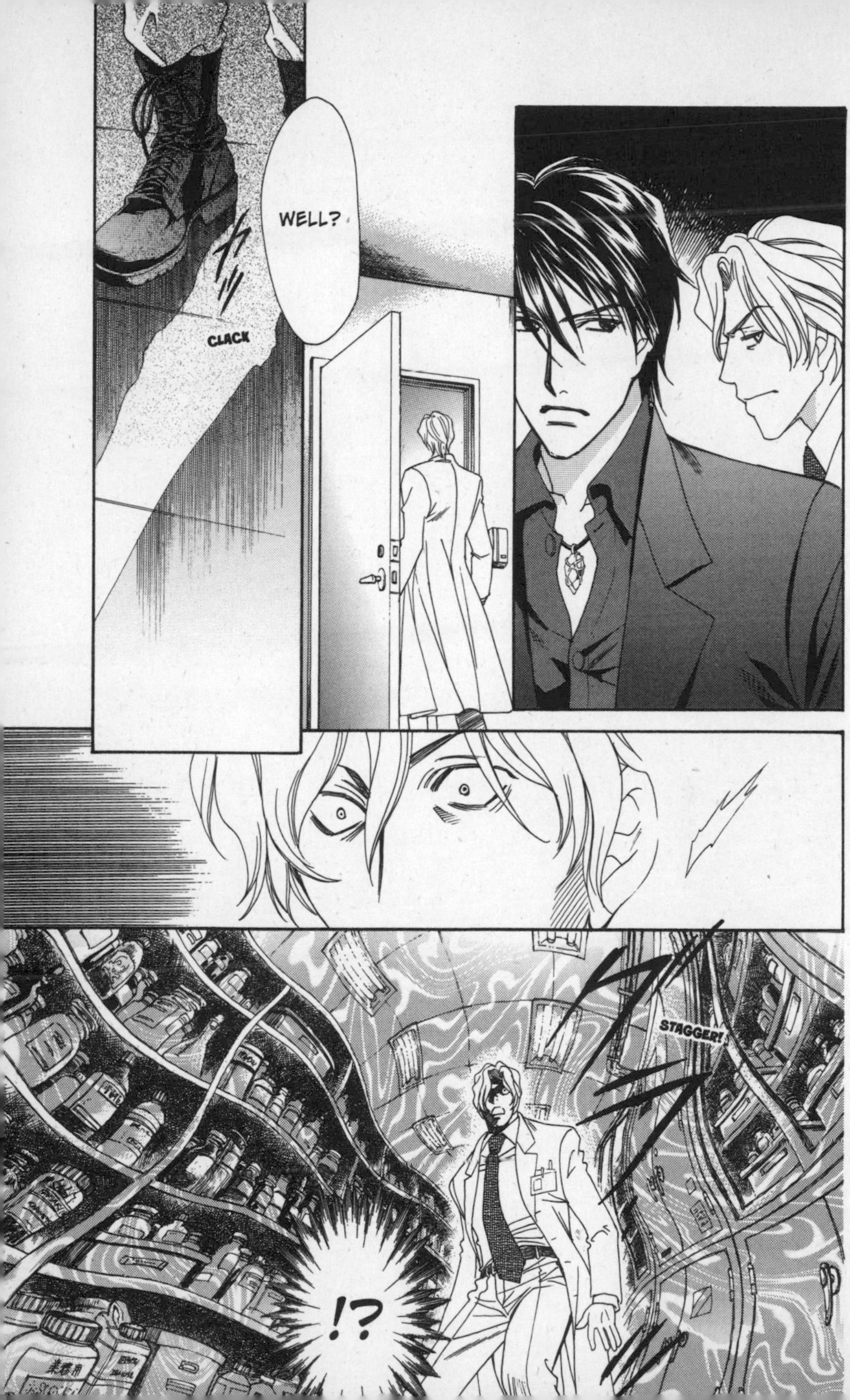
WELL?
CLACK
STAGGER!
!?

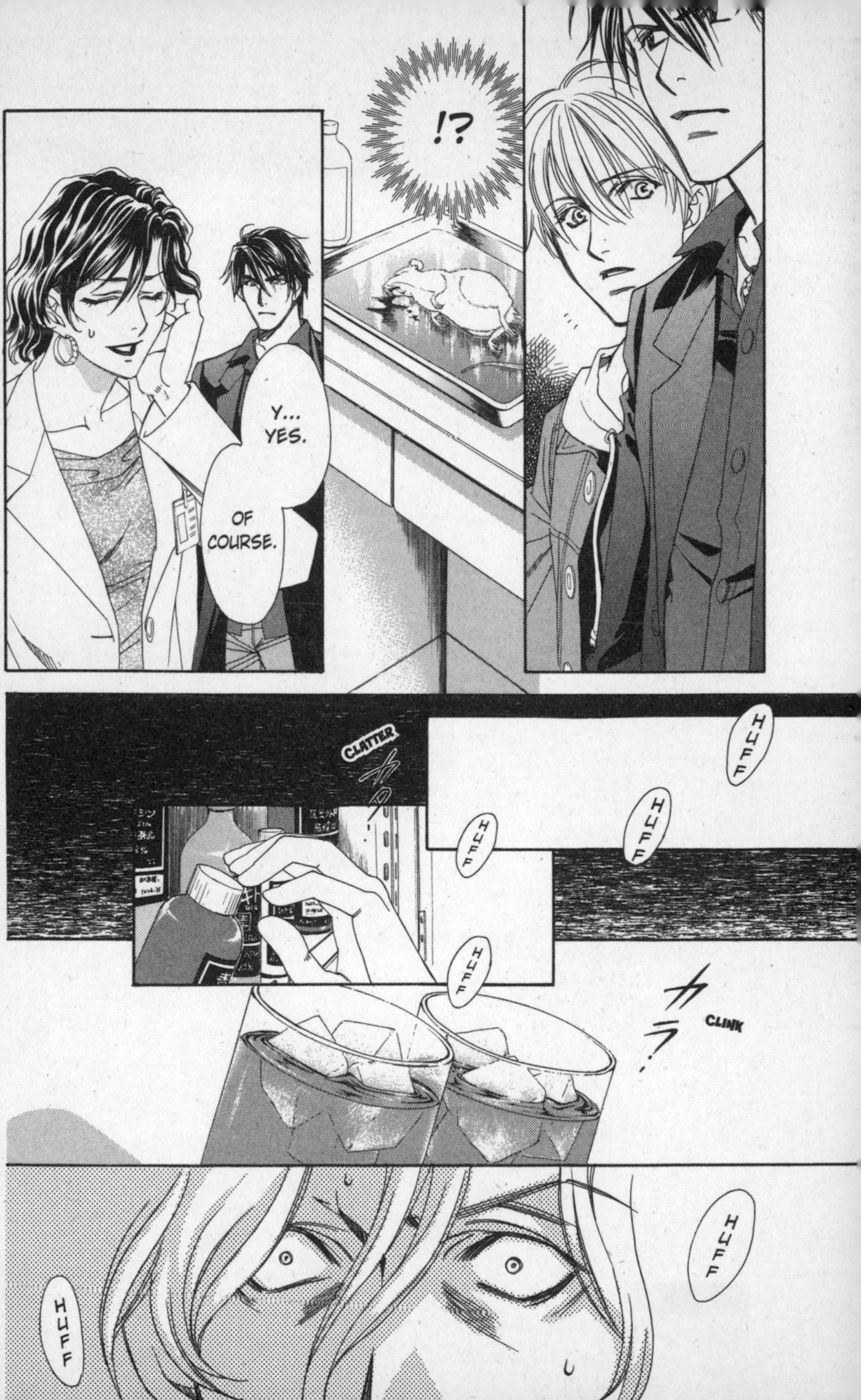
!?
Y... YES.
OF COURSE.
HUFF
HUFF
HUFF
CLATTER
HUFF
CLINK
HUFF
HUFF

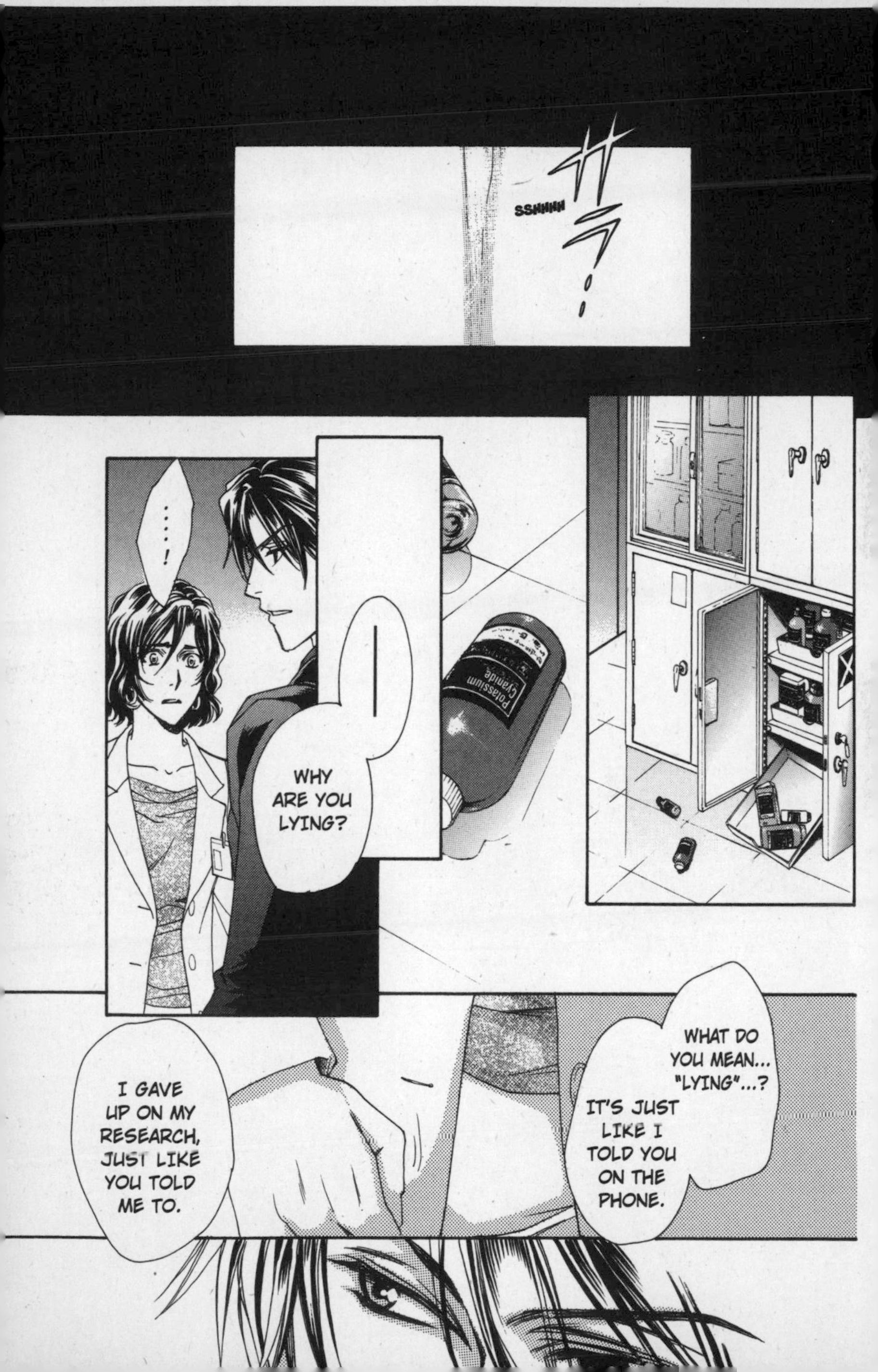
SSHHHH
....!
—
WHY ARE YOU LYING?
Potassium Cyanide
WHAT DO YOU MEAN... "LYING"...?
IT'S JUST LIKE I TOLD YOU ON THE PHONE.
I GAVE UP ON MY RESEARCH, JUST LIKE YOU TOLD ME TO.

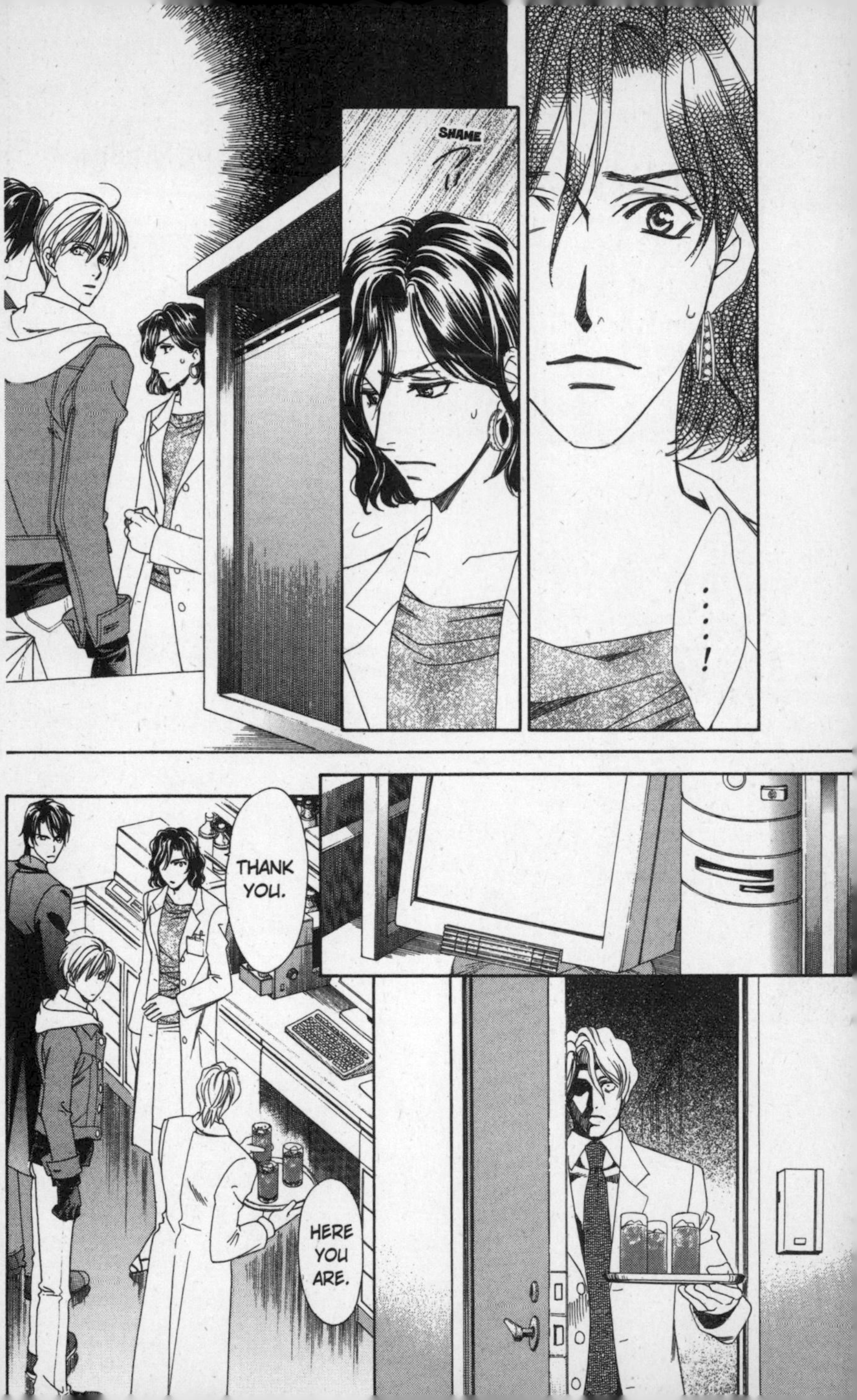
....!
SHAME
THANK YOU.
HERE YOU ARE.

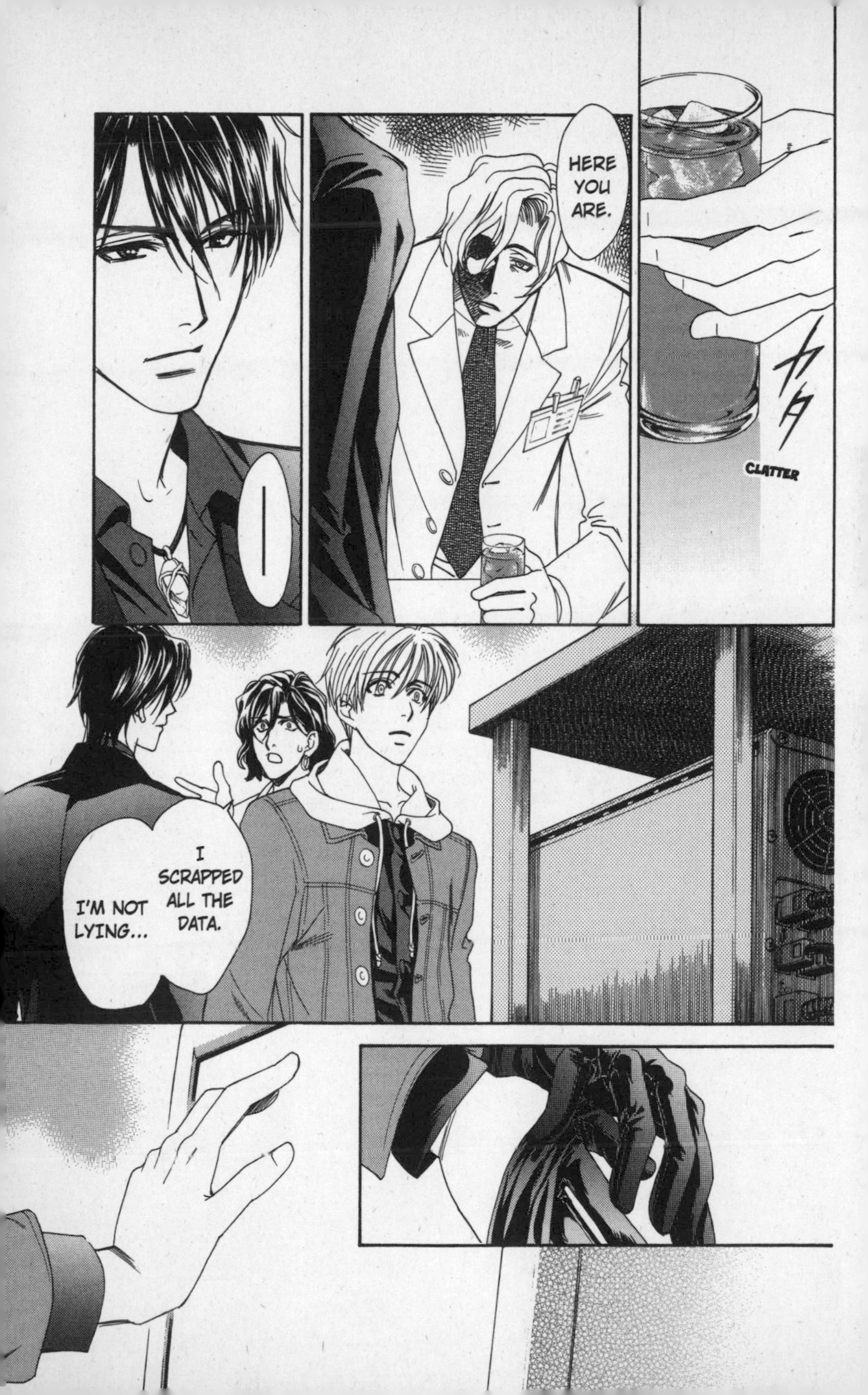
カタ
CLATTER
HERE YOU ARE.
I SCRAPPED ALL THE DATA.
I'M NOT LYING...

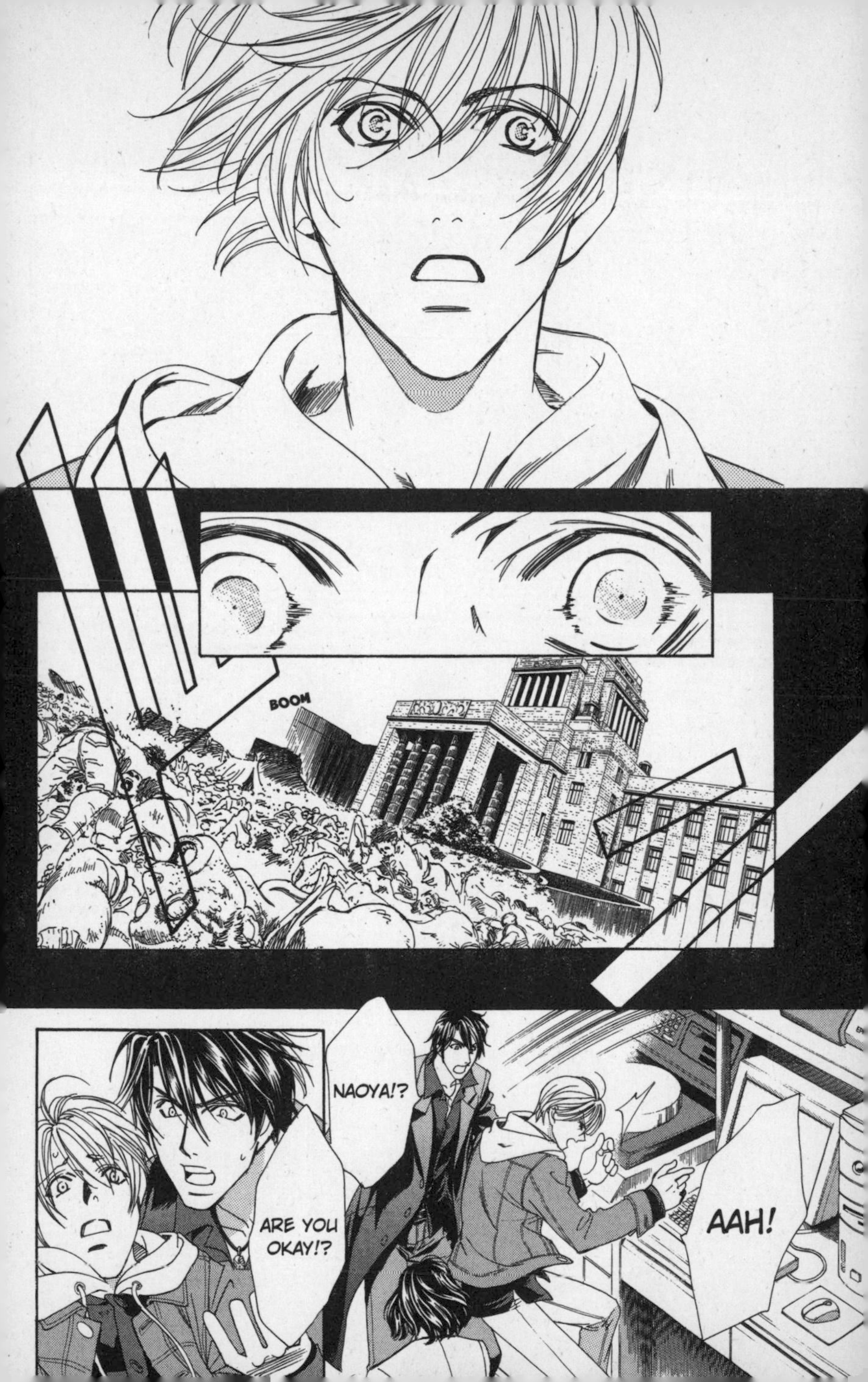
BOOM
AAH!
NAOYA!?
ARE YOU OKAY!?

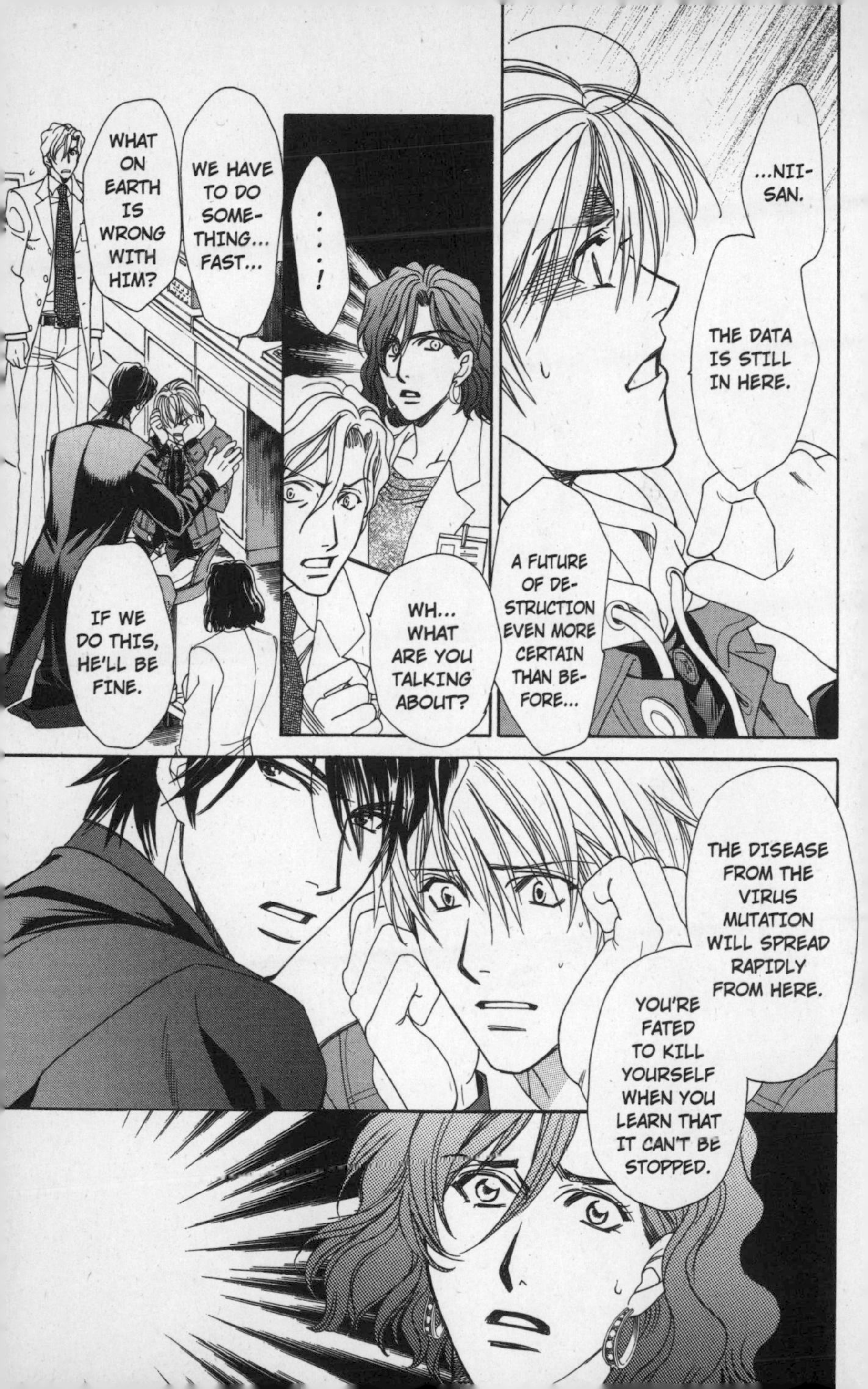
...NII-SAN.
THE DATA IS STILL IN HERE.
A FUTURE OF DESTRUCTION EVEN MORE CERTAIN THAN BEFORE...
....!
WH... WHAT ARE YOU TALKING ABOUT?
WE HAVE TO DO SOMETHING... FAST...
WHAT ON EARTH IS WRONG WITH HIM?
IF WE DO THIS, HE'LL BE FINE.
THE DISEASE FROM THE VIRUS MUTATION WILL SPREAD RAPIDLY FROM HERE.
YOU'RE FATED TO KILL YOURSELF WHEN YOU LEARN THAT IT CAN'T BE STOPPED.

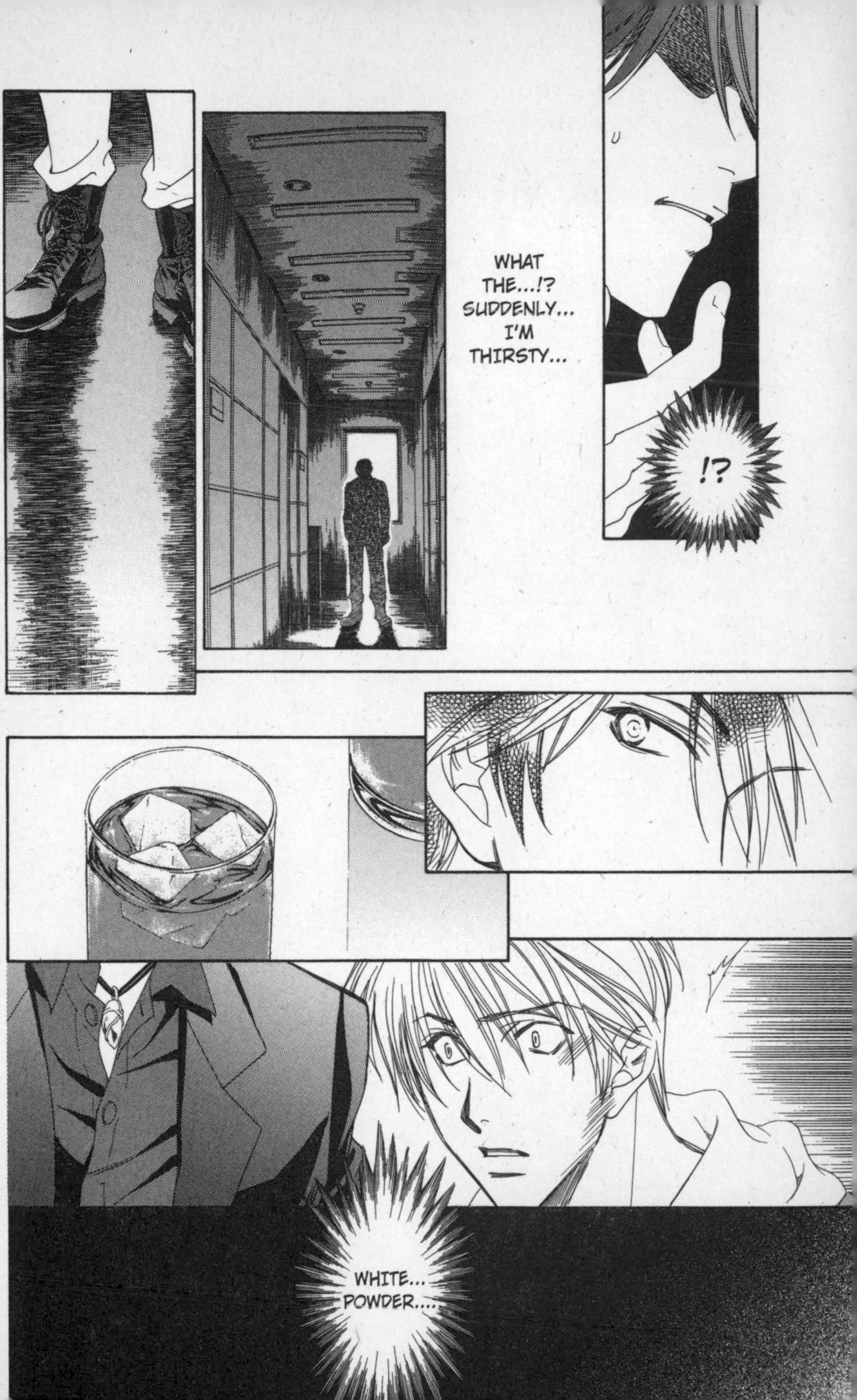
WHAT THE...!? SUDDENLY... I'M THIRSTY...
!?
WHITE... POWDER....

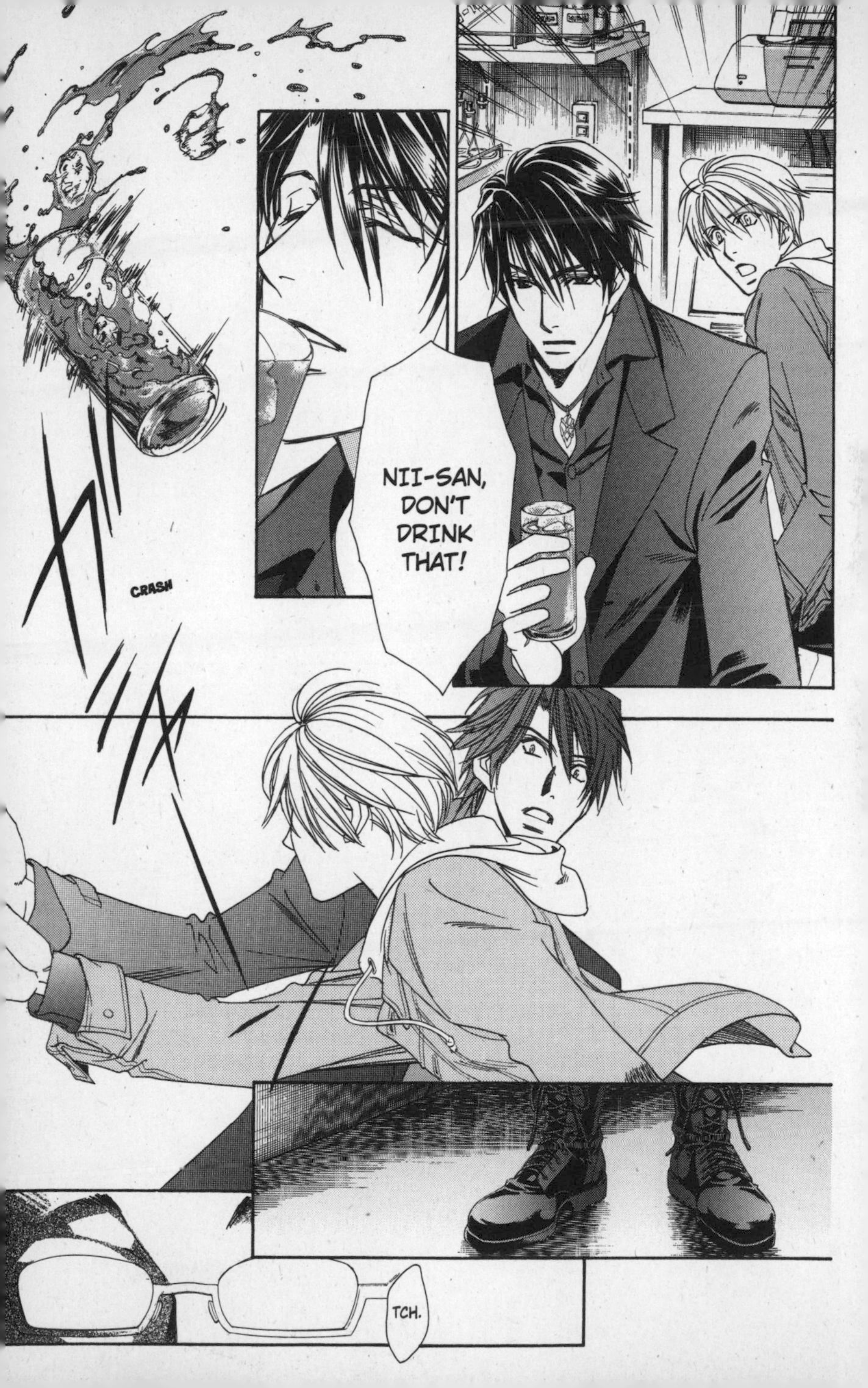
NII-SAN, DON'T DRINK THAT!
CRASH
TCH.

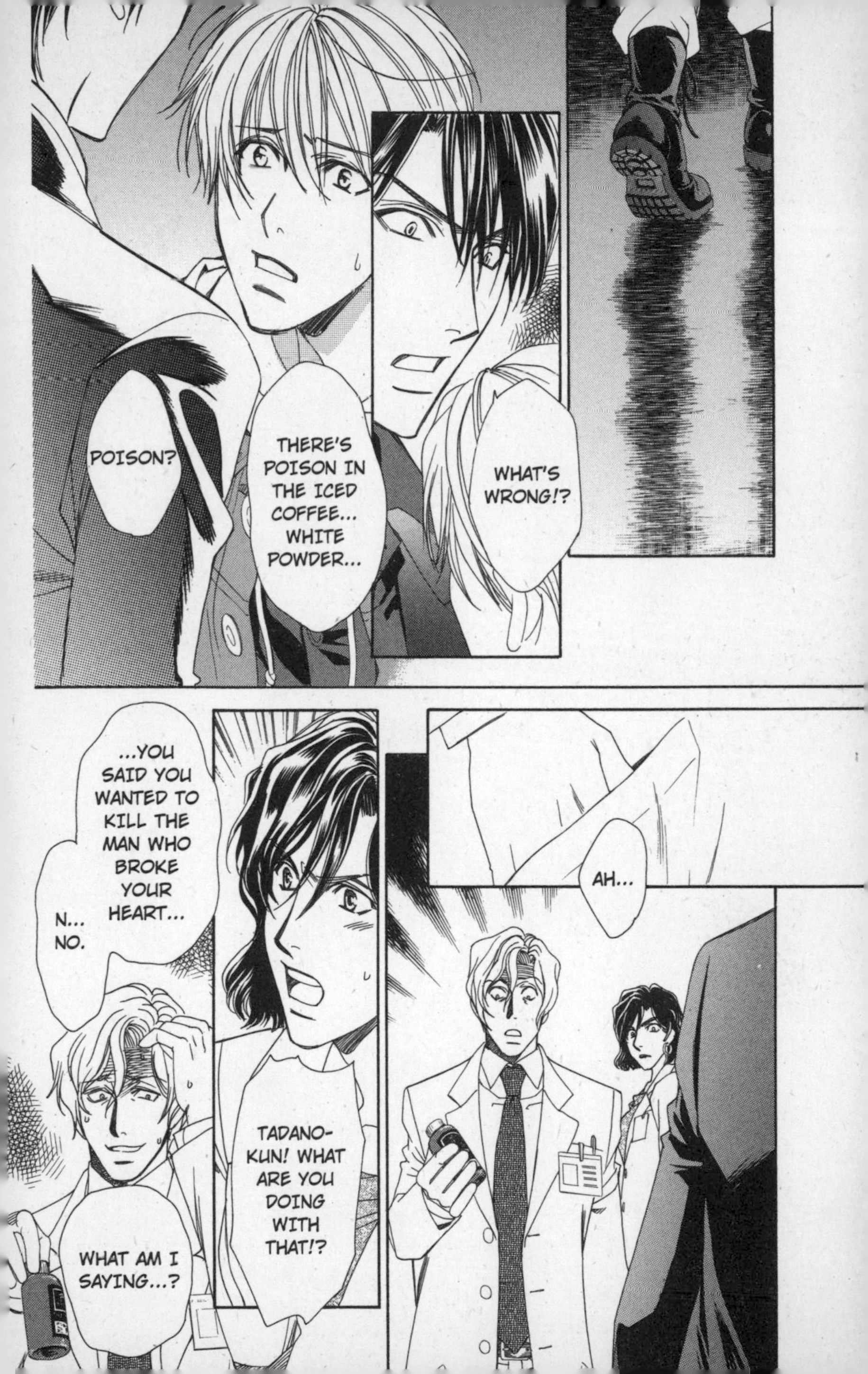
WHAT'S WRONG!?
THERE'S POISON IN THE ICED COFFEE... WHITE POWDER...
POISON?
AH...
TADANO-KUN! WHAT ARE YOU DOING WITH THAT!?
...YOU SAID YOU WANTED TO KILL THE MAN WHO BROKE YOUR HEART...
N... NO.
WHAT AM I SAYING...?

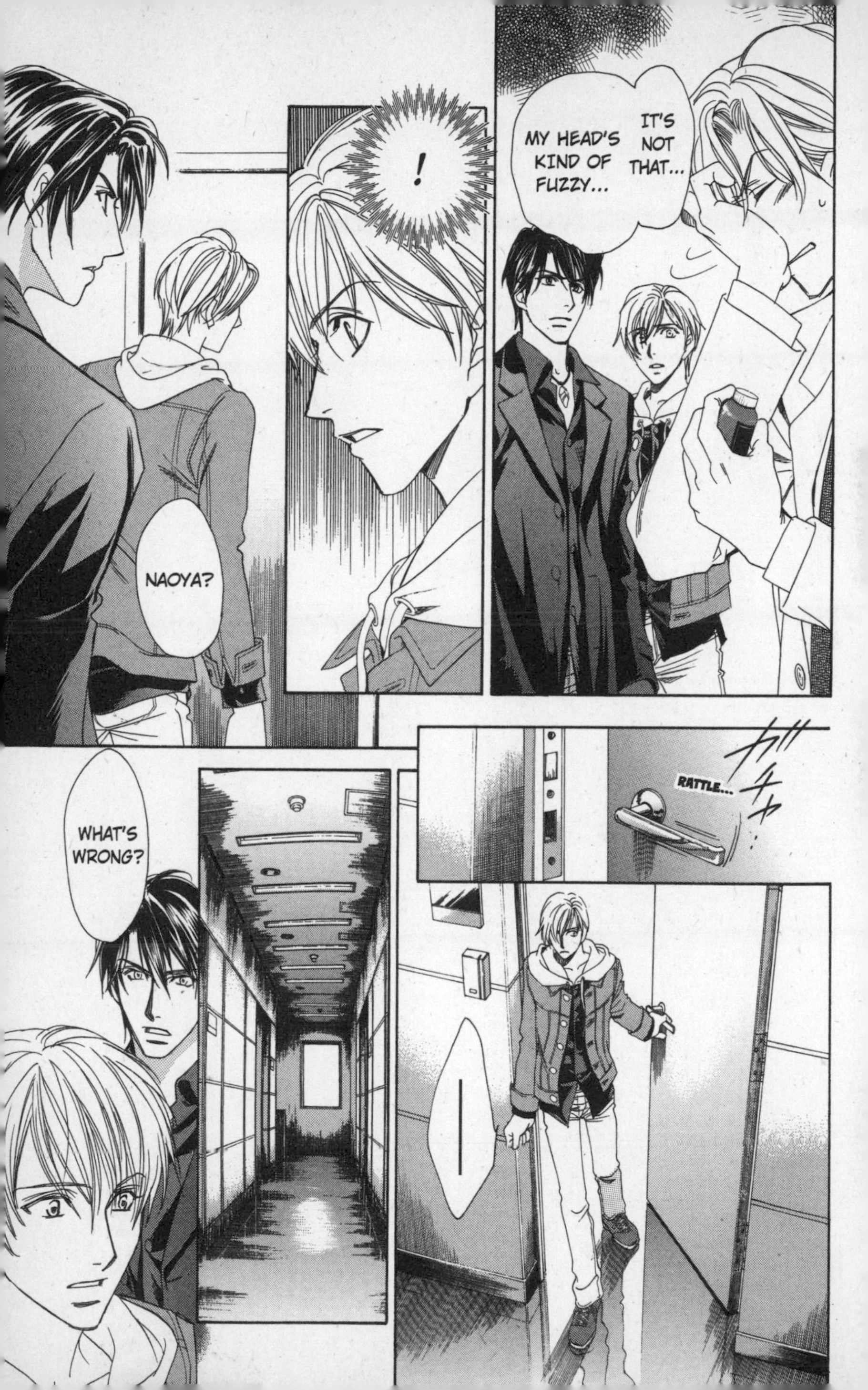
IT'S NOT THAT...
MY HEAD'S KIND OF FUZZY...
!
NAOYA?
RATTLE...
—
WHAT'S WRONG?

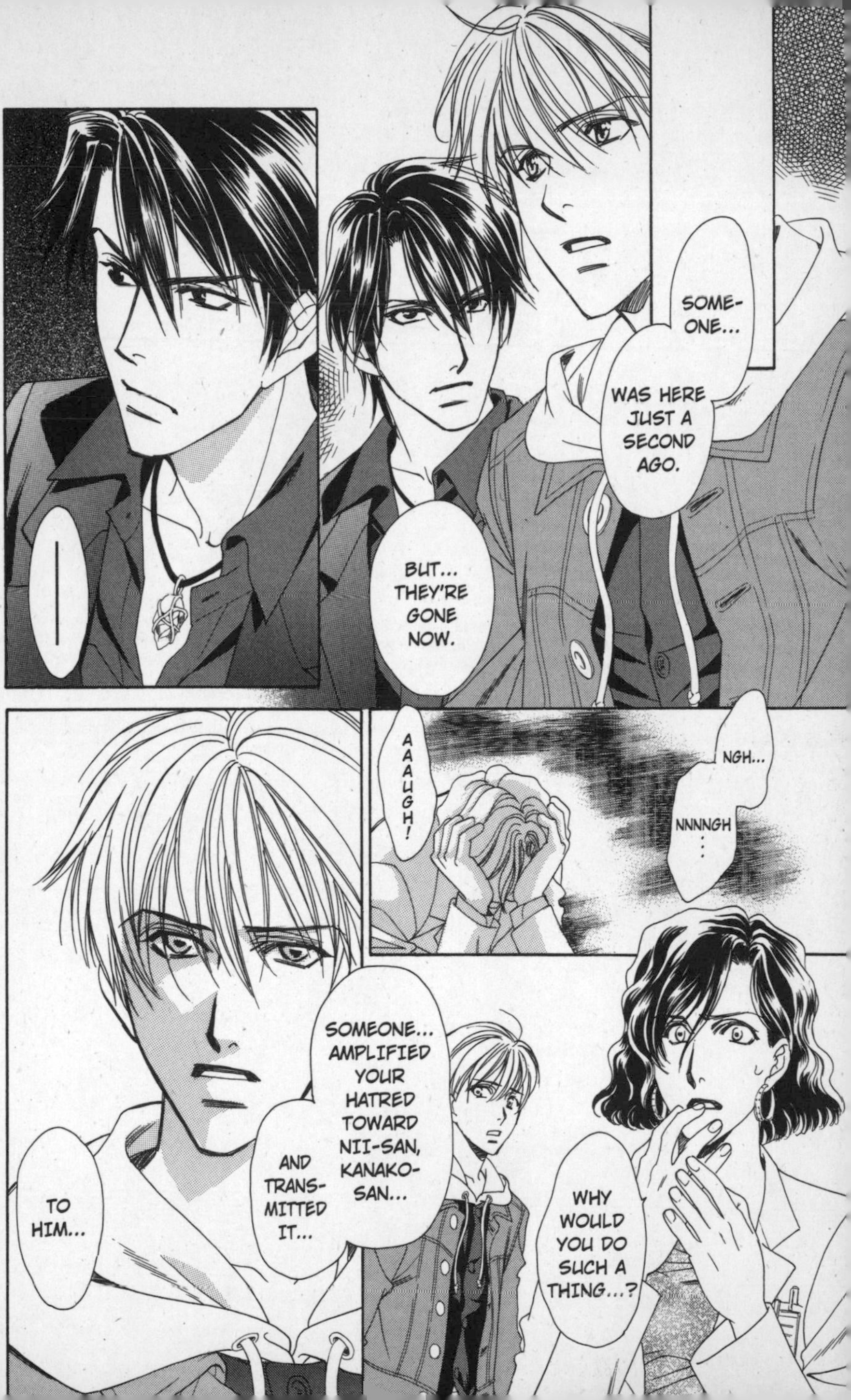
SOME-ONE...
WAS HERE JUST A SECOND AGO.
BUT... THEY'RE GONE NOW.
—
NGH...
NNNNGH...
AAAAUGH!
WHY WOULD YOU DO SUCH A THING...?
SOMEONE... AMPLIFIED YOUR HATRED TOWARD NII-SAN, KANAKO-SAN...
AND TRANS-MITTED IT...
TO HIM...

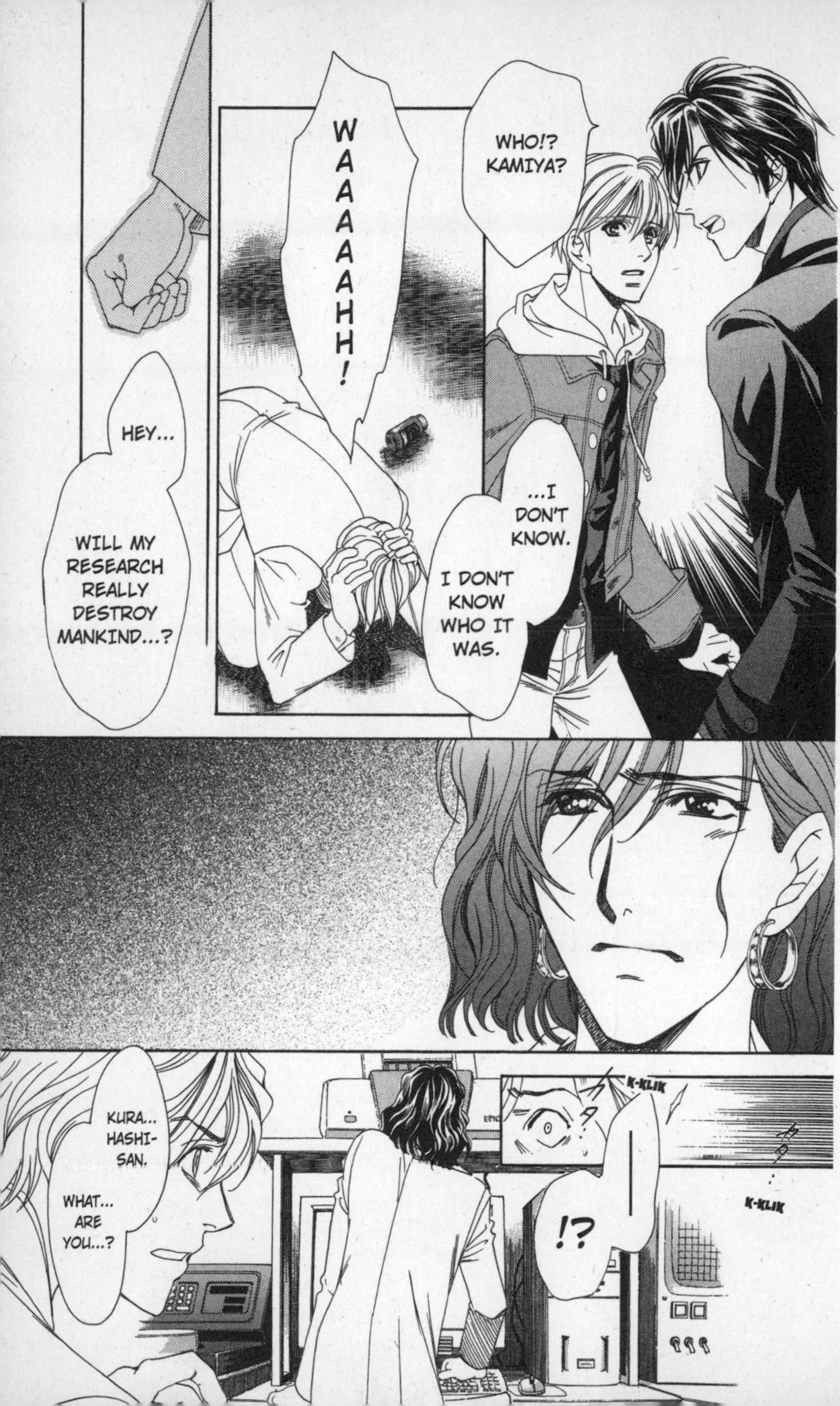
WHO!? KAMIYA?
...I DON'T KNOW.
I DON'T KNOW WHO IT WAS.
WAAAAAAAHH!
HEY...
WILL MY RESEARCH REALLY DESTROY MANKIND...?
K-KLIK
!?
K-KLIK
KURA... HASHI-SAN.
WHAT... ARE YOU...?

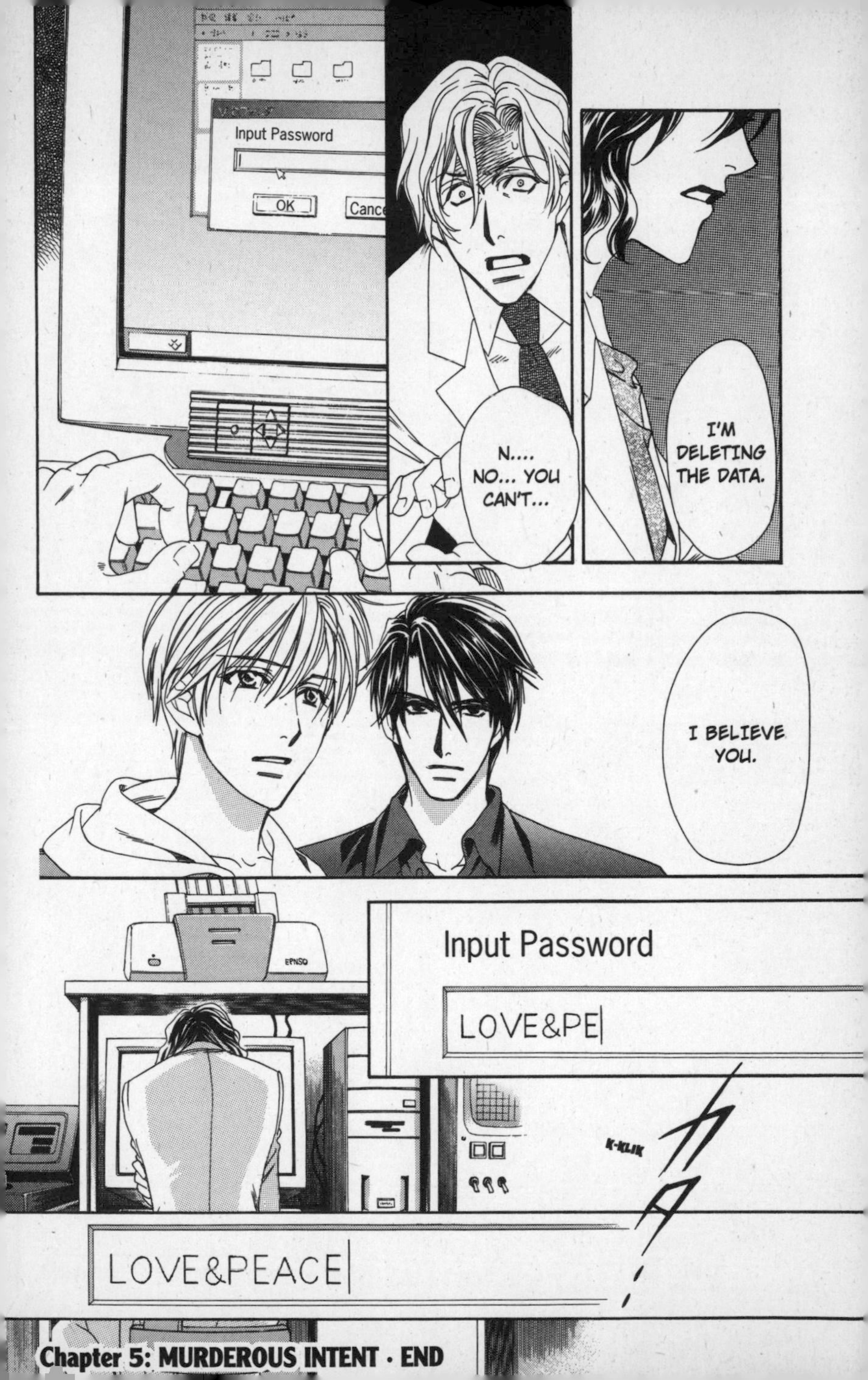
I'M DELETING THE DATA.
N.... NO... YOU CAN'T...
Input Password
OK
Cance
I BELIEVE YOU.
Input Password
LOVE&PE
K-KLIK
EPNSO
LOVE&PEACE

Chapter 5: MURDEROUS INTENT · END

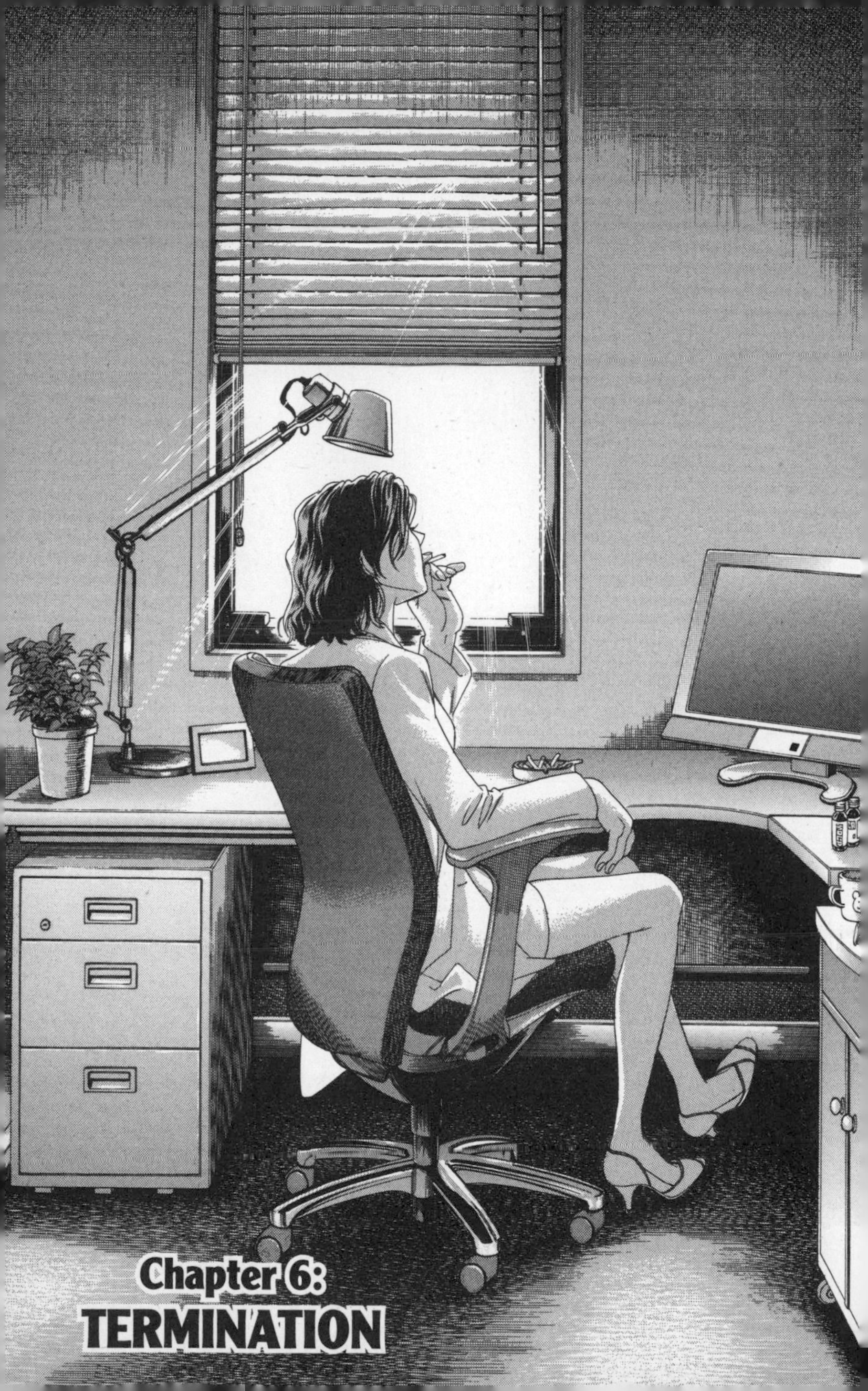

Chapter 6: TERMINATION

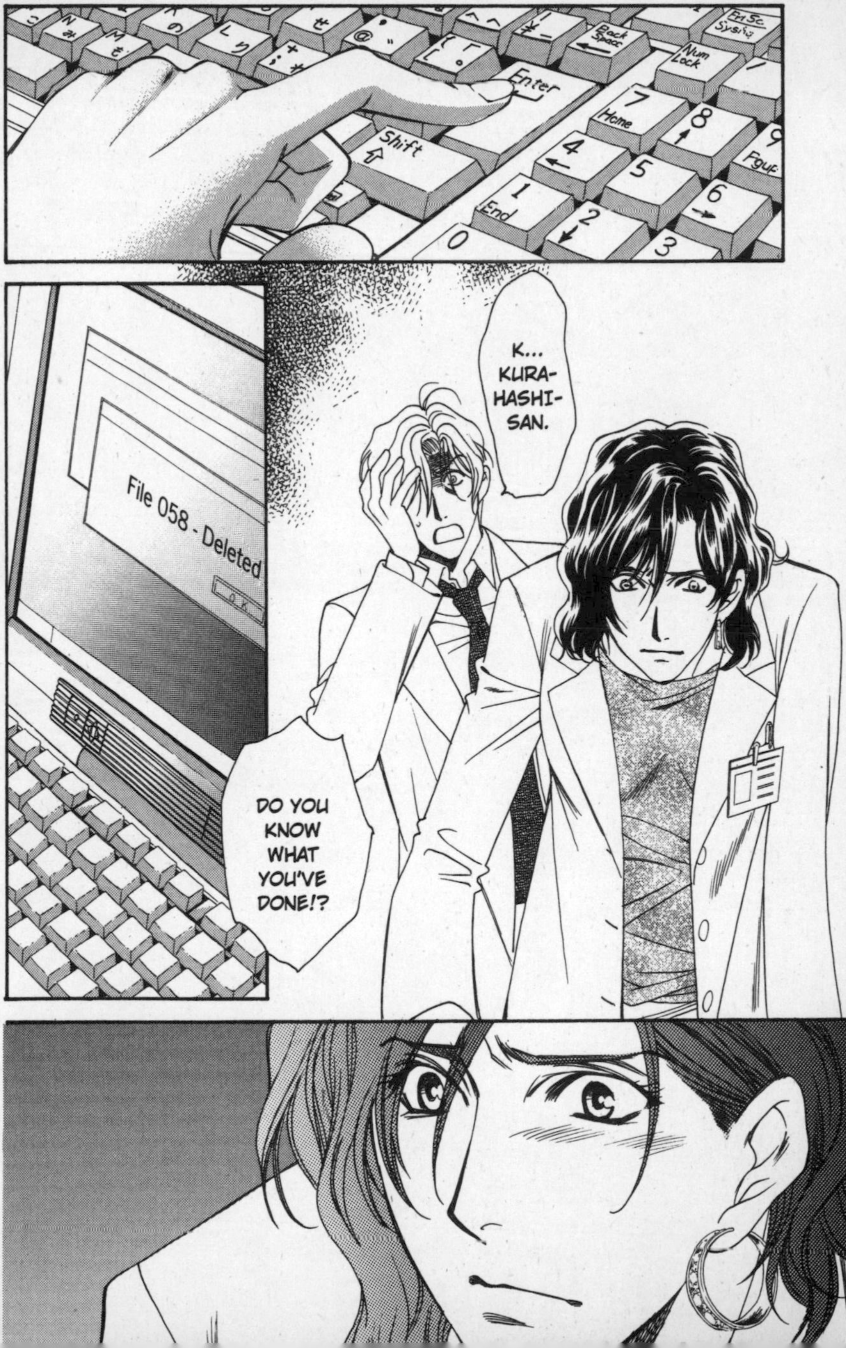
K... KURA-HASHI-SAN.
File 058 - Deleted
DO YOU KNOW WHAT YOU'VE DONE!?

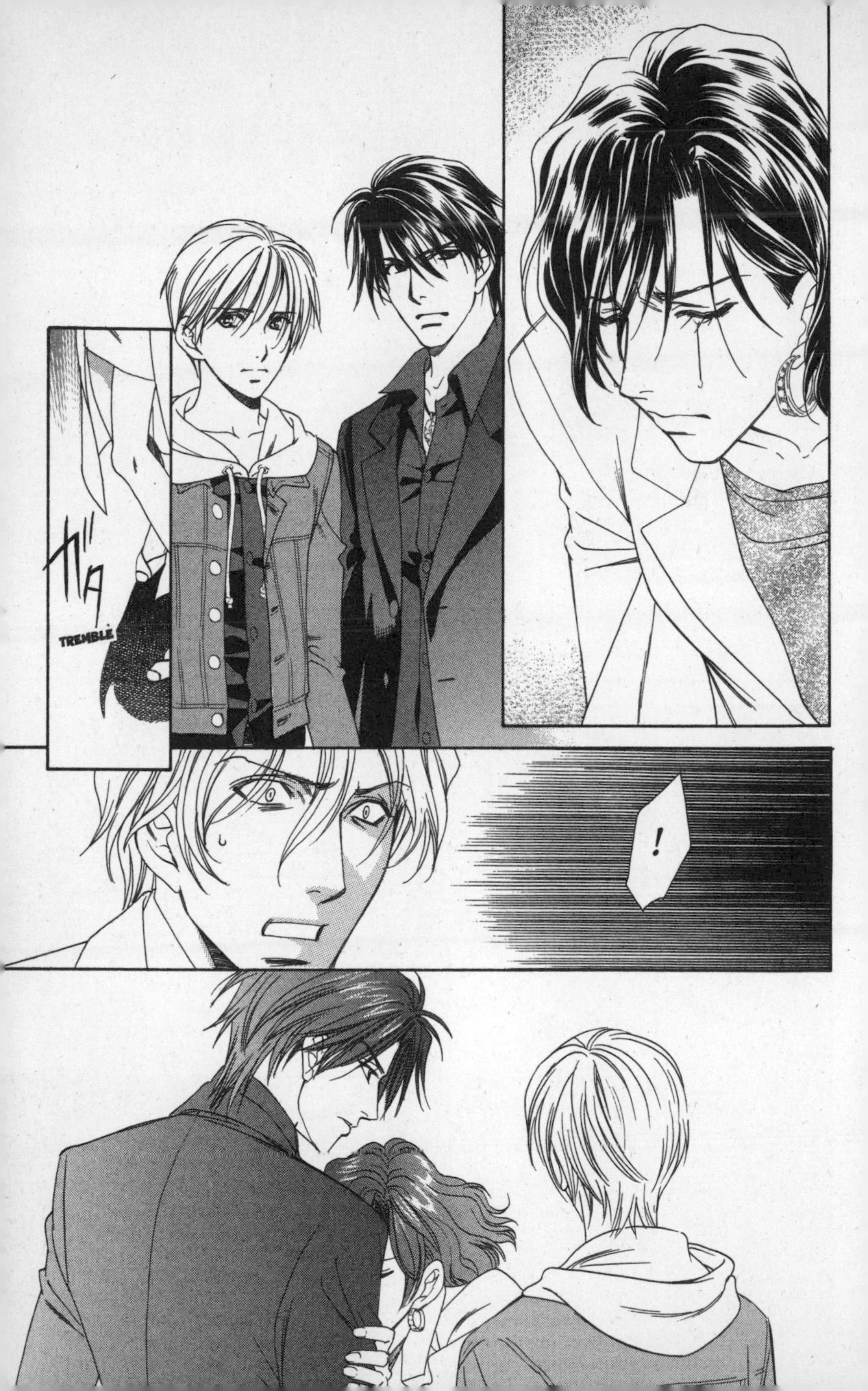

ガタ
TREMBLE
!

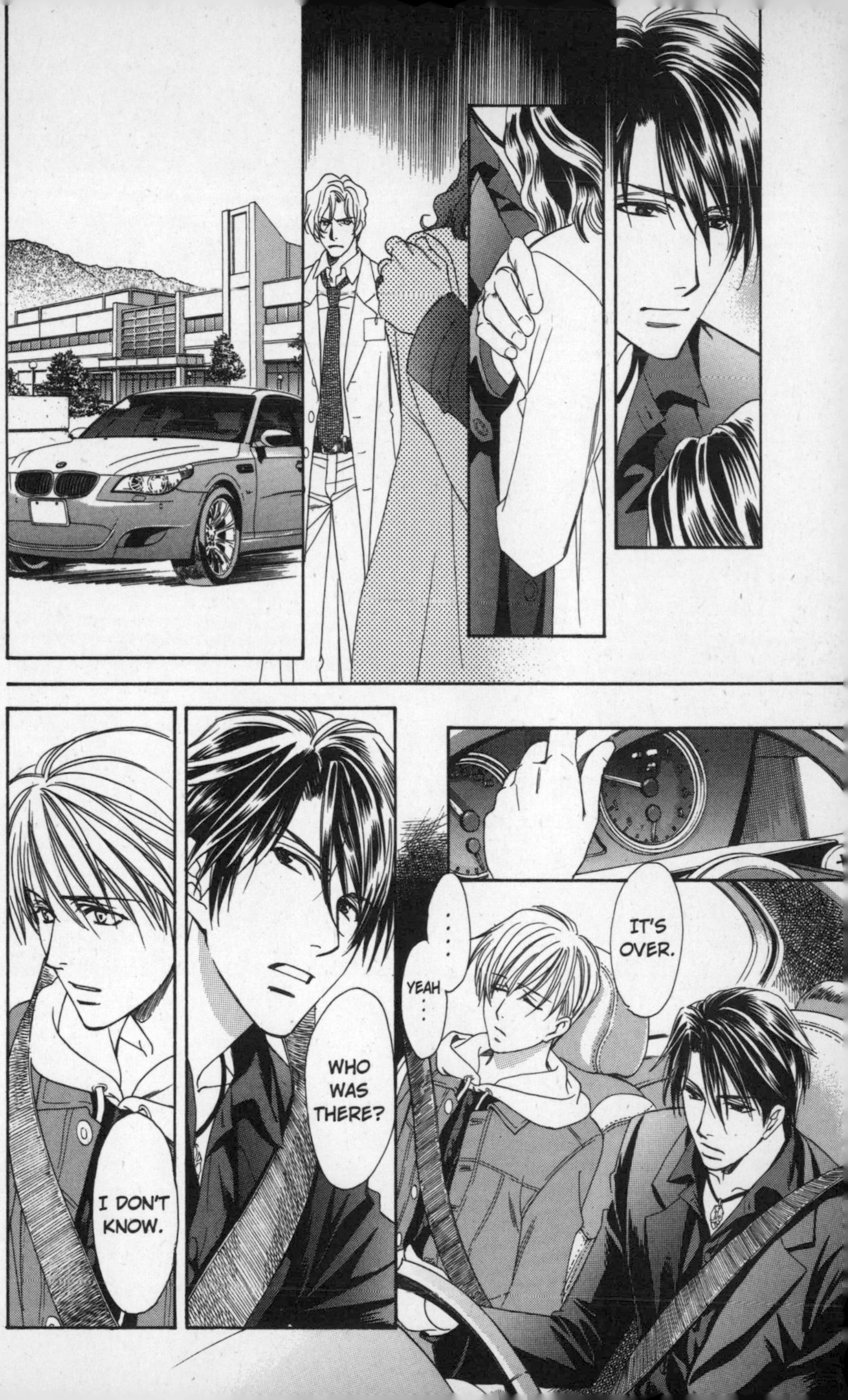
IT'S OVER.
....YEAH...
WHO WAS THERE?
I DON'T KNOW.

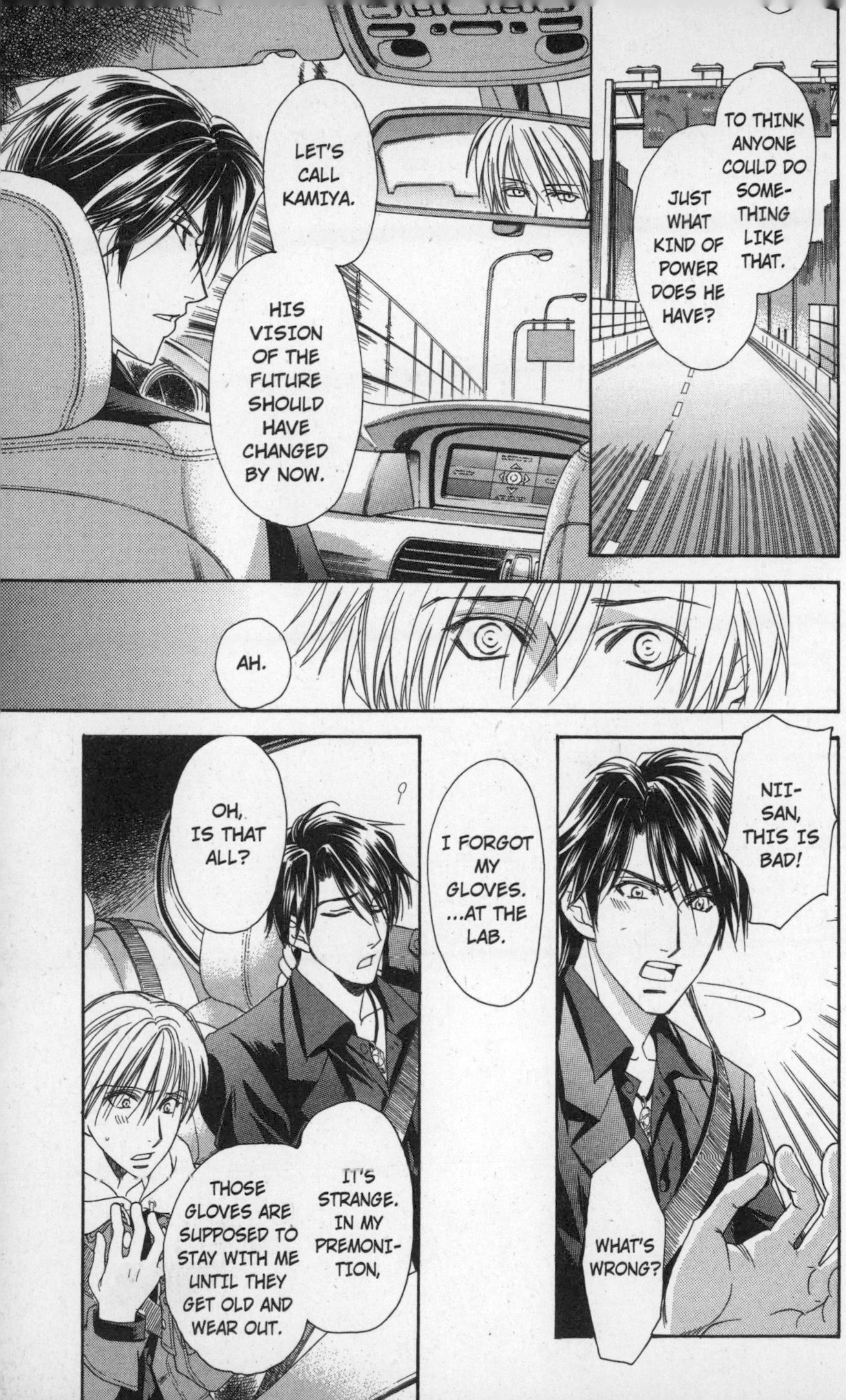
TO THINK ANYONE COULD DO SOME-THING LIKE THAT.
JUST WHAT KIND OF POWER DOES HE HAVE?
LET'S CALL KAMIYA.
HIS VISION OF THE FUTURE SHOULD HAVE CHANGED BY NOW.
AH.
NII-SAN, THIS IS BAD!
WHAT'S WRONG?
I FORGOT MY GLOVES. ...AT THE LAB.
OH, IS THAT ALL?
IT'S STRANGE. IN MY PREMONI-TION,
THOSE GLOVES ARE SUPPOSED TO STAY WITH ME UNTIL THEY GET OLD AND WEAR OUT.

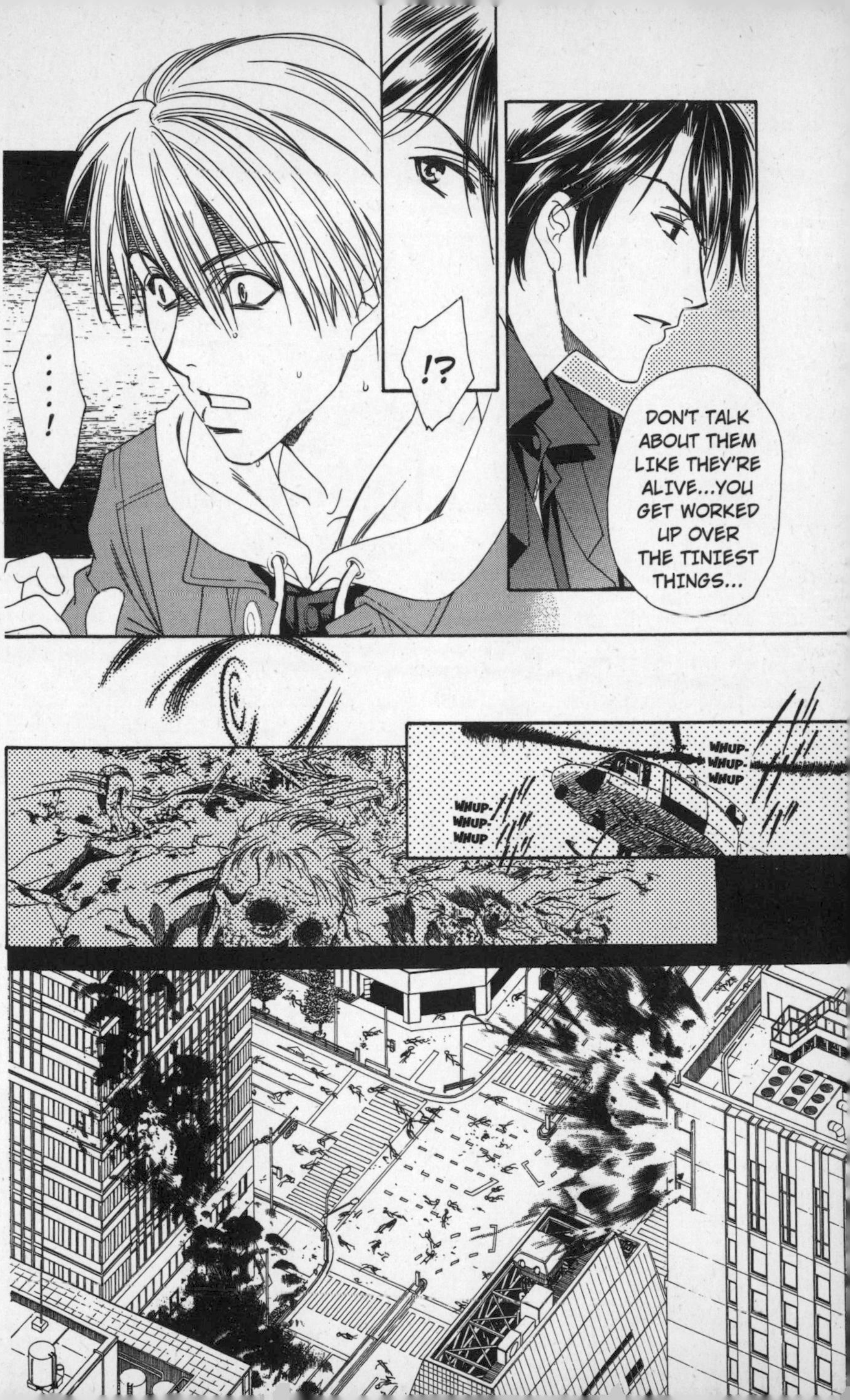
DON'T TALK ABOUT THEM LIKE THEY'RE ALIVE...YOU GET WORKED UP OVER THE TINIEST THINGS...
!?
....!
WHUP-WHUP-WHUP
WHUP-WHUP-WHUP

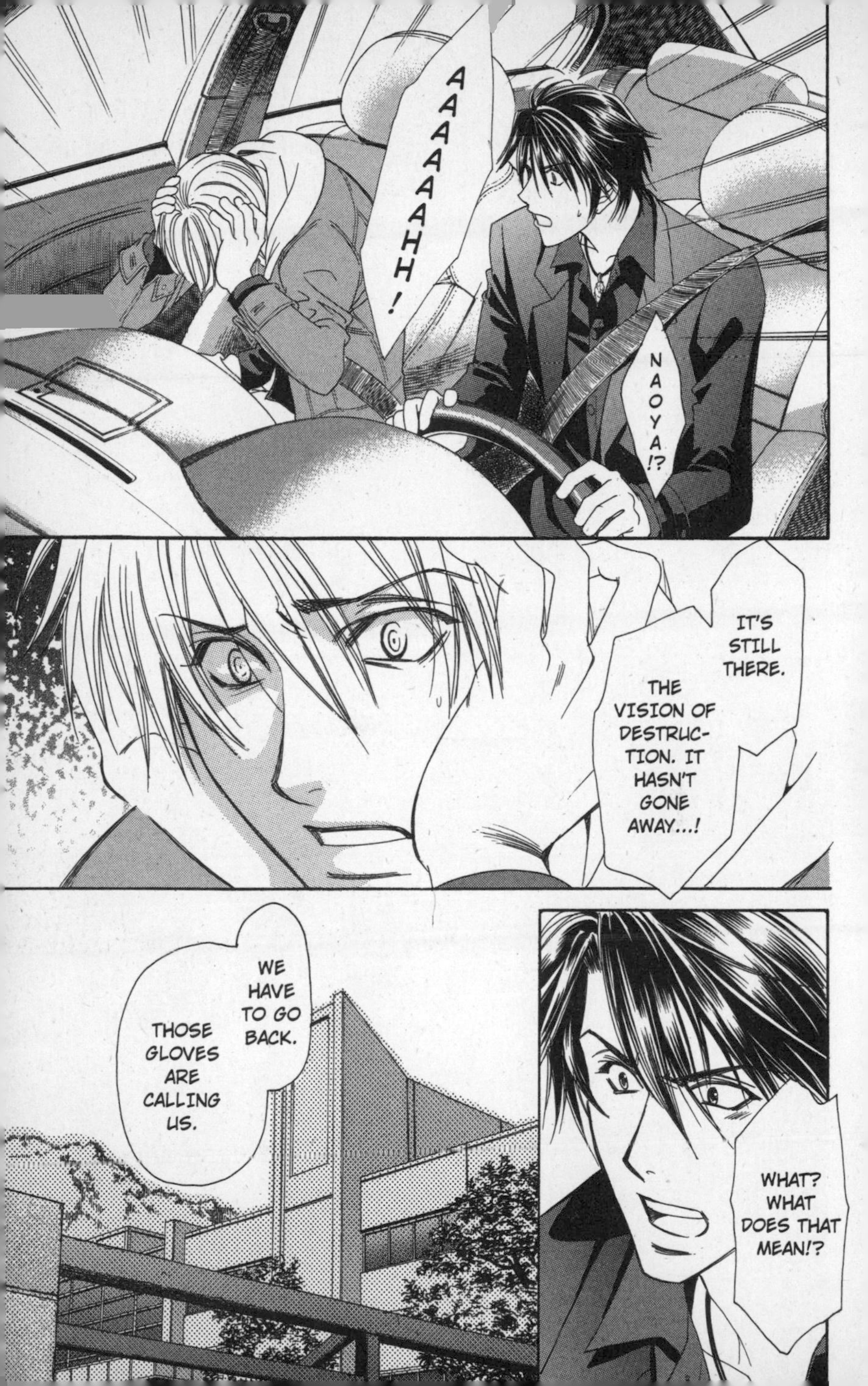
AAAAAAAAH!
NAOYA!?
IT'S STILL THERE.
THE VISION OF DESTRUCTION. IT HASN'T GONE AWAY...!
WHAT? WHAT DOES THAT MEAN!?
WE HAVE TO GO BACK.
THOSE GLOVES ARE CALLING US.

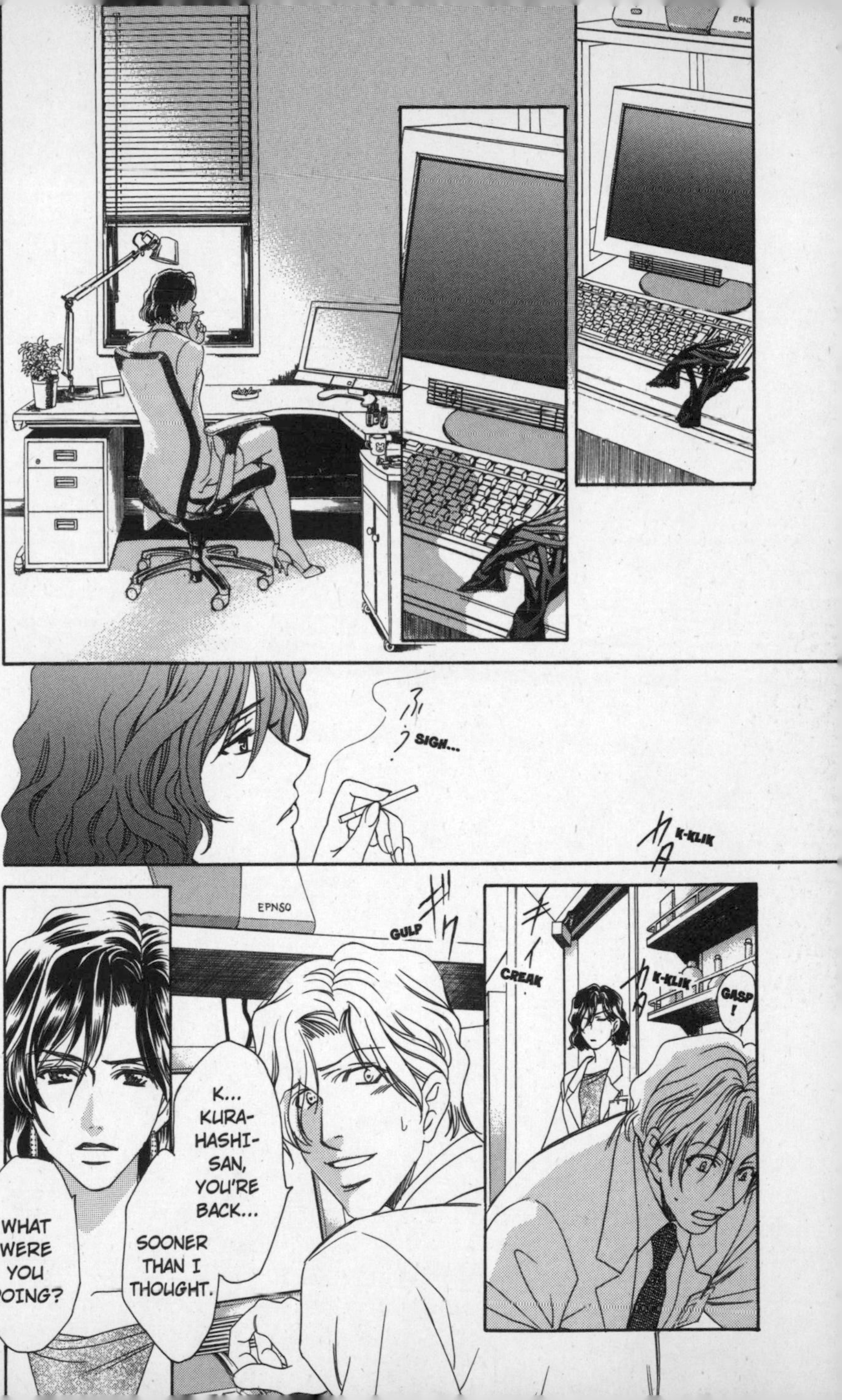
SIGH...
K-KLIK
CREAK
K-KLIK
GASP!
EPNSO
GULP
K... KURA-HASHI-SAN, YOU'RE BACK...
SOONER THAN I THOUGHT.
WHAT WERE YOU DOING?

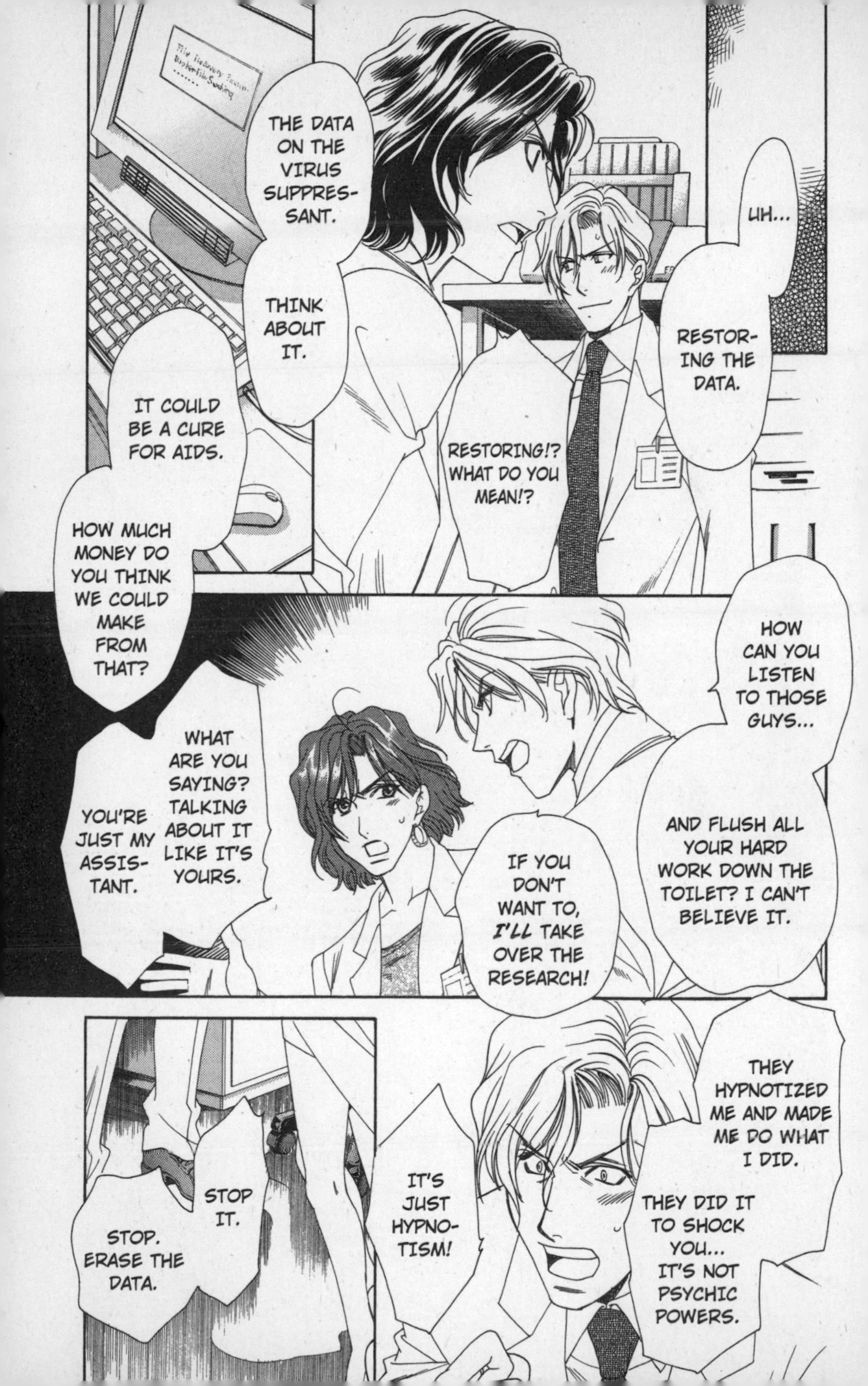
UH...
RESTORING THE DATA.
RESTORING!? WHAT DO YOU MEAN!?
THE DATA ON THE VIRUS SUPPRES-SANT.
THINK ABOUT IT.
IT COULD BE A CURE FOR AIDS.
HOW MUCH MONEY DO YOU THINK WE COULD MAKE FROM THAT?
HOW CAN YOU LISTEN TO THOSE GUYS...
AND FLUSH ALL YOUR HARD WORK DOWN THE TOILET? I CAN'T BELIEVE IT.
IF YOU DON'T WANT TO, *I'LL* TAKE OVER THE RESEARCH!
WHAT ARE YOU SAYING? TALKING ABOUT IT LIKE IT'S YOURS.
YOU'RE JUST MY ASSIS-TANT.
THEY HYPNOTIZED ME AND MADE ME DO WHAT I DID.
THEY DID IT TO SHOCK YOU... IT'S NOT PSYCHIC POWERS.
IT'S JUST HYPNO-TISM!
STOP IT.
STOP. ERASE THE DATA.

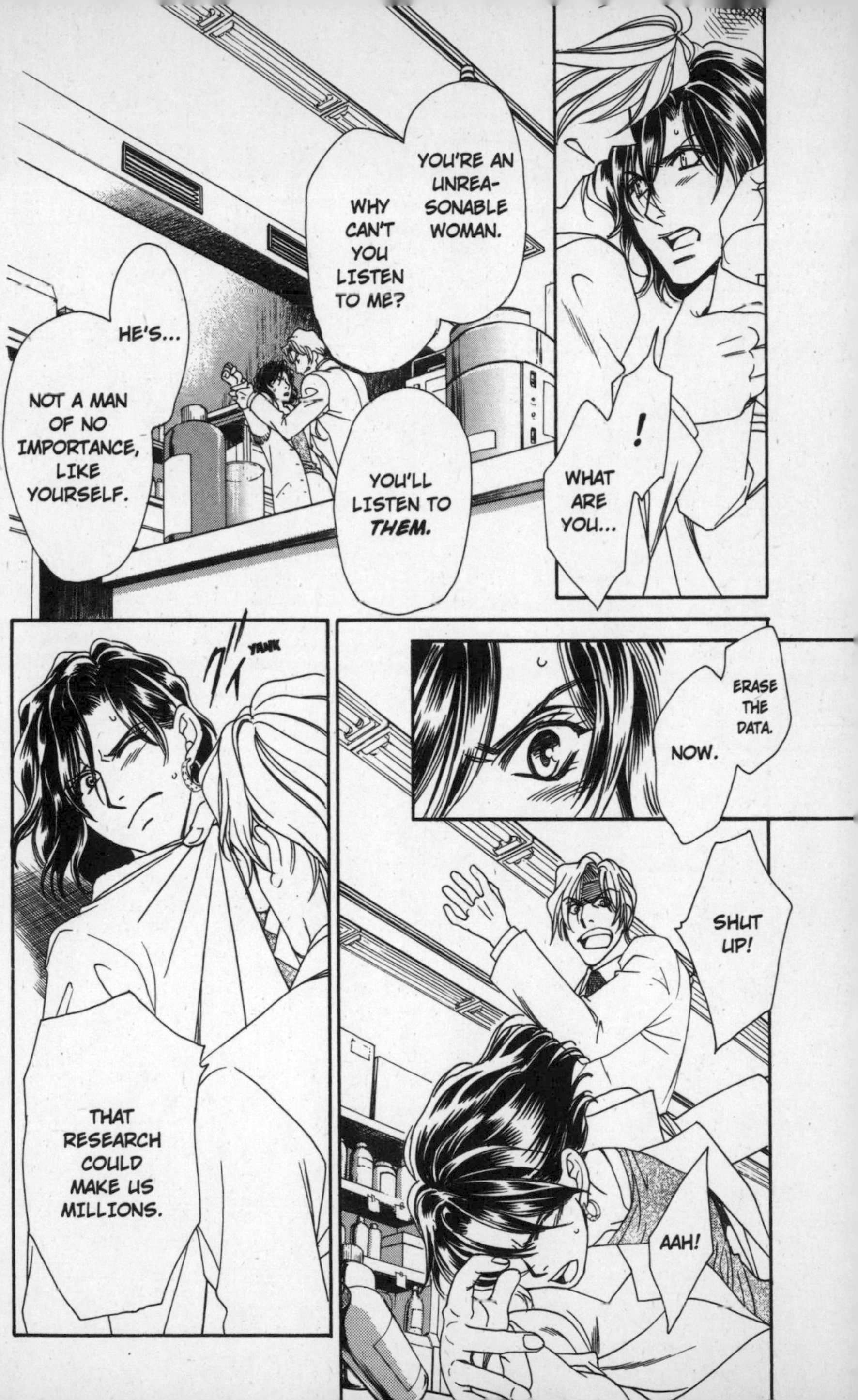
!
WHAT ARE YOU...
YOU'RE AN UNREA-SONABLE WOMAN. WHY CAN'T YOU LISTEN TO ME?
HE'S... NOT A MAN OF NO IMPORTANCE, LIKE YOURSELF.
YOU'LL LISTEN TO *THEM.*
ERASE THE DATA. NOW.
SHUT UP!
AAH!
YANK
THAT RESEARCH COULD MAKE US MILLIONS.

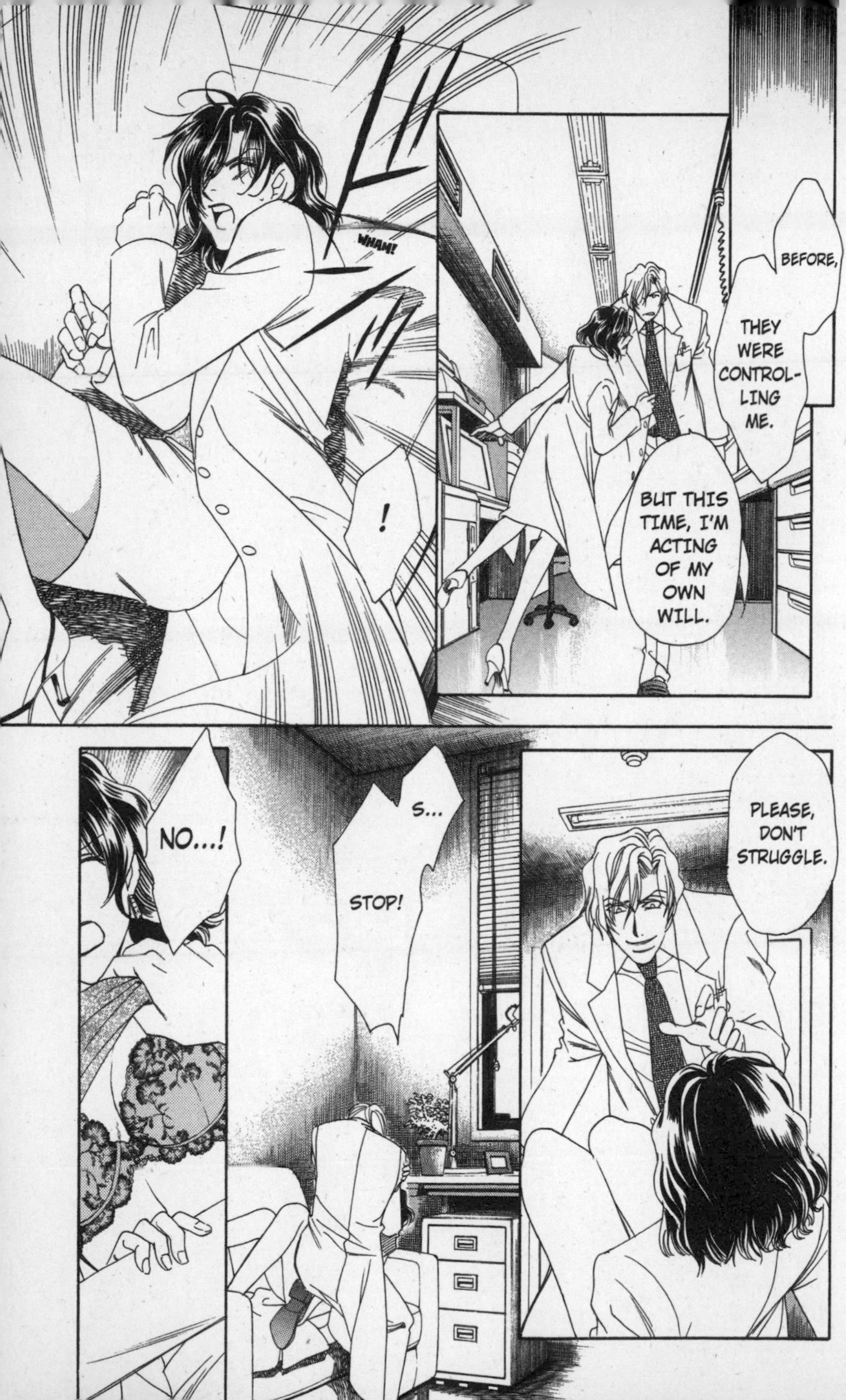
BEFORE,
THEY WERE CONTROLLING ME.
BUT THIS TIME, I'M ACTING OF MY OWN WILL.
WHAM!
!
PLEASE, DON'T STRUGGLE.
S...
STOP!
NO...!

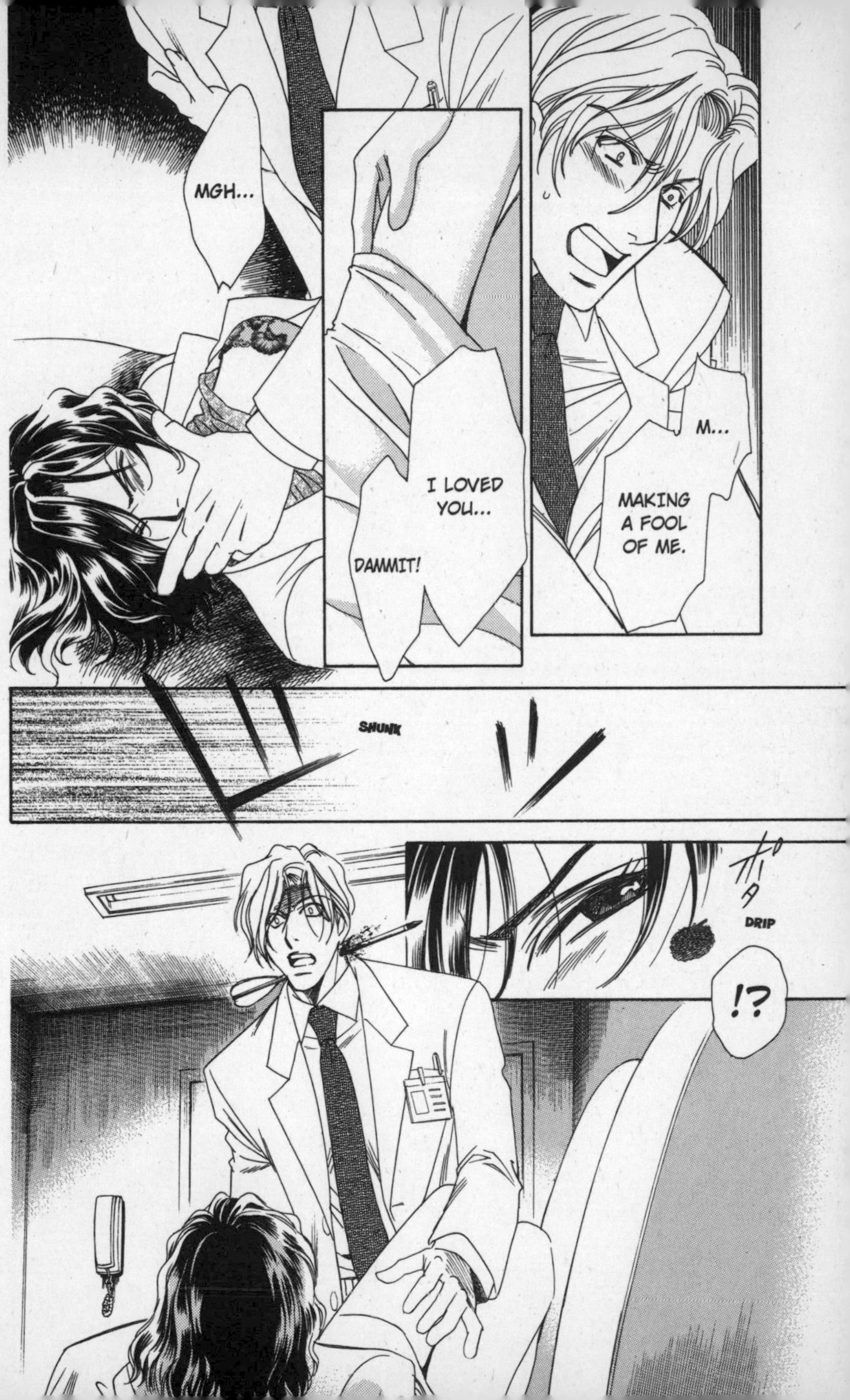
M...
MAKING A FOOL OF ME.
I LOVED YOU...
DAMMIT!
MGH...
SHUNK
DRIP
!?

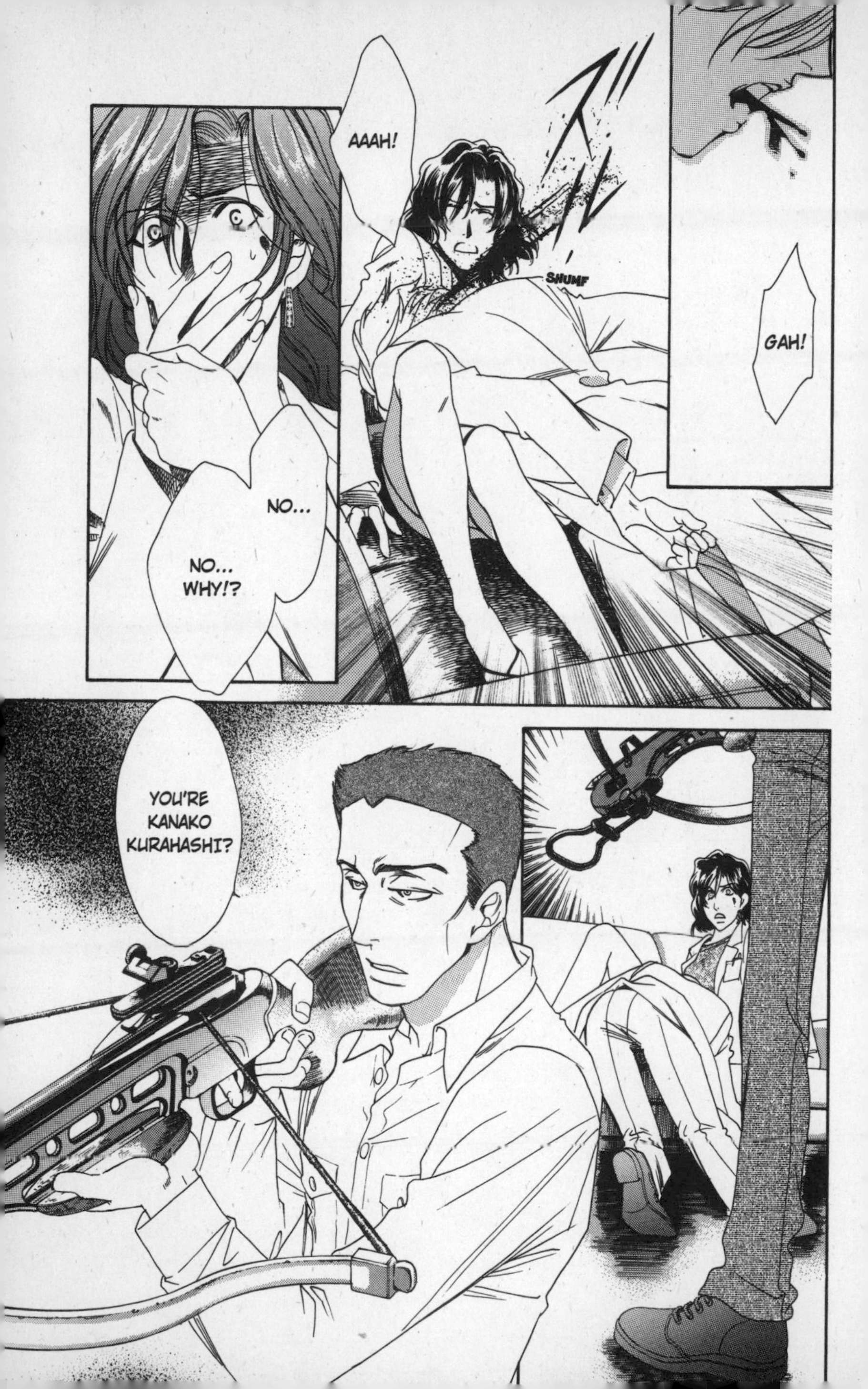
GAH!
AAAH!
SHUMF
NO...
NO... WHY!?
YOU'RE KANAKO KURAHASHI?

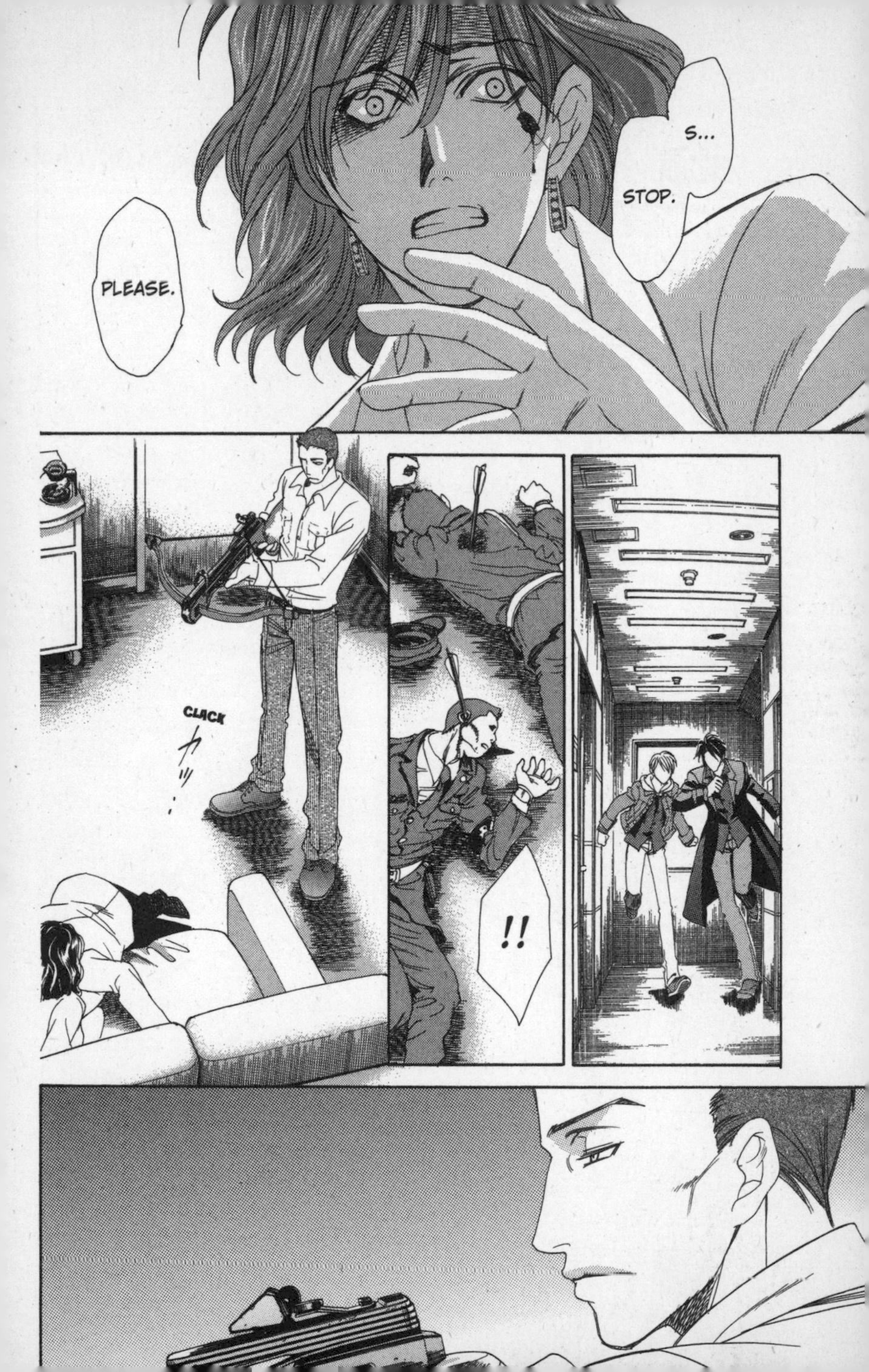
S...
STOP.
PLEASE.
!!
CLACK
カッ…

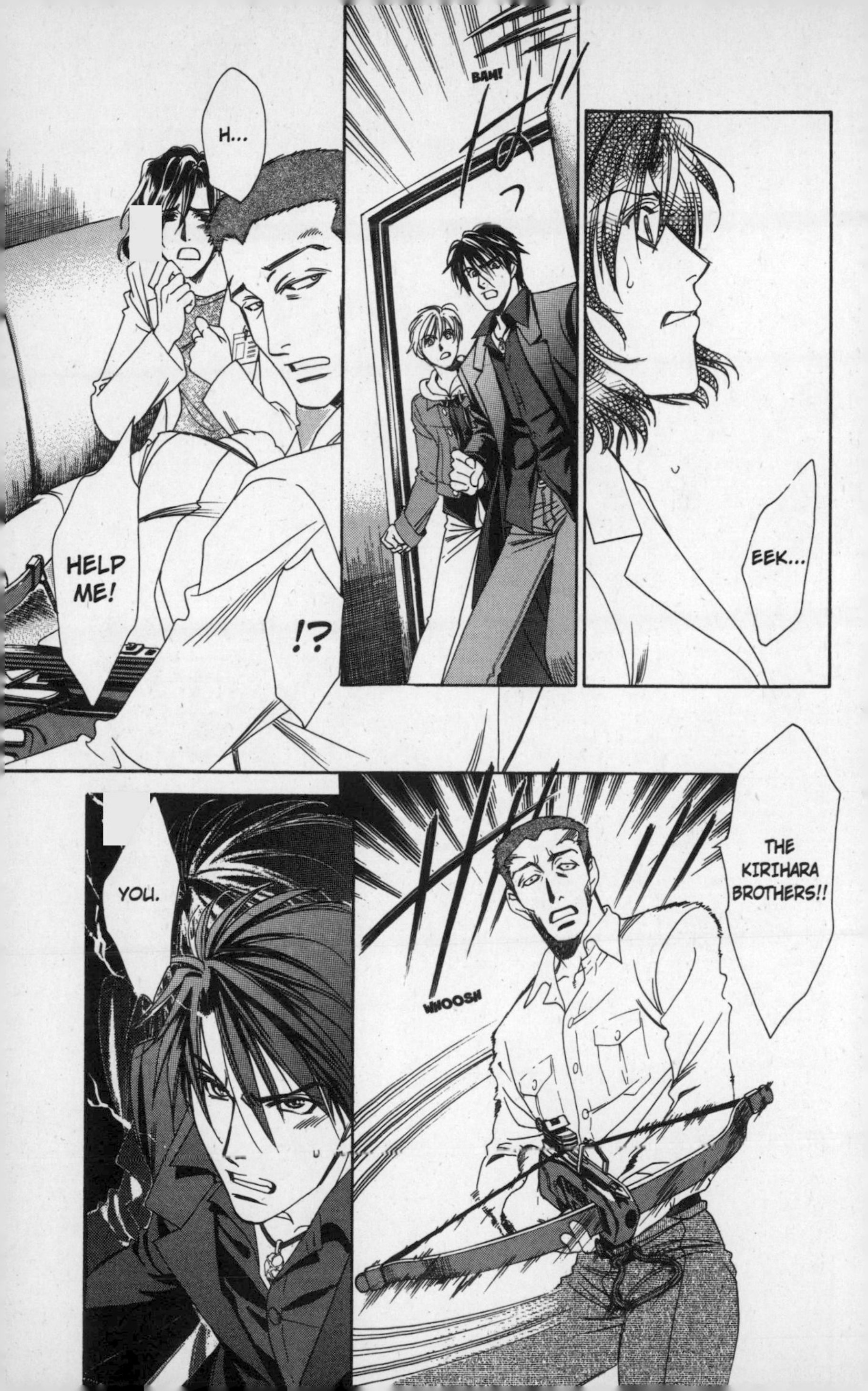
EEK...
BAM!
H...
HELP ME!
!?
THE KIRIHARA BROTHERS!!
WHOOSH
YOU.

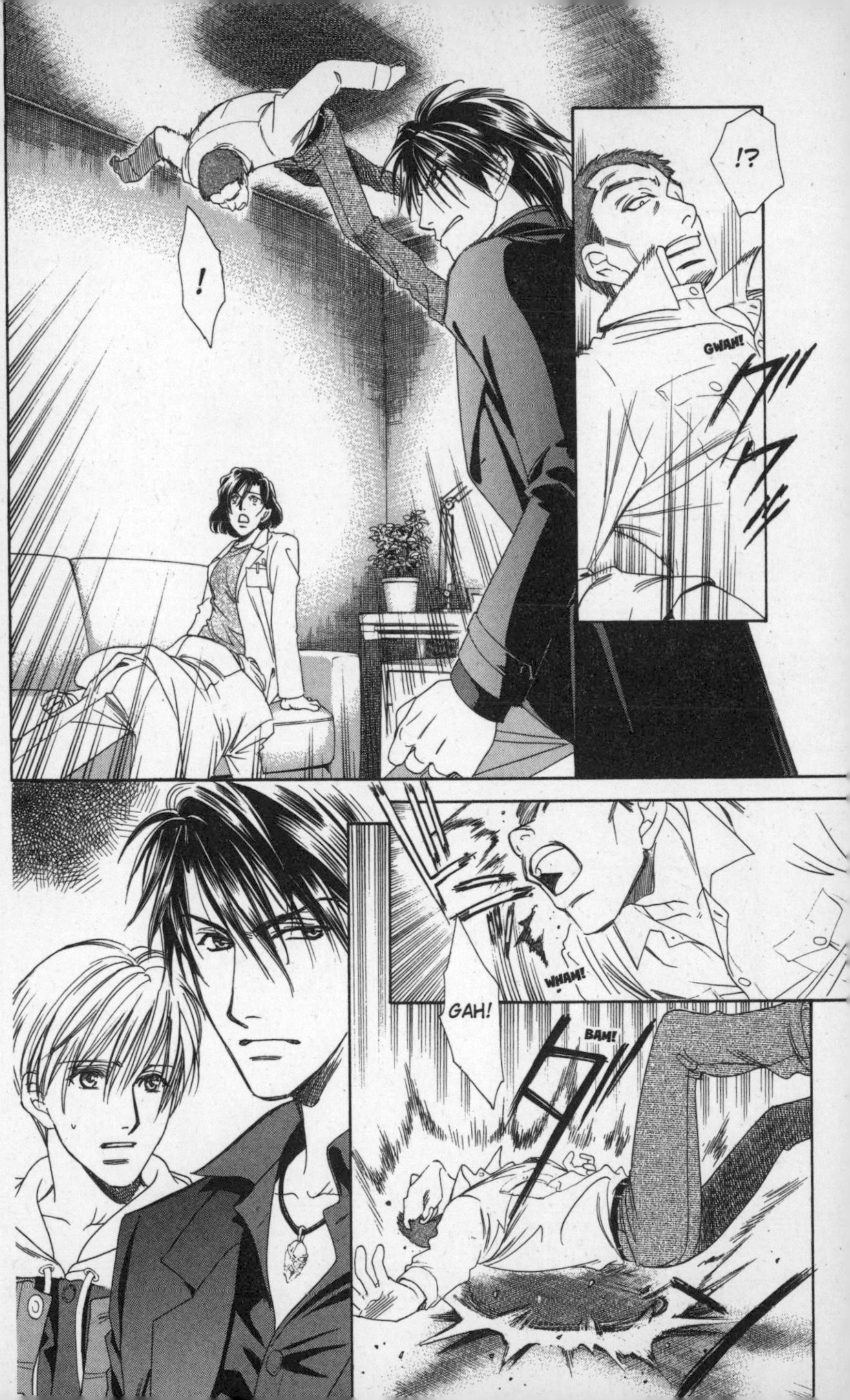
!?
GWAH!
!
WHAM!
GAH!
BAM!

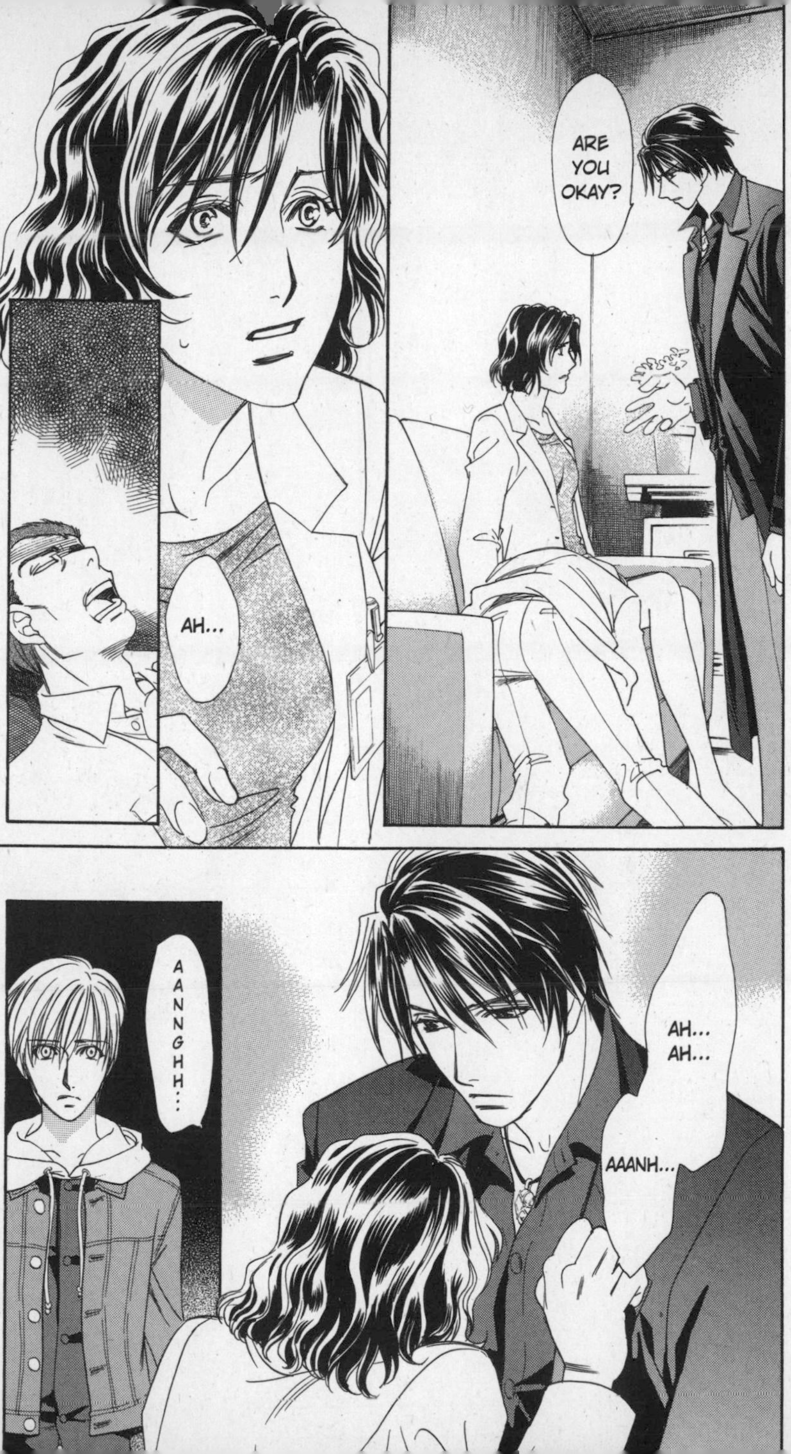
ARE YOU OKAY?
AH...
AH... AH...
AAANH...
AANNGHH...

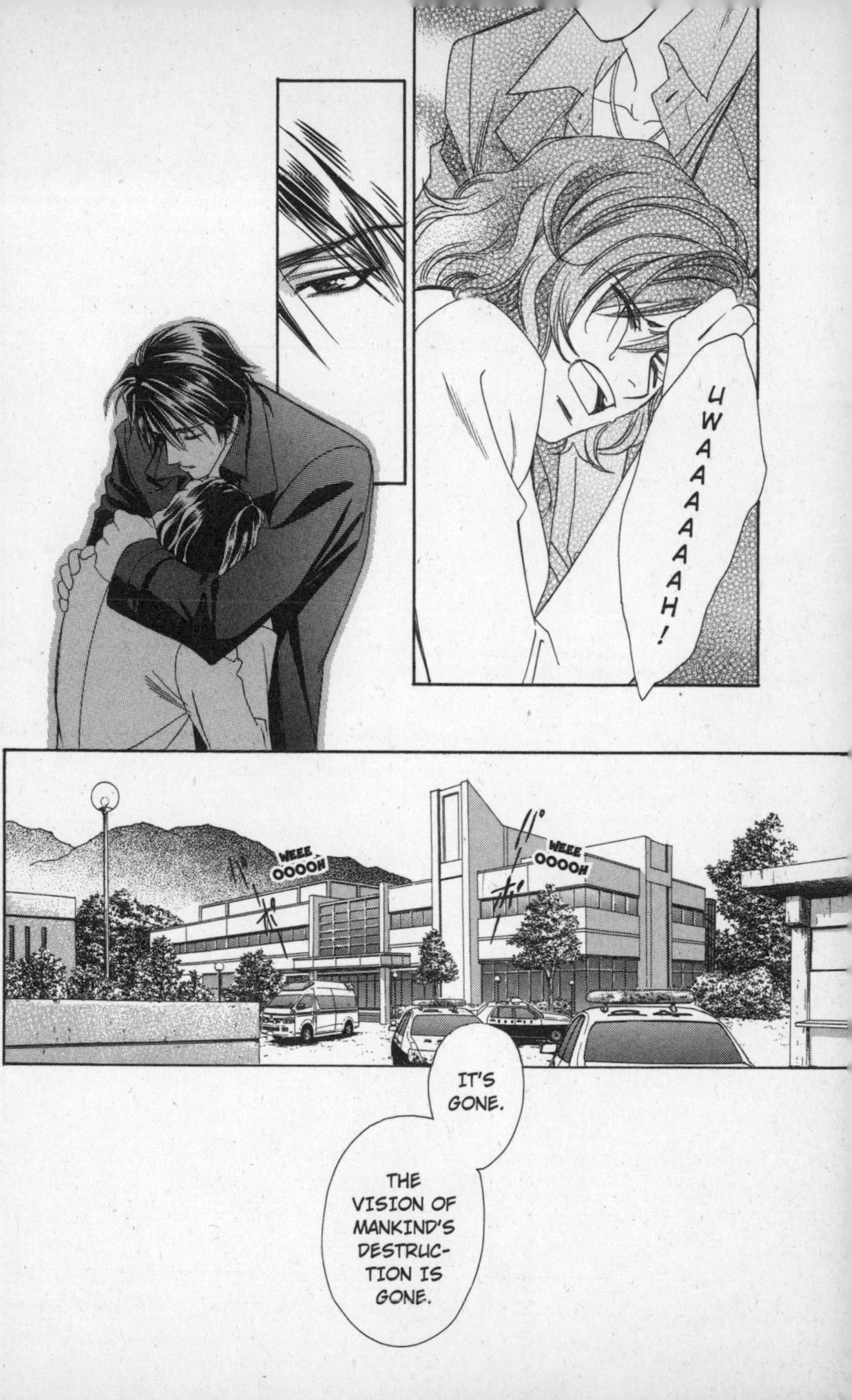
UWAAAAAAAH!
WEEE OOOOH
WEEE OOOOH
IT'S GONE.
THE VISION OF MANKIND'S DESTRUCTION IS GONE.

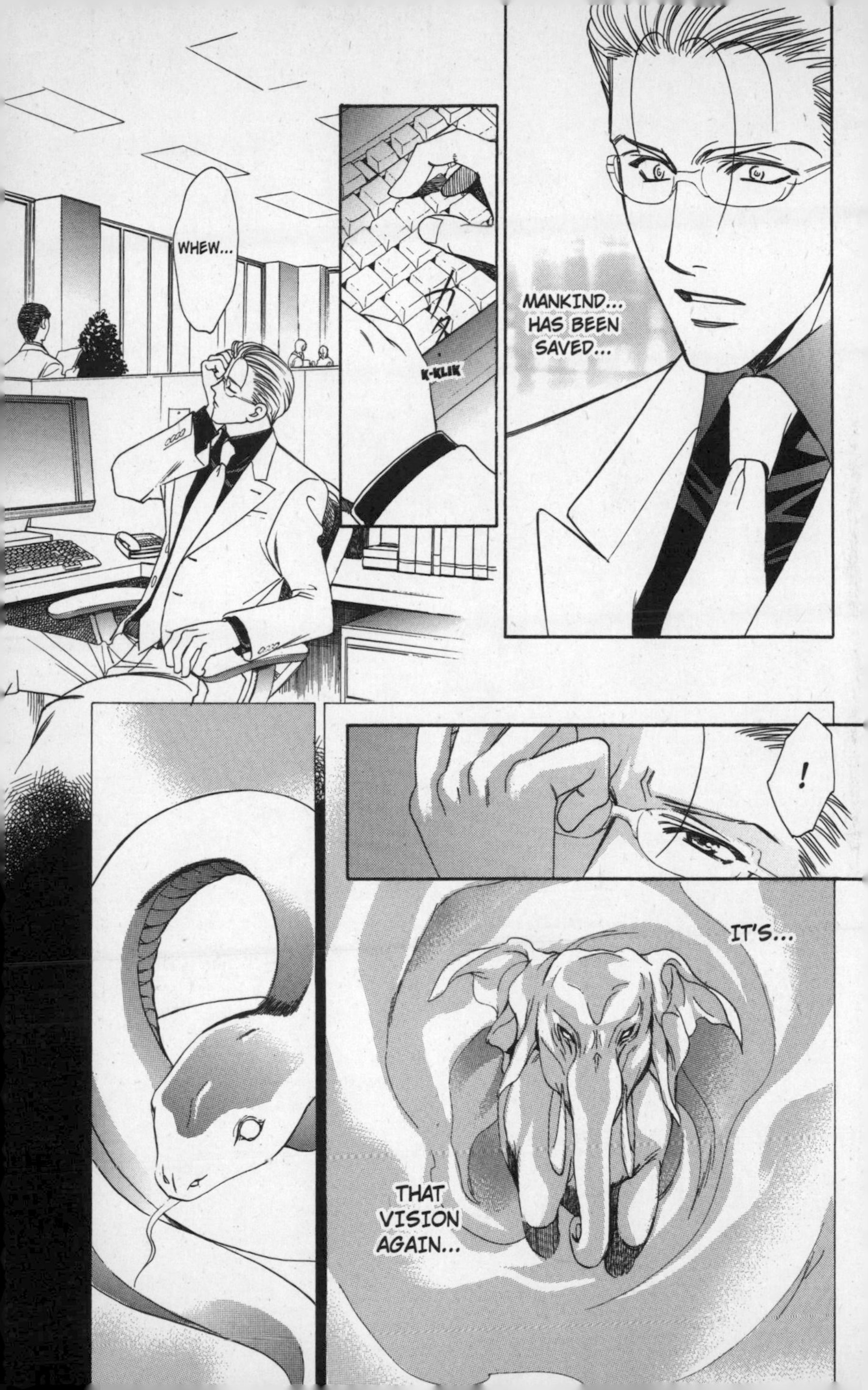
MANKIND... HAS BEEN SAVED...
K-KLIK
WHEW...
!
IT'S...
THAT VISION AGAIN...

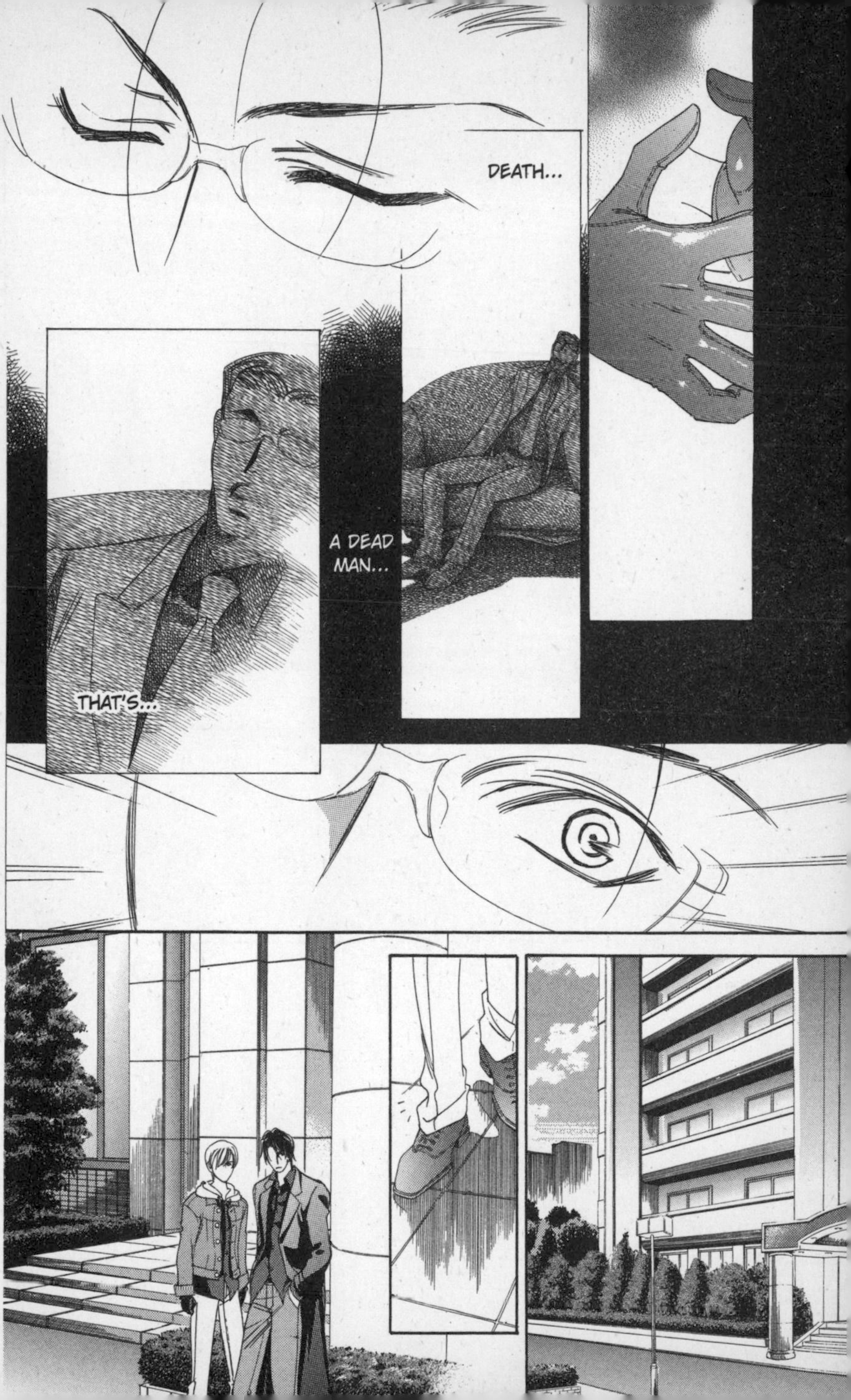
DEATH...
A DEAD MAN...
THAT'S...

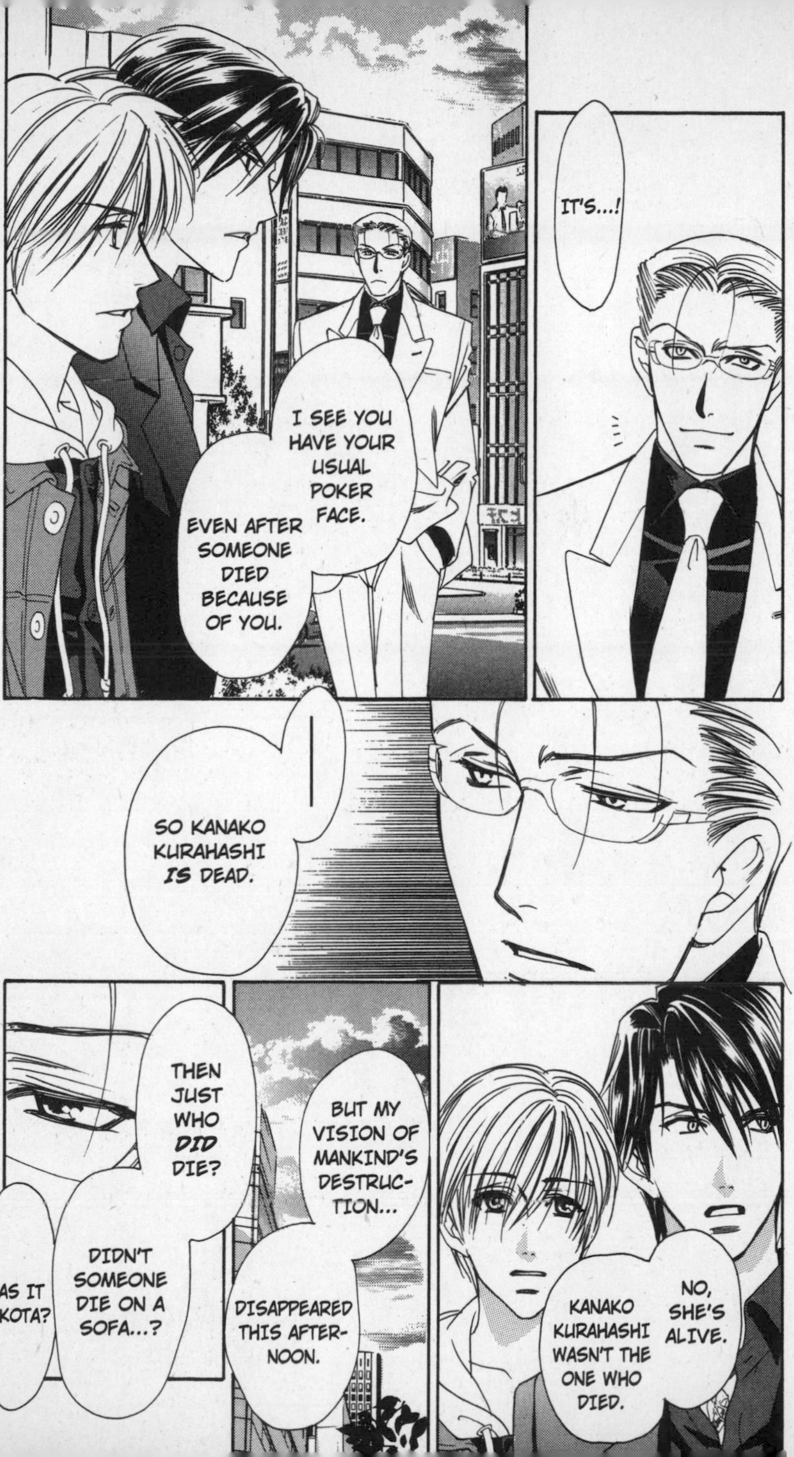
IT'S...!
I SEE YOU HAVE YOUR USUAL POKER FACE.
EVEN AFTER SOMEONE DIED BECAUSE OF YOU.
—
SO KANAKO KURAHASHI *IS* DEAD.
NO, SHE'S ALIVE.
KANAKO KURAHASHI WASN'T THE ONE WHO DIED.
BUT MY VISION OF MANKIND'S DESTRUCTION...
DISAPPEARED THIS AFTERNOON.
THEN JUST WHO *DID* DIE?
DIDN'T SOMEONE DIE ON A SOFA...?
WAS IT SAKOTA?

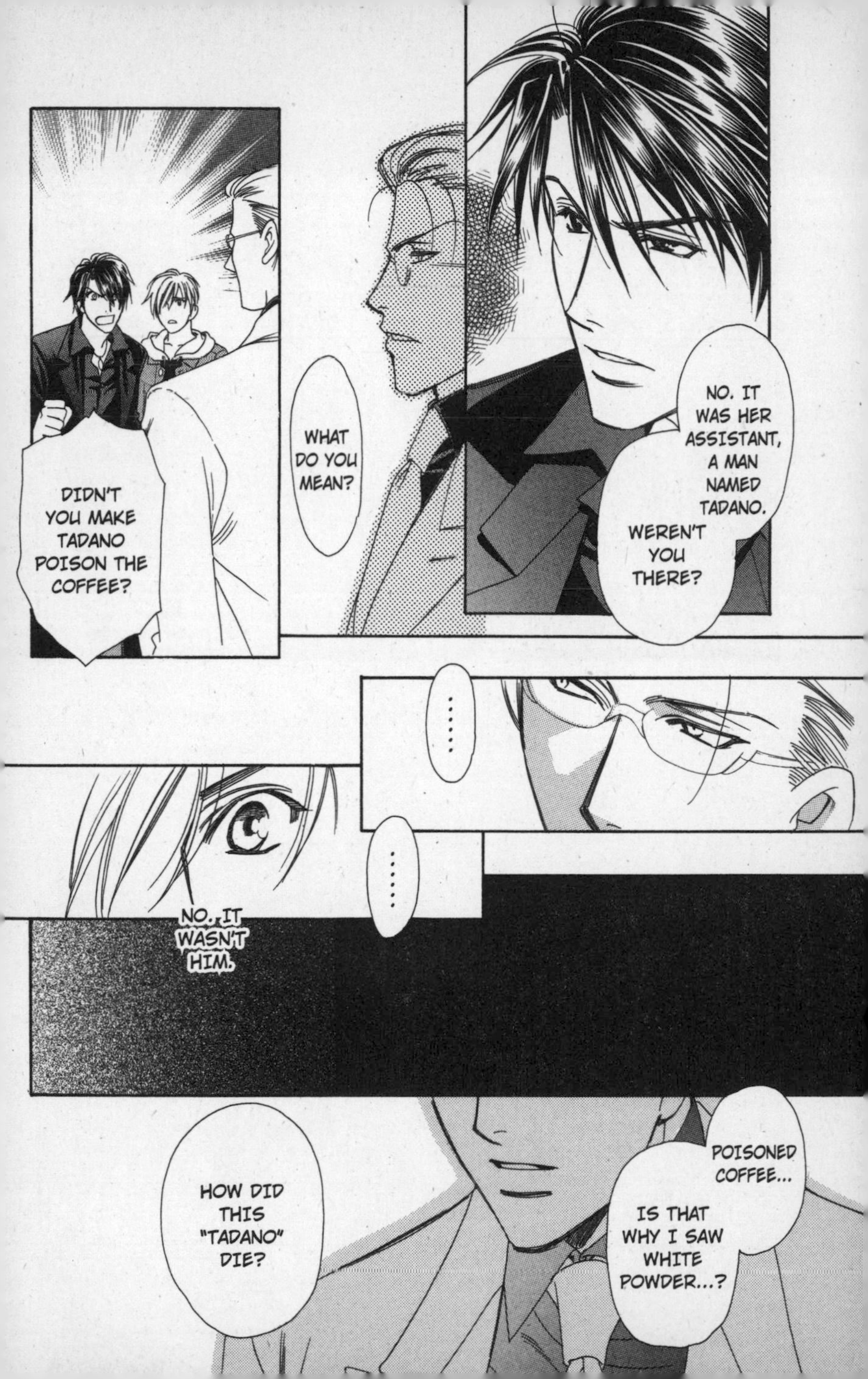
NO. IT WAS HER ASSISTANT, A MAN NAMED TADANO.
WEREN'T YOU THERE?
WHAT DO YOU MEAN?
DIDN'T YOU MAKE TADANO POISON THE COFFEE?
......
......
NO. IT WASN'T HIM.
POISONED COFFEE...
IS THAT WHY I SAW WHITE POWDER...?
HOW DID THIS "TADANO" DIE?

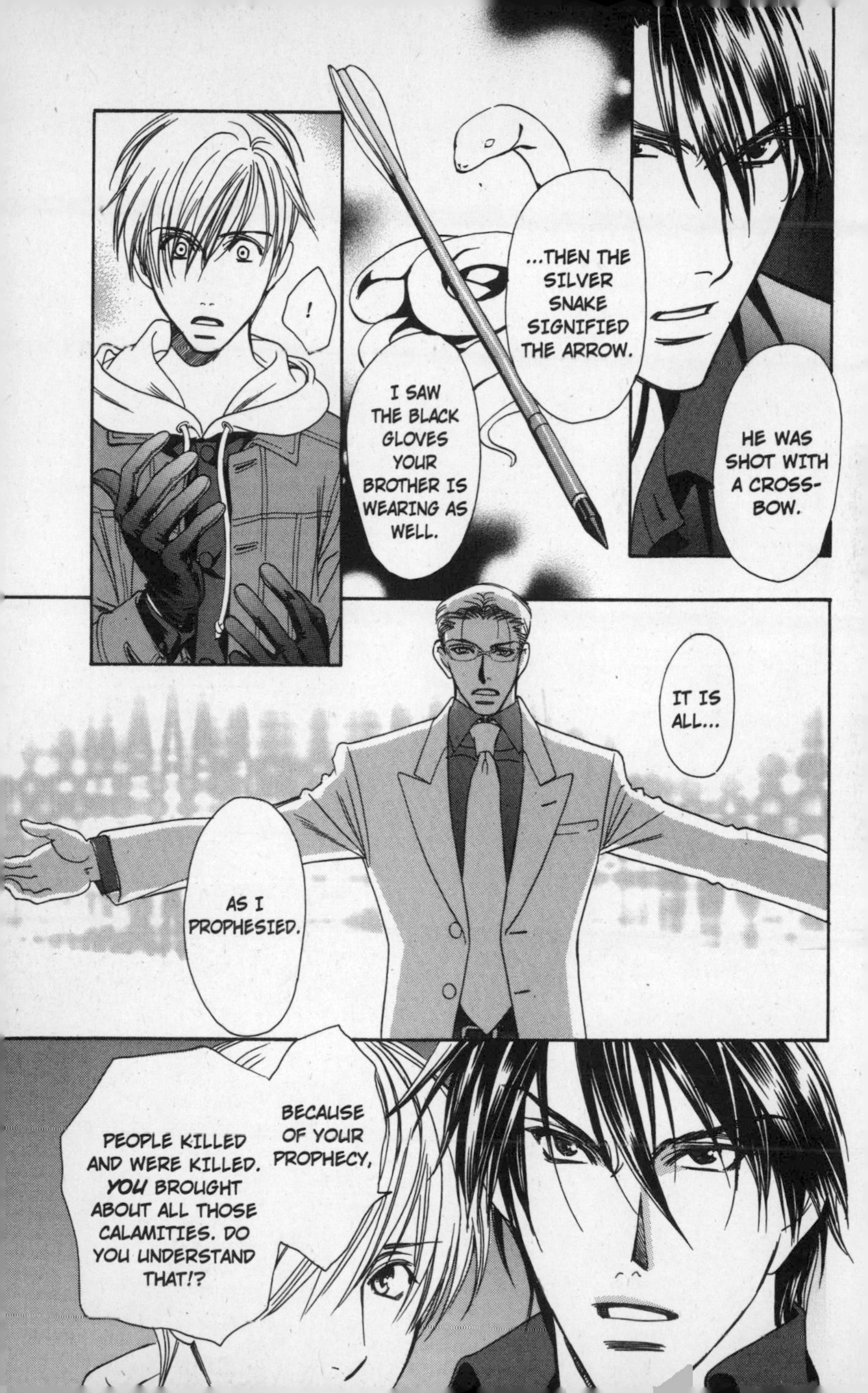
...THEN THE SILVER SNAKE SIGNIFIED THE ARROW.
HE WAS SHOT WITH A CROSS-BOW.
!
I SAW THE BLACK GLOVES YOUR BROTHER IS WEARING AS WELL.
IT IS ALL...
AS I PROPHESIED.
BECAUSE OF YOUR PROPHECY,
PEOPLE KILLED AND WERE KILLED. *YOU* BROUGHT ABOUT ALL THOSE CALAMITIES. DO YOU UNDERSTAND THAT!?

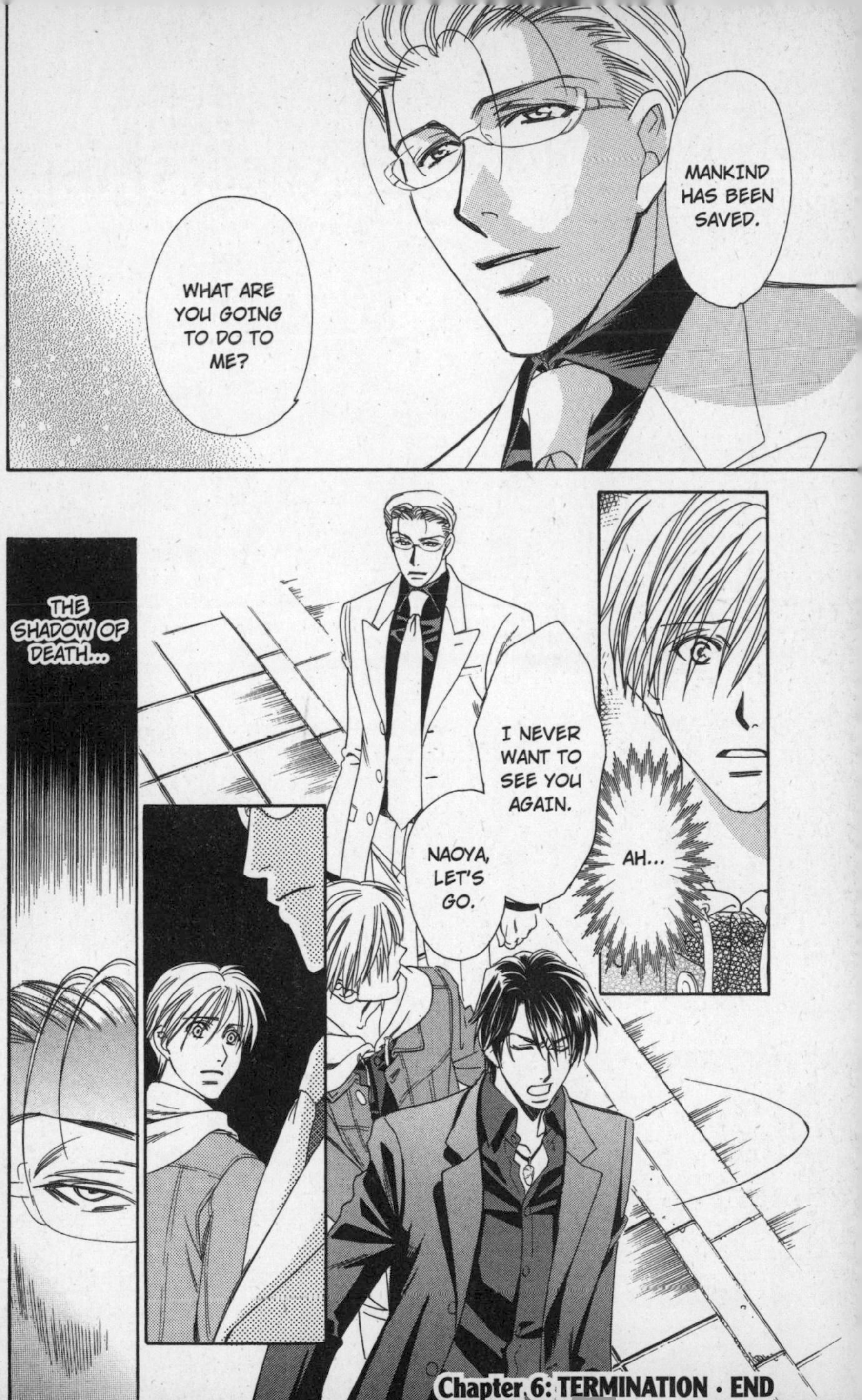
MANKIND HAS BEEN SAVED.
WHAT ARE YOU GOING TO DO TO ME?
AH...
I NEVER WANT TO SEE YOU AGAIN.
NAOYA, LET'S GO.
THE SHADOW OF DEATH...
Chapter 6: TERMINATION · END

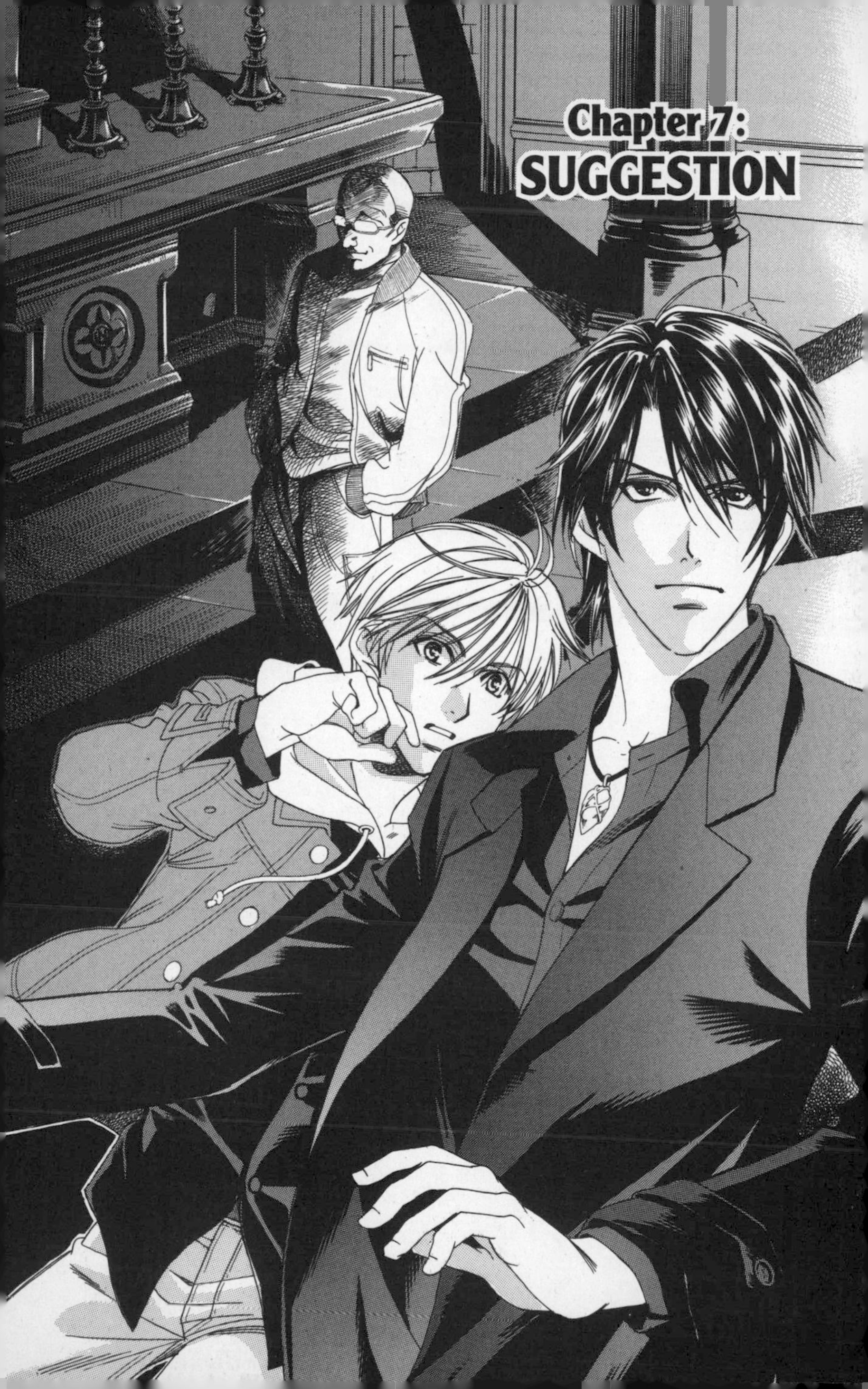
Chapter 7:
SUGGESTION

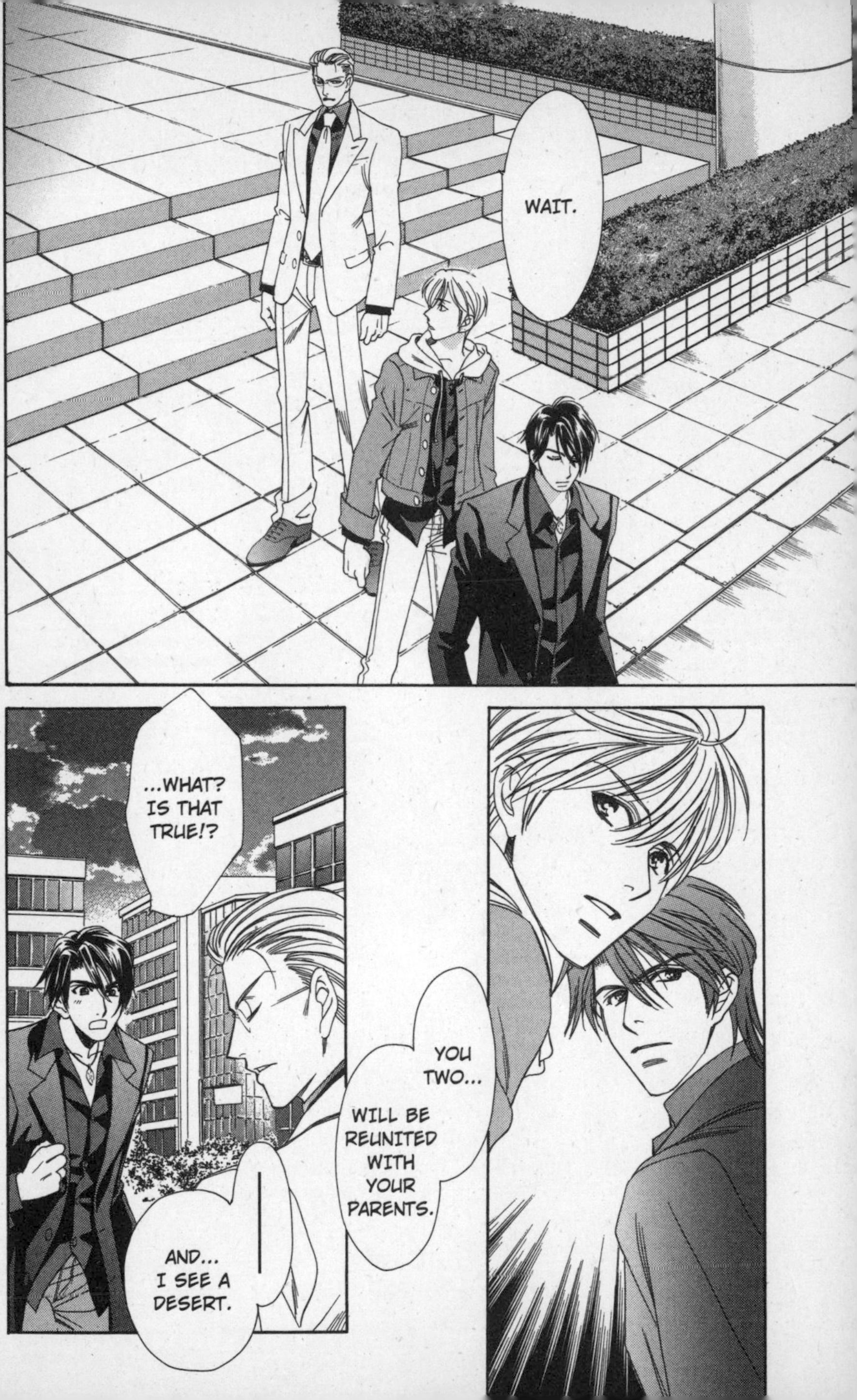
WAIT.
YOU TWO...
WILL BE REUNITED WITH YOUR PARENTS.
...WHAT? IS THAT TRUE!?
AND... I SEE A DESERT.

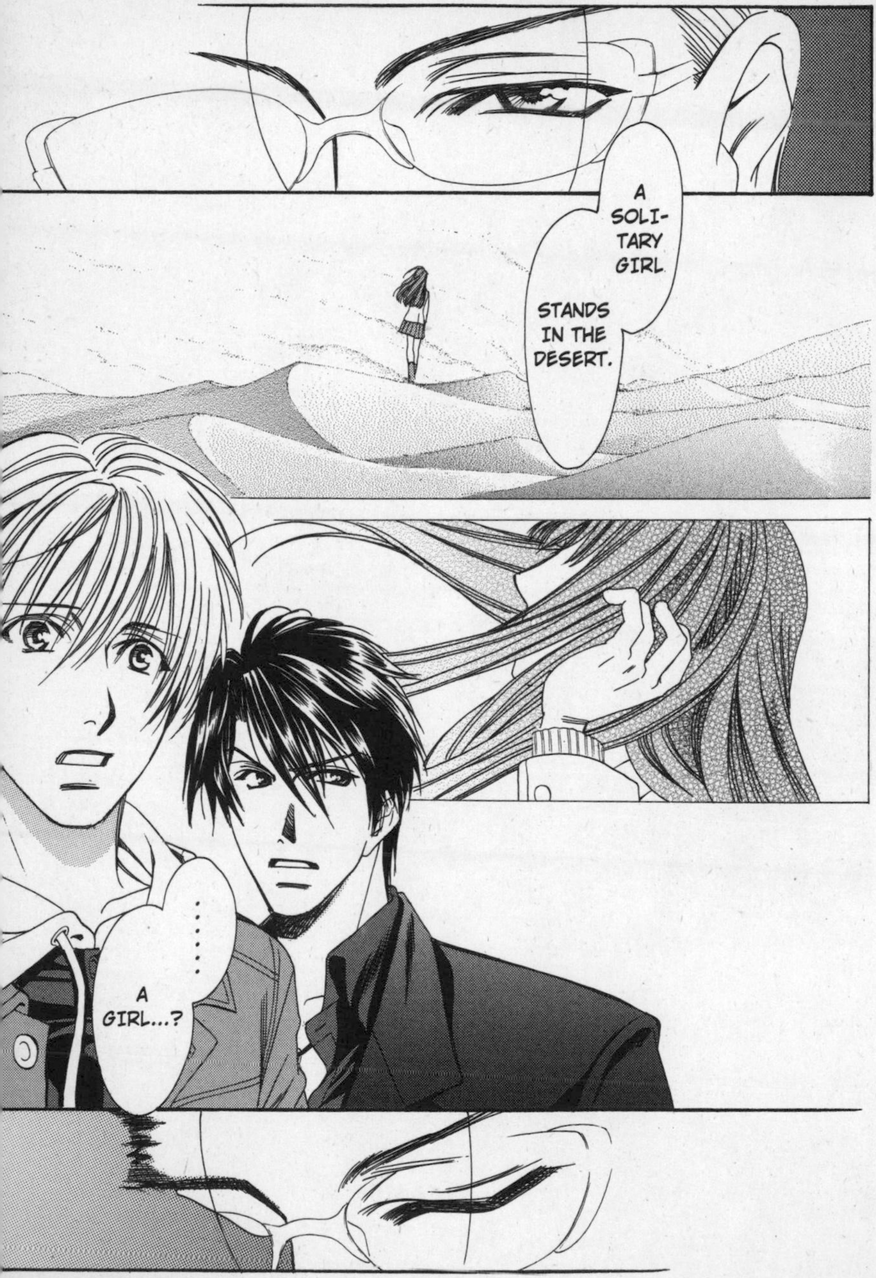
A SOLI- TARY GIRL
STANDS IN THE DESERT.
...... A GIRL...?

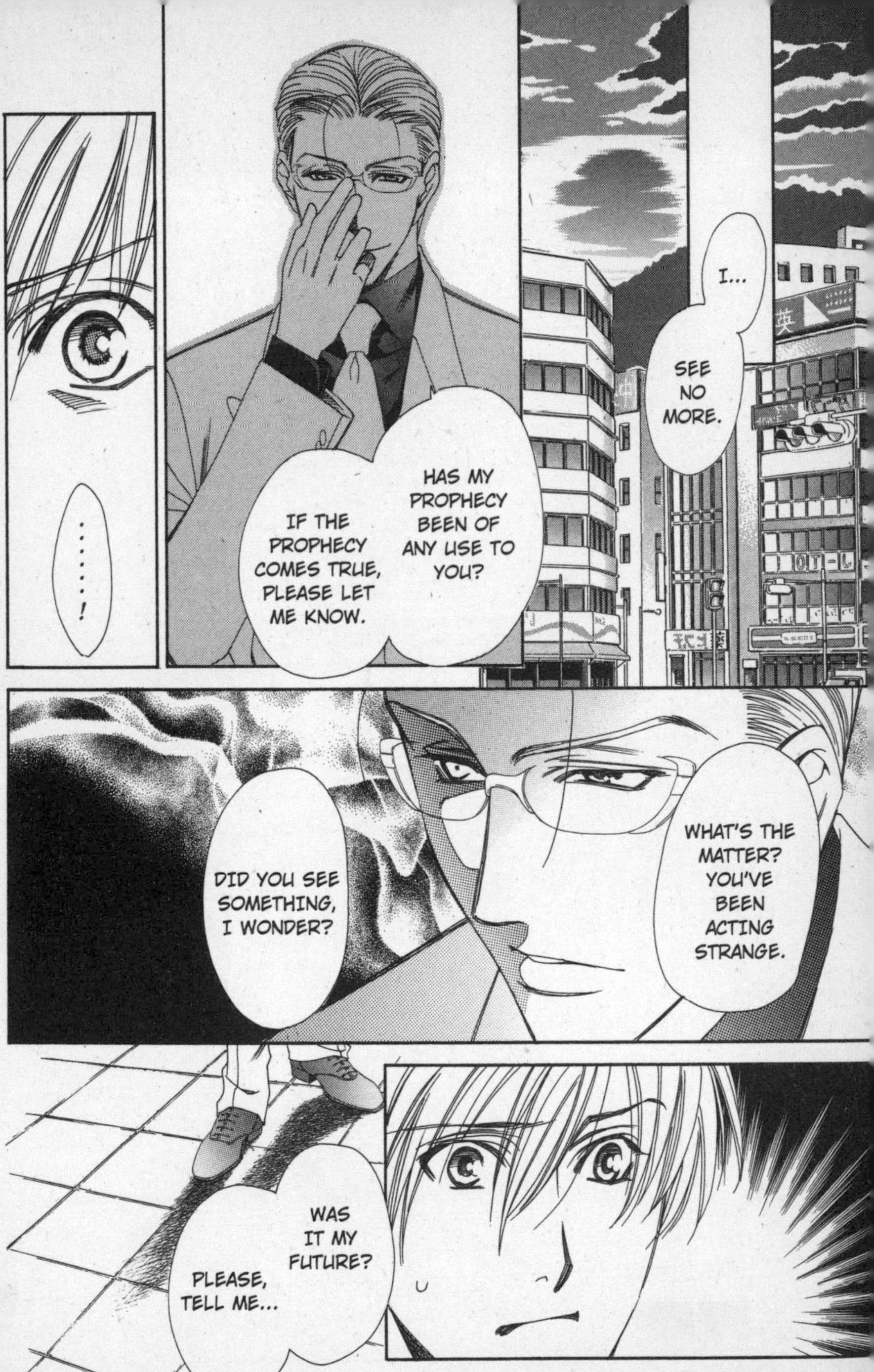
I...
SEE NO MORE.
HAS MY PROPHECY BEEN OF ANY USE TO YOU?
IF THE PROPHECY COMES TRUE, PLEASE LET ME KNOW.
......!
WHAT'S THE MATTER? YOU'VE BEEN ACTING STRANGE.
DID YOU SEE SOMETHING, I WONDER?
WAS IT MY FUTURE?
PLEASE, TELL ME...

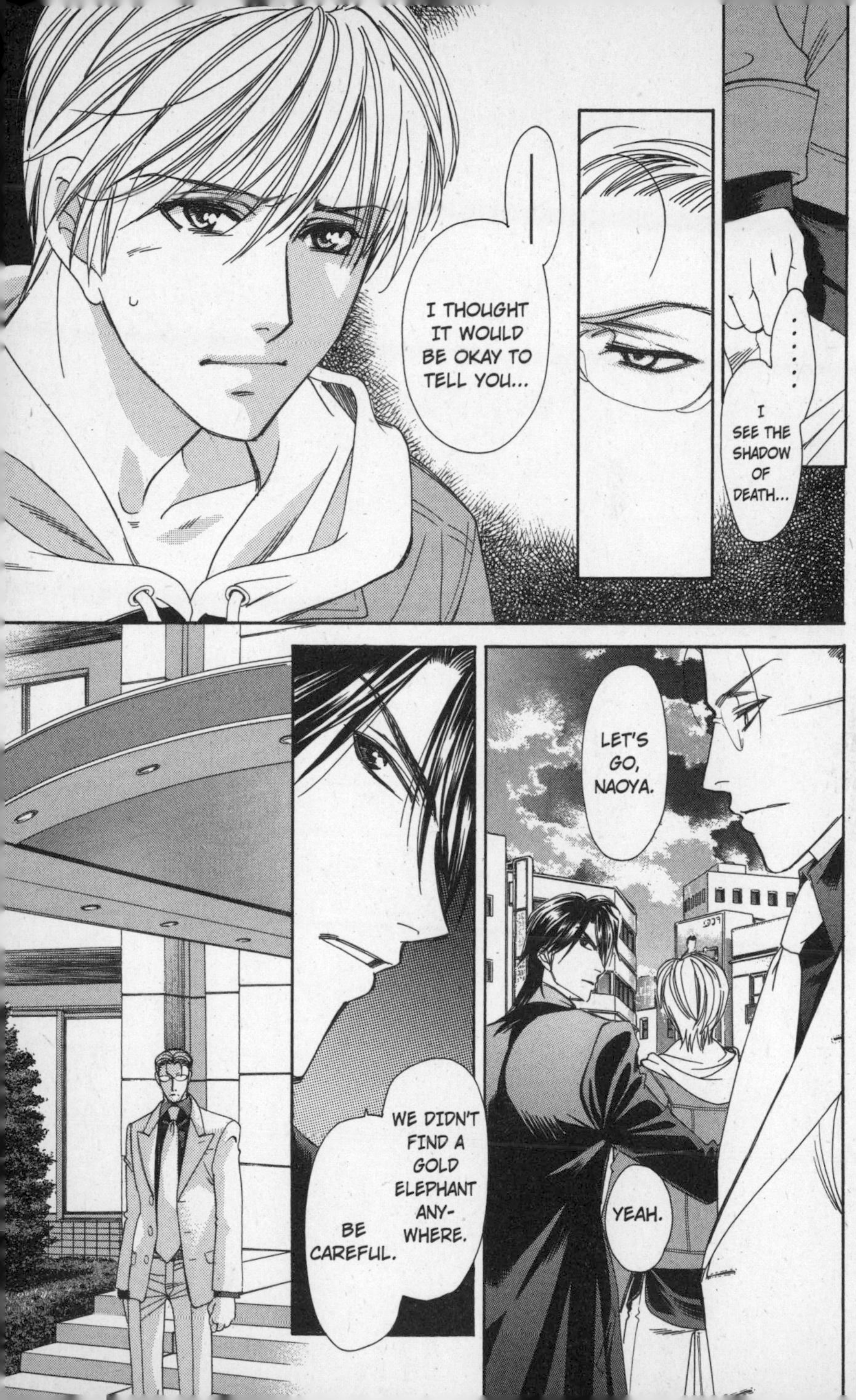
......
I SEE THE SHADOW OF DEATH...
I THOUGHT IT WOULD BE OKAY TO TELL YOU...
LET'S GO, NAOYA.
YEAH.
WE DIDN'T FIND A GOLD ELEPHANT ANY-WHERE.
BE CAREFUL.

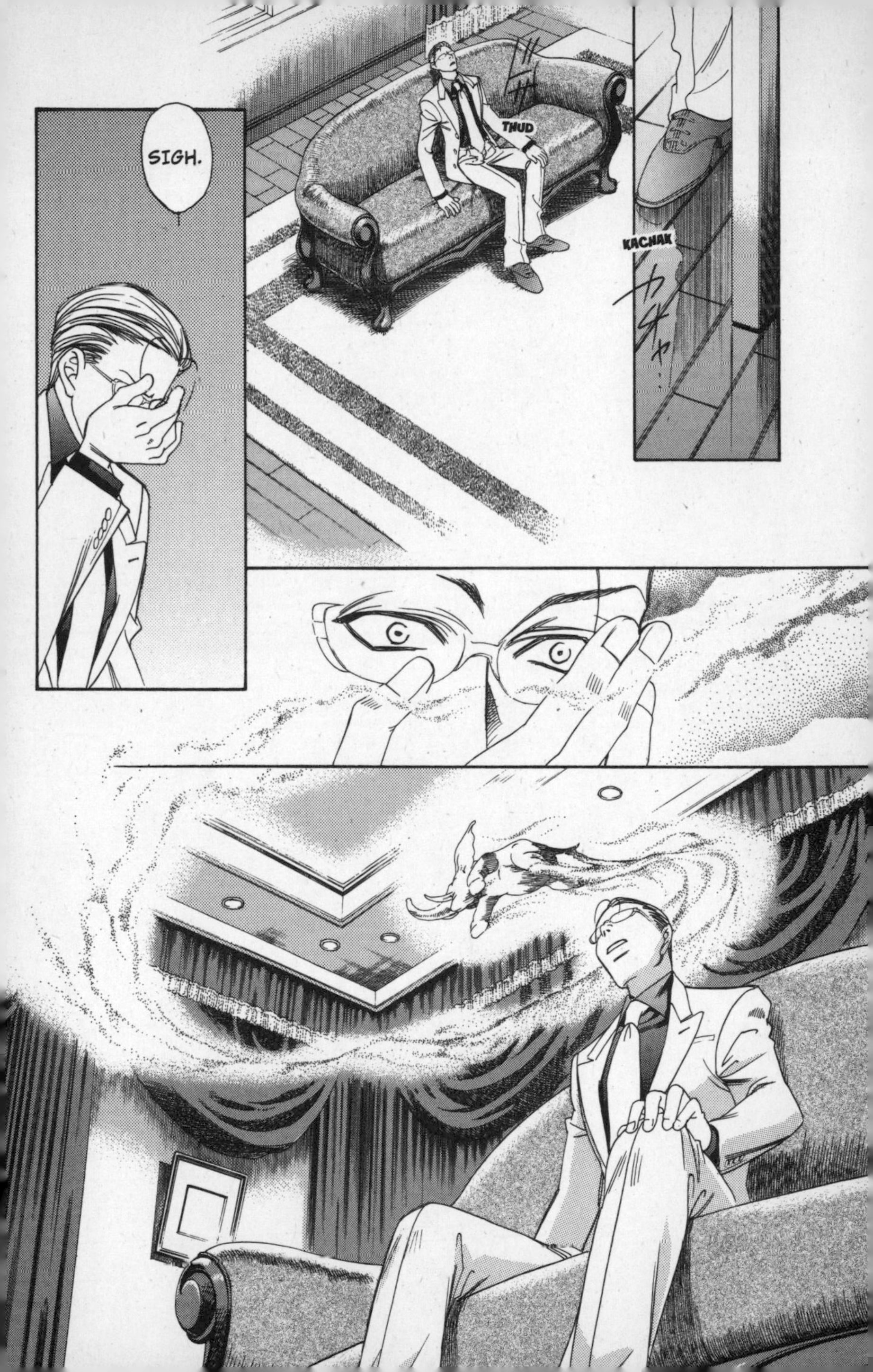
KACHAK
カチャッ
THUD
SIGH.

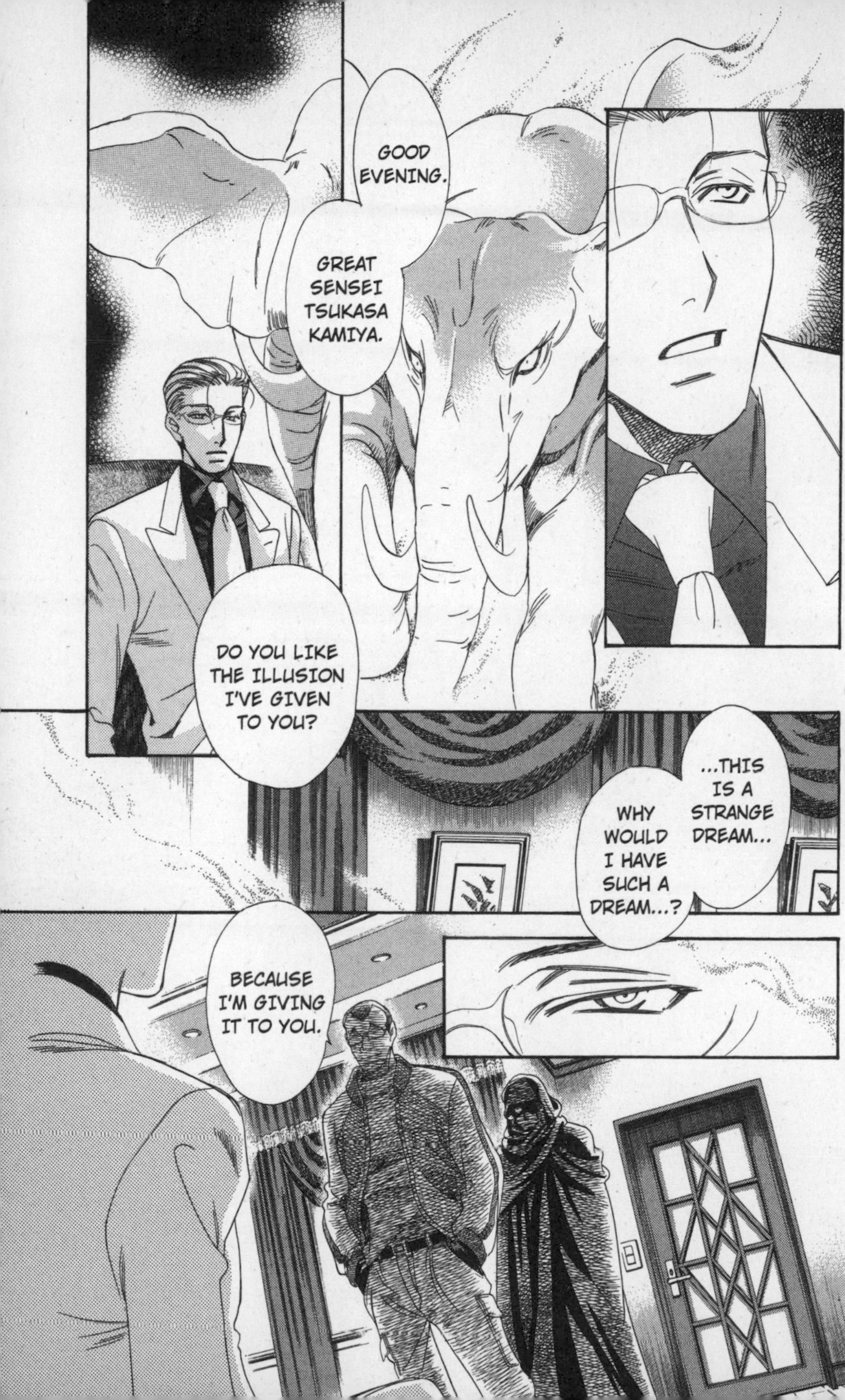
GOOD EVENING.
GREAT SENSEI TSUKASA KAMIYA.
DO YOU LIKE THE ILLUSION I'VE GIVEN TO YOU?
...THIS IS A STRANGE DREAM...
WHY WOULD I HAVE SUCH A DREAM...?
BECAUSE I'M GIVING IT TO YOU.

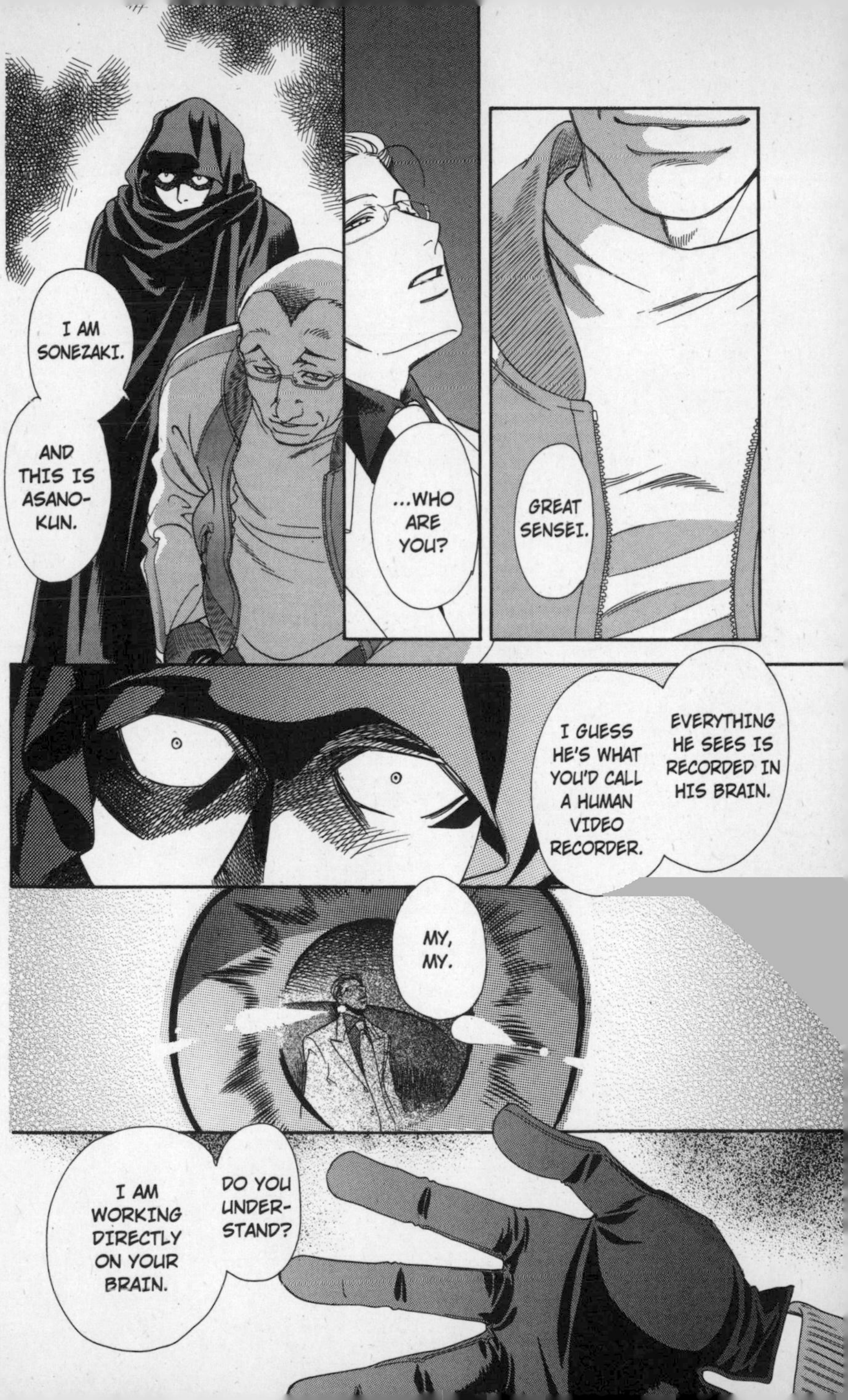
GREAT SENSEI.
...WHO ARE YOU?
I AM SONEZAKI.
AND THIS IS ASANO-KUN.
EVERYTHING HE SEES IS RECORDED IN HIS BRAIN.
I GUESS HE'S WHAT YOU'D CALL A HUMAN VIDEO RECORDER.
MY, MY.
DO YOU UNDER-STAND?
I AM WORKING DIRECTLY ON YOUR BRAIN.

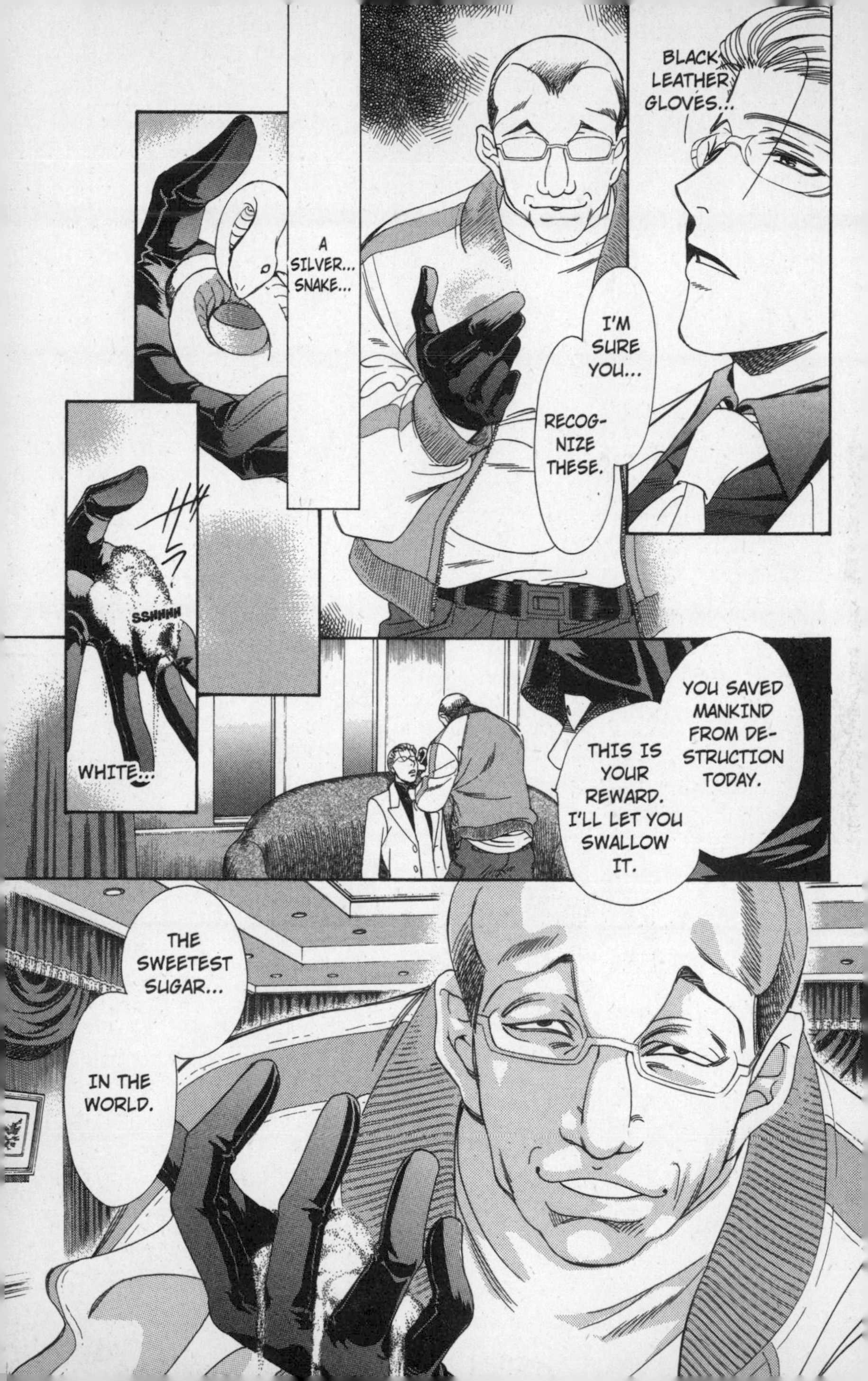
BLACK LEATHER GLOVES...
I'M SURE YOU...
RECOGNIZE THESE.
A SILVER... SNAKE...
SSHHHH
WHITE...
YOU SAVED MANKIND FROM DESTRUCTION TODAY.
THIS IS YOUR REWARD. I'LL LET YOU SWALLOW IT.
THE SWEETEST SUGAR...
IN THE WORLD.

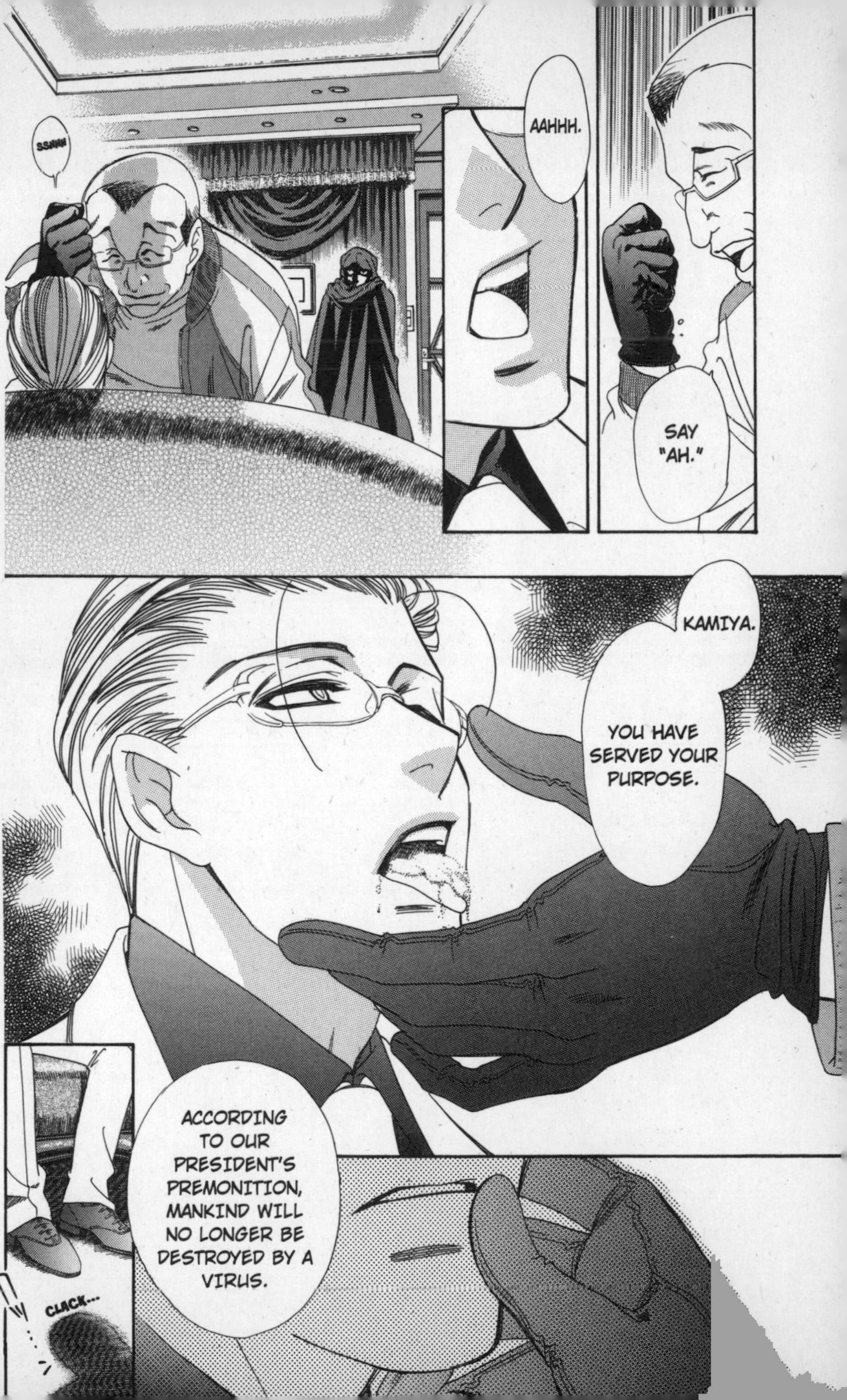
SAY "AH."
AAHHH.
SSHHH
KAMIYA.
YOU HAVE SERVED YOUR PURPOSE.
ACCORDING TO OUR PRESIDENT'S PREMONITION, MANKIND WILL NO LONGER BE DESTROYED BY A VIRUS.
CLACK...

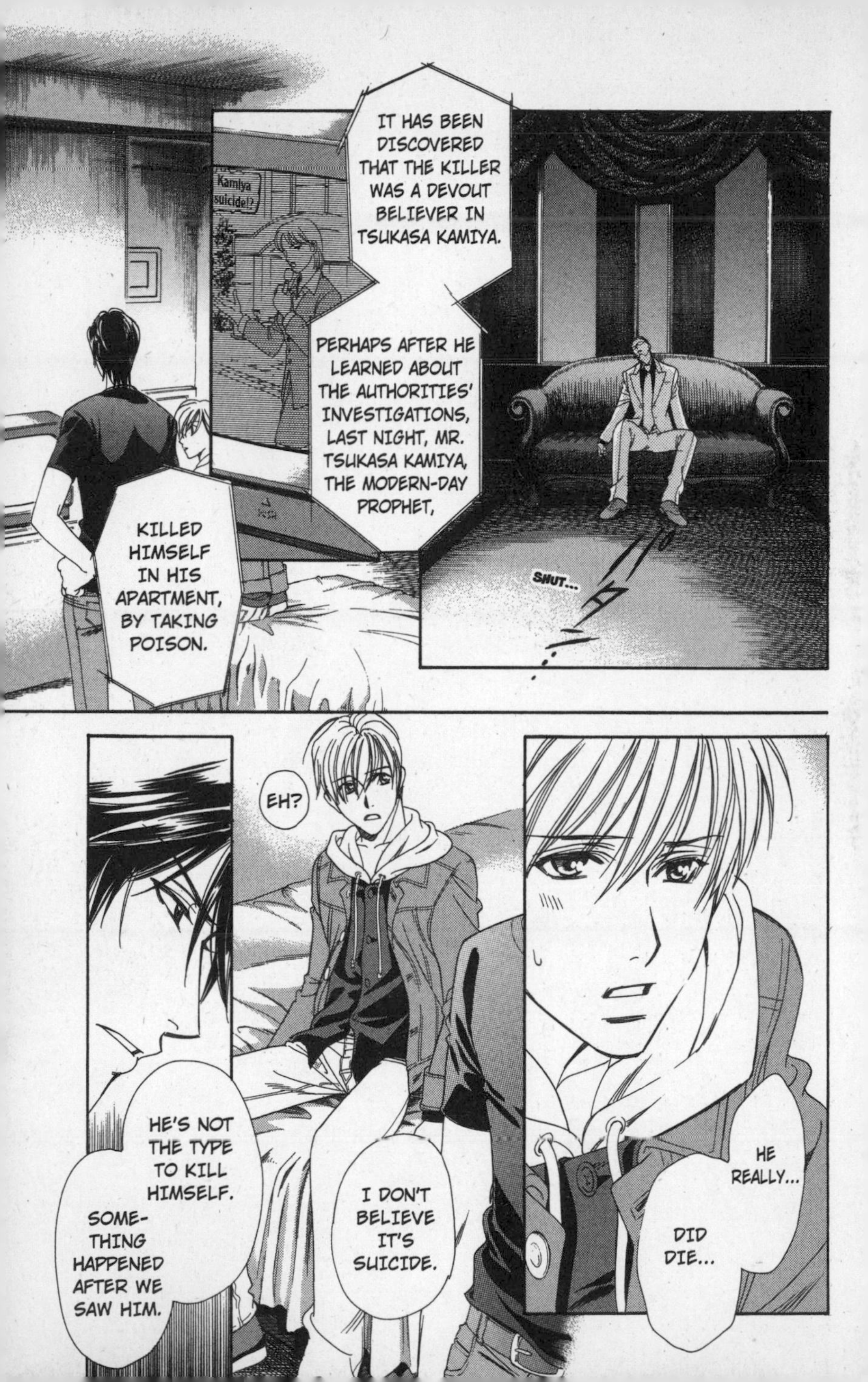
IT HAS BEEN DISCOVERED THAT THE KILLER WAS A DEVOUT BELIEVER IN TSUKASA KAMIYA.
PERHAPS AFTER HE LEARNED ABOUT THE AUTHORITIES' INVESTIGATIONS, LAST NIGHT, MR. TSUKASA KAMIYA, THE MODERN-DAY PROPHET,
SHUT...
Kamiya suicide!?
KILLED HIMSELF IN HIS APARTMENT, BY TAKING POISON.
HE REALLY...
DID DIE...
EH?
I DON'T BELIEVE IT'S SUICIDE.
HE'S NOT THE TYPE TO KILL HIMSELF.
SOME-THING HAPPENED AFTER WE SAW HIM.

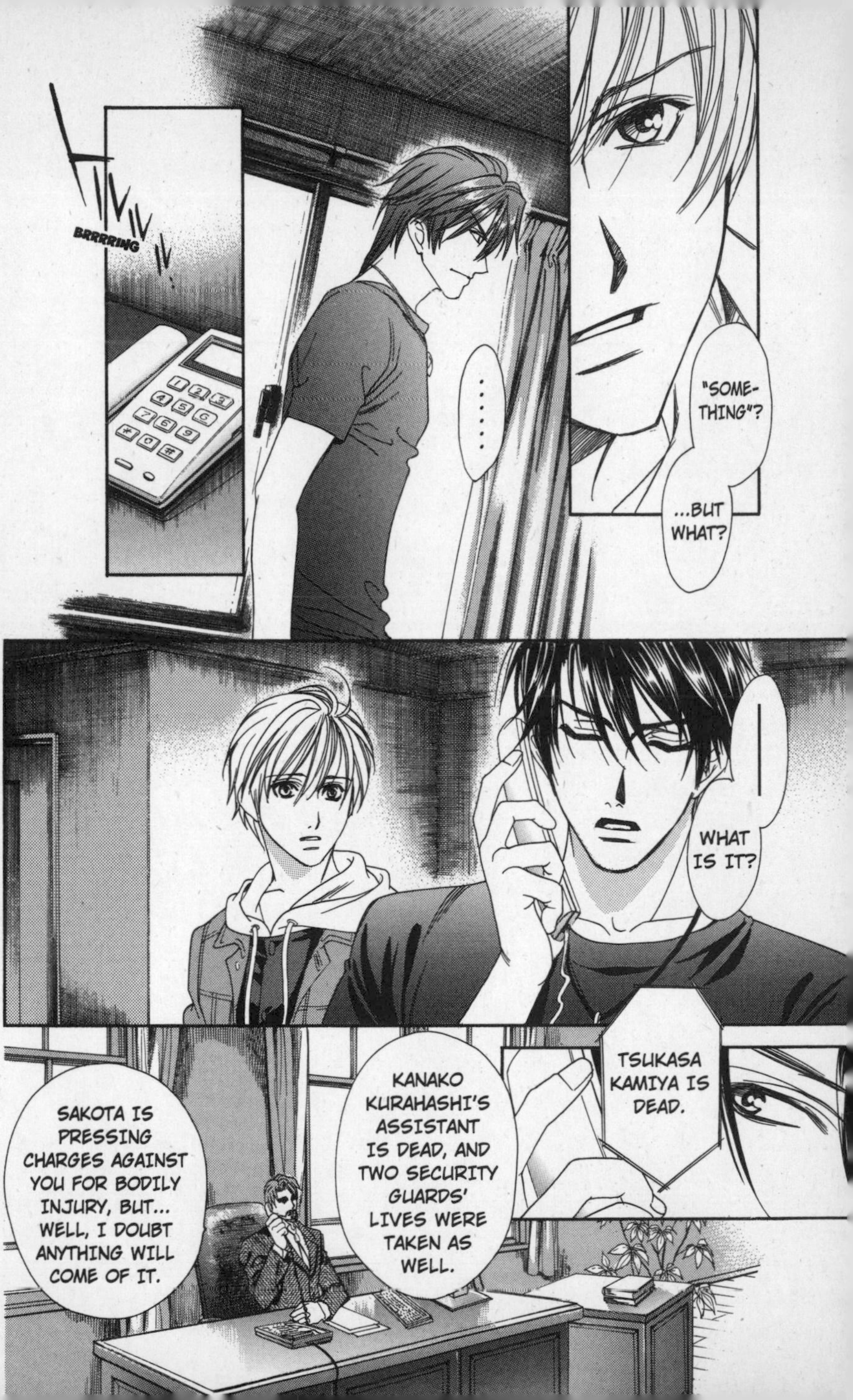
"SOME-THING"?
...BUT WHAT?
......
BRRRRING
WHAT IS IT?
TSUKASA KAMIYA IS DEAD.
KANAKO KURAHASHI'S ASSISTANT IS DEAD, AND TWO SECURITY GUARDS' LIVES WERE TAKEN AS WELL.
SAKOTA IS PRESSING CHARGES AGAINST YOU FOR BODILY INJURY, BUT... WELL, I DOUBT ANYTHING WILL COME OF IT.

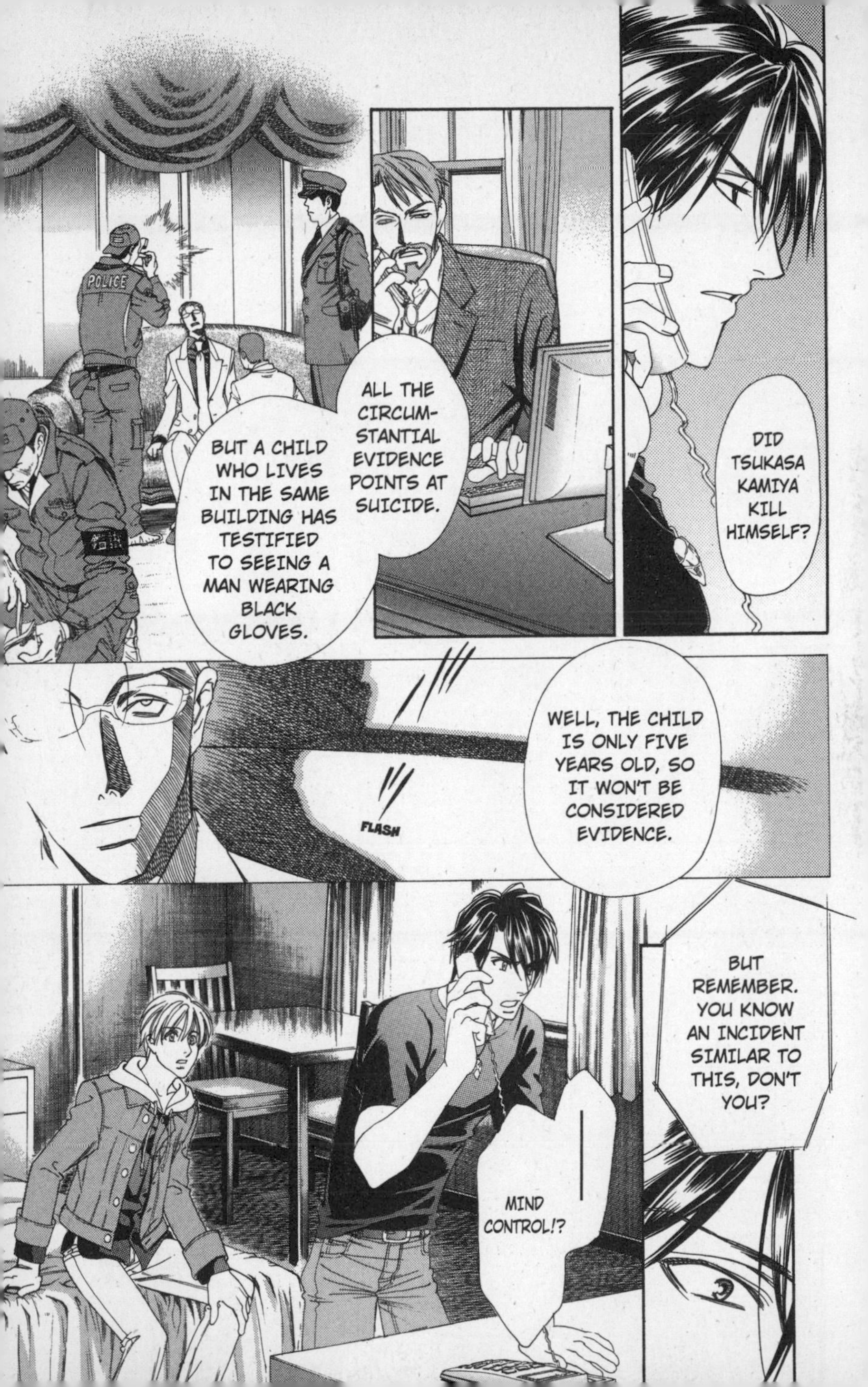
DID TSUKASA KAMIYA KILL HIMSELF?
ALL THE CIRCUM-STANTIAL EVIDENCE POINTS AT SUICIDE.
BUT A CHILD WHO LIVES IN THE SAME BUILDING HAS TESTIFIED TO SEEING A MAN WEARING BLACK GLOVES.
POLICE
WELL, THE CHILD IS ONLY FIVE YEARS OLD, SO IT WON'T BE CONSIDERED EVIDENCE.
FLASH
BUT REMEMBER. YOU KNOW AN INCIDENT SIMILAR TO THIS, DON'T YOU?
MIND CONTROL!?

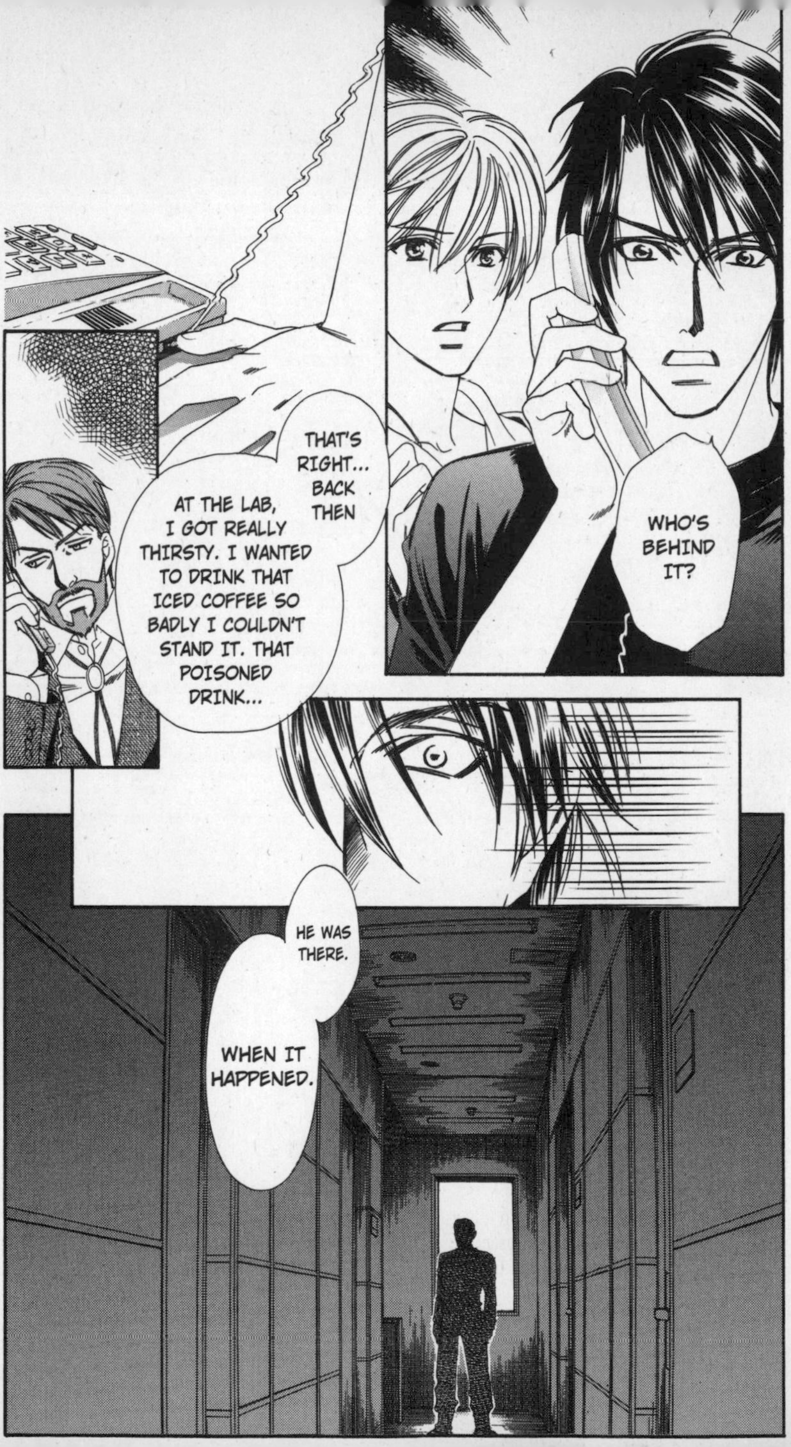
WHO'S BEHIND IT?
THAT'S RIGHT... BACK THEN
AT THE LAB, I GOT REALLY THIRSTY. I WANTED TO DRINK THAT ICED COFFEE SO BADLY I COULDN'T STAND IT. THAT POISONED DRINK...
HE WAS THERE.
WHEN IT HAPPENED.

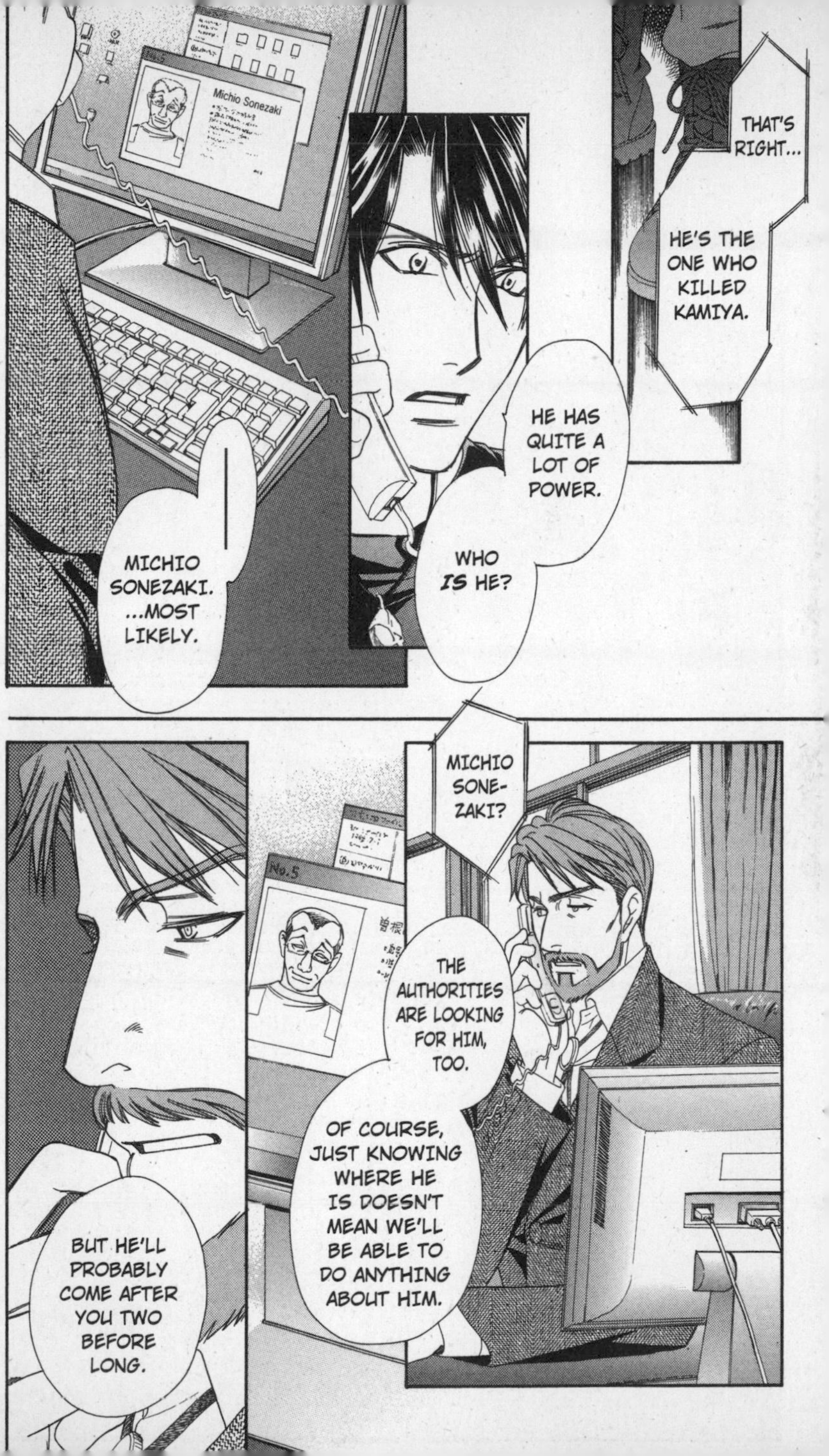
THAT'S RIGHT...
HE'S THE ONE WHO KILLED KAMIYA.
HE HAS QUITE A LOT OF POWER.
WHO *IS* HE?
Michio Sonezaki
MICHIO SONEZAKI. ...MOST LIKELY.
MICHIO SONE-ZAKI?
THE AUTHORITIES ARE LOOKING FOR HIM, TOO.
OF COURSE, JUST KNOWING WHERE HE IS DOESN'T MEAN WE'LL BE ABLE TO DO ANYTHING ABOUT HIM.
No.5
BUT HE'LL PROBABLY COME AFTER YOU TWO BEFORE LONG.

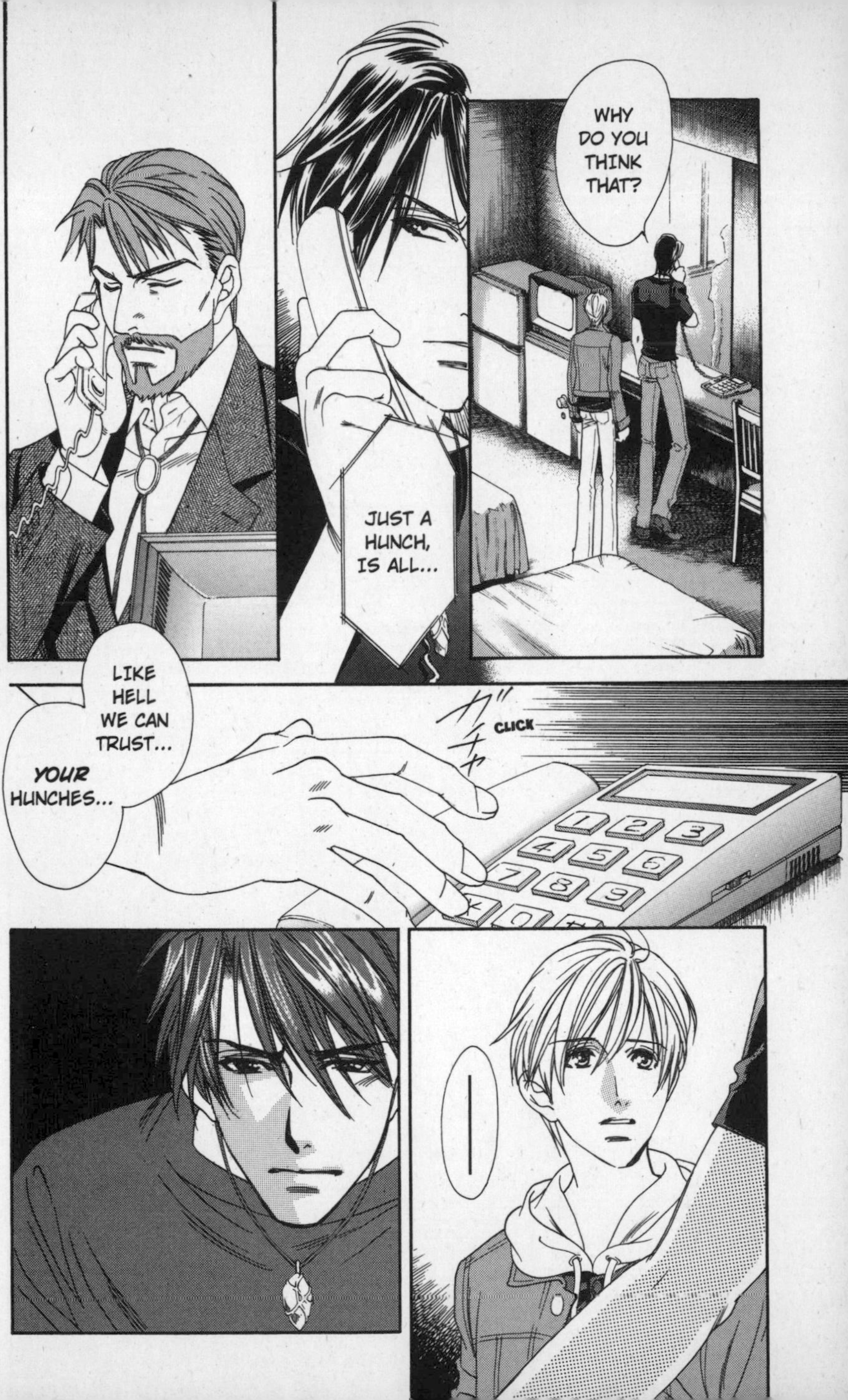
WHY DO YOU THINK THAT?
JUST A HUNCH, IS ALL...
CLICK
ガチャ
LIKE HELL WE CAN TRUST... *YOUR* HUNCHES...

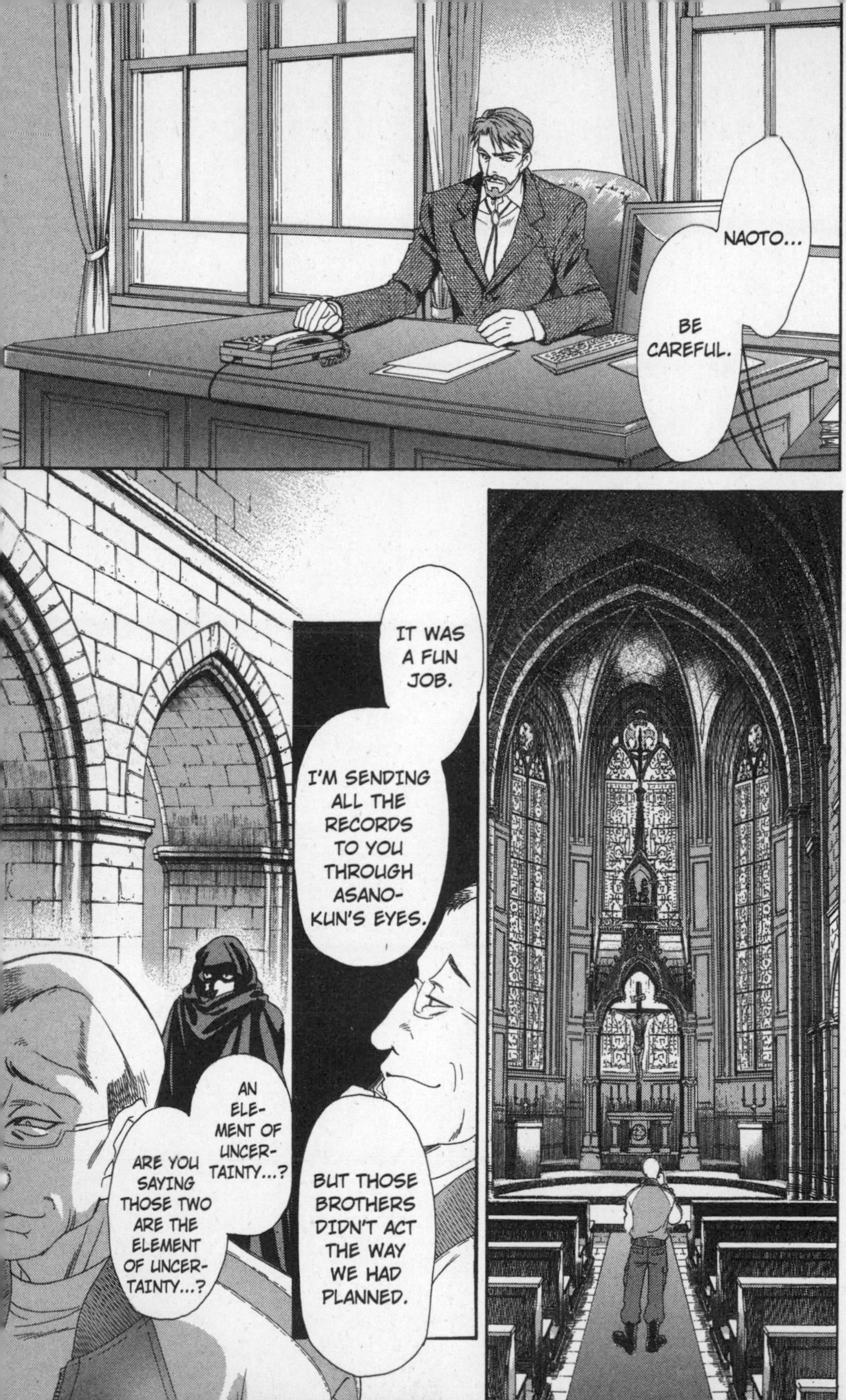
NAOTO...
BE CAREFUL.
IT WAS A FUN JOB.
I'M SENDING ALL THE RECORDS TO YOU THROUGH ASANO-KUN'S EYES.
BUT THOSE BROTHERS DIDN'T ACT THE WAY WE HAD PLANNED.
AN ELEMENT OF UNCERTAINTY...?
ARE YOU SAYING THOSE TWO ARE THE ELEMENT OF UNCERTAINTY...?

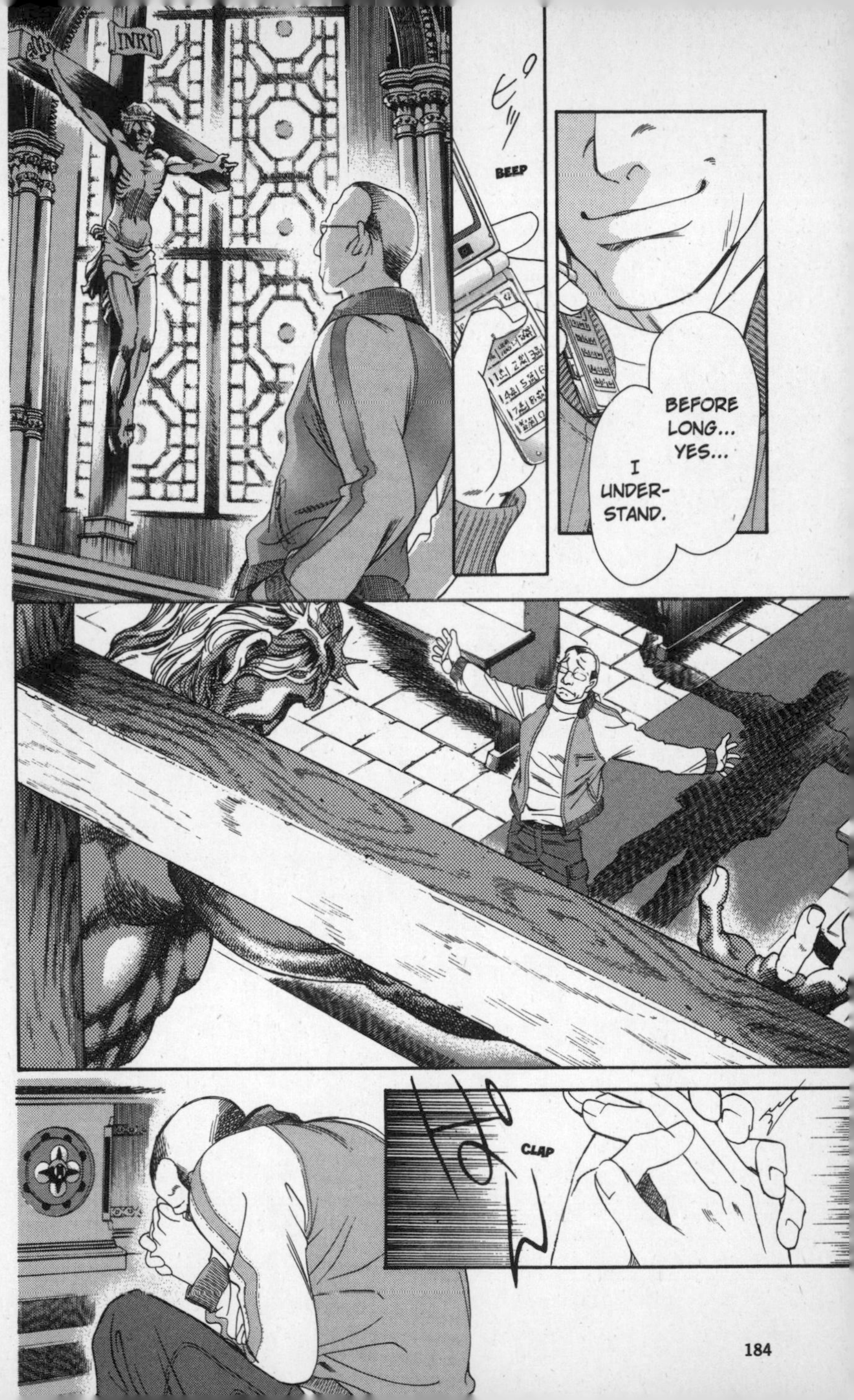
BEFORE LONG... YES... I UNDERSTAND.
BEEP
CLAP

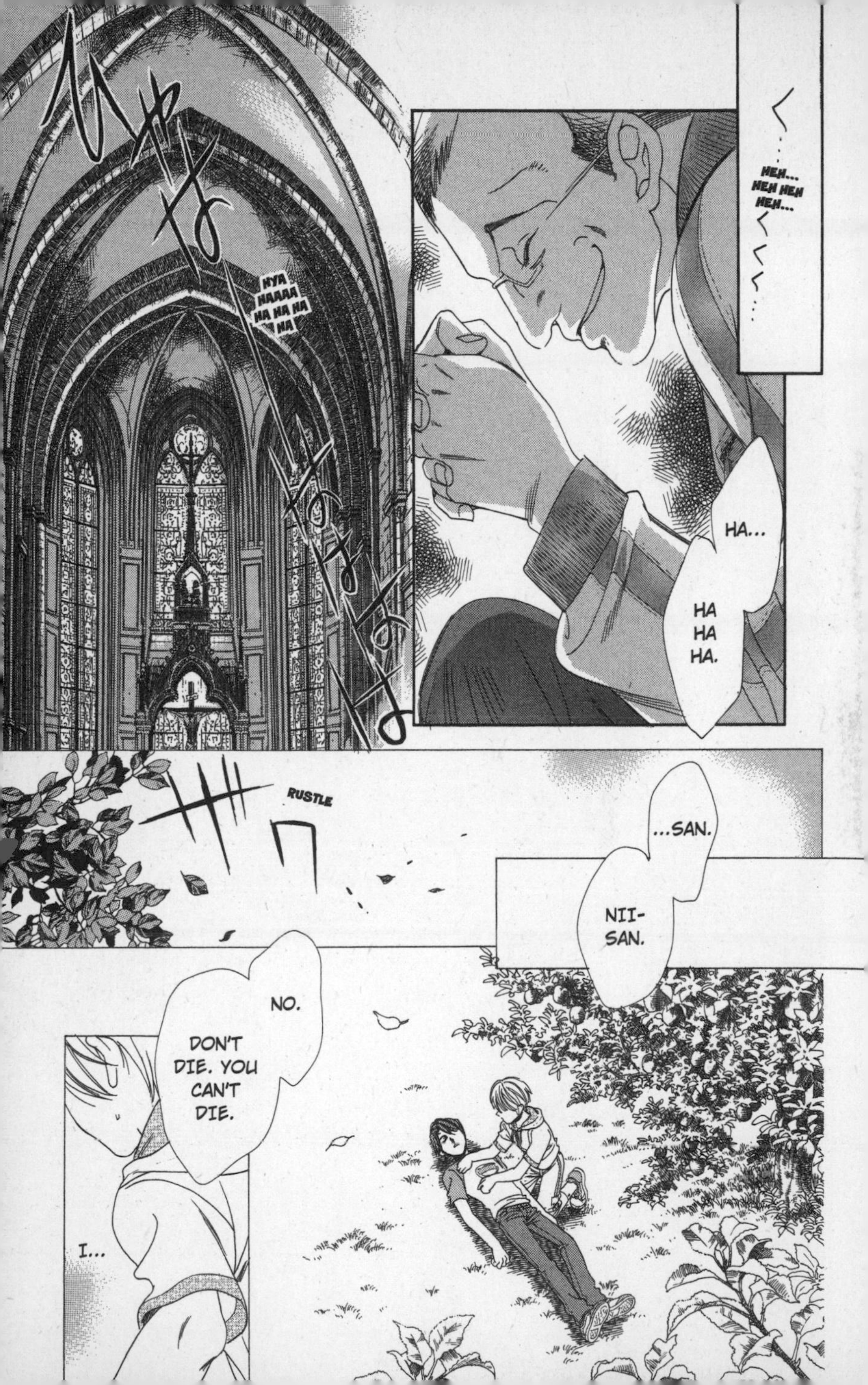
HEH... HEH HEH HEH...
HA...
HA HA HA.
HYA HAAAA HA HA HA HA
...SAN.
NII-SAN.
RUSTLE
NO.
DON'T DIE. YOU CAN'T DIE.
I...

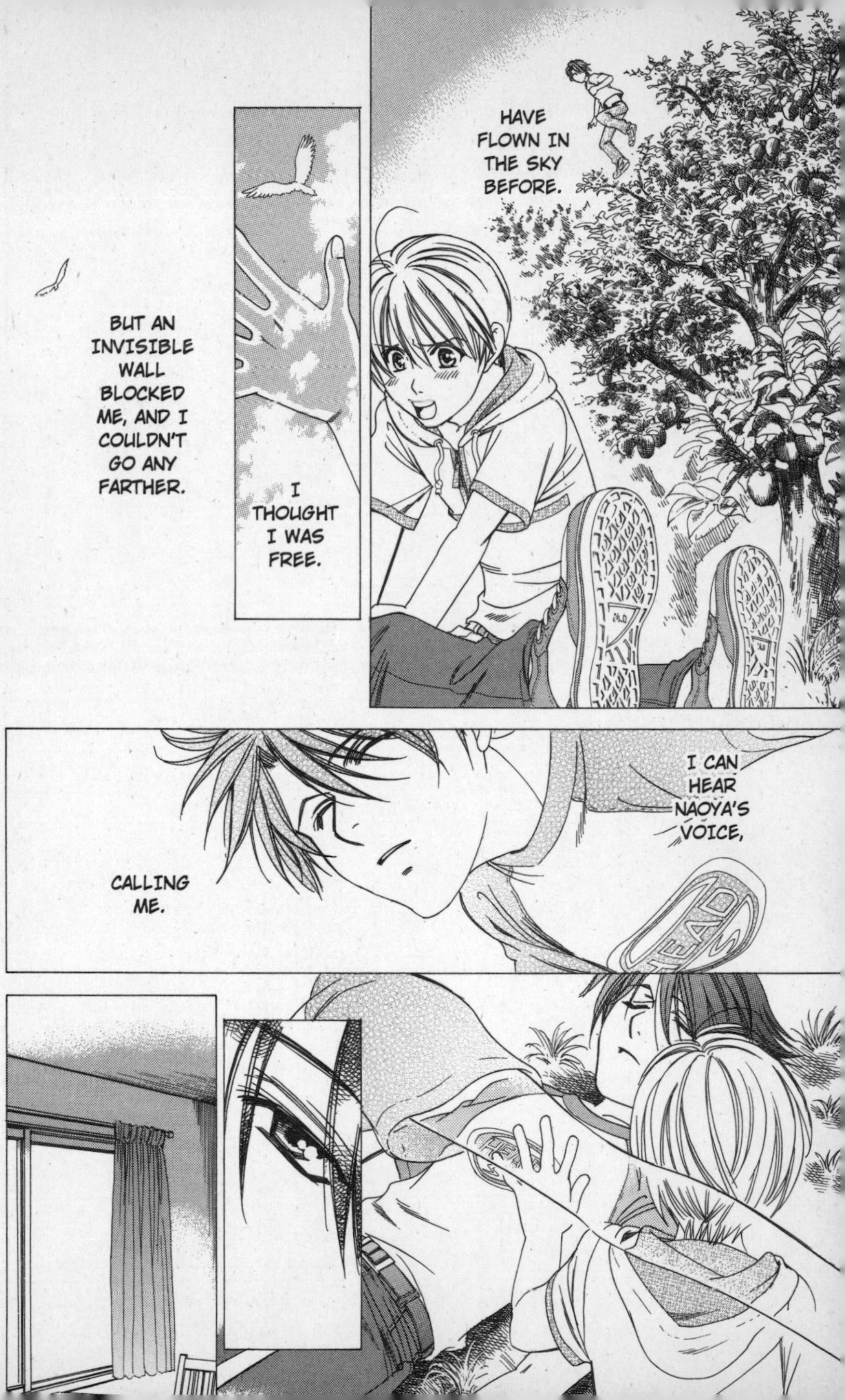
HAVE FLOWN IN THE SKY BEFORE.
I THOUGHT I WAS FREE.
BUT AN INVISIBLE WALL BLOCKED ME, AND I COULDN'T GO ANY FARTHER.
I CAN HEAR NAOYA'S VOICE,
CALLING ME.

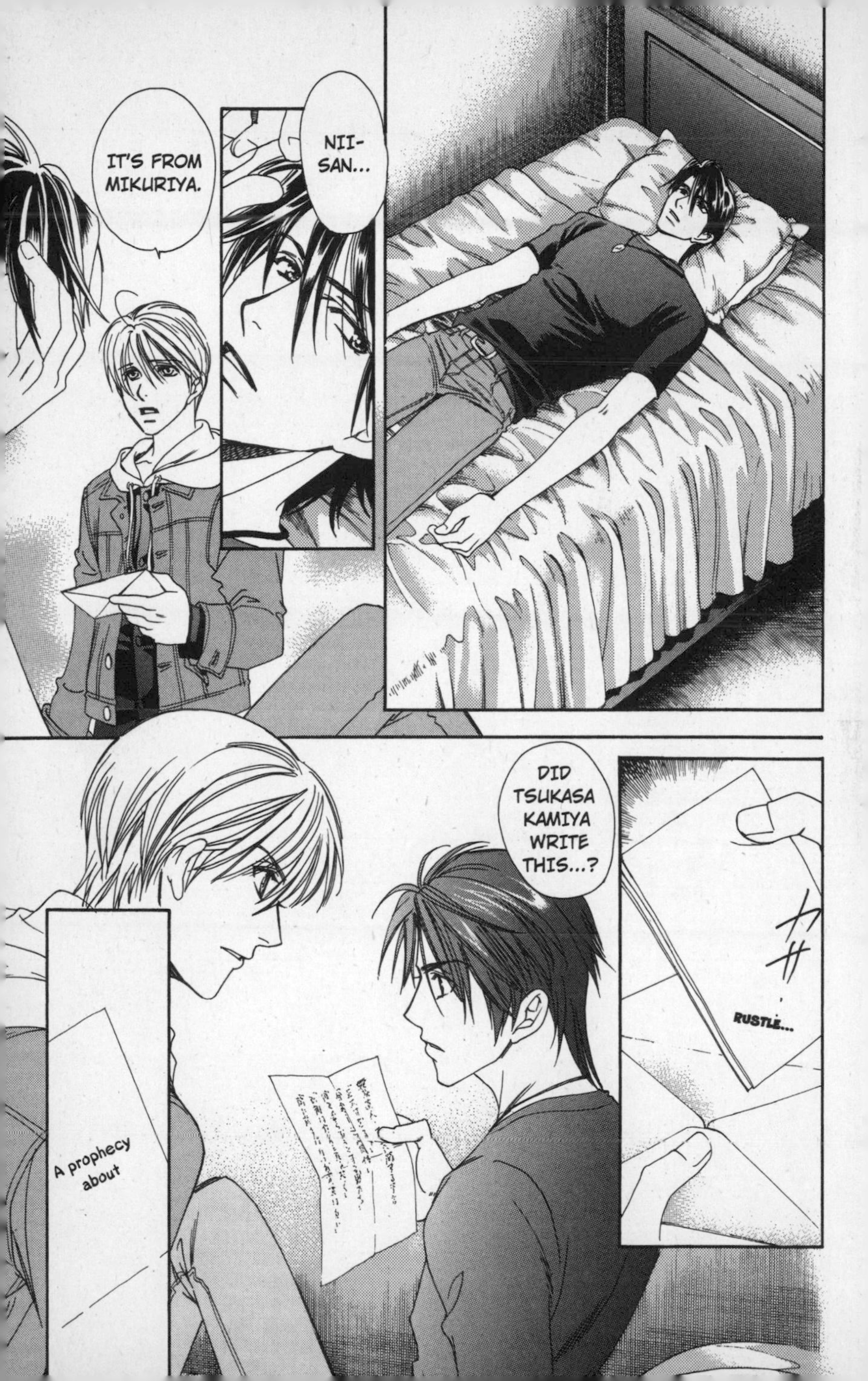
NII-SAN...
IT'S FROM MIKURIYA.
RUSTLE...
DID TSUKASA KAMIYA WRITE THIS...?
A prophecy about

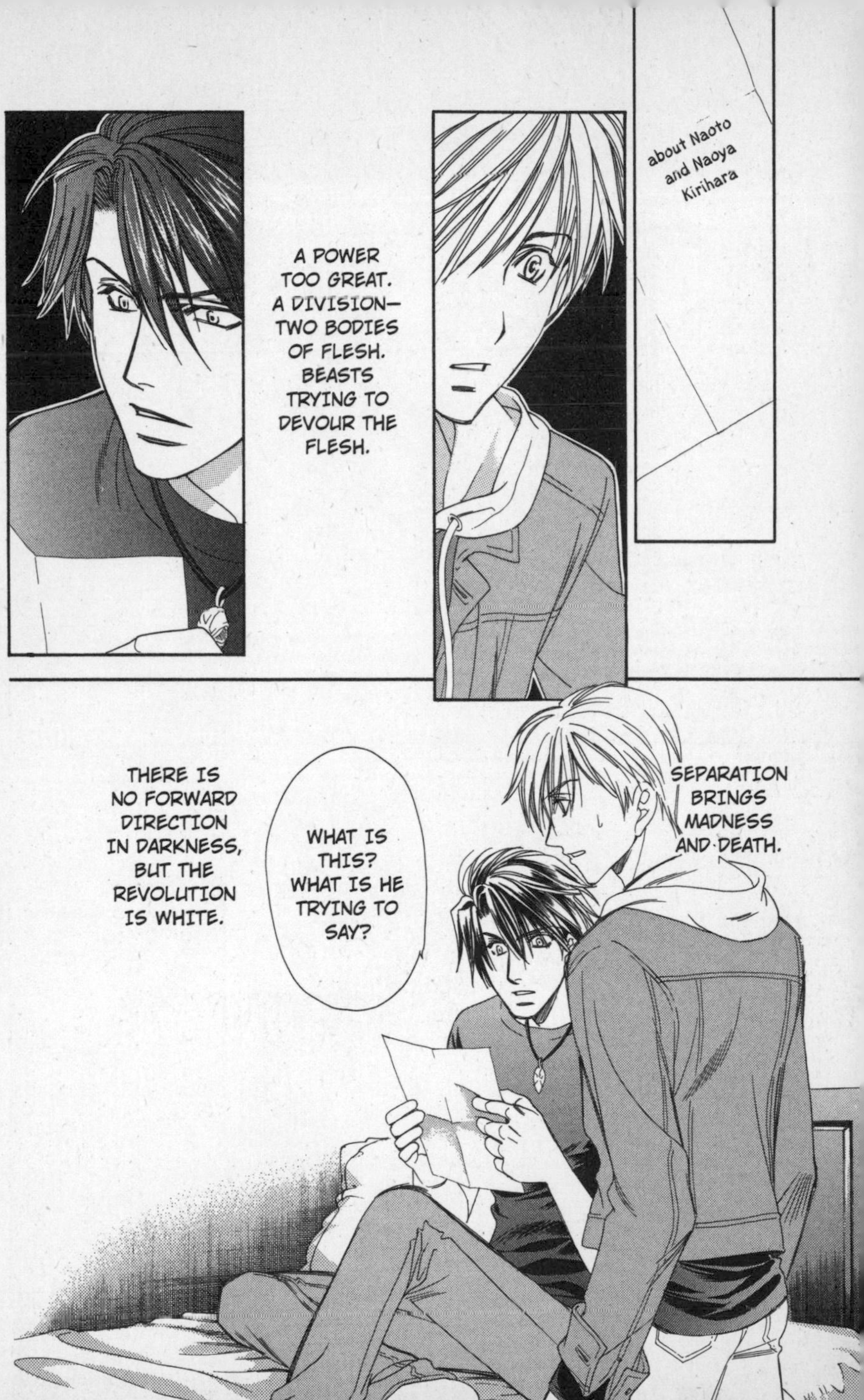
about Naoto and Naoya Kirihara
A POWER TOO GREAT. A DIVISION— TWO BODIES OF FLESH. BEASTS TRYING TO DEVOUR THE FLESH.
SEPARATION BRINGS MADNESS AND DEATH.
WHAT IS THIS? WHAT IS HE TRYING TO SAY?
THERE IS NO FORWARD DIRECTION IN DARKNESS, BUT THE REVOLUTION IS WHITE.

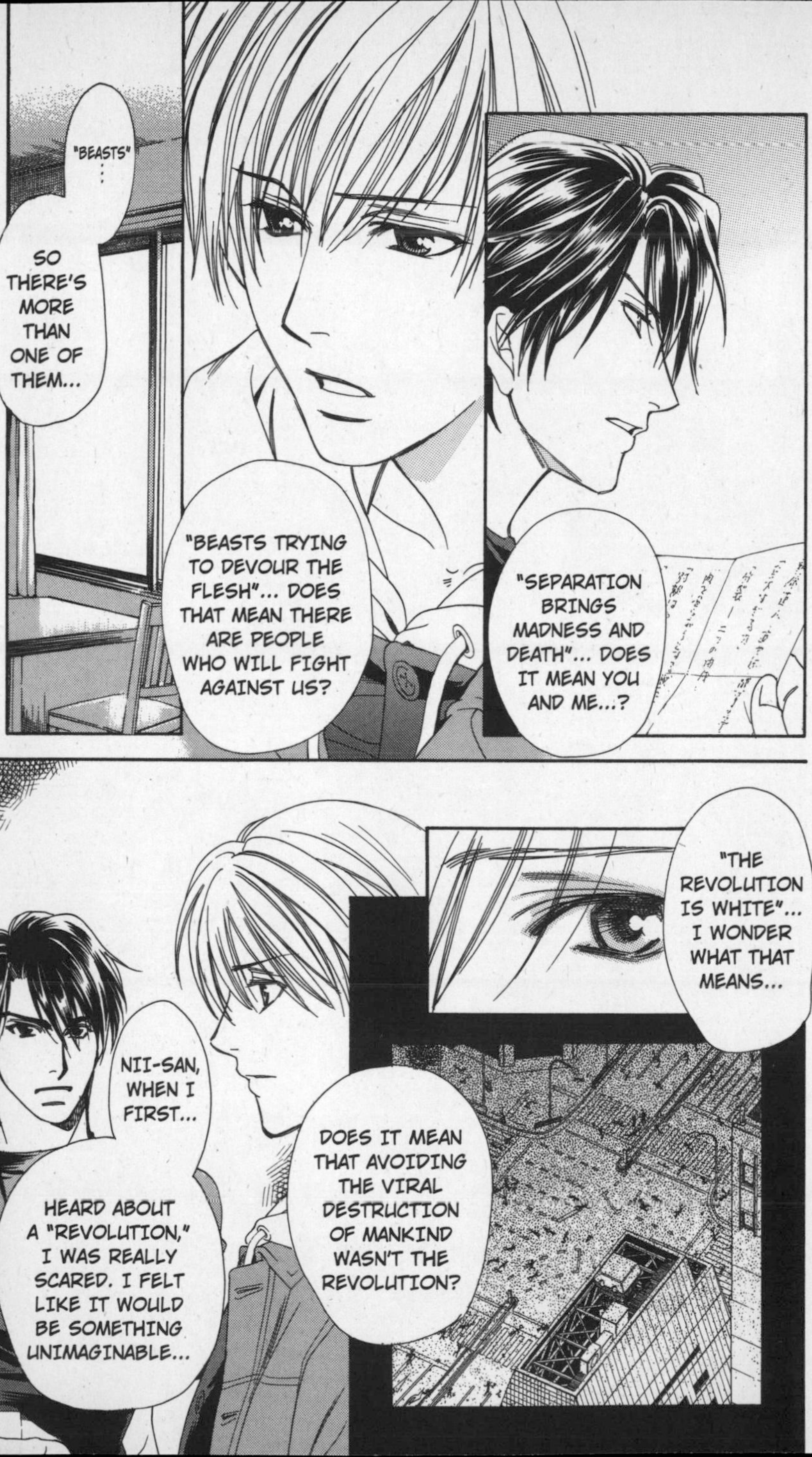
"SEPARATION BRINGS MADNESS AND DEATH"... DOES IT MEAN YOU AND ME...?
"BEASTS TRYING TO DEVOUR THE FLESH"... DOES THAT MEAN THERE ARE PEOPLE WHO WILL FIGHT AGAINST US?
"BEASTS" ...
SO THERE'S MORE THAN ONE OF THEM...
"THE REVOLUTION IS WHITE"... I WONDER WHAT THAT MEANS...
DOES IT MEAN THAT AVOIDING THE VIRAL DESTRUCTION OF MANKIND WASN'T THE REVOLUTION?
NII-SAN, WHEN I FIRST...
HEARD ABOUT A "REVOLUTION," I WAS REALLY SCARED. I FELT LIKE IT WOULD BE SOMETHING UNIMAGINABLE...

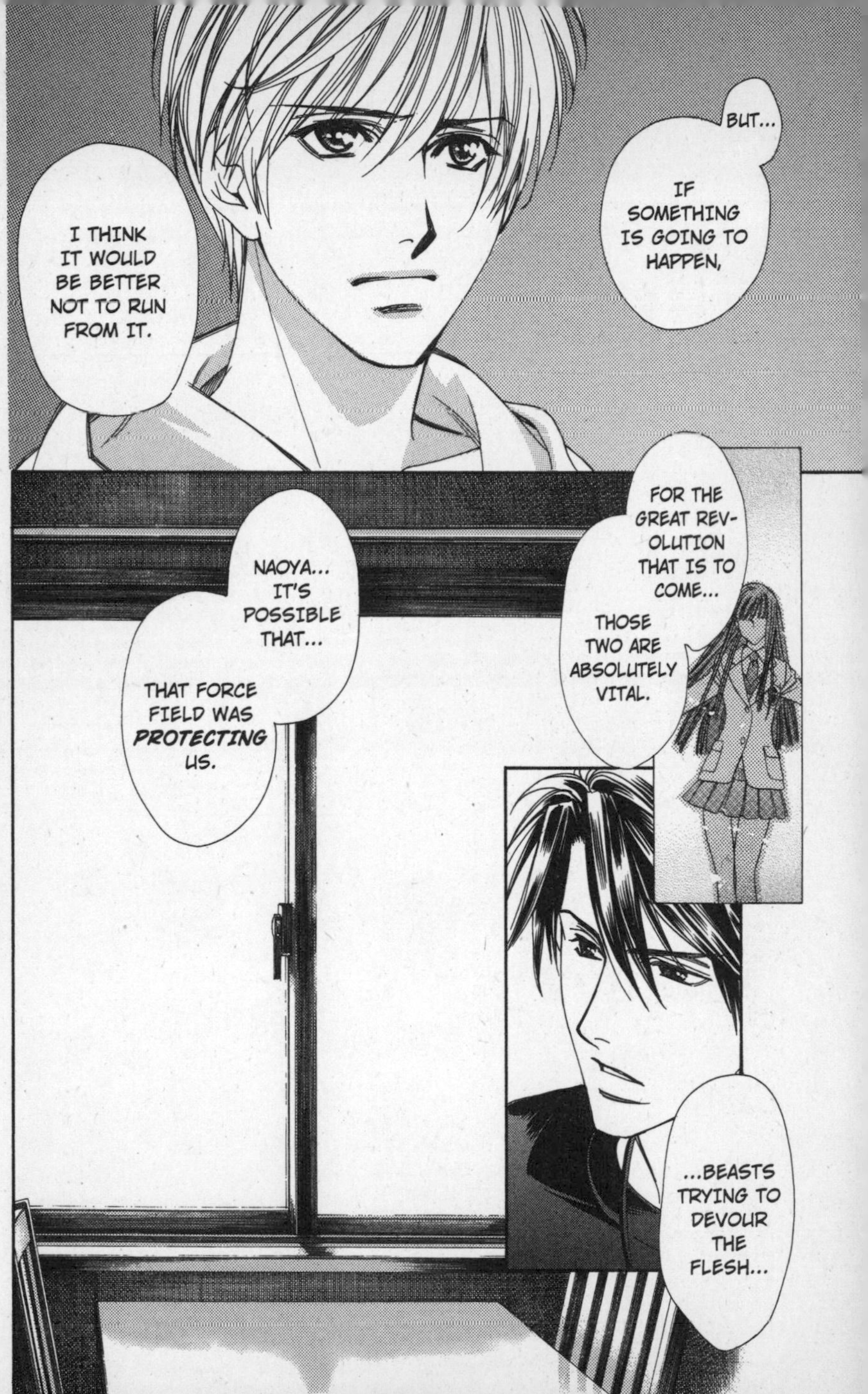
BUT...
IF SOMETHING IS GOING TO HAPPEN,
I THINK IT WOULD BE BETTER NOT TO RUN FROM IT.
FOR THE GREAT REV-OLUTION THAT IS TO COME...
THOSE TWO ARE ABSOLUTELY VITAL.
NAOYA... IT'S POSSIBLE THAT...
THAT FORCE FIELD WAS *PROTECTING* US.
...BEASTS TRYING TO DEVOUR THE FLESH...

Night Head Genesis volume 1 • END

A word from the manga creator:

Hello. Pleased to meet you. I am You Higuri, and I was in charge of the manga and the character designs for the anime version of *Night Head Genesis*.

Thank you very much for picking up this book.

I always write for magazines geared toward women, so I was surprised to hear that the series would be published in *Magazine Z*. This is a good experience.

I was given the assignment of making this series—which was created in such fine detail—understandable to people seeing it for the first time, and still making it shorter . . . and so, very unfortunately, I had to cut out a lot of really good episodes.

Now I'm hoping that it will sum up nicely in the end. . . . I hope you'll stay with it and enjoy it to the end.

Everyone who helped me with drawing this book: Hijiri Izumi-san, Naoko Nakatsuji-san, Kazuyuki Ônishi-san, Gyôshô-san, Aoi Ichinose-san, Mitsuru Fuyutsuki-san, Akito Aizawa-san, Chief Oda, and N-san from *Magazine Z's* editorial department.

You Higuri's official home page, Electronic Brain Higurin Information Channel TIARA:

http://www.diana.dti.ne.jp/~higuri

Translation Notes

Japanese is a tricky language for most Westerners, and translation is often more art than science. For your edification and reading pleasure, here are notes on some of the places where we could have gone in a different direction in our translation of the work, or where a Japanese cultural reference is used.

NII-CHAN...
THEY'RE ALL
LYING...

Nii-chan, page 9

Nii-san means "older brother." Here, because Naoya is still little, he calls Naoto "*Nii-chan*," which is a little more immature. When he grows up, he calls Naoto "*Nii-chan*."

WOULD YOU LIKE SOME DRY ICE WITH THAT?

Dry ice and cake, page 42

Sachie is asking her customer if she wants some dry ice in the box with the cake to keep it from going bad. Dry ice works well for this, because it doesn't make things wet. But if the customer is planning to eat the cake soon, she won't need any, and so she just can't decide whether or not to get some.

Magazine Z, page 192

Magazine Z is a manga magazine aimed at older boys.

Preview of Volume 2

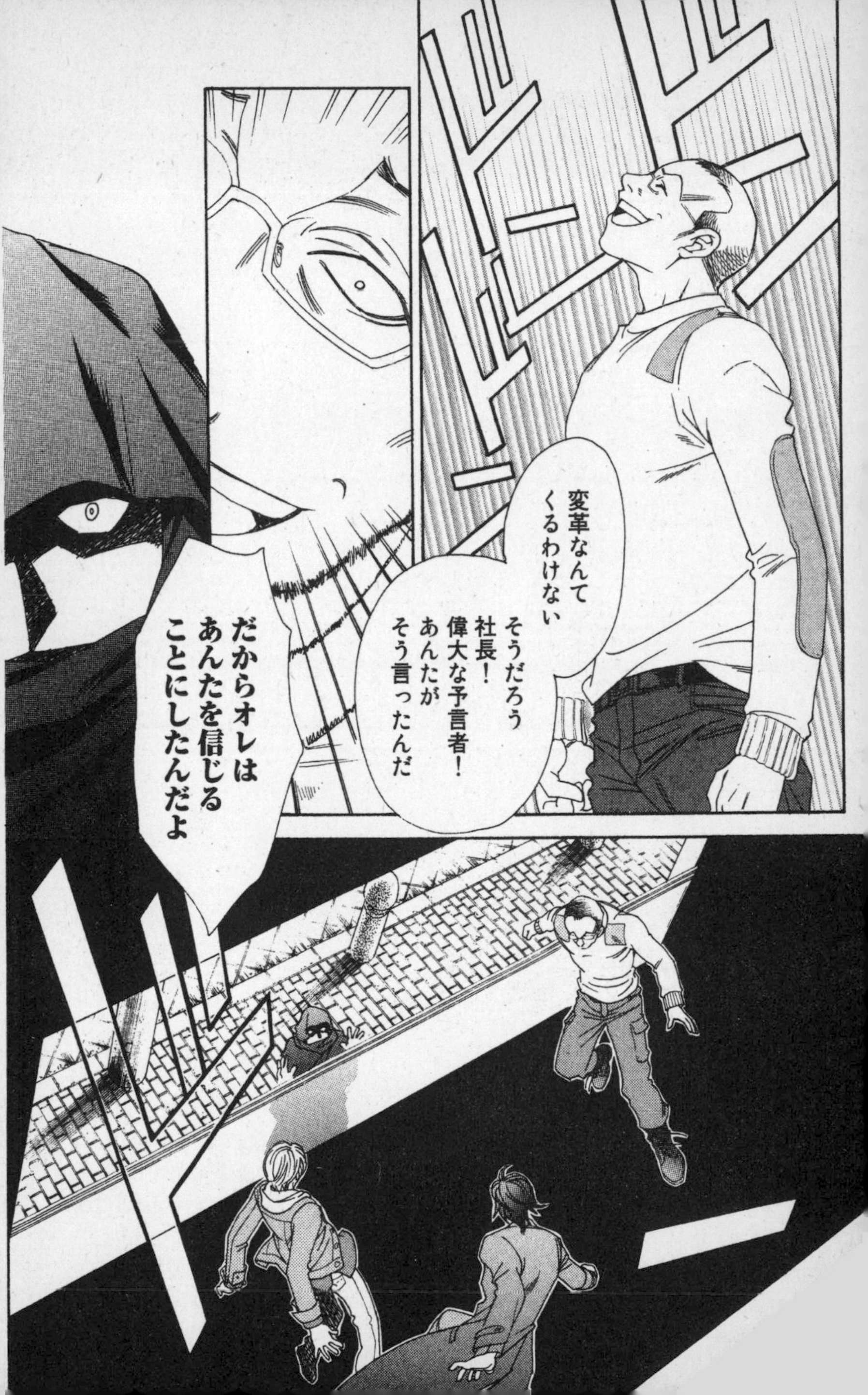
変革なんてくるわけない
そうだろう社長！偉大な予言者！あんたがそう言ったんだ
だからオレはあんたを信じることにしたんだよ

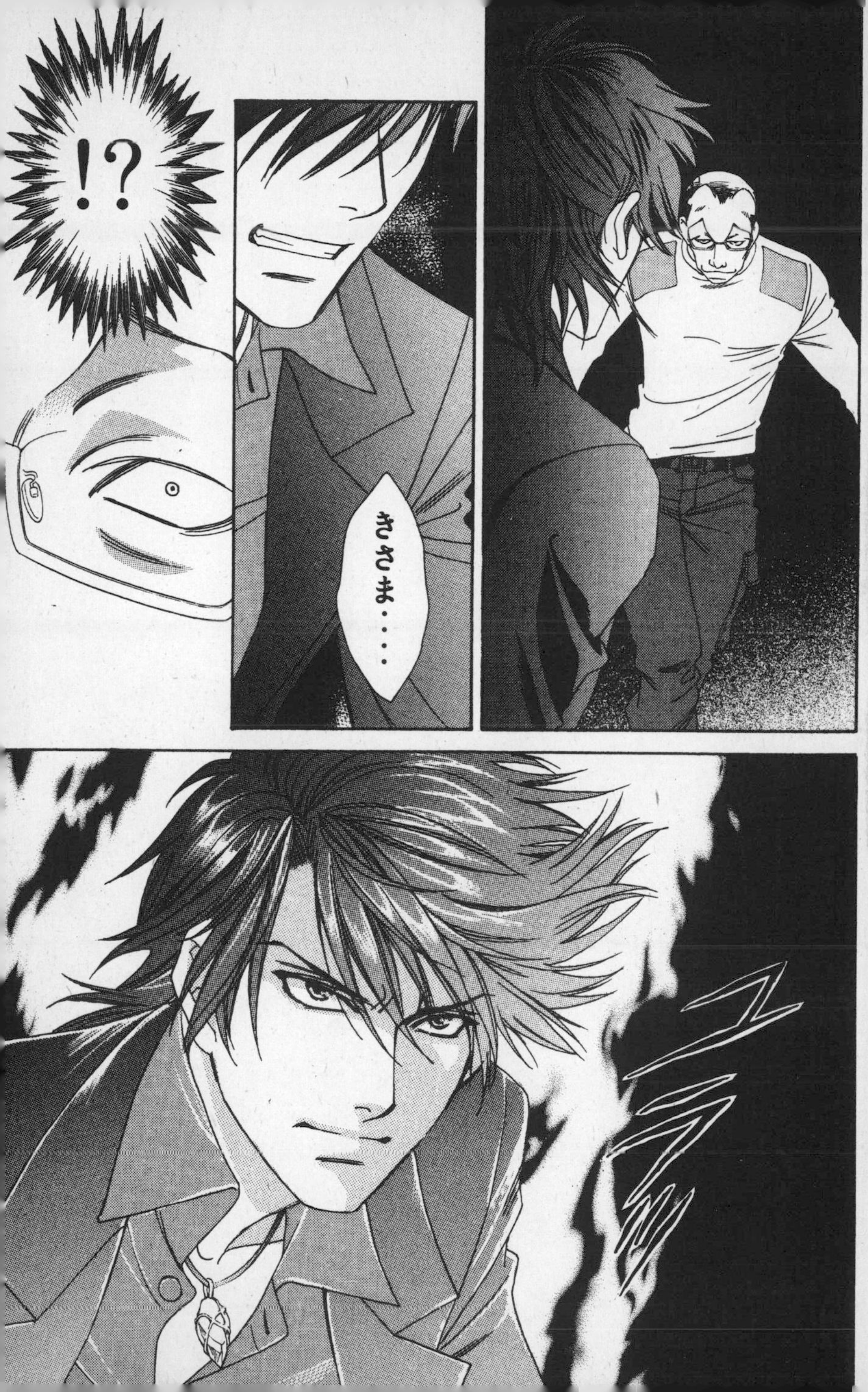
きさま・・・・
!?

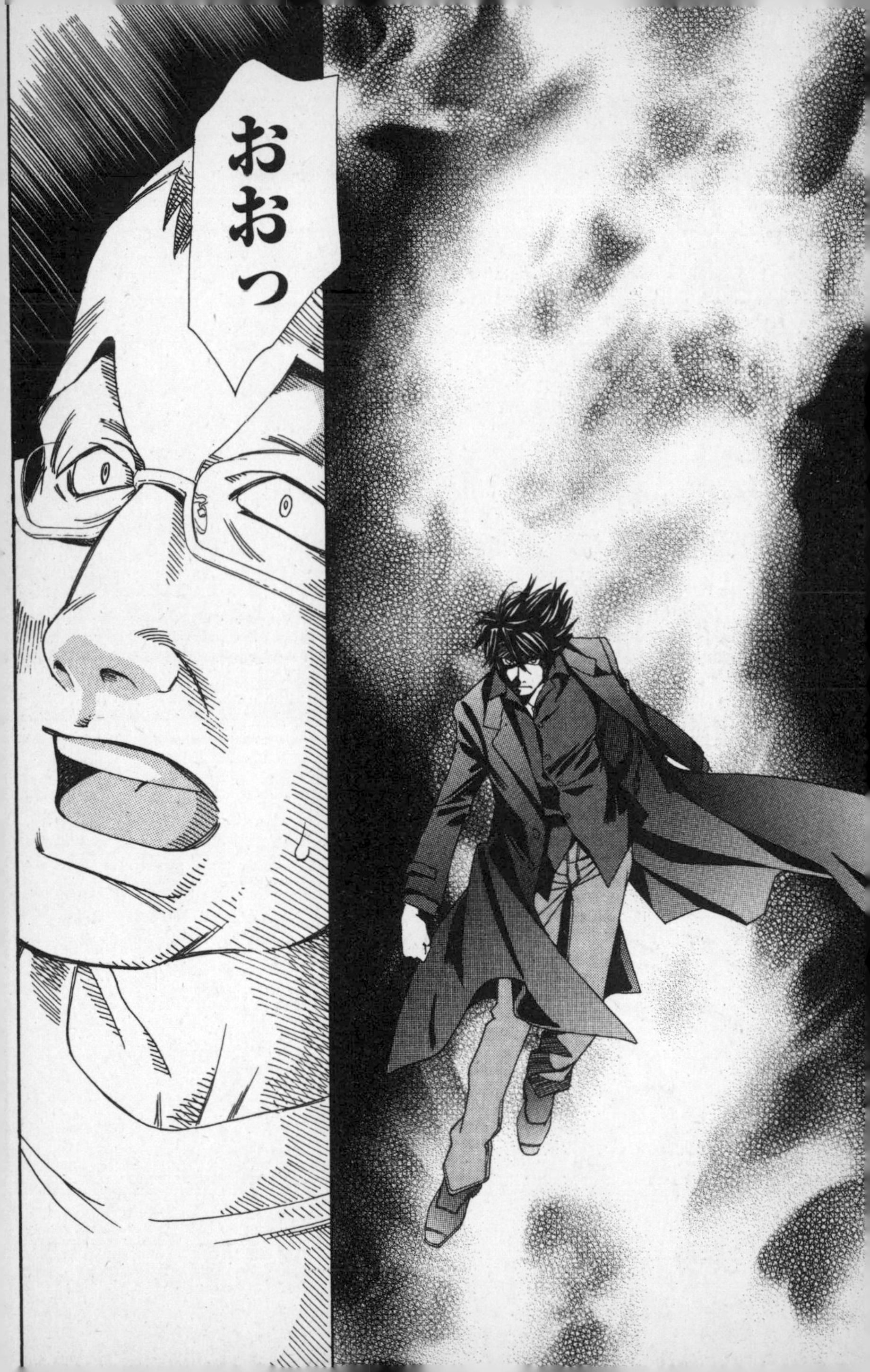
おおっ

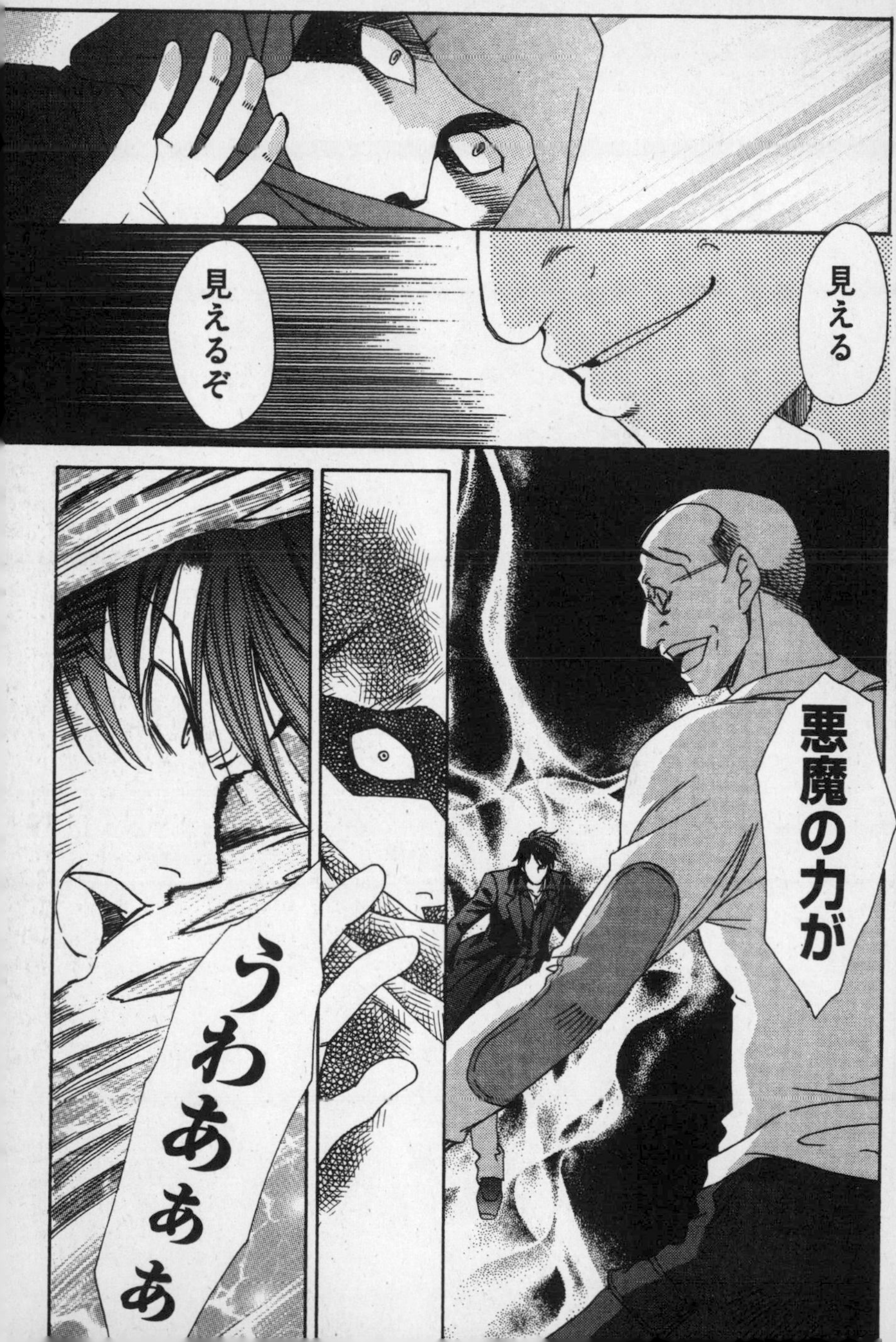
見える
見えるぞ
悪魔の力が
うわあぁぁ

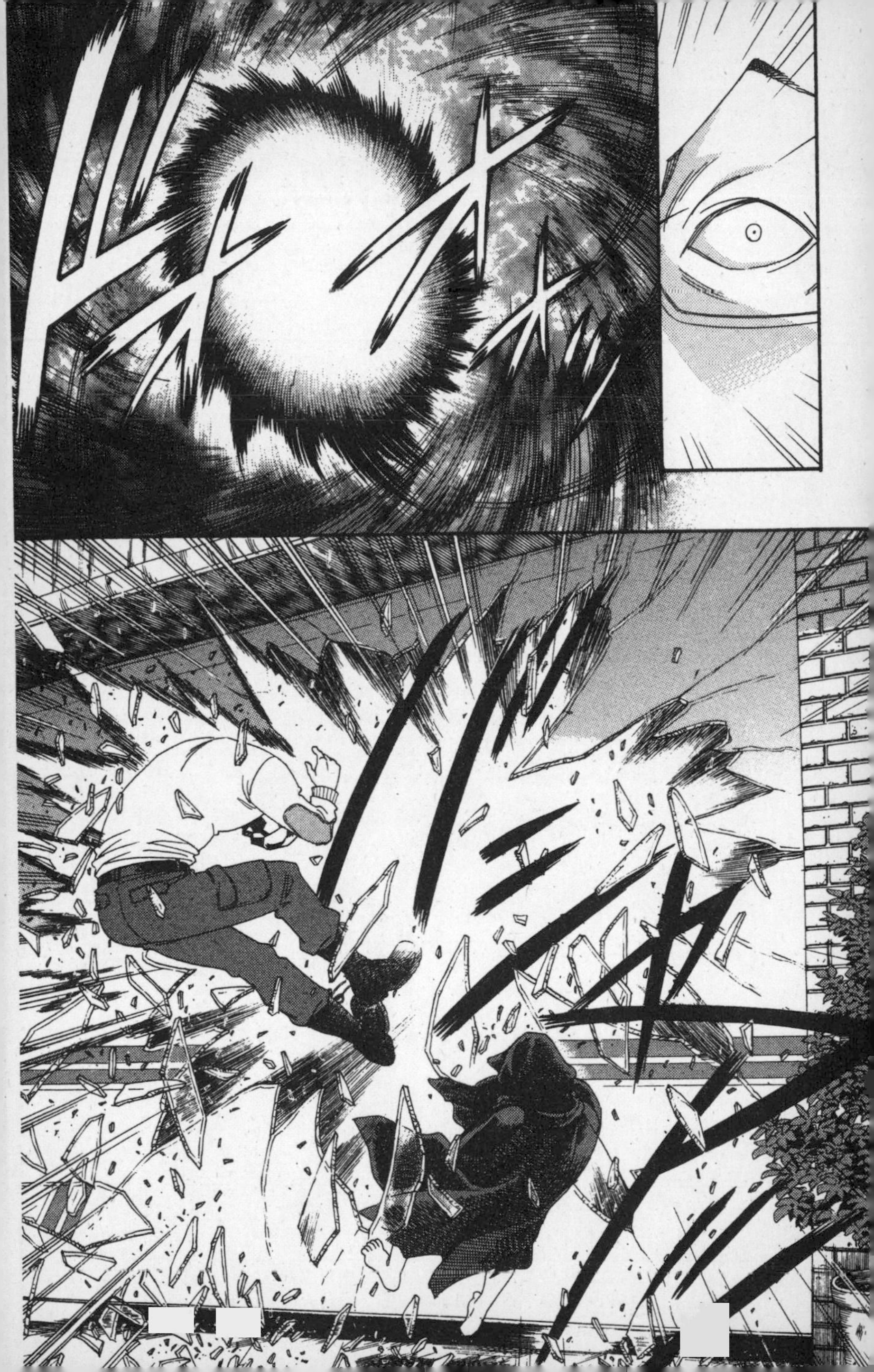

STOP!
TOMARE!

You're going the wrong way!

Manga is a completely different type of reading experience.

To start at the *beginning*, go to the *end*!

That's right! Authentic manga is read the traditional Japanese way—from right to left. Exactly the *opposite* of how American books are read. It's easy to follow: Just go to the other end of the book, and read each page—and each panel—from right side to left side, starting at the top right. Now you're experiencing manga as it was meant to be!